+Vampire
Season II

AKIHISA IKEDA

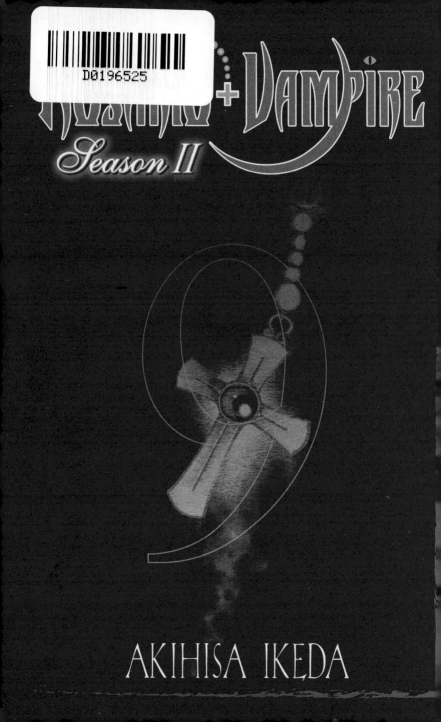

Horror Story Thus Far

Tsukune Aono accidentally enrolls in Yokai Academy, a high school for monsters! After befriending the school's cutest girl, Moka Akashiya, he decides to stay...even though Yokai has a zero-tolerance policy toward humans. (A *fatal* policy.) Tsukune has to hide his true identity while fending off attacks by monster gangs. He survives with the help of his News Club friends—Moka, Kurumu, Yukari and Mizore.

Now Tsukune and his friends are sophomores and starting to think about their futures, while at the same time battling a mysterious organization called Fairy Tale. They've learned that Moka's Rosario seal is beginning to weaken and have gone to Hong Kong to get it fixed...but when the great sorcerer Tohofuhai touches the Rosario to repair it, a bizarre force drags Tsukune, Mizore and Tohofuhai into Moka's mind, where they witness traumatic memories from her past.

Meanwhile, in the real world, Moka's estranged sister Aqua Shuzen attacks the Huang Family mansion...

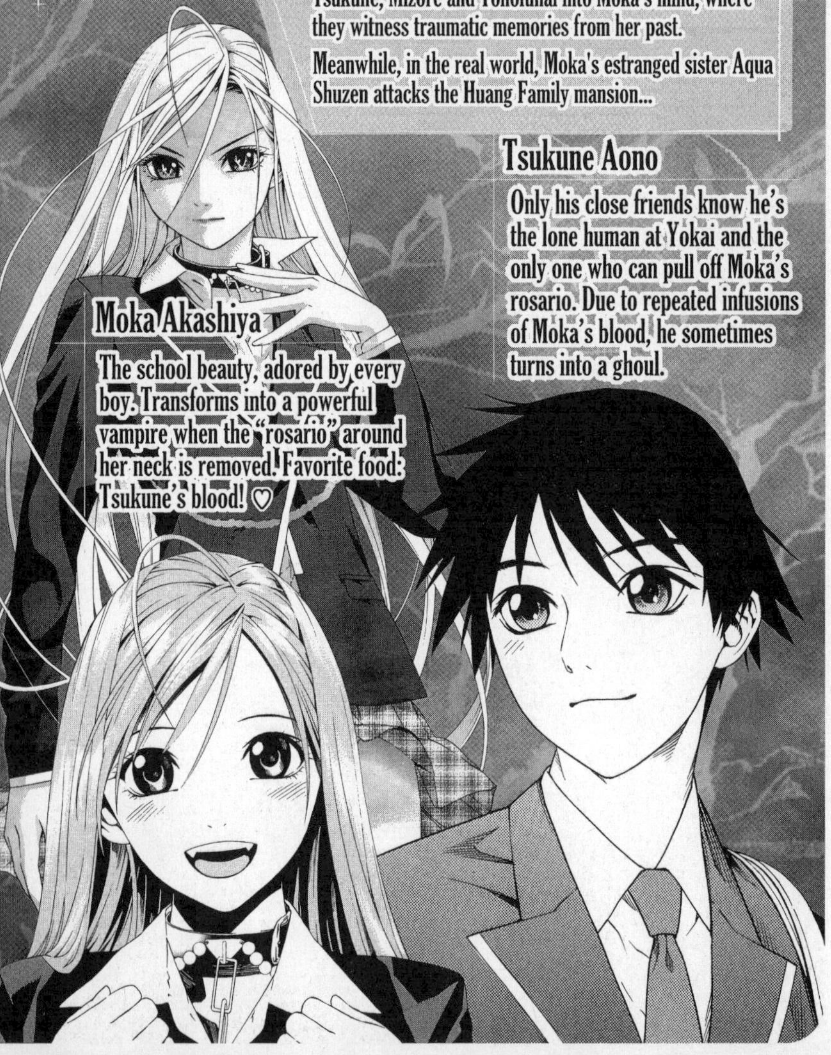

Tsukune Aono

Only his close friends know he's the lone human at Yokai and the only one who can pull off Moka's rosario. Due to repeated infusions of Moka's blood, he sometimes turns into a ghoul.

Moka Akashiya

The school beauty, adored by every boy. Transforms into a powerful vampire when the "rosario" around her neck is removed. Favorite food: Tsukune's blood! ♡

Kurumu Kurono

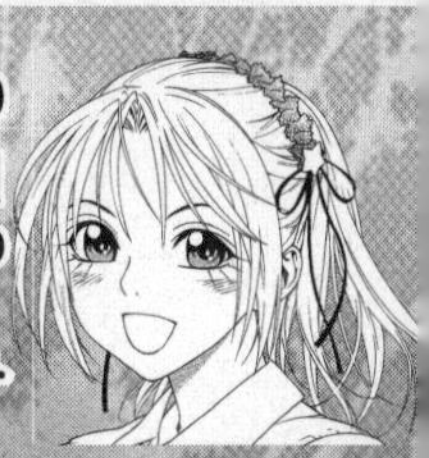

A succubus. Also adored by all the boys—for two obvious reasons. Fights with Moka over Tsukune.

Yukari Sendo

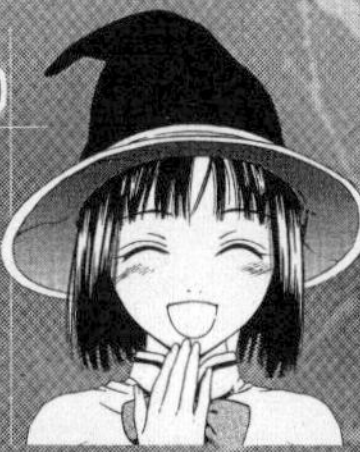

A mischievous witch. Much younger than the others but a real genius, she skipped several grades to get into the Academy. A sharp tongue for such a cute little thing.

Mizore Shirayuki

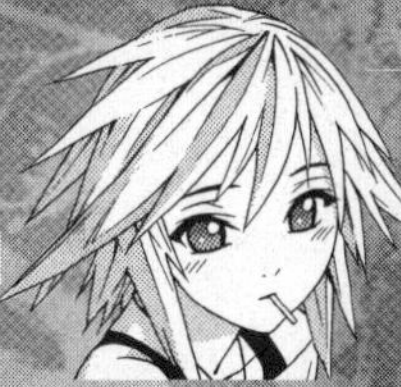

A snow fairy who manipulates ice. She fell in love with Tsukune after reading his newspaper articles.

Ruby Tojo

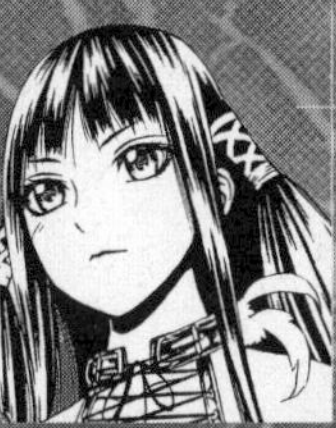

A witch who only learned to trust humans after meeting Tsukune. Now employed as Yokai's headmaster's assistant. A bit of a masochist.

Koko Shuzen

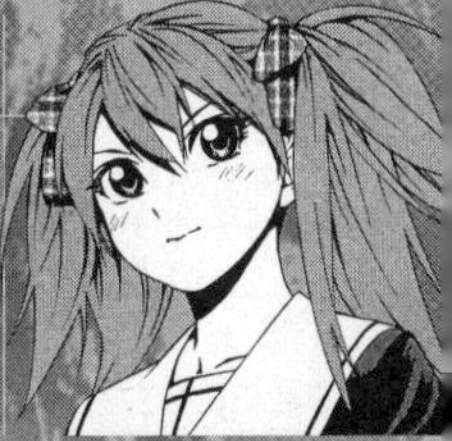

Moka's stubborn little sister. Koko worships Moka's inner vampiric self but hates her sweet exterior. Koko's pet bat transforms into a weapon.

Aqua Shuzen

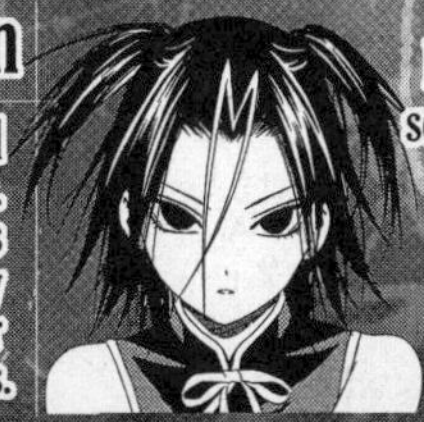

Moka's elder sister and the eldest daughter. Having lost her mother as a child, she was raised by relatives in China. A master of Chinese martial arts.

Fangfang Huang

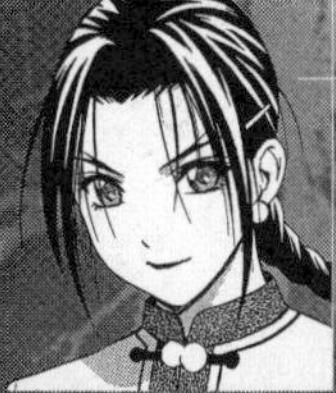

Freshman at Yokai Academy, the only son of a Chinese Mafia family that controls China's most dangerous monsters. Also a "Yasha," a Chinese demon who excels at transformation and sorcery. In awe of Tsukune.

Lingling Huang

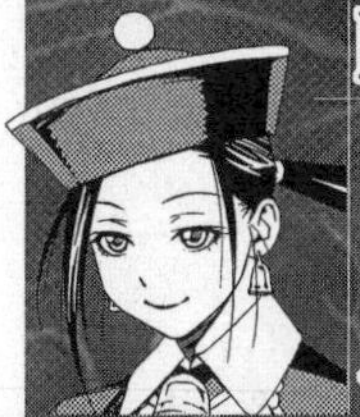

Fangfang's elder sister, who is also late. Because she's dead. Reanimated as a Jiang Shi, a hopping zombie. A junior transfer student at Yokai.

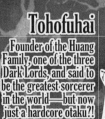

Ginei Morioka

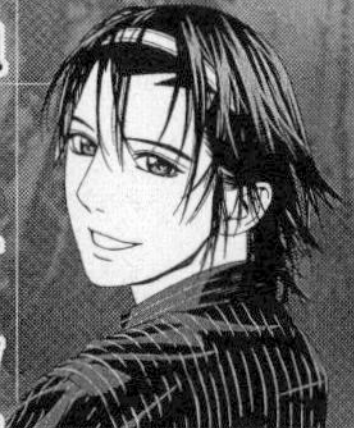

President of the News Club. Although his true form is a werewolf, he's more notorious as a wolf of a different kind—one who chases every girl in sight.

Tohofuhai

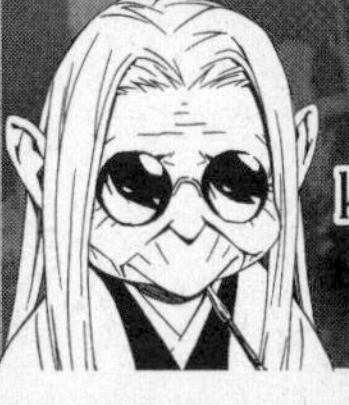

Founder of the Huang Family, one of the three Dark Lords, and said to be the greatest sorcerer in the world—but now just a hardcore otaku?!

ROSARIO+VAMPIRE
Season II

9

Contents

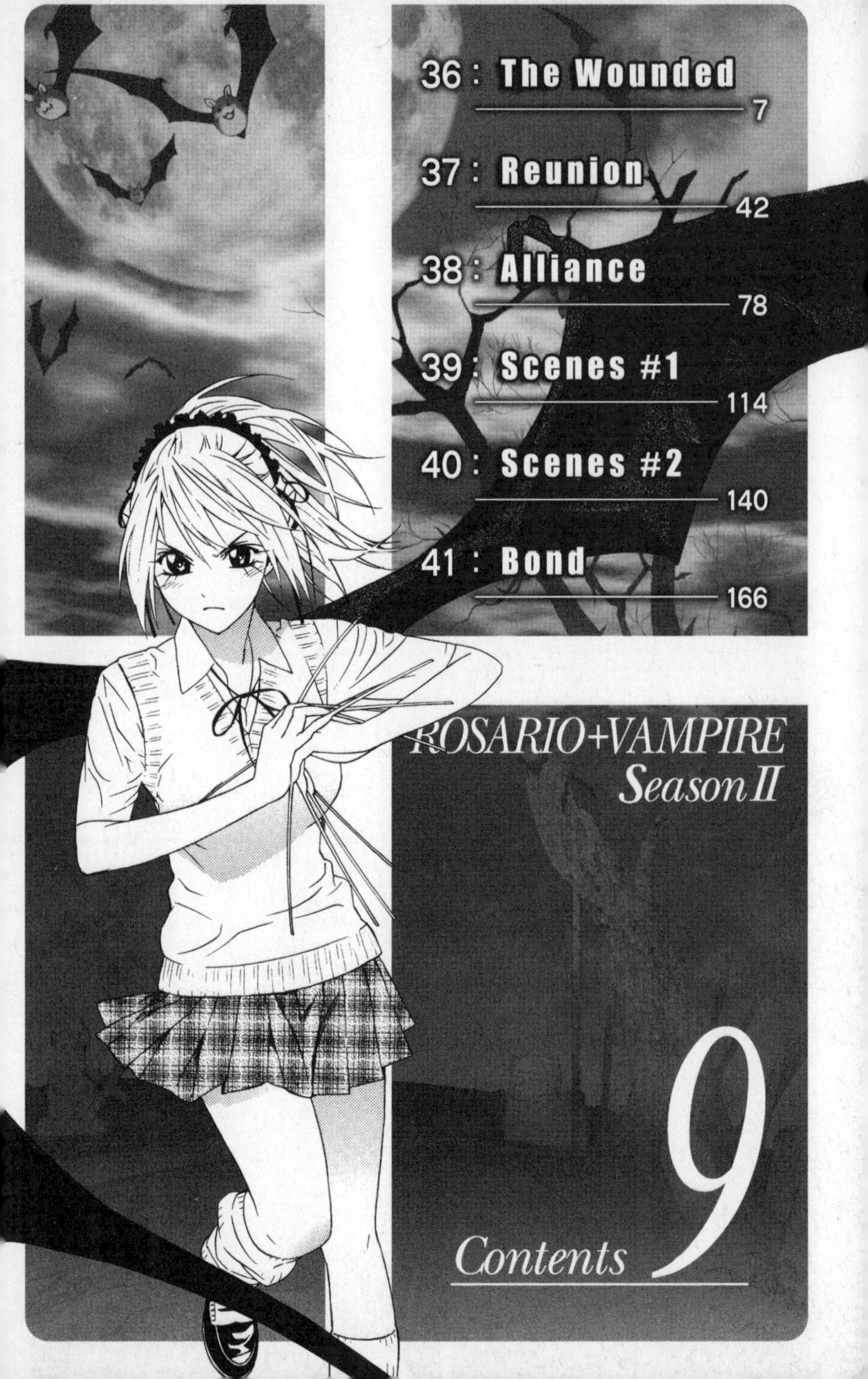

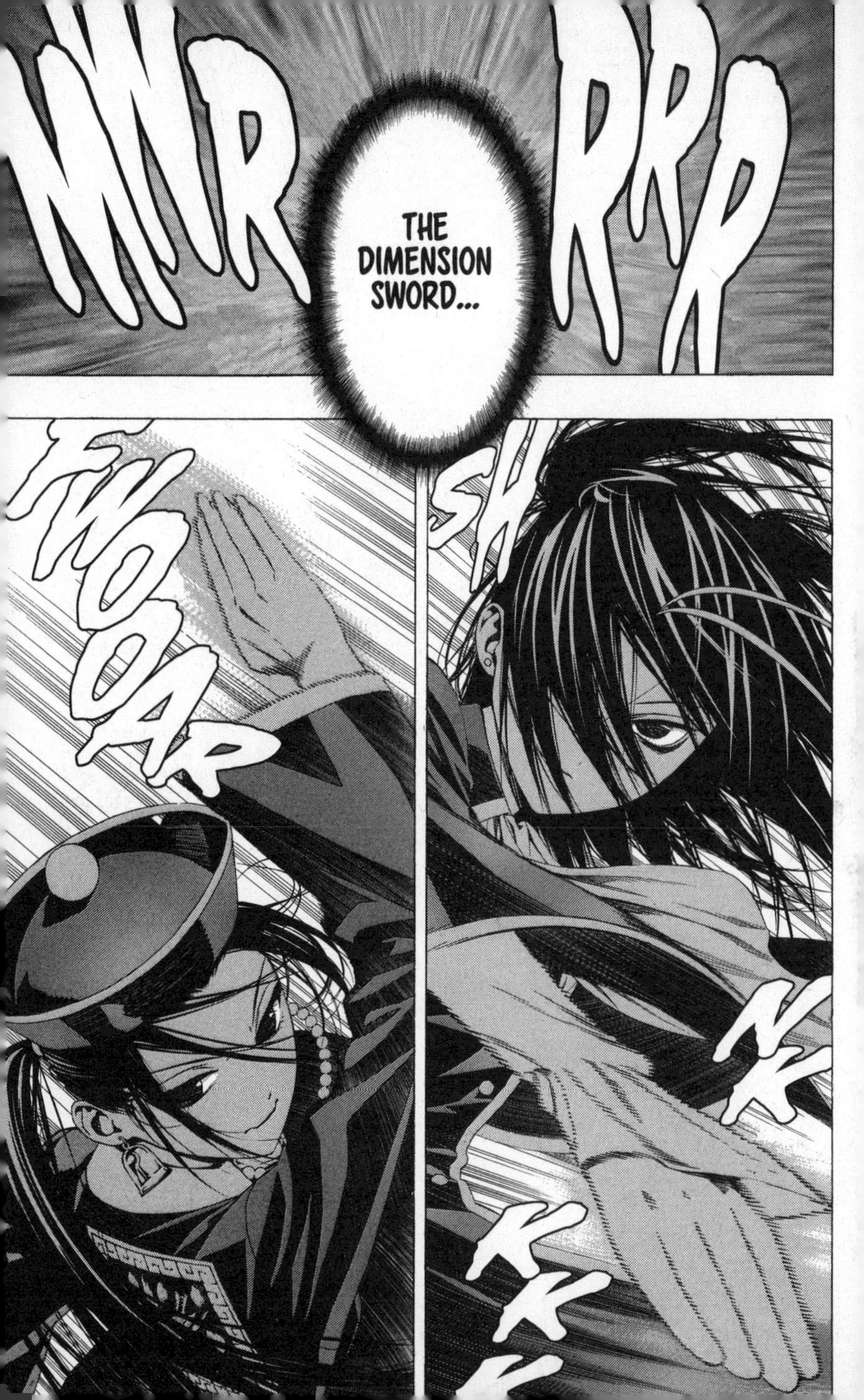
THE DIMENSION SWORD...

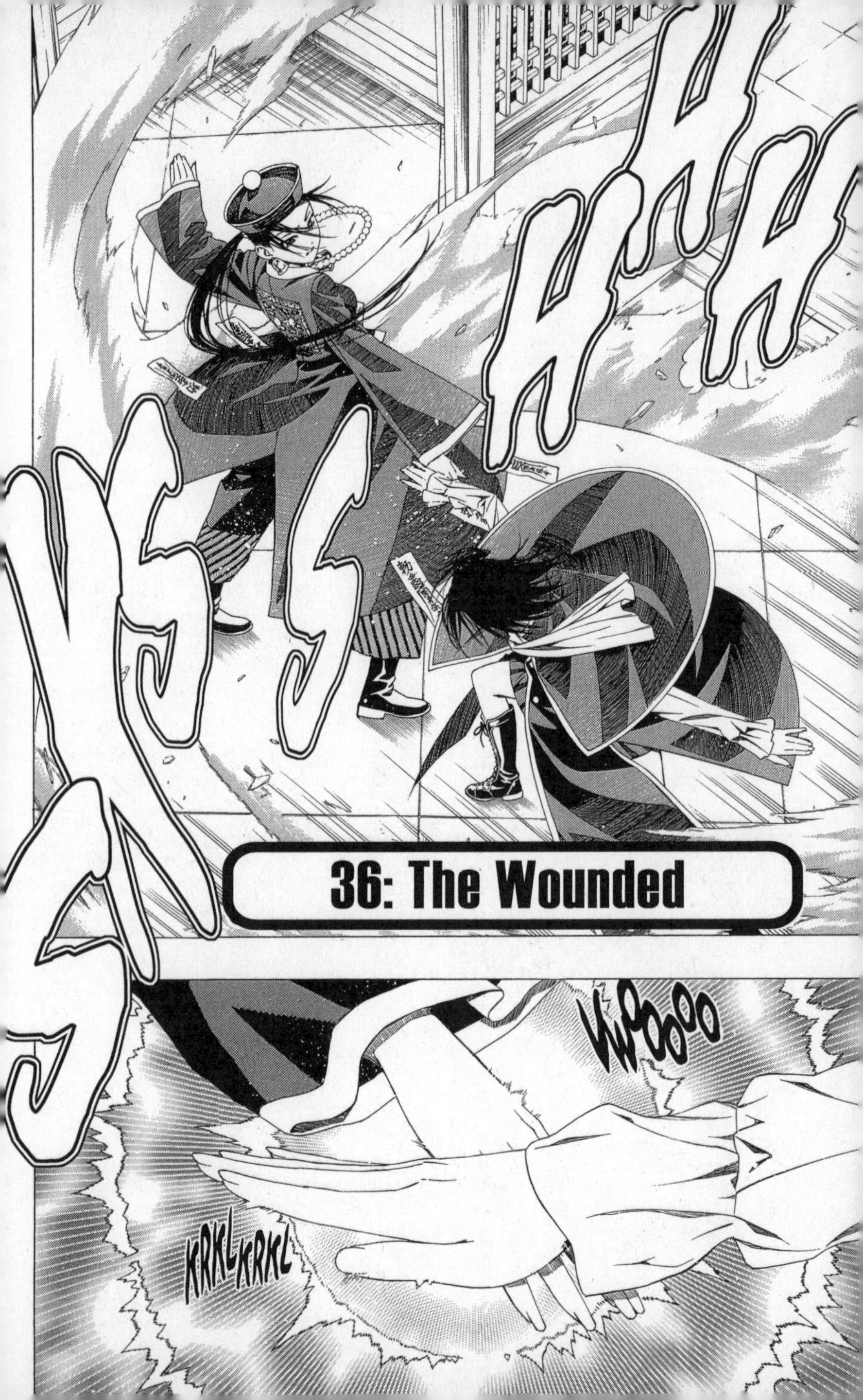
36: The Wounded
KRKLKRKL

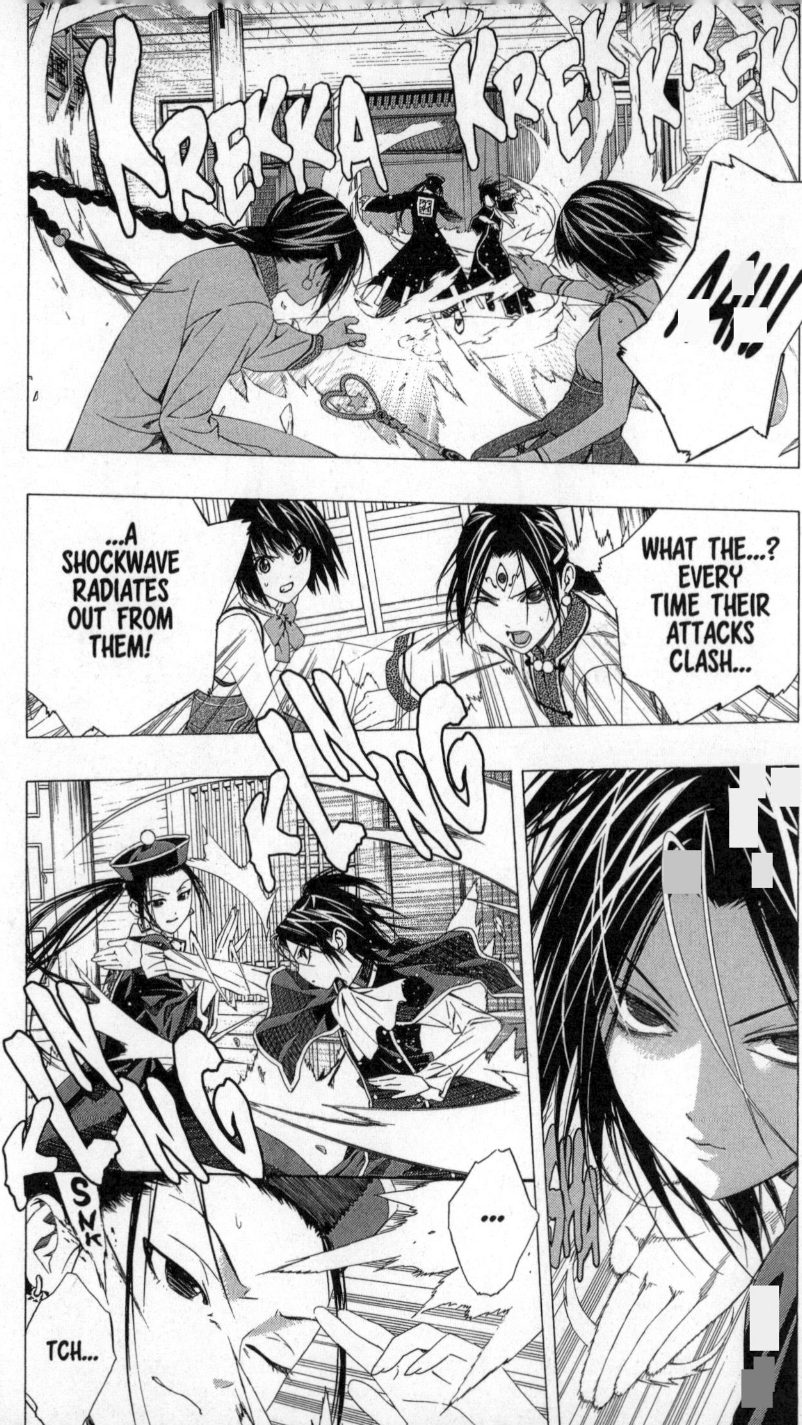
KREKKA KREK KREK
WHAT THE...? EVERY TIME THEIR ATTACKS CLASH...
...A SHOCKWAVE RADIATES OUT FROM THEM!
KLING KLING
KLING KLING
...
SNK
TCH...

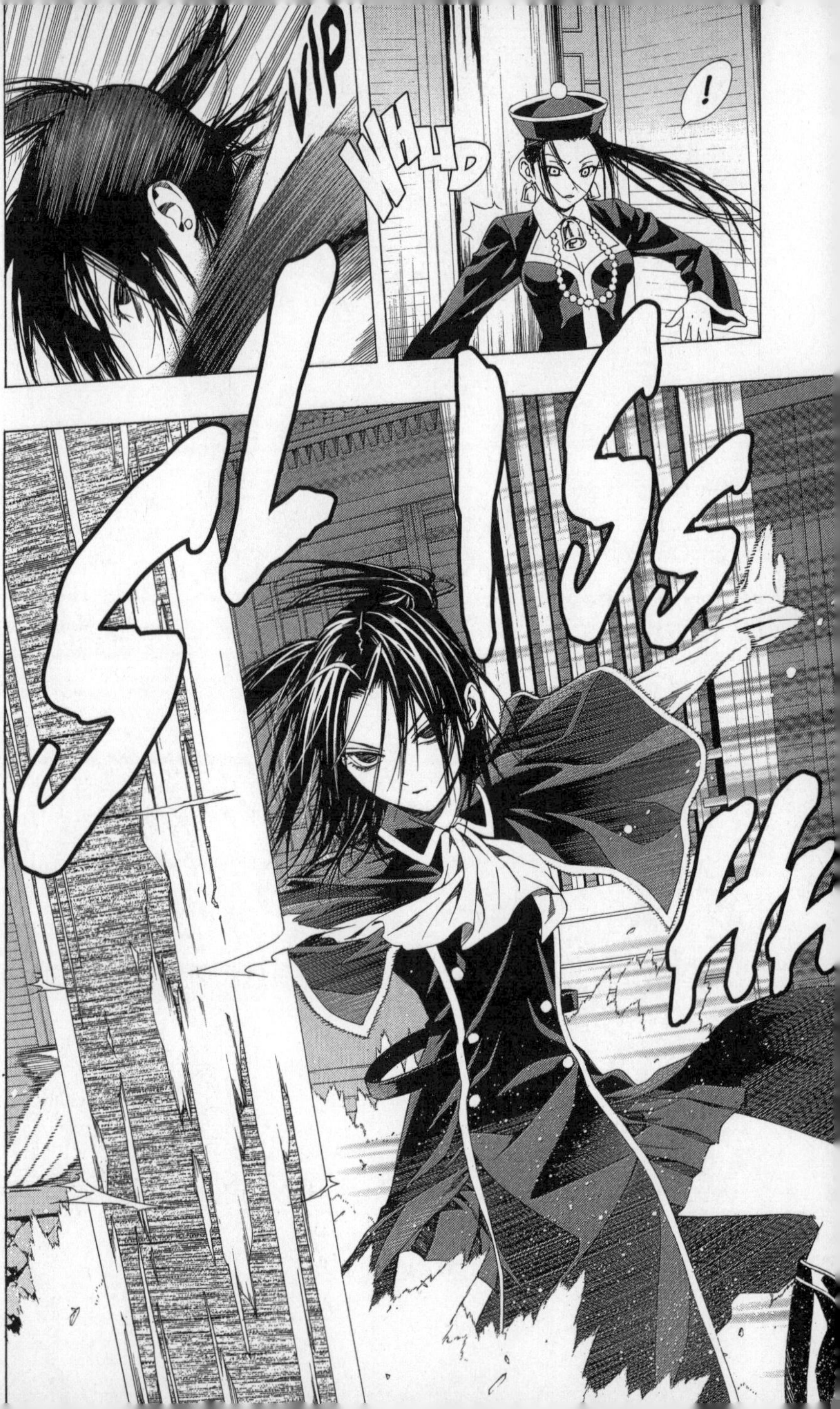
!
WHUD
VIP
SLISSH

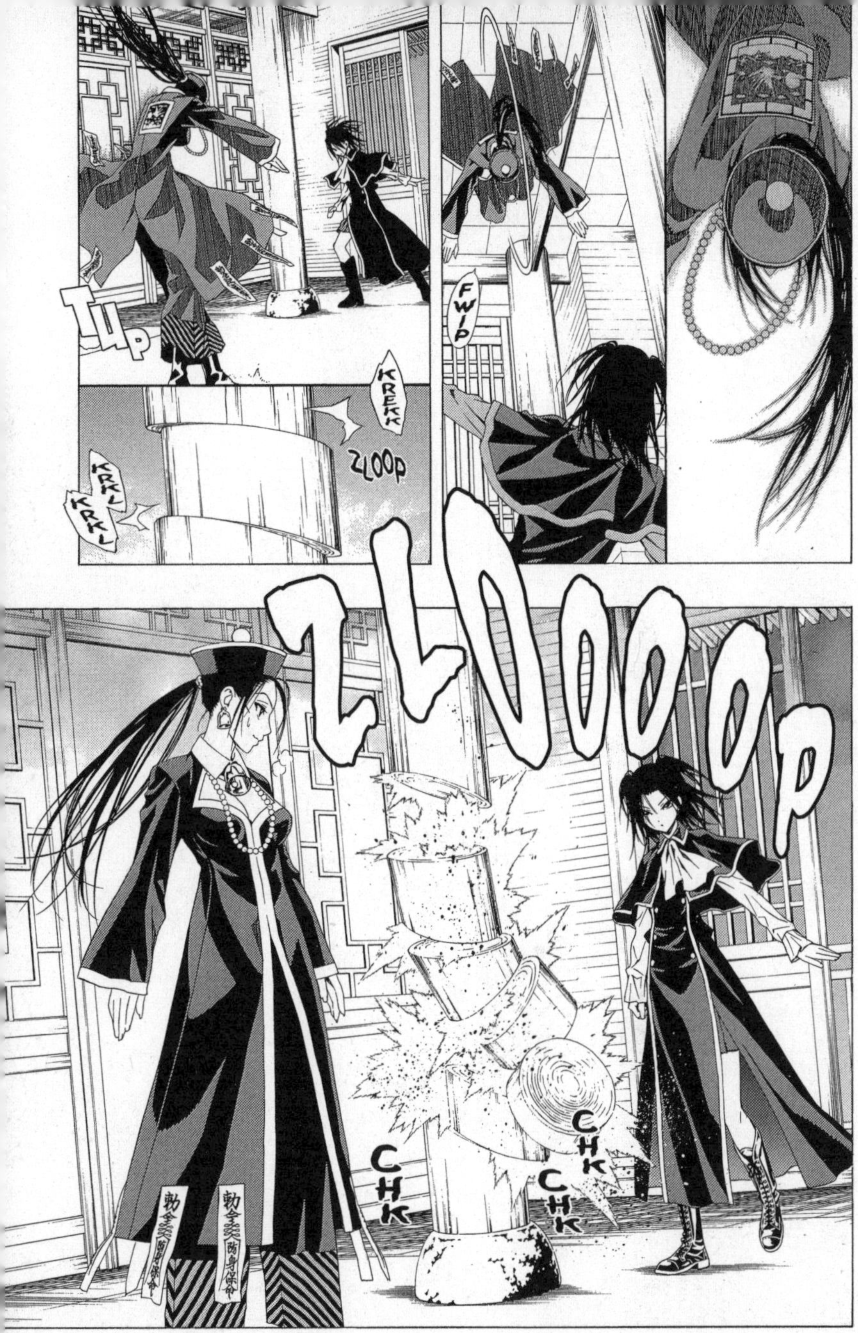
FWIP
TUP
KREKK
ZLOOP
KRKL
KRKL
ZLOOOOP
CHK
CHK
CHK
CHK

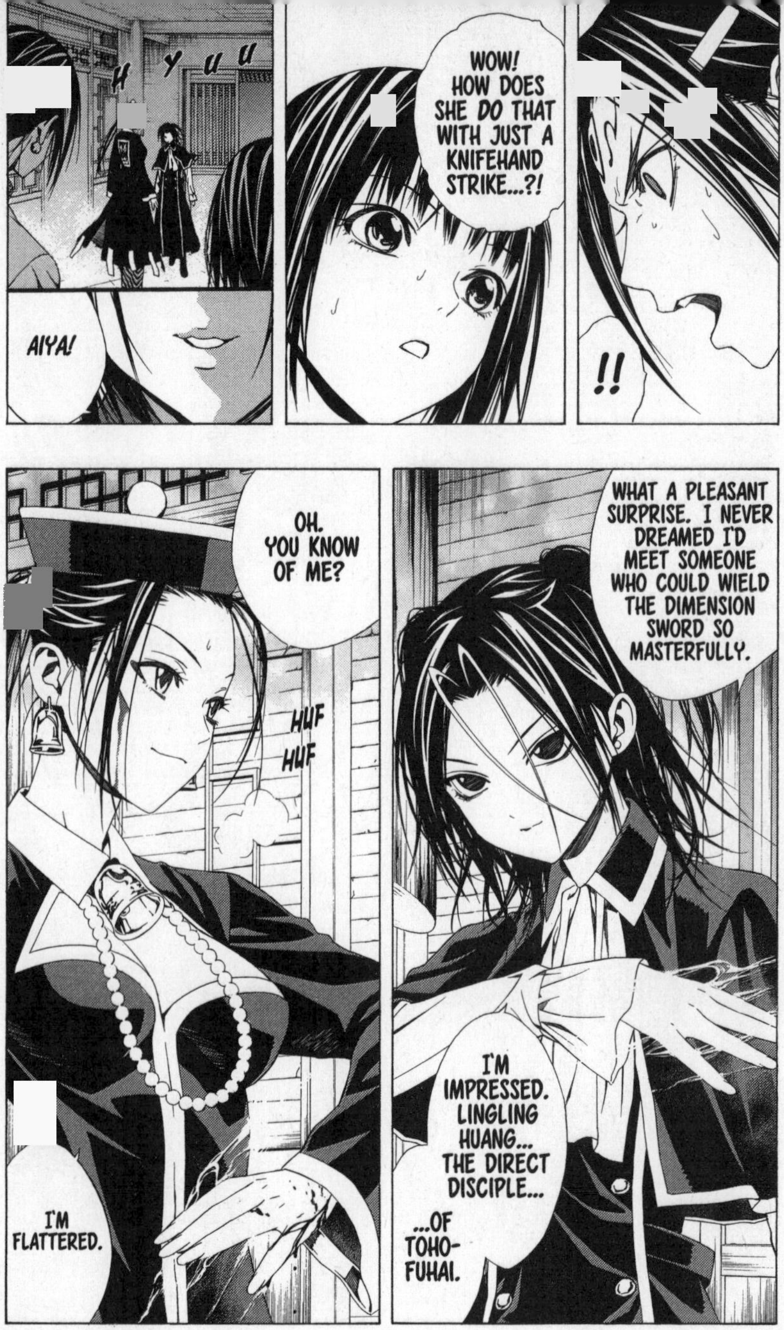
!!
WOW! HOW DOES SHE DO THAT WITH JUST A KNIFEHAND STRIKE...?!
HYUU
AIYA!
WHAT A PLEASANT SURPRISE. I NEVER DREAMED I'D MEET SOMEONE WHO COULD WIELD THE DIMENSION SWORD SO MASTERFULLY.
I'M IMPRESSED. LINGLING HUANG... THE DIRECT DISCIPLE...
...OF TOHO-FUHAI.
OH. YOU KNOW OF ME?
HUF HUF
I'M FLATTERED.

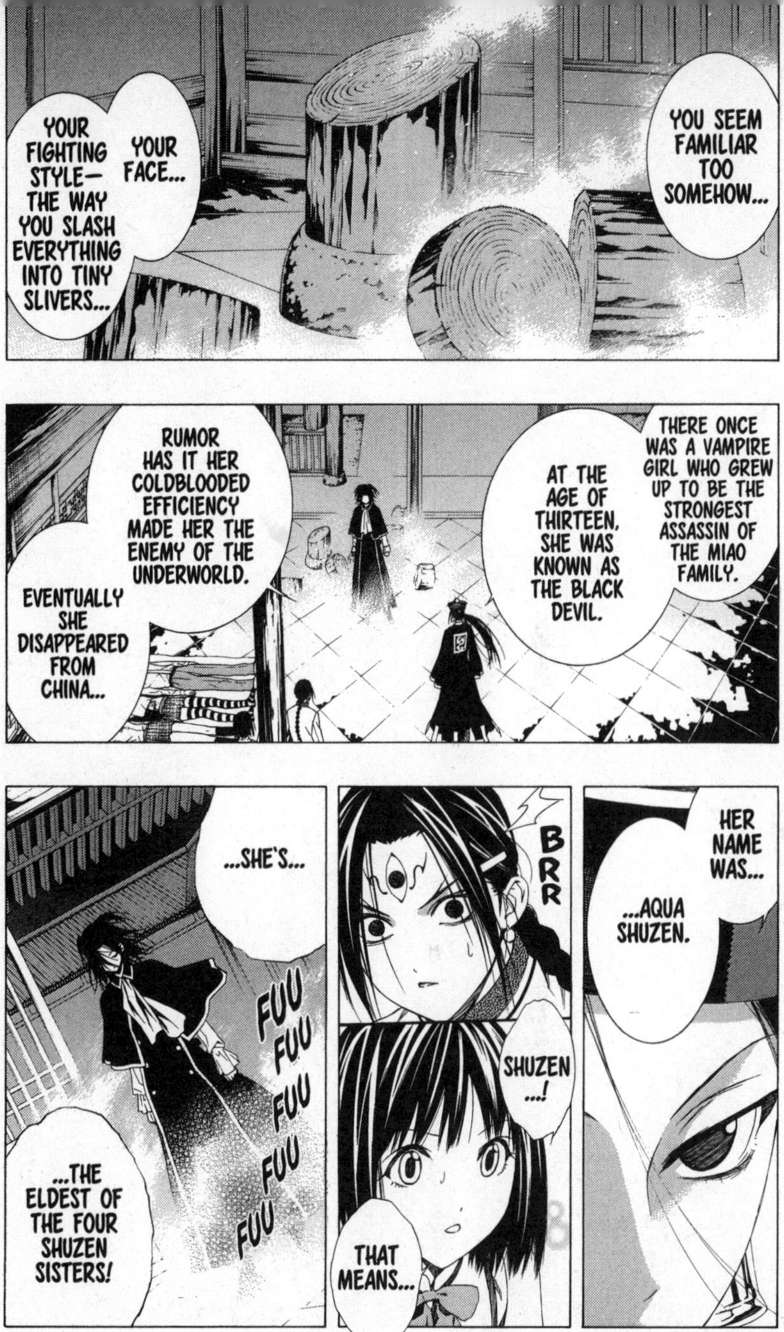
YOU SEEM FAMILIAR TOO SOMEHOW...
YOUR FACE...
YOUR FIGHTING STYLE—THE WAY YOU SLASH EVERYTHING INTO TINY SLIVERS...
THERE ONCE WAS A VAMPIRE GIRL WHO GREW UP TO BE THE STRONGEST ASSASSIN OF THE MIAO FAMILY.
AT THE AGE OF THIRTEEN, SHE WAS KNOWN AS THE BLACK DEVIL.
RUMOR HAS IT HER COLDBLOODED EFFICIENCY MADE HER THE ENEMY OF THE UNDERWORLD.
EVENTUALLY SHE DISAPPEARED FROM CHINA...
HER NAME WAS...
...AQUA SHUZEN.
BRR
SHUZEN...!
THAT MEANS...
...SHE'S...
FUU FUU FUU FUU FUU
...THE ELDEST OF THE FOUR SHUZEN SISTERS!

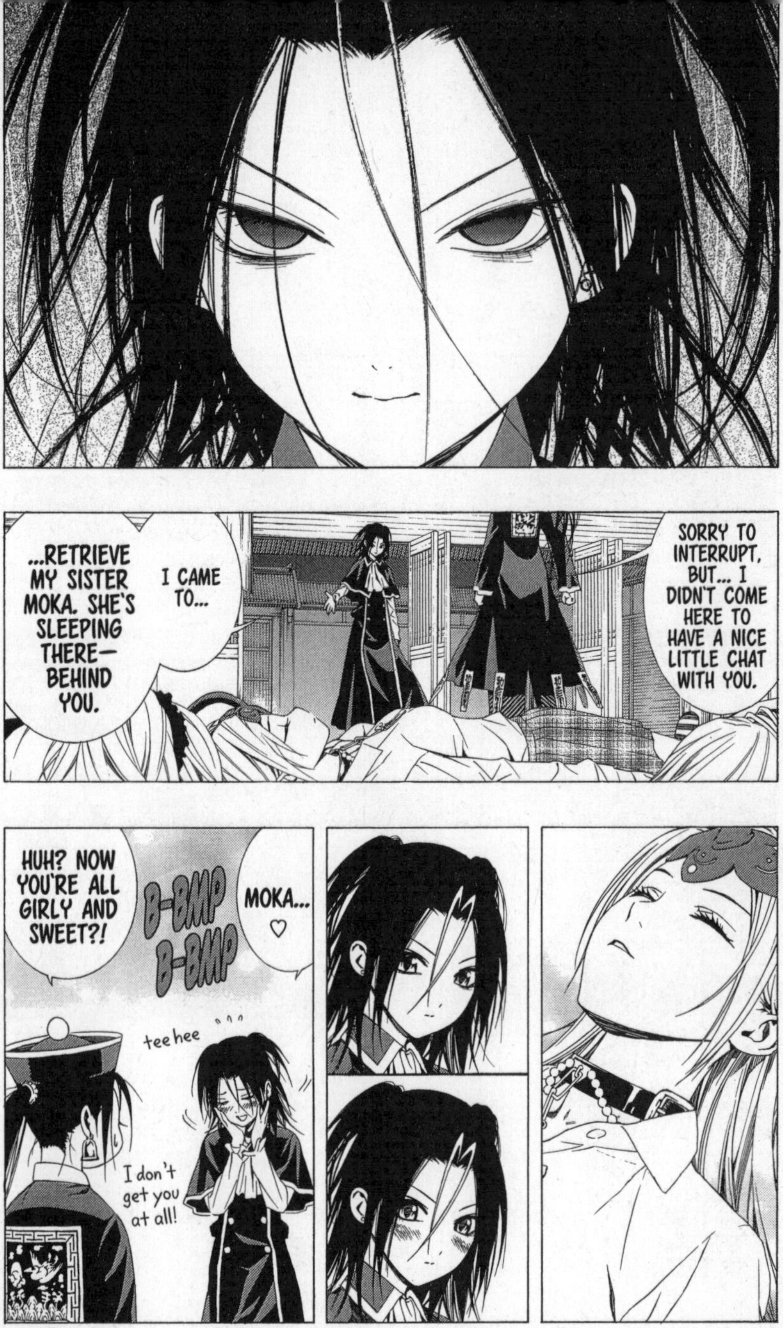
SORRY TO INTERRUPT, BUT... I DIDN'T COME HERE TO HAVE A NICE LITTLE CHAT WITH YOU.
I CAME TO...
...RETRIEVE MY SISTER MOKA. SHE'S SLEEPING THERE— BEHIND YOU.
MOKA... ♡
B-BMP B-BMP
HUH? NOW YOU'RE ALL GIRLY AND SWEET?!
tee hee
I don't get you at all!

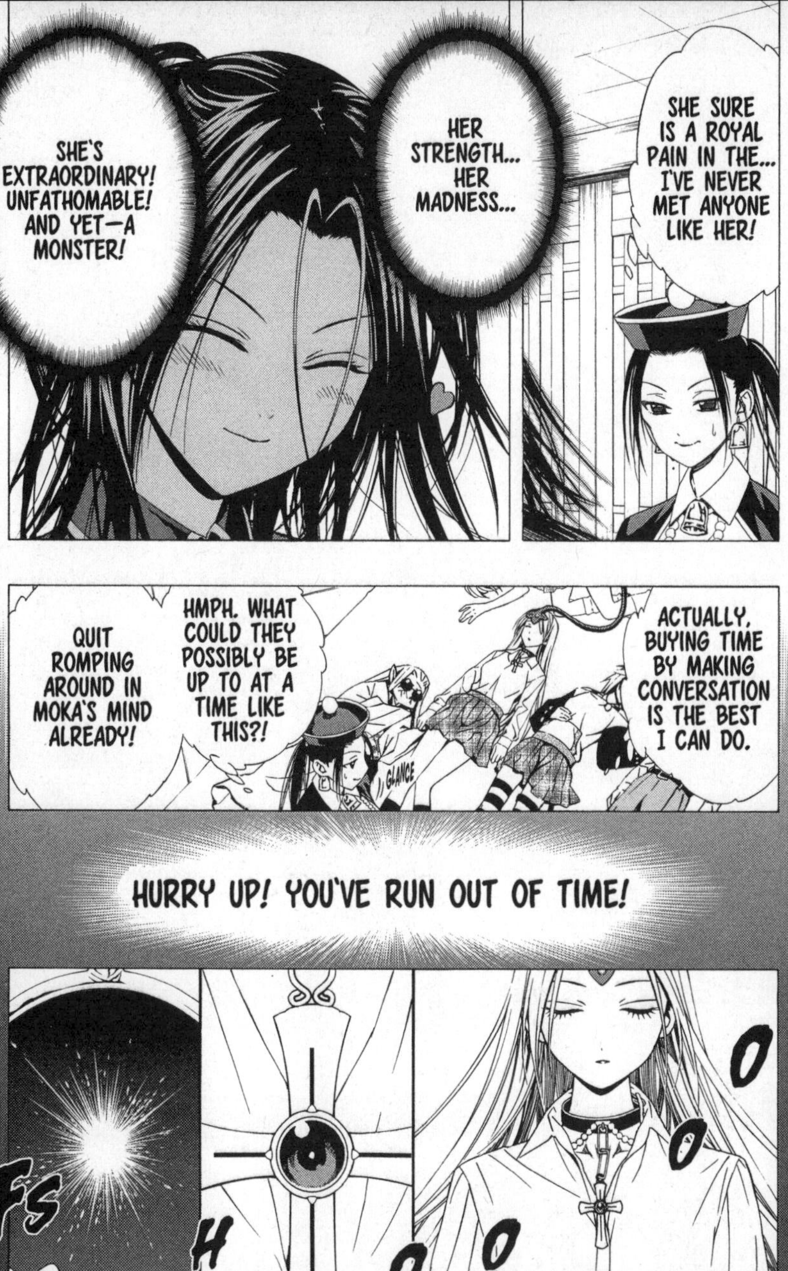
SHE SURE IS A ROYAL PAIN IN THE... I'VE NEVER MET ANYONE LIKE HER!
HER STRENGTH... HER MADNESS...
SHE'S EXTRAORDINARY! UNFATHOMABLE! AND YET—A MONSTER!
ACTUALLY, BUYING TIME BY MAKING CONVERSATION IS THE BEST I CAN DO.
GLANCE
HMPH. WHAT COULD THEY POSSIBLY BE UP TO AT A TIME LIKE THIS?!
QUIT ROMPING AROUND IN MOKA'S MIND ALREADY!
HURRY UP! YOU'VE RUN OUT OF TIME!
FSHOOOOO
BLBL GLBBL

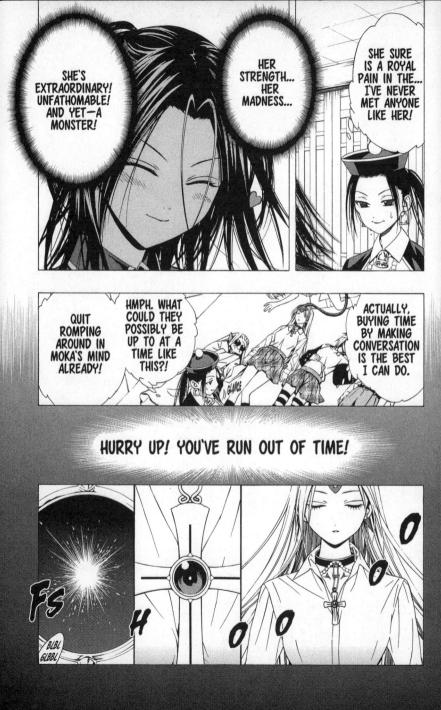

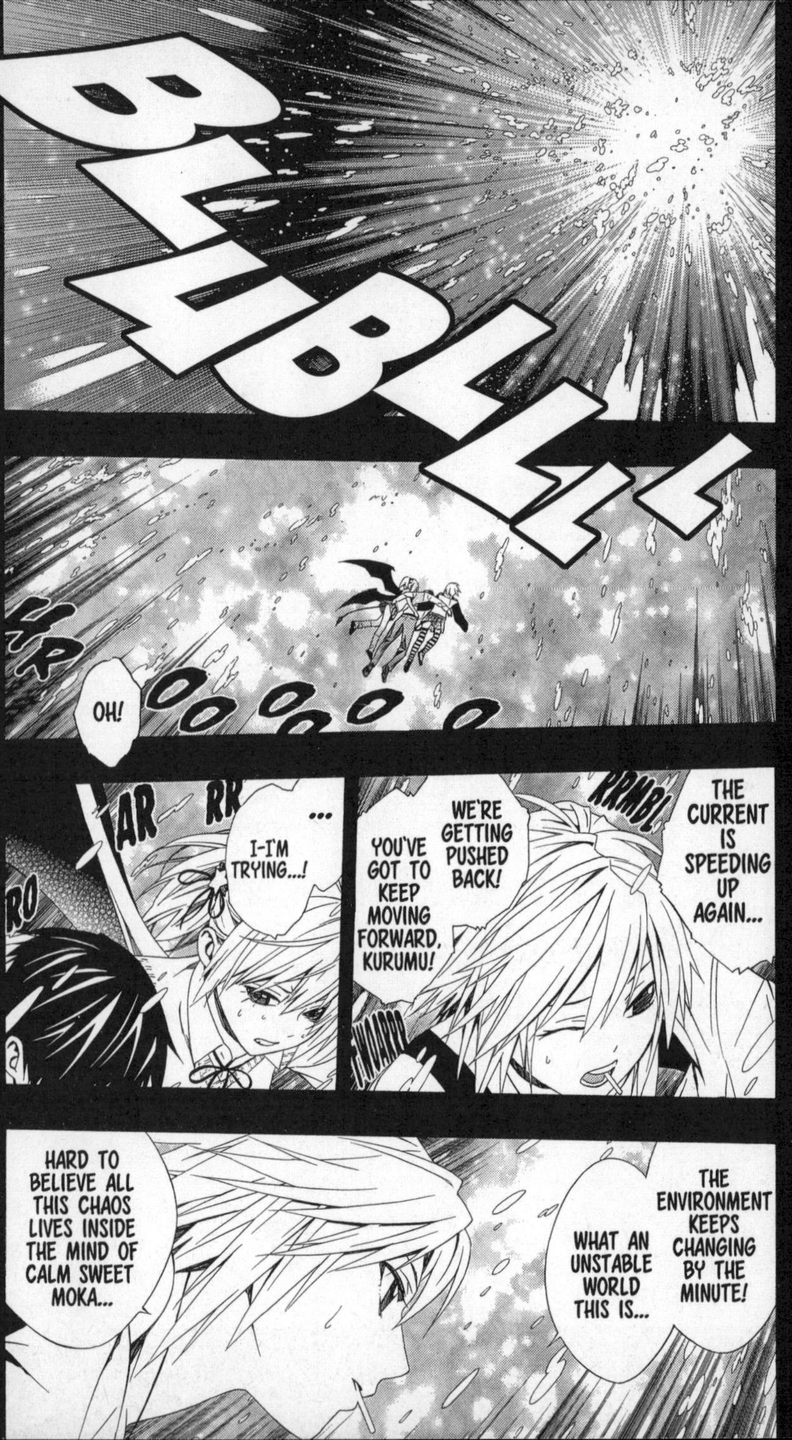
OH!
THE CURRENT IS SPEEDING UP AGAIN...
WE'RE GETTING PUSHED BACK!
YOU'VE GOT TO KEEP MOVING FORWARD, KURUMU!
...
I-I'M TRYING...!
THE ENVIRONMENT KEEPS CHANGING BY THE MINUTE!
WHAT AN UNSTABLE WORLD THIS IS...
HARD TO BELIEVE ALL THIS CHAOS LIVES INSIDE THE MIND OF CALM SWEET MOKA...

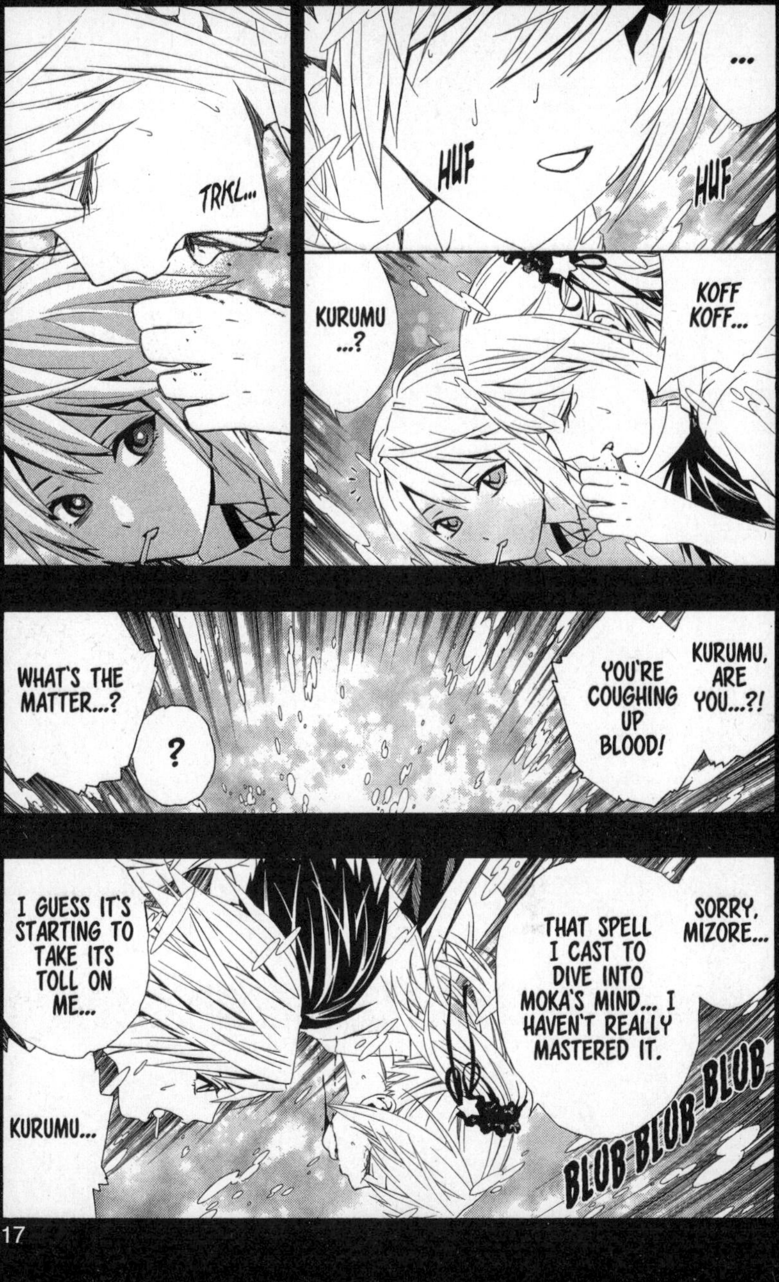
...
HUF
HUF
KOFF KOFF...
KURUMU ...?
TRKL...
KURUMU, ARE YOU...?!
YOU'RE COUGHING UP BLOOD!
WHAT'S THE MATTER...?
?
SORRY, MIZORE...
THAT SPELL I CAST TO DIVE INTO MOKA'S MIND... I HAVEN'T REALLY MASTERED IT.
I GUESS IT'S STARTING TO TAKE ITS TOLL ON ME...
BLUB BLUB BLUB
KURUMU...

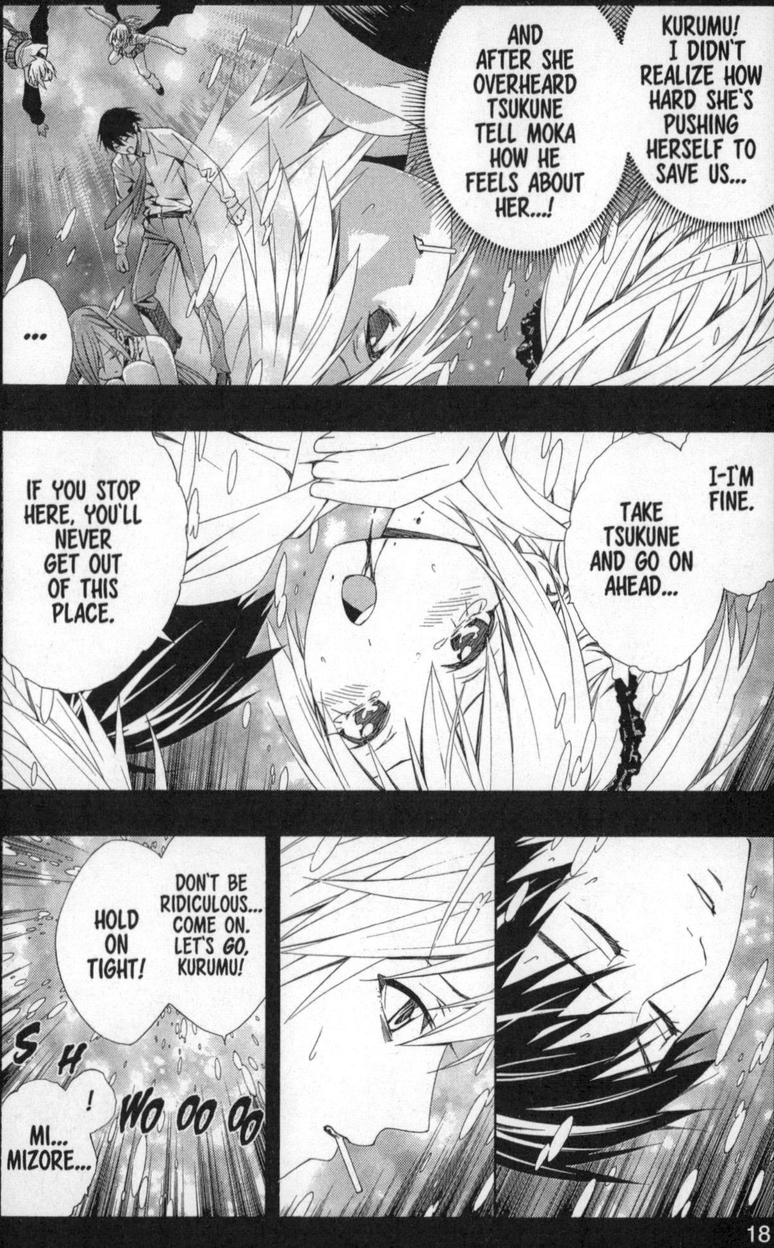
KURUMU! I DIDN'T REALIZE HOW HARD SHE'S PUSHING HERSELF TO SAVE US...
AND AFTER SHE OVERHEARD TSUKUNE TELL MOKA HOW HE FEELS ABOUT HER...!
...
I-I'M FINE.
TAKE TSUKUNE AND GO ON AHEAD...
IF YOU STOP HERE, YOU'LL NEVER GET OUT OF THIS PLACE.
DON'T BE RIDICULOUS... COME ON. LET'S GO, KURUMU!
HOLD ON TIGHT!
SH!
WOOOOO
MI... MIZORE...

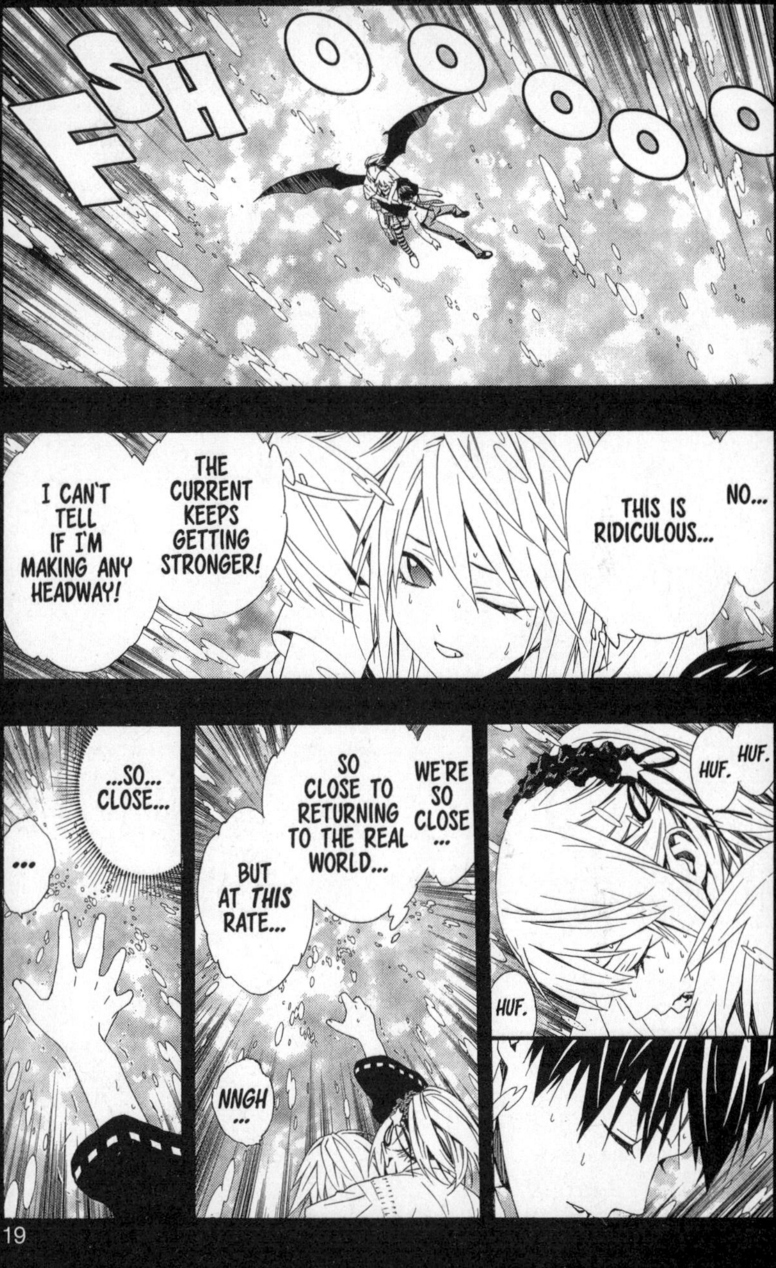
FSHOOOOO
NO...
THIS IS RIDICULOUS...
THE CURRENT KEEPS GETTING STRONGER!
I CAN'T TELL IF I'M MAKING ANY HEADWAY!
HUF.
HUF.
HUF.
WE'RE SO CLOSE...
SO CLOSE TO RETURNING TO THE REAL WORLD...
BUT AT *THIS* RATE...
NNGH...
...SO... CLOSE...
...

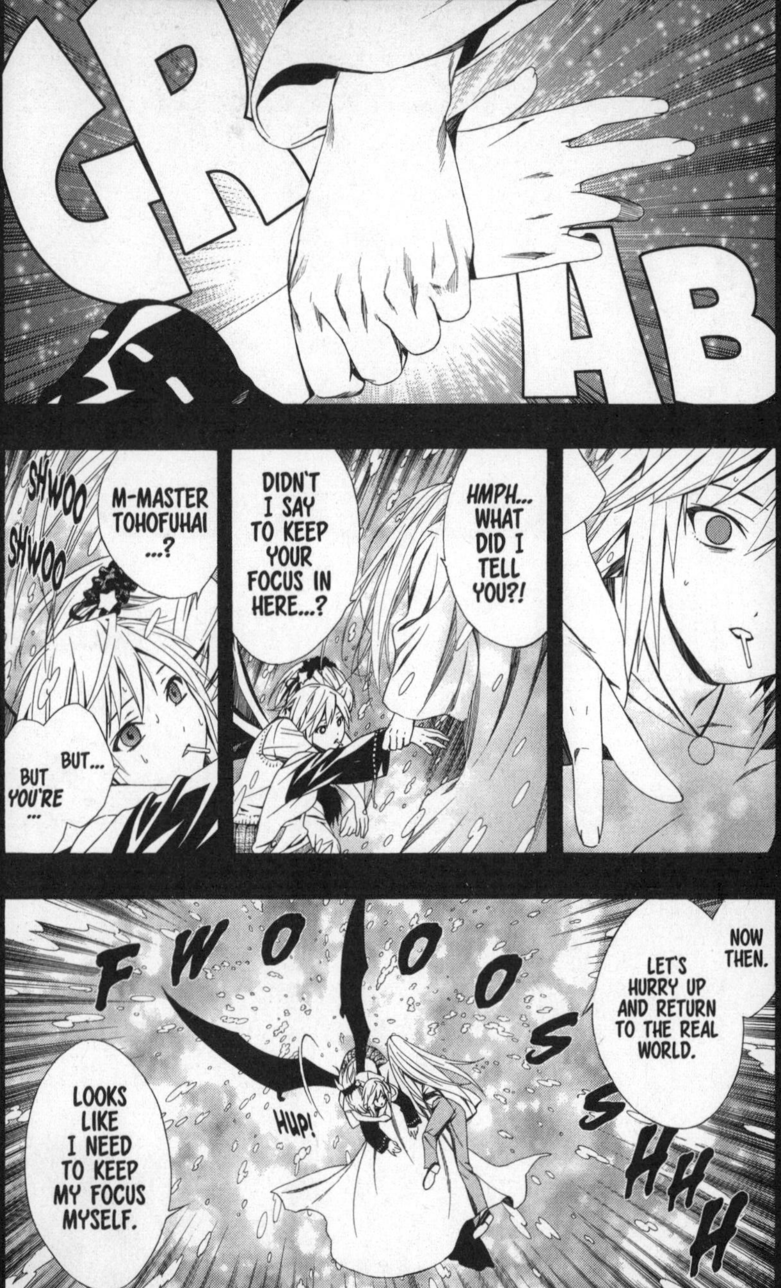
GRAB
HMPH... WHAT DID I TELL YOU?!
DIDN'T I SAY TO KEEP YOUR FOCUS IN HERE...?
M-MASTER TOHOFUHAI ...?
SHWOO SHWOO
BUT... BUT YOU'RE ...
NOW THEN.
LET'S HURRY UP AND RETURN TO THE REAL WORLD.
FWOOOSSHHHH
HUP!
LOOKS LIKE I NEED TO KEEP MY FOCUS MYSELF.

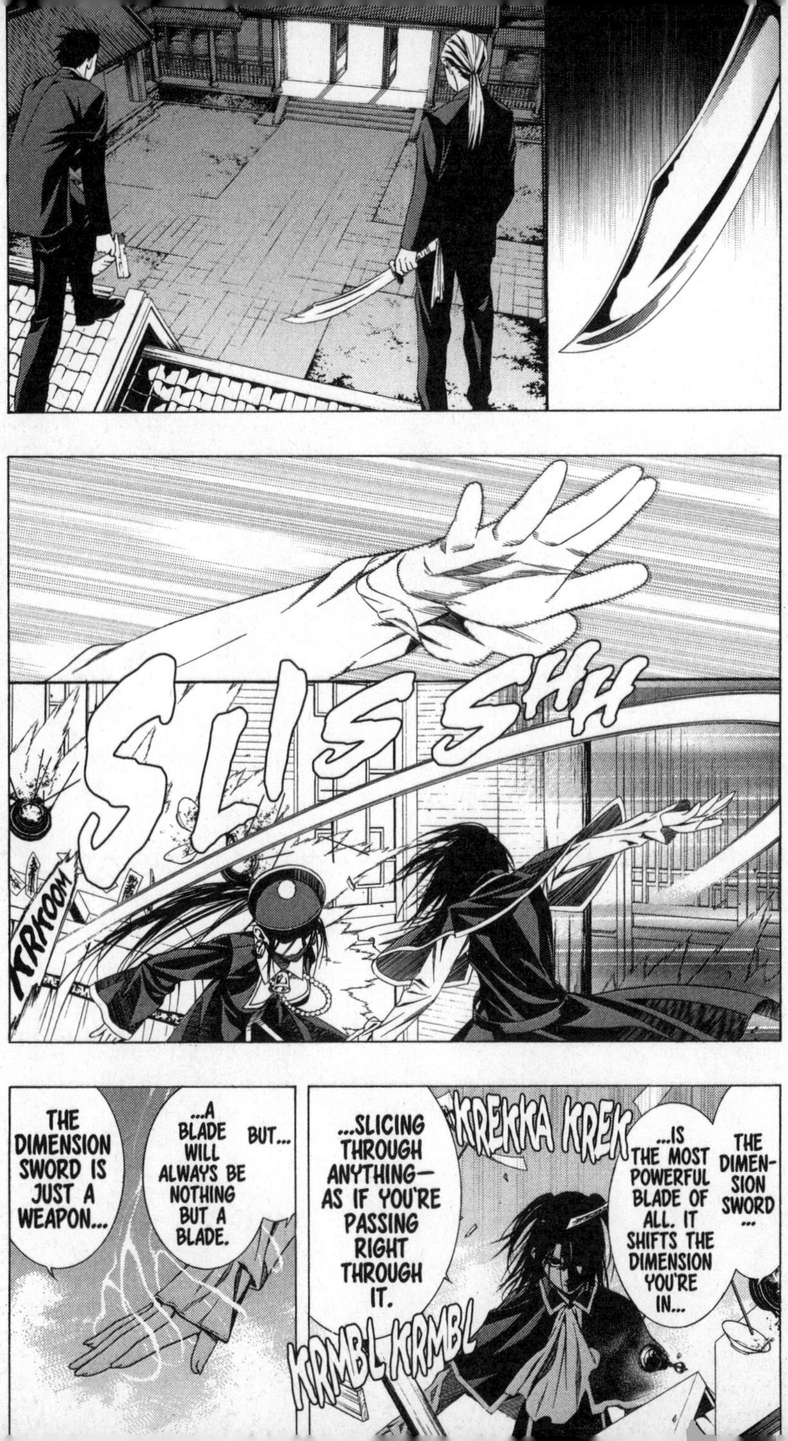
SLISSHH
KRKOOM
THE DIMENSION SWORD...
...IS THE MOST POWERFUL BLADE OF ALL. IT SHIFTS THE DIMENSION YOU'RE IN...
KREKKA KREK
...SLICING THROUGH ANYTHING— AS IF YOU'RE PASSING RIGHT THROUGH IT.
KRMBL KRMBL
BUT...
...A BLADE WILL ALWAYS BE NOTHING BUT A BLADE.
THE DIMENSION SWORD IS JUST A WEAPON...

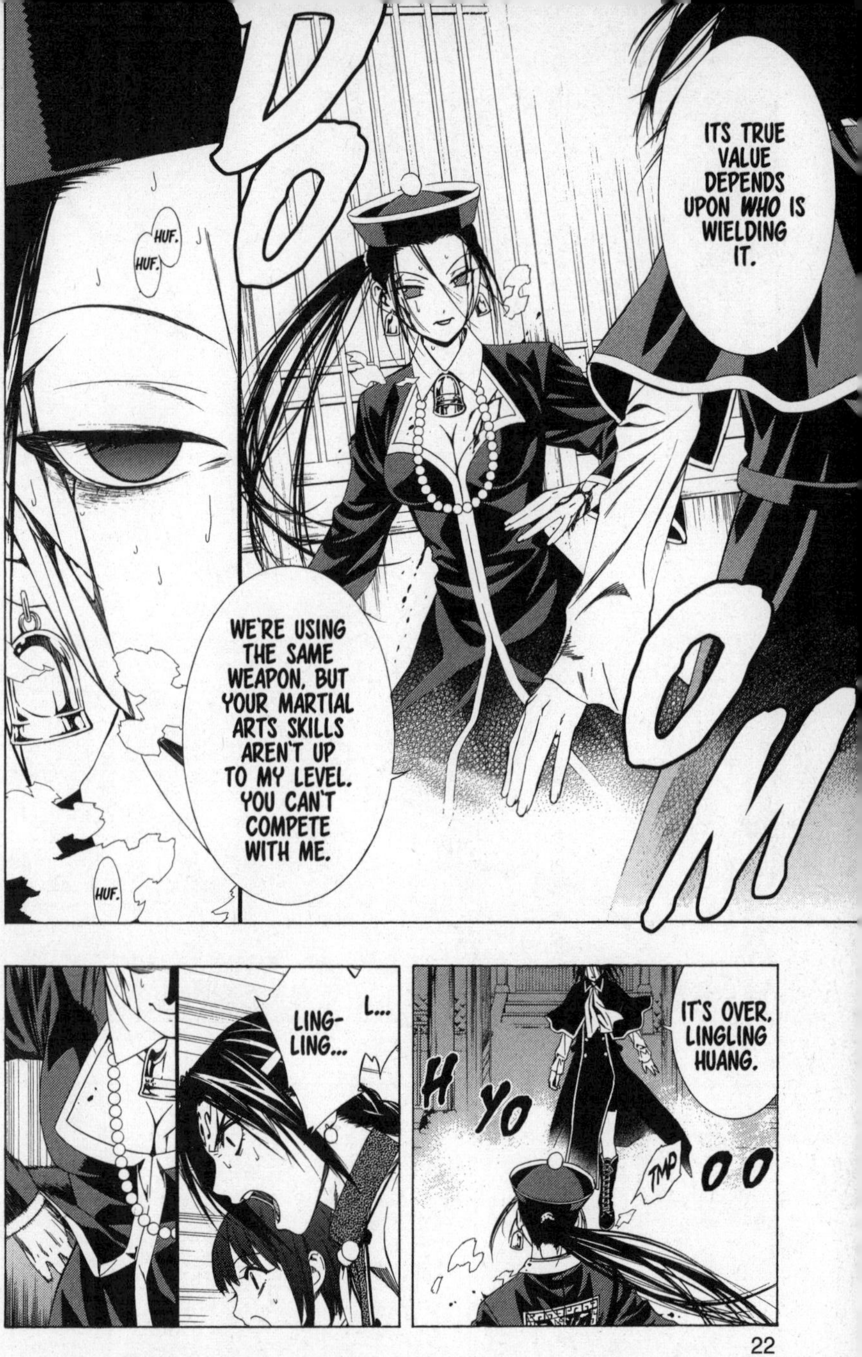
ITS TRUE VALUE DEPENDS UPON WHO IS WIELDING IT.
DOOM
WE'RE USING THE SAME WEAPON, BUT YOUR MARTIAL ARTS SKILLS AREN'T UP TO MY LEVEL. YOU CAN'T COMPETE WITH ME.
HUF.
HUF.
HUF.
IT'S OVER, LINGLING HUANG.
HYOO
TMP
L...
LING-LING...

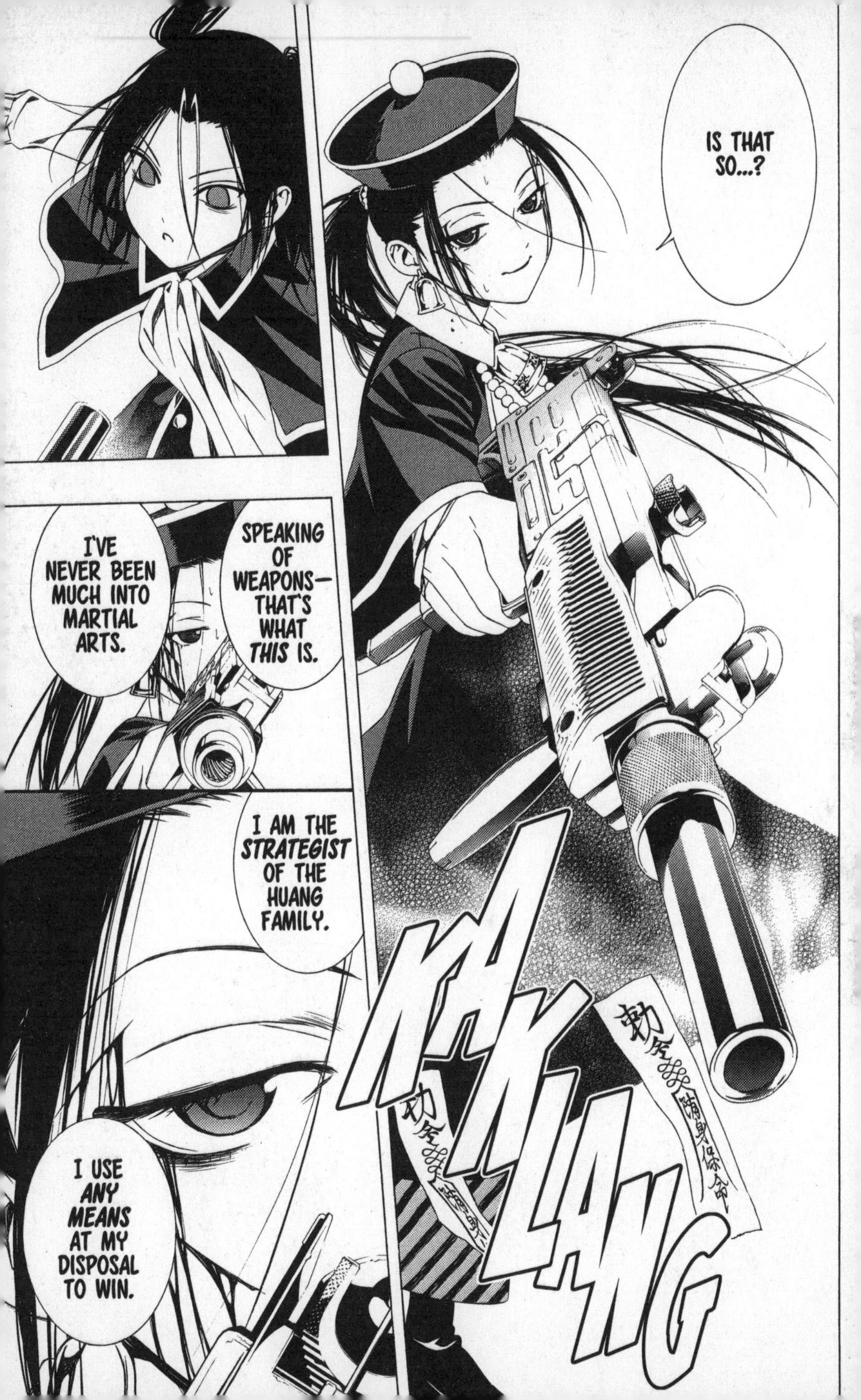
IS THAT SO...?
SPEAKING OF WEAPONS— THAT'S WHAT *THIS* IS.
I'VE NEVER BEEN MUCH INTO MARTIAL ARTS.
I AM THE *STRATEGIST* OF THE HUANG FAMILY.
I USE *ANY MEANS* AT MY DISPOSAL TO WIN.

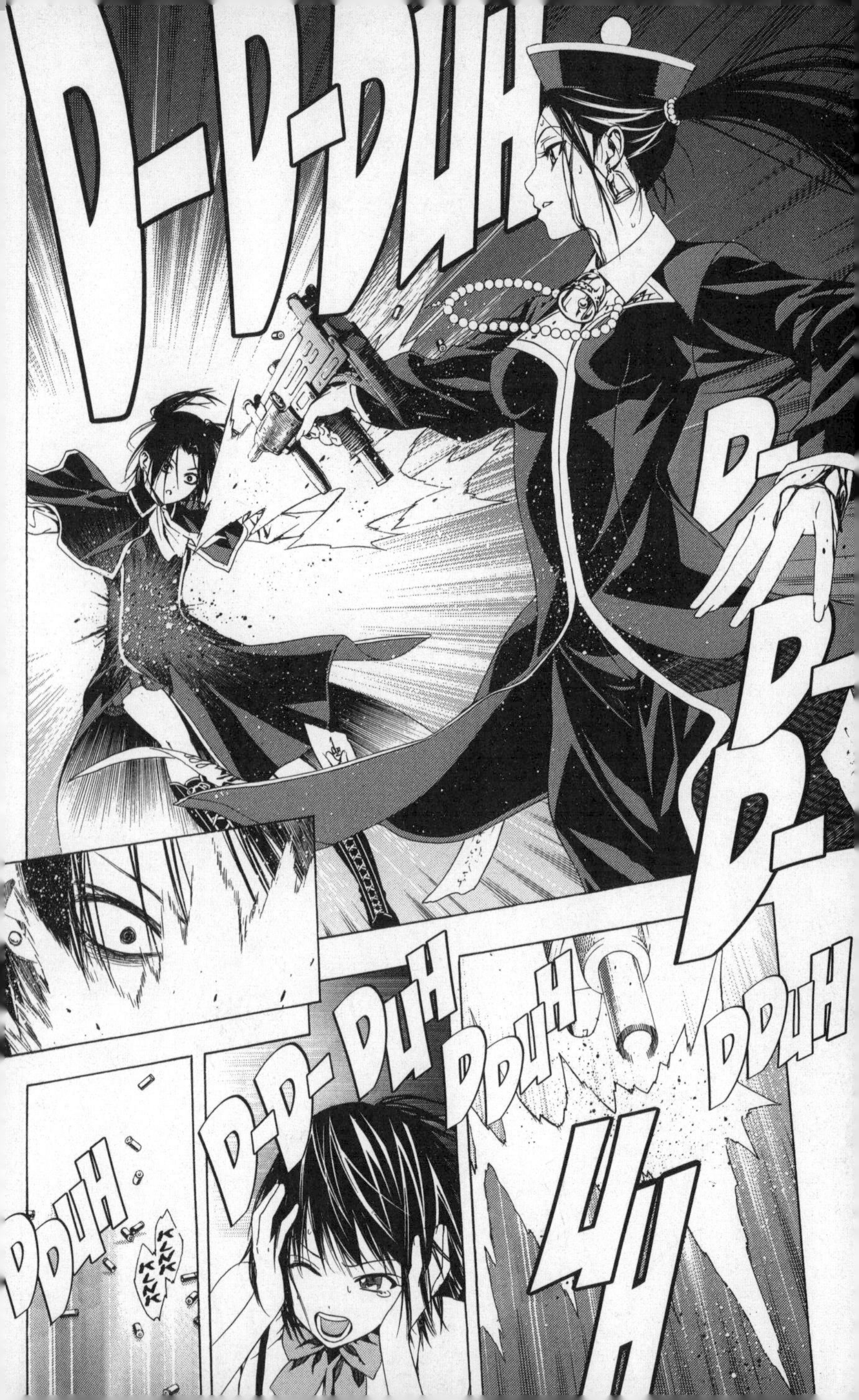
D-D-DUH
D-
D-D-D-
DDUH
UH
DDUH
D-D-DUH
DDUH
KLNK
KLNK

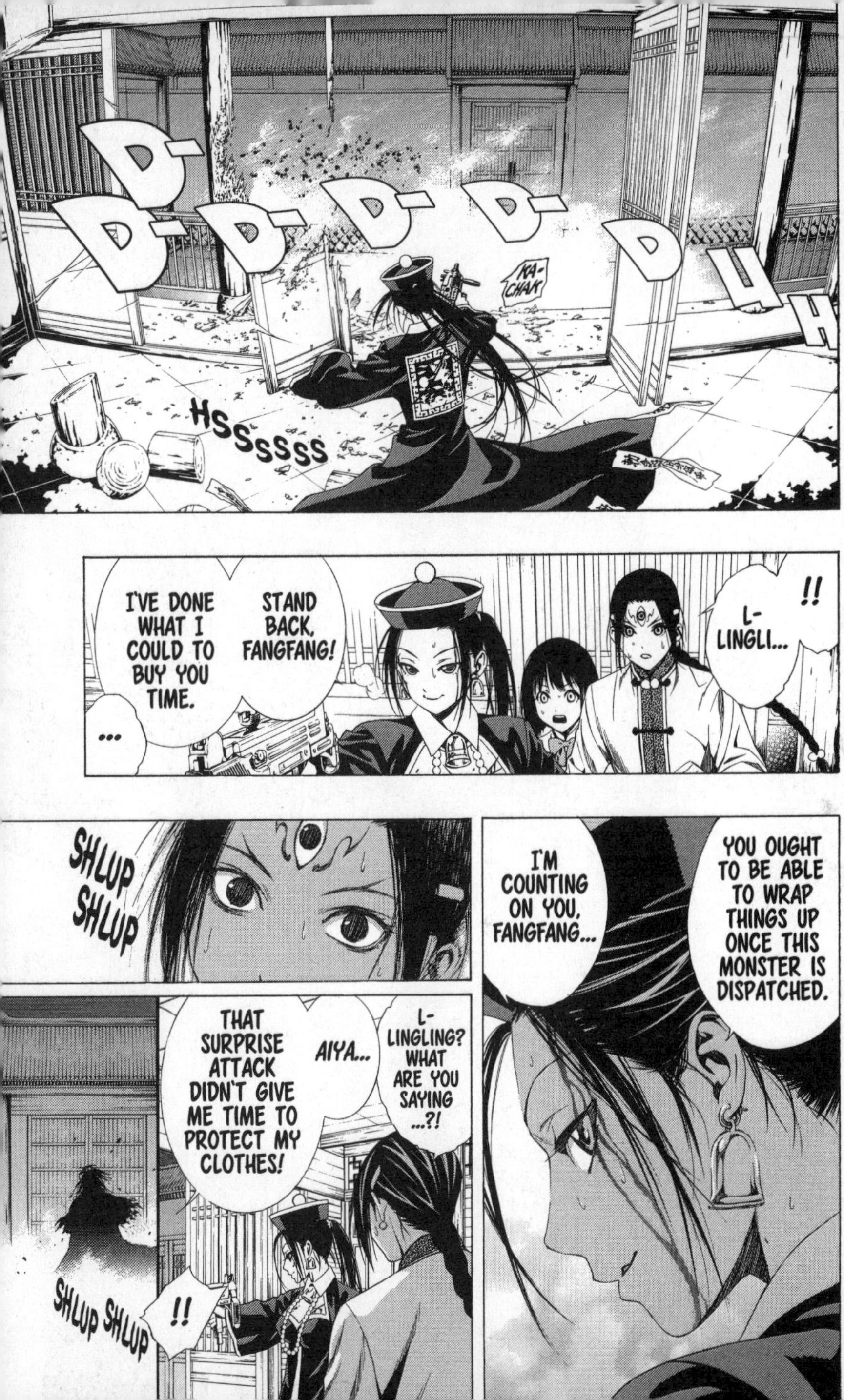
D-D-D-D-D-DUH
KA-CHAK
HSSSSSS
!!
L-LINGLI...
STAND BACK, FANGFANG!
I'VE DONE WHAT I COULD TO BUY YOU TIME.
...
YOU OUGHT TO BE ABLE TO WRAP THINGS UP ONCE THIS MONSTER IS DISPATCHED.
I'M COUNTING ON YOU, FANGFANG...
SHLUP SHLUP
L-LINGLING? WHAT ARE YOU SAYING ...?!
AIYA...
THAT SURPRISE ATTACK DIDN'T GIVE ME TIME TO PROTECT MY CLOTHES!
!!
SHLUP SHLUP

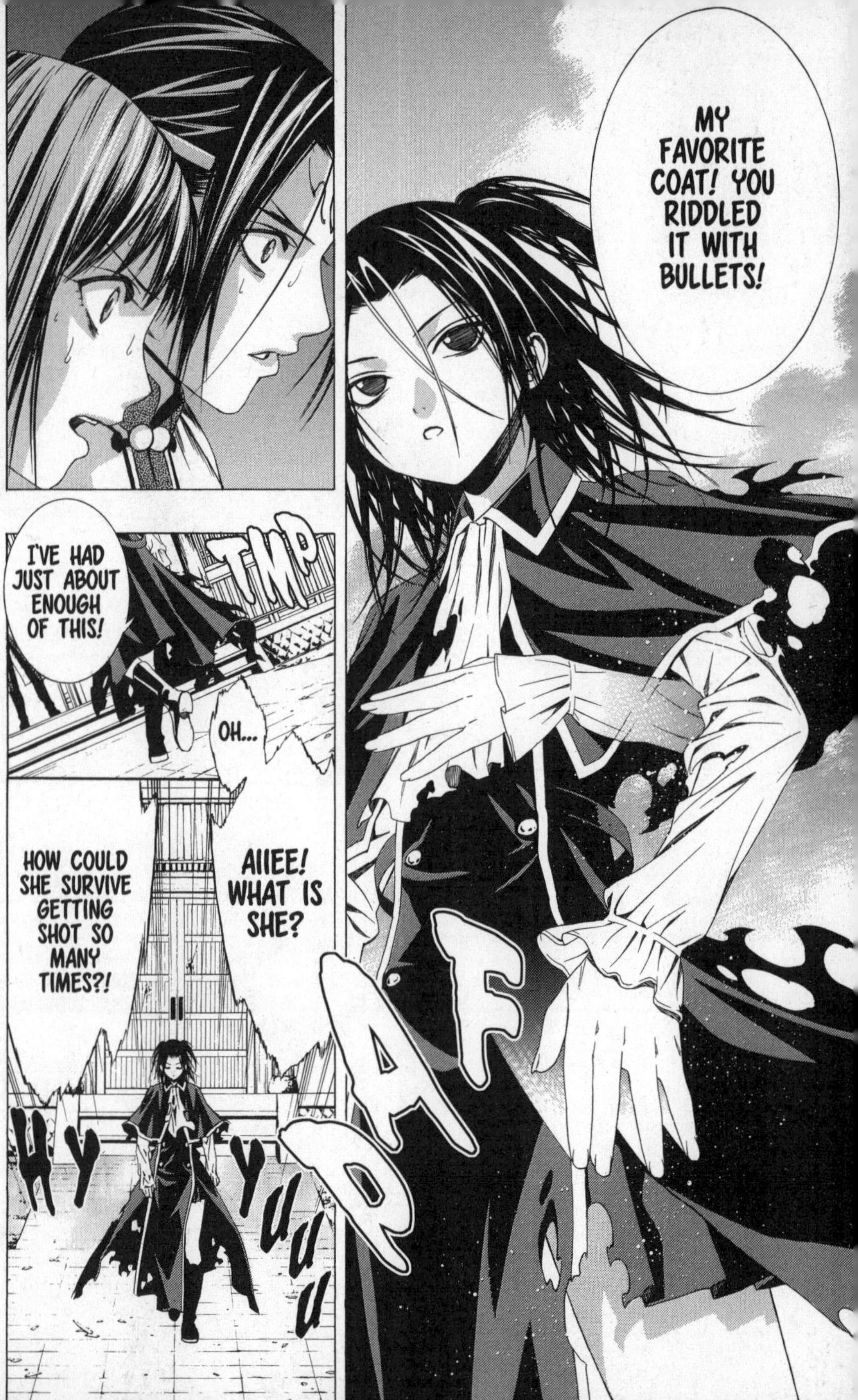
MY FAVORITE COAT! YOU RIDDLED IT WITH BULLETS!
RAF
TMP
I'VE HAD JUST ABOUT ENOUGH OF THIS!
OH...
AIIEE! WHAT IS SHE?
HOW COULD SHE SURVIVE GETTING SHOT SO MANY TIMES?!
HYUUUU

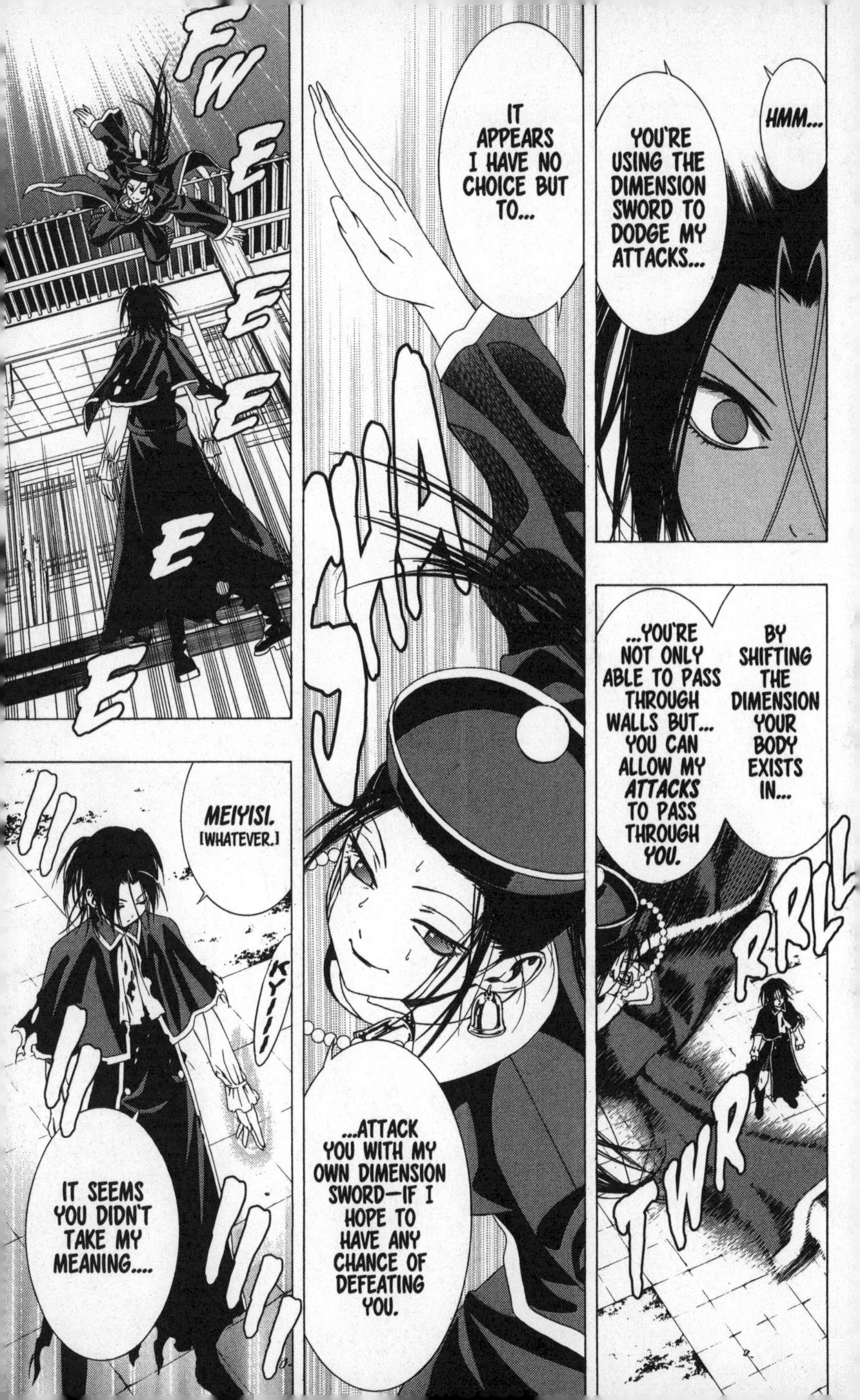
HMM...
YOU'RE USING THE DIMENSION SWORD TO DODGE MY ATTACKS...
BY SHIFTING THE DIMENSION YOUR BODY EXISTS IN...
...YOU'RE NOT ONLY ABLE TO PASS THROUGH WALLS BUT... YOU CAN ALLOW MY ATTACKS TO PASS THROUGH YOU.
TWRRRLL
IT APPEARS I HAVE NO CHOICE BUT TO...
...ATTACK YOU WITH MY OWN DIMENSION SWORD—IF I HOPE TO HAVE ANY CHANCE OF DEFEATING YOU.
FWEEEEE
MEIYISI.
[WHATEVER.]
IT SEEMS YOU DIDN'T TAKE MY MEANING....

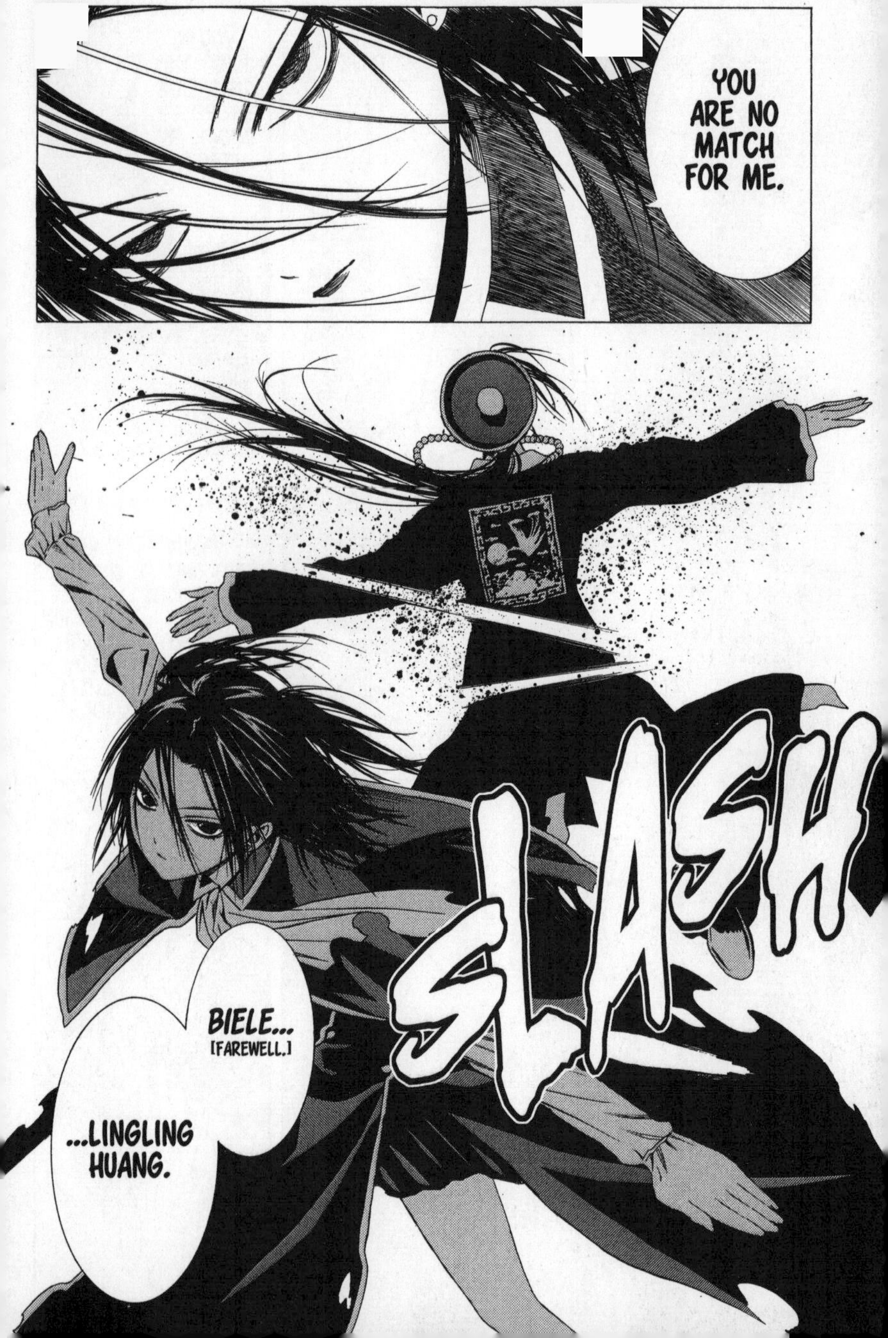
YOU ARE NO MATCH FOR ME.
BIELE... [FAREWELL.]
...LINGLING HUANG.
SLASH

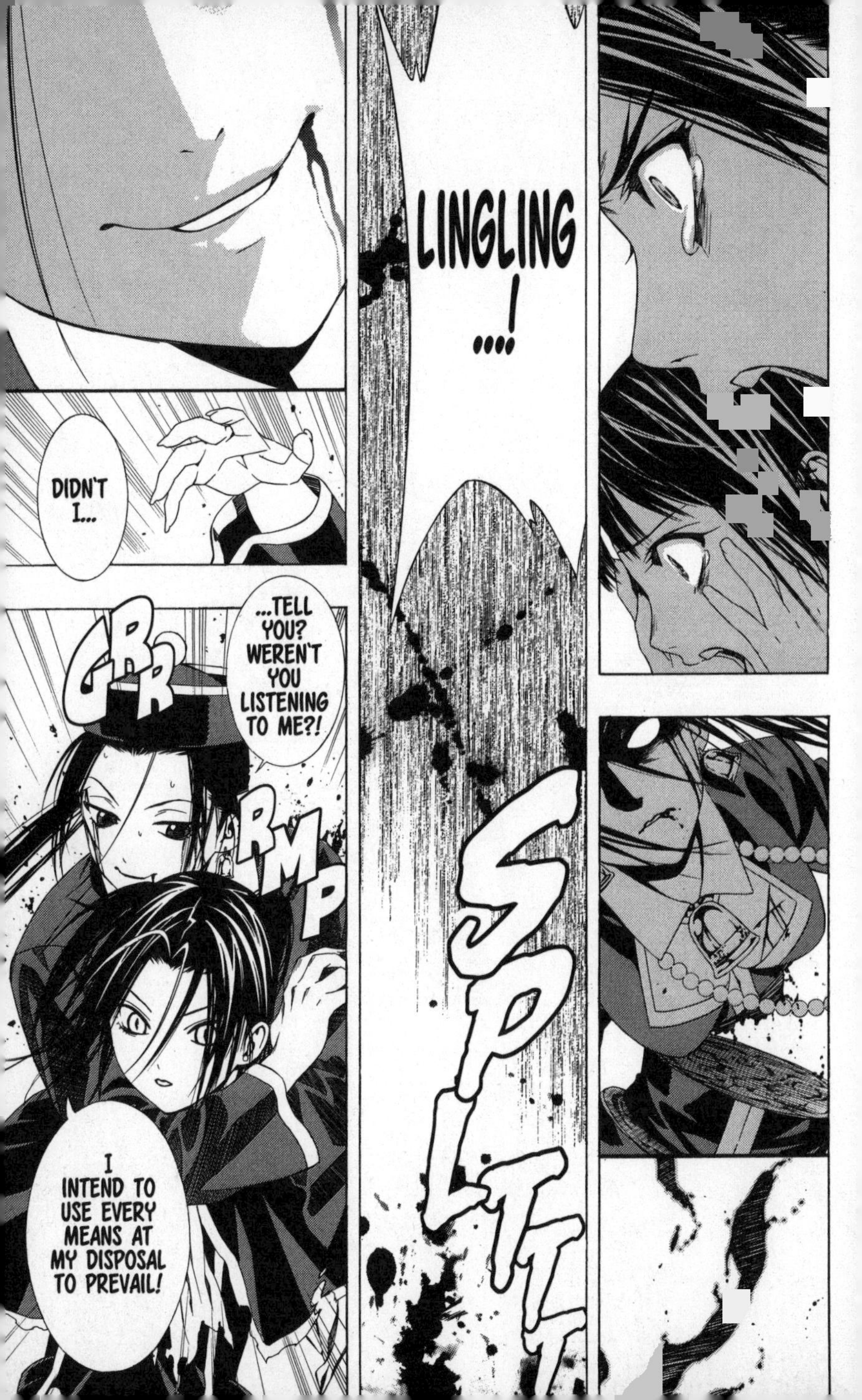
LINGLING ...!
SPLIT
DIDN'T I...
...TELL YOU? WEREN'T YOU LISTENING TO ME?!
GRR
RMP
I INTEND TO USE EVERY MEANS AT MY DISPOSAL TO PREVAIL!

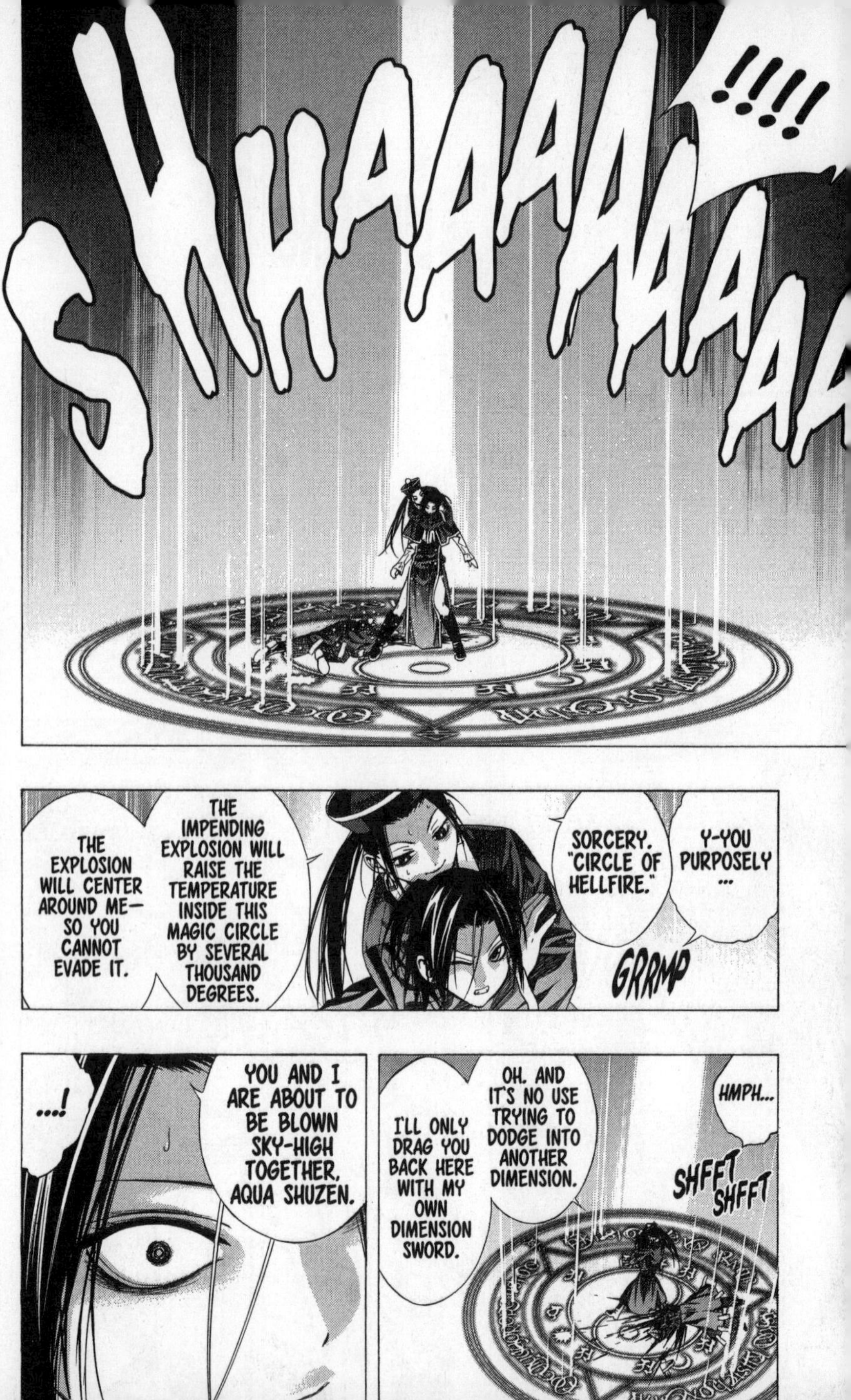

SHHAAAAAAAAA!!!!!
Y-YOU PURPOSELY ...
SORCERY. "CIRCLE OF HELLFIRE."
GRRMP
THE IMPENDING EXPLOSION WILL RAISE THE TEMPERATURE INSIDE THIS MAGIC CIRCLE BY SEVERAL THOUSAND DEGREES.
THE EXPLOSION WILL CENTER AROUND ME— SO YOU CANNOT EVADE IT.
HMPH...
SHFFT SHFFT
OH. AND IT'S NO USE TRYING TO DODGE INTO ANOTHER DIMENSION.
I'LL ONLY DRAG YOU BACK HERE WITH MY OWN DIMENSION SWORD.
YOU AND I ARE ABOUT TO BE BLOWN SKY-HIGH TOGETHER, AQUA SHUZEN.
...!

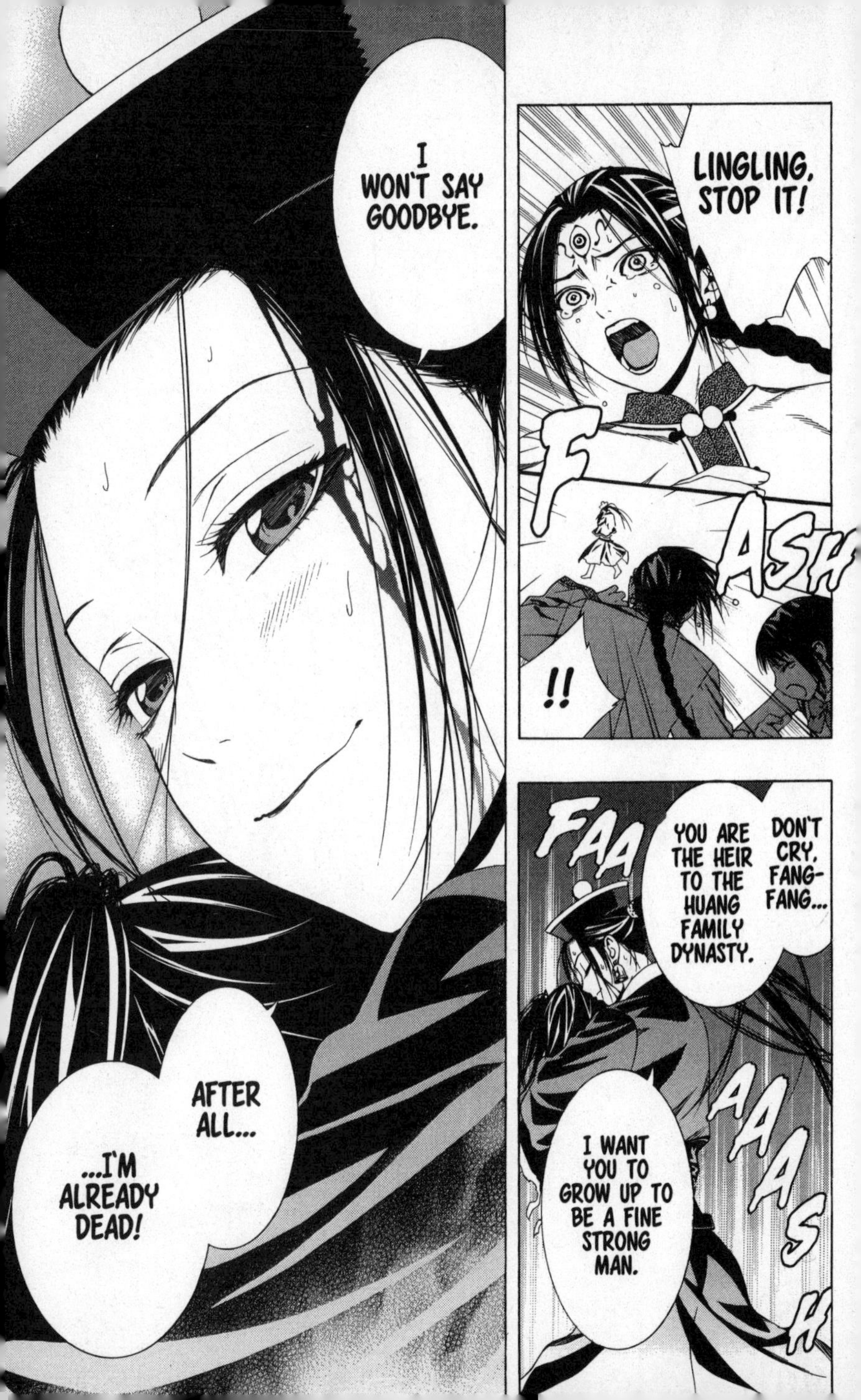
LINGLING, STOP IT!
F
ASH
!!
DON'T CRY, FANG-FANG...
YOU ARE THE HEIR TO THE HUANG FAMILY DYNASTY.
FAA
I WANT YOU TO GROW UP TO BE A FINE STRONG MAN.
AAAASH
I WON'T SAY GOODBYE.
AFTER ALL...
...I'M ALREADY DEAD!

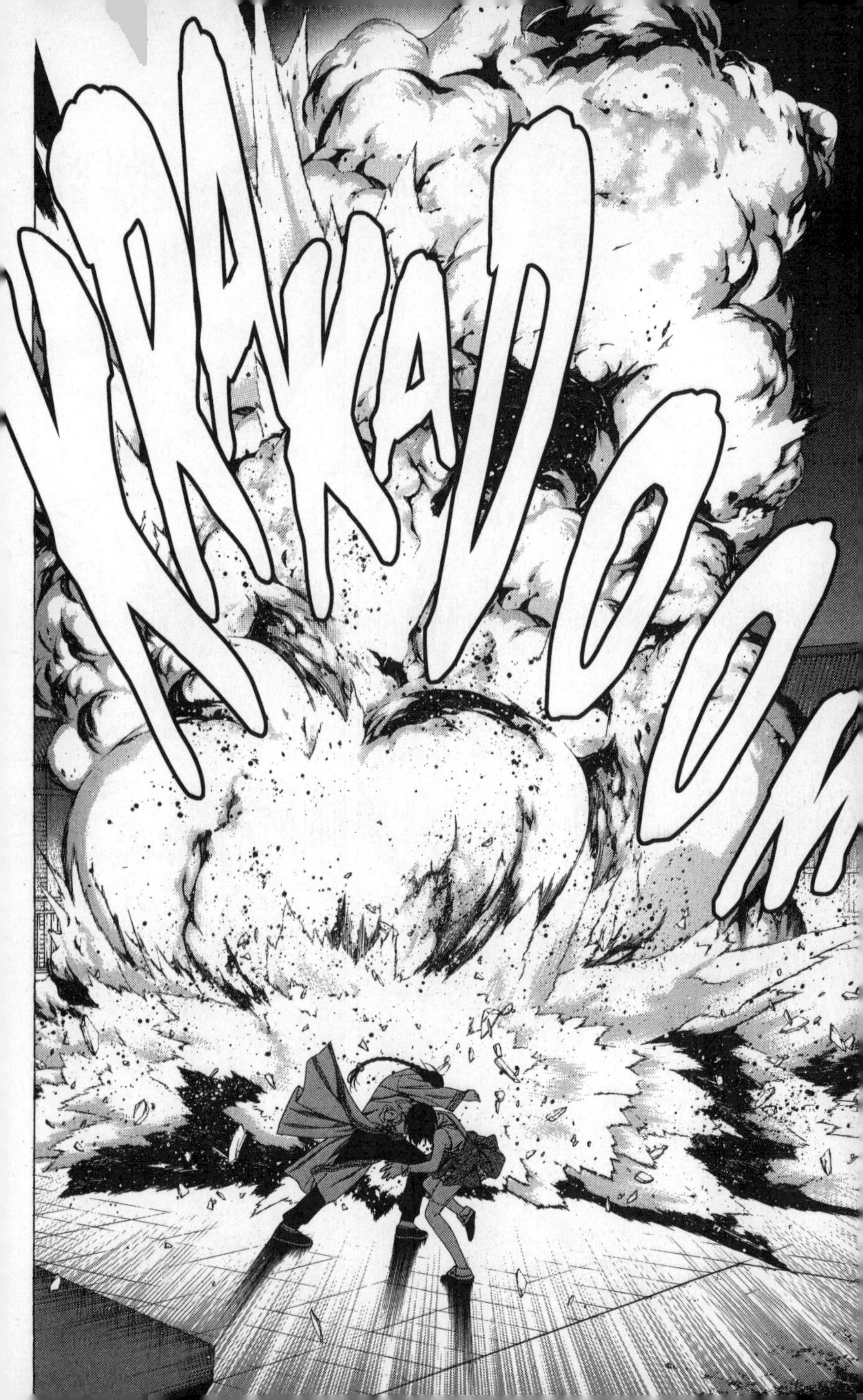
KRAKADOOM

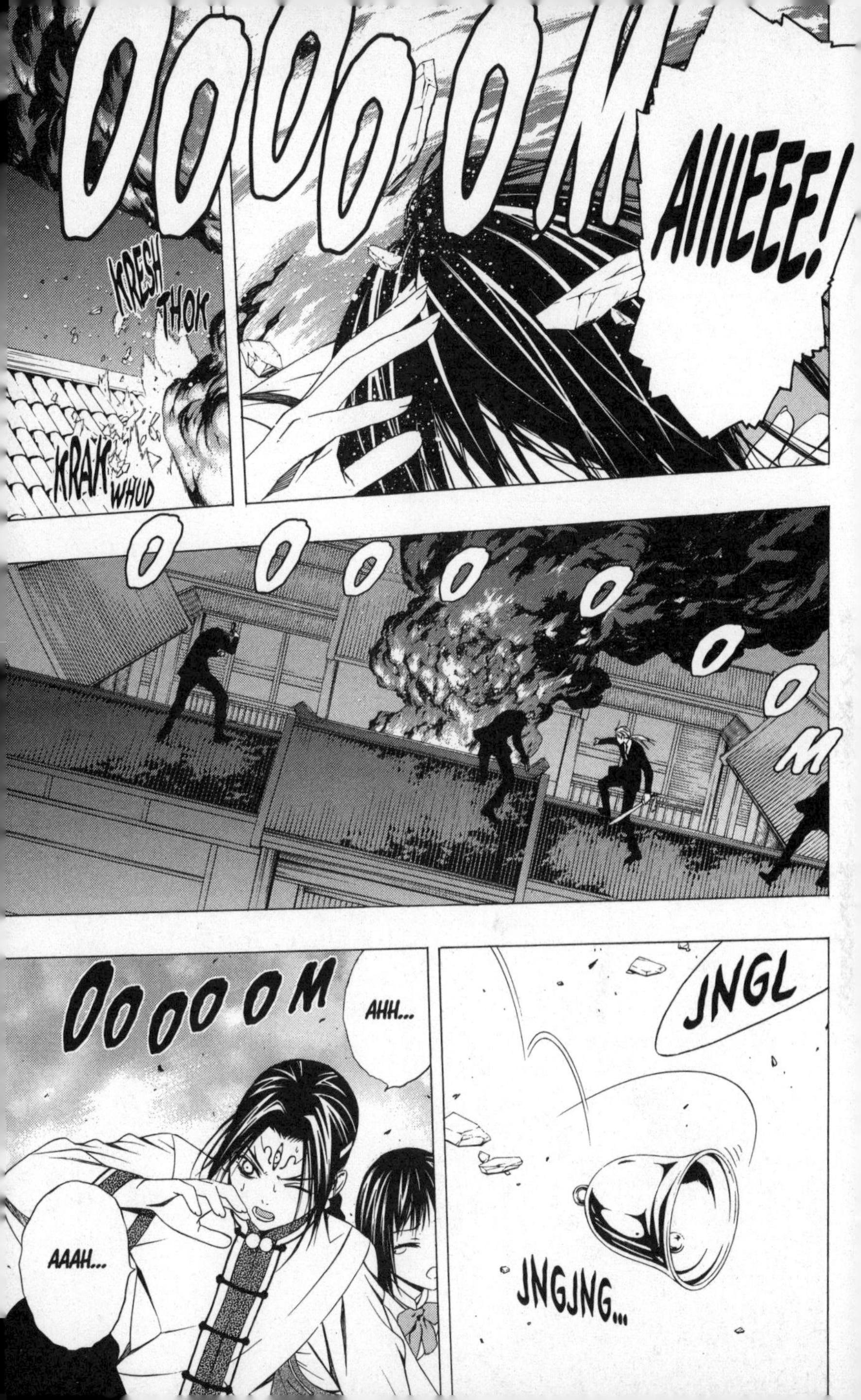
OOOOOM
AIIIEEE!
KRESH
THOK
KRAK
WHUD
OOOOOOOM
JNGL
JNGJNG...
OOOOOM
AHH...
AAAH...

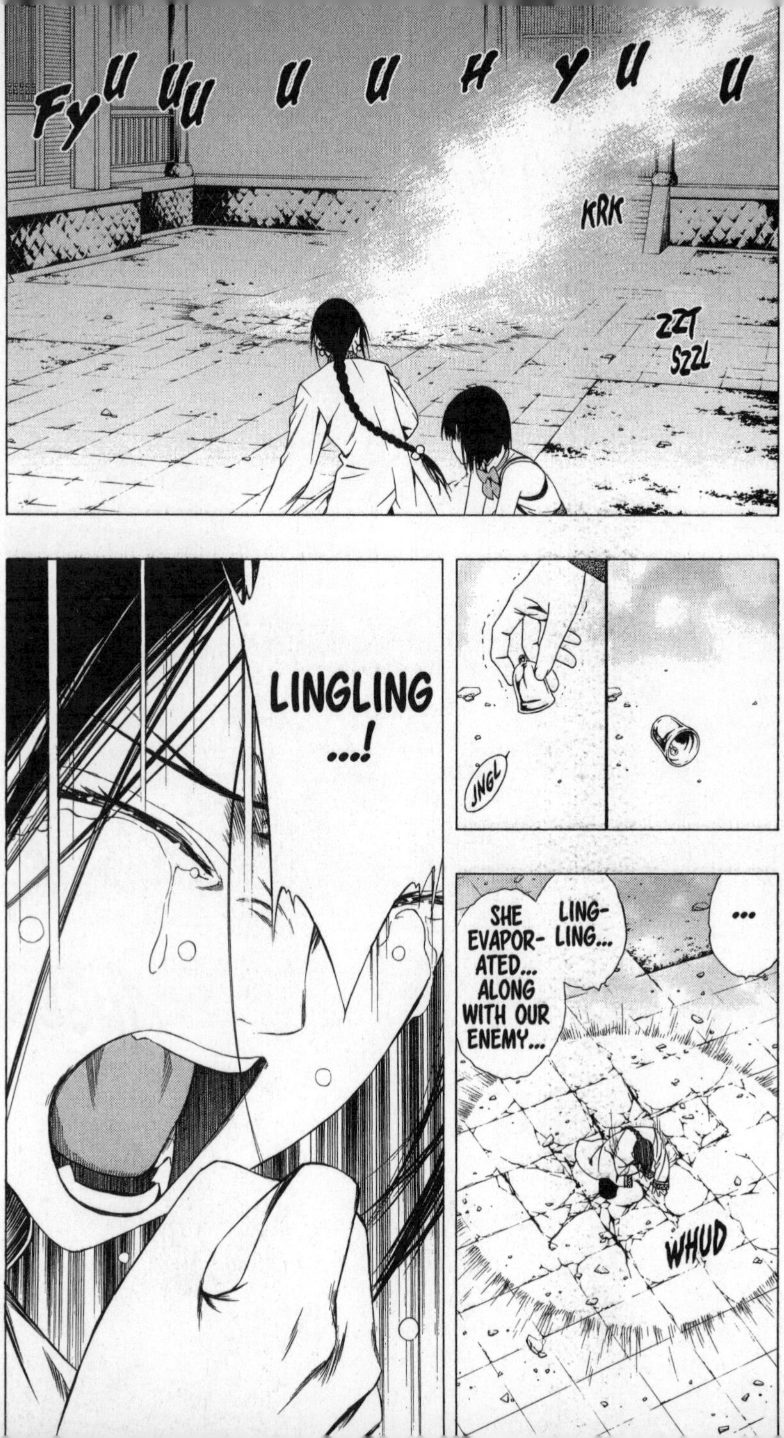
Fyuuuuuhyuu
KRK
ZZT
SZZL
JNGL
...
LING-LING...
SHE EVAPORATED... ALONG WITH OUR ENEMY...
WHUD
LINGLING ...!

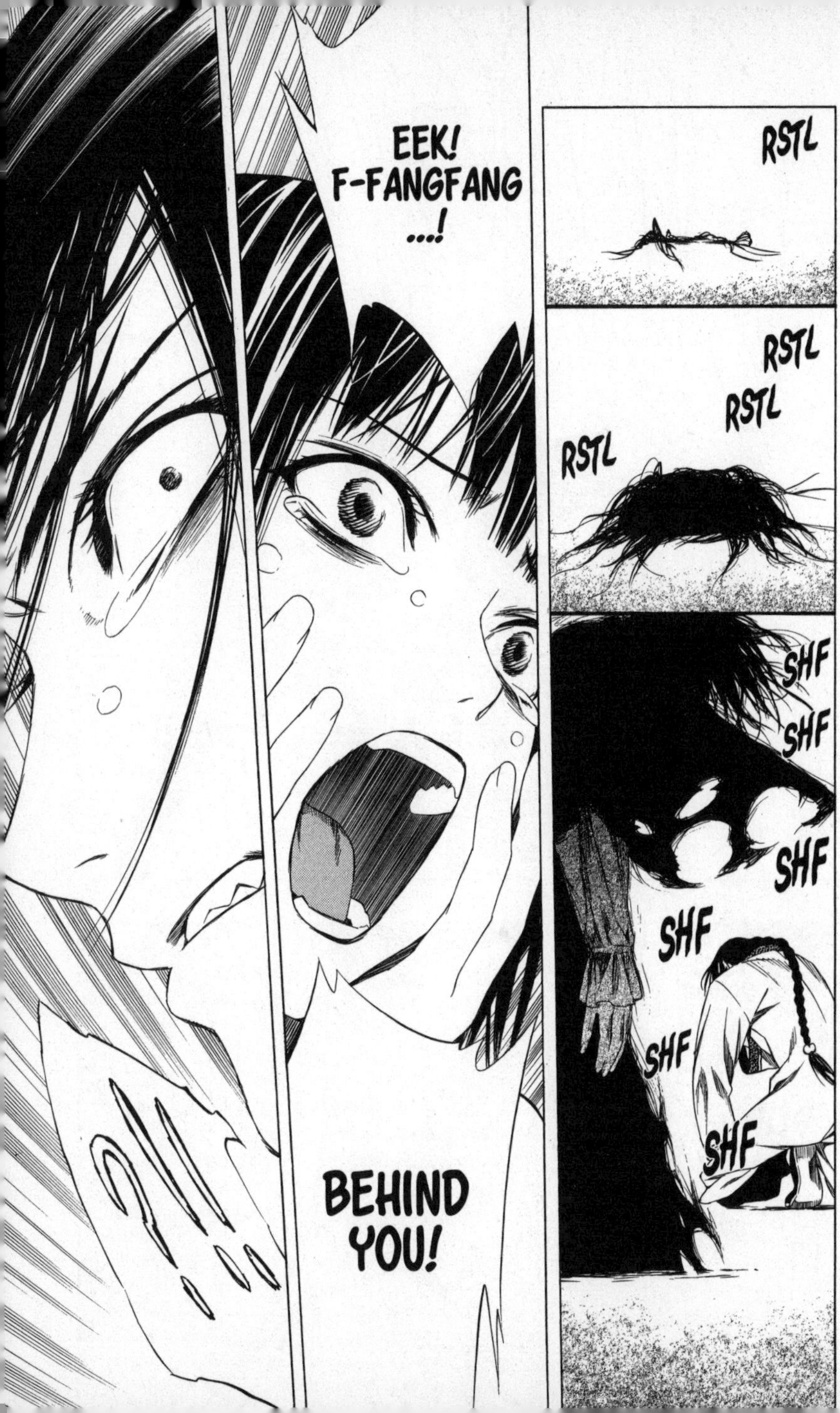
RSTL
RSTL
RSTL
RSTL
SHF
SHF
SHF
SHF
SHF
SHF
EEK! F-FANGFANG ...!
BEHIND YOU!

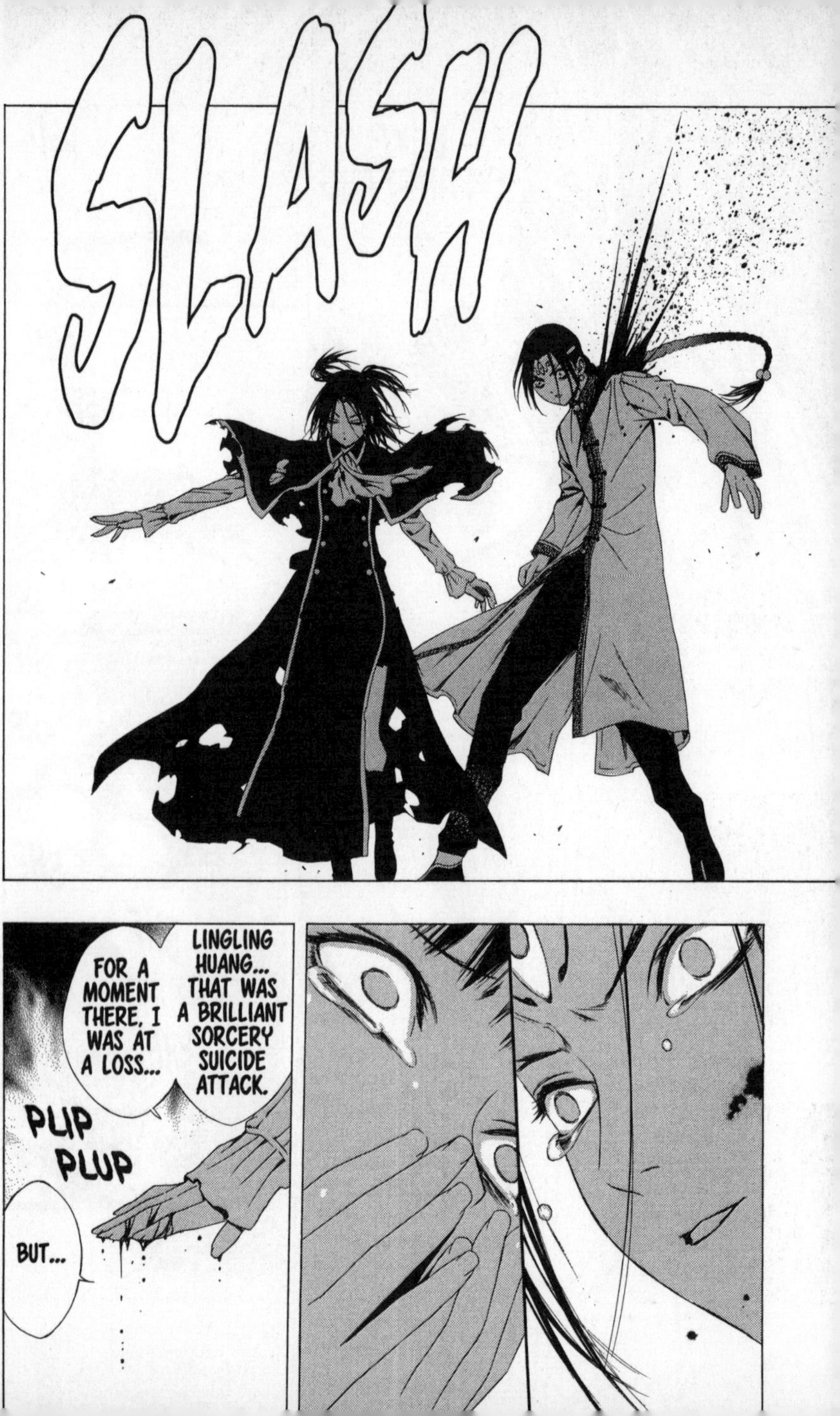
SLASH
LINGLING HUANG... THAT WAS A BRILLIANT SORCERY SUICIDE ATTACK.
FOR A MOMENT THERE, I WAS AT A LOSS...
PLIP PLUP
BUT...

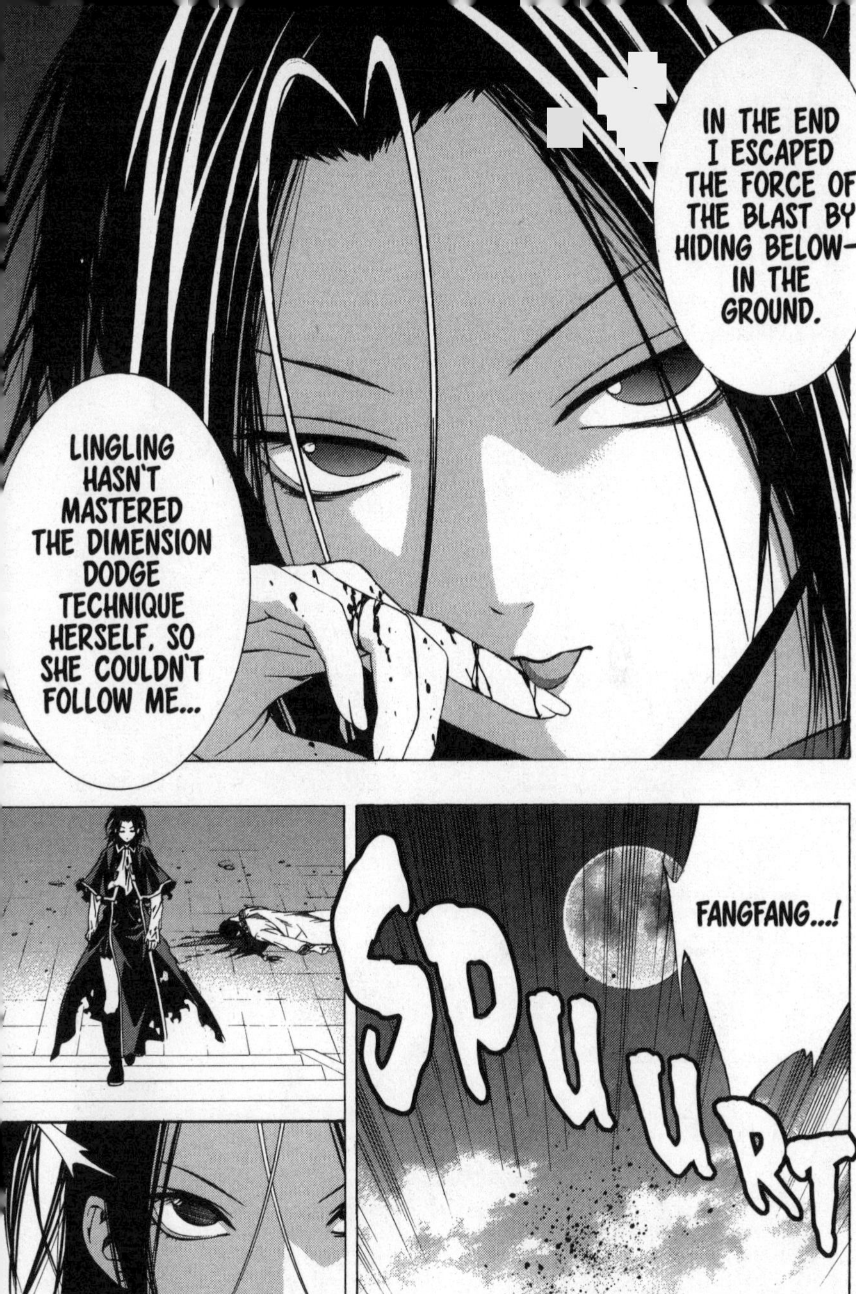
IN THE END I ESCAPED THE FORCE OF THE BLAST BY HIDING BELOW— IN THE GROUND.
LINGLING HASN'T MASTERED THE DIMENSION DODGE TECHNIQUE HERSELF, SO SHE COULDN'T FOLLOW ME...
FANGFANG...!
SPUURT

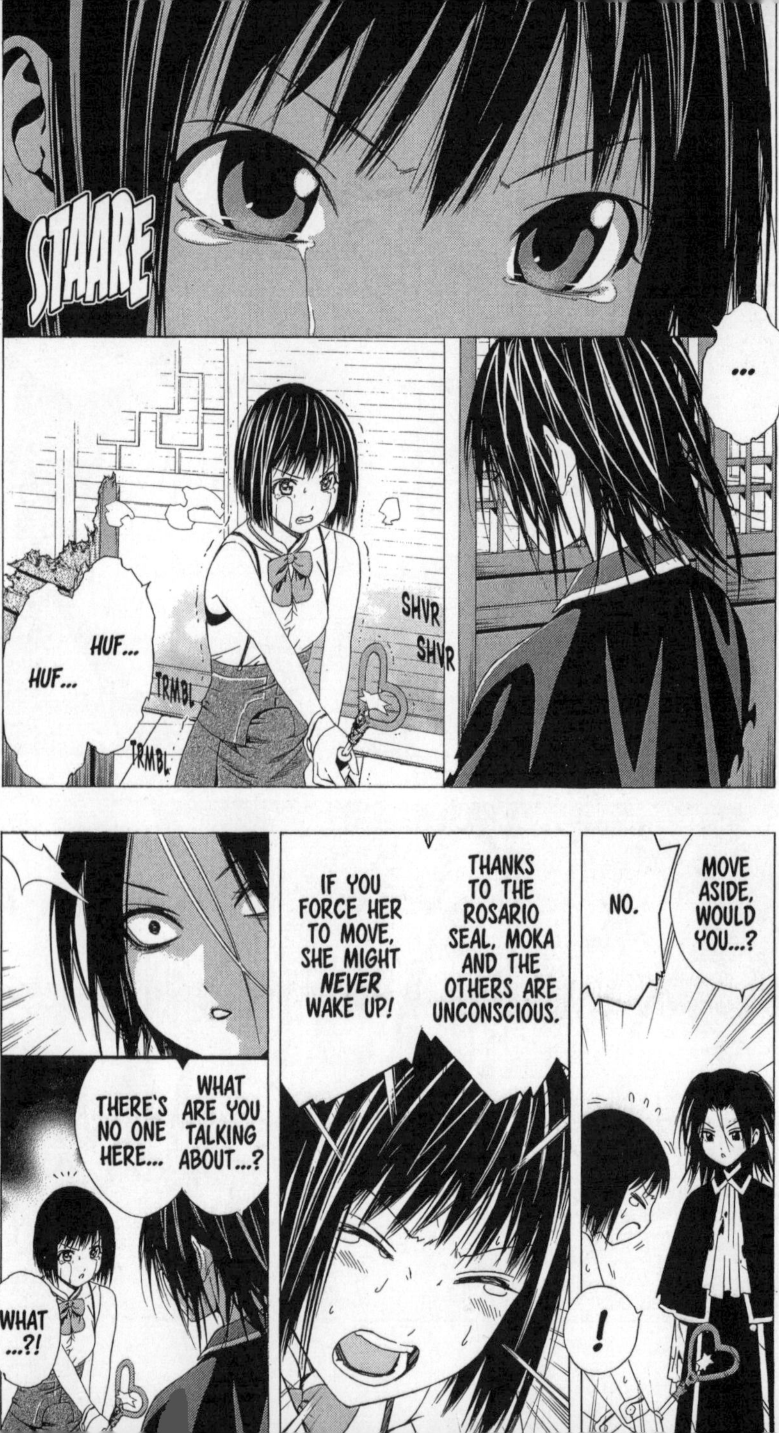
STAARE
...
SHVR
SHVR
HUF...
HUF...
TRMBL
TRMBL
MOVE ASIDE, WOULD YOU...?
NO.
THANKS TO THE ROSARIO SEAL, MOKA AND THE OTHERS ARE UNCONSCIOUS.
IF YOU FORCE HER TO MOVE, SHE MIGHT *NEVER* WAKE UP!
!
WHAT ARE YOU TALKING ABOUT...?
THERE'S NO ONE HERE...
WHAT ...?!

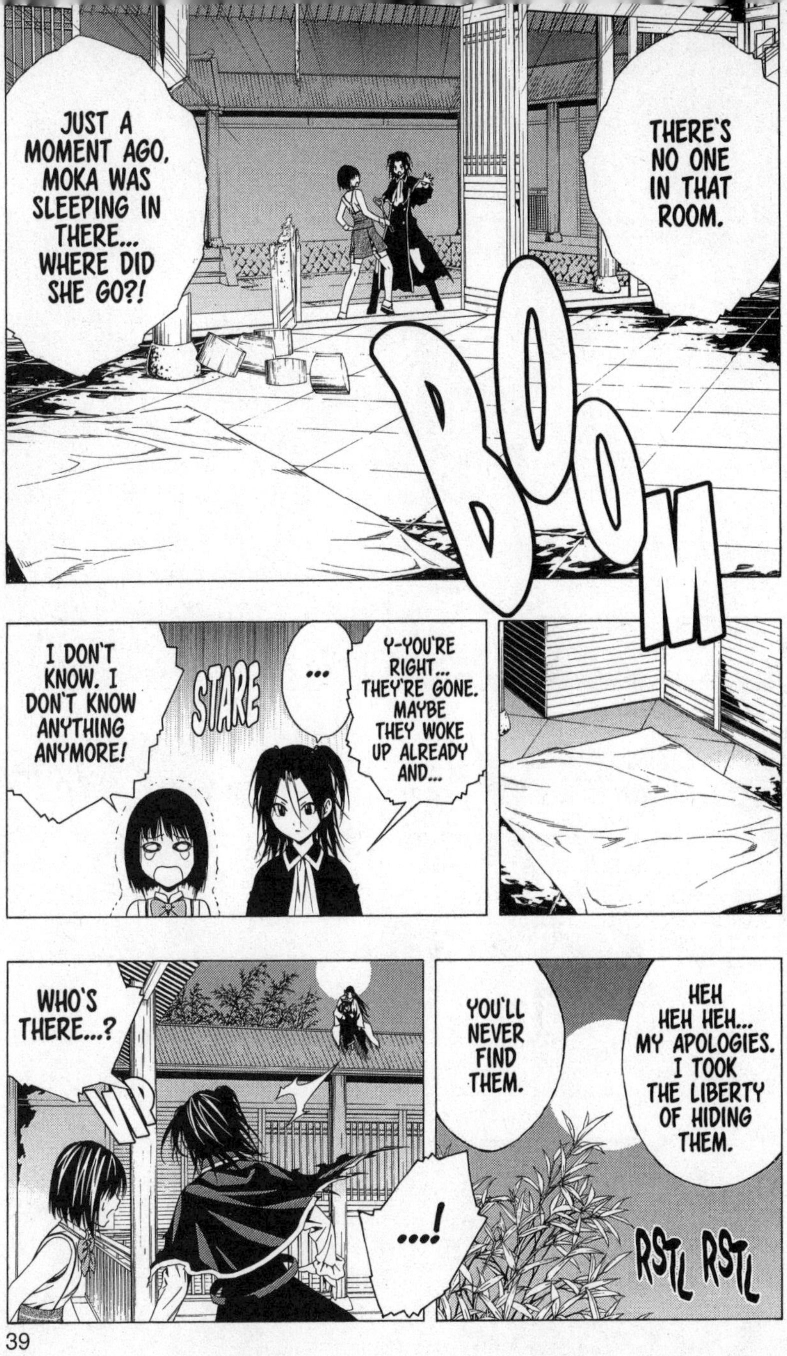
THERE'S NO ONE IN THAT ROOM.
JUST A MOMENT AGO, MOKA WAS SLEEPING IN THERE... WHERE DID SHE GO?!
BOOM
Y-YOU'RE RIGHT... THEY'RE GONE. MAYBE THEY WOKE UP ALREADY AND...
...
STARE
I DON'T KNOW. I DON'T KNOW ANYTHING ANYMORE!
HEH HEH HEH... MY APOLOGIES. I TOOK THE LIBERTY OF HIDING THEM.
YOU'LL NEVER FIND THEM.
RSTL RSTL
...!
WHO'S THERE...?
VIP

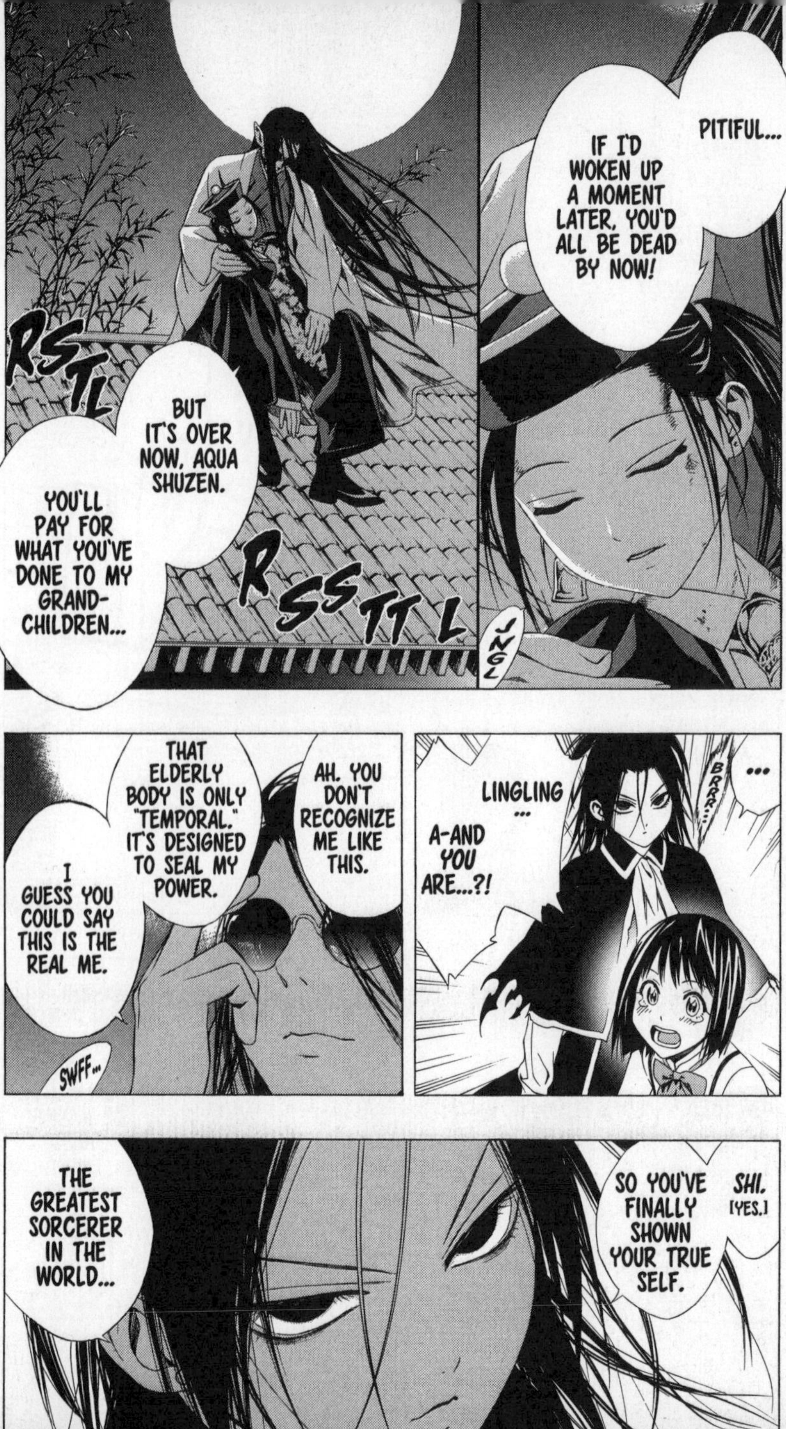
PITIFUL...
IF I'D WOKEN UP A MOMENT LATER, YOU'D ALL BE DEAD BY NOW!
JNGL
BUT IT'S OVER NOW, AQUA SHUZEN.
RSTL
YOU'LL PAY FOR WHAT YOU'VE DONE TO MY GRAND-CHILDREN...
RSSTTL
...
BRRR...
LINGLING...
A-AND YOU ARE...?!
AH. YOU DON'T RECOGNIZE ME LIKE THIS.
THAT ELDERLY BODY IS ONLY "TEMPORAL." IT'S DESIGNED TO SEAL MY POWER.
I GUESS YOU COULD SAY THIS IS THE REAL ME.
SWFF...
SHI. [YES.]
SO YOU'VE FINALLY SHOWN YOUR TRUE SELF.
THE GREATEST SORCERER IN THE WORLD...

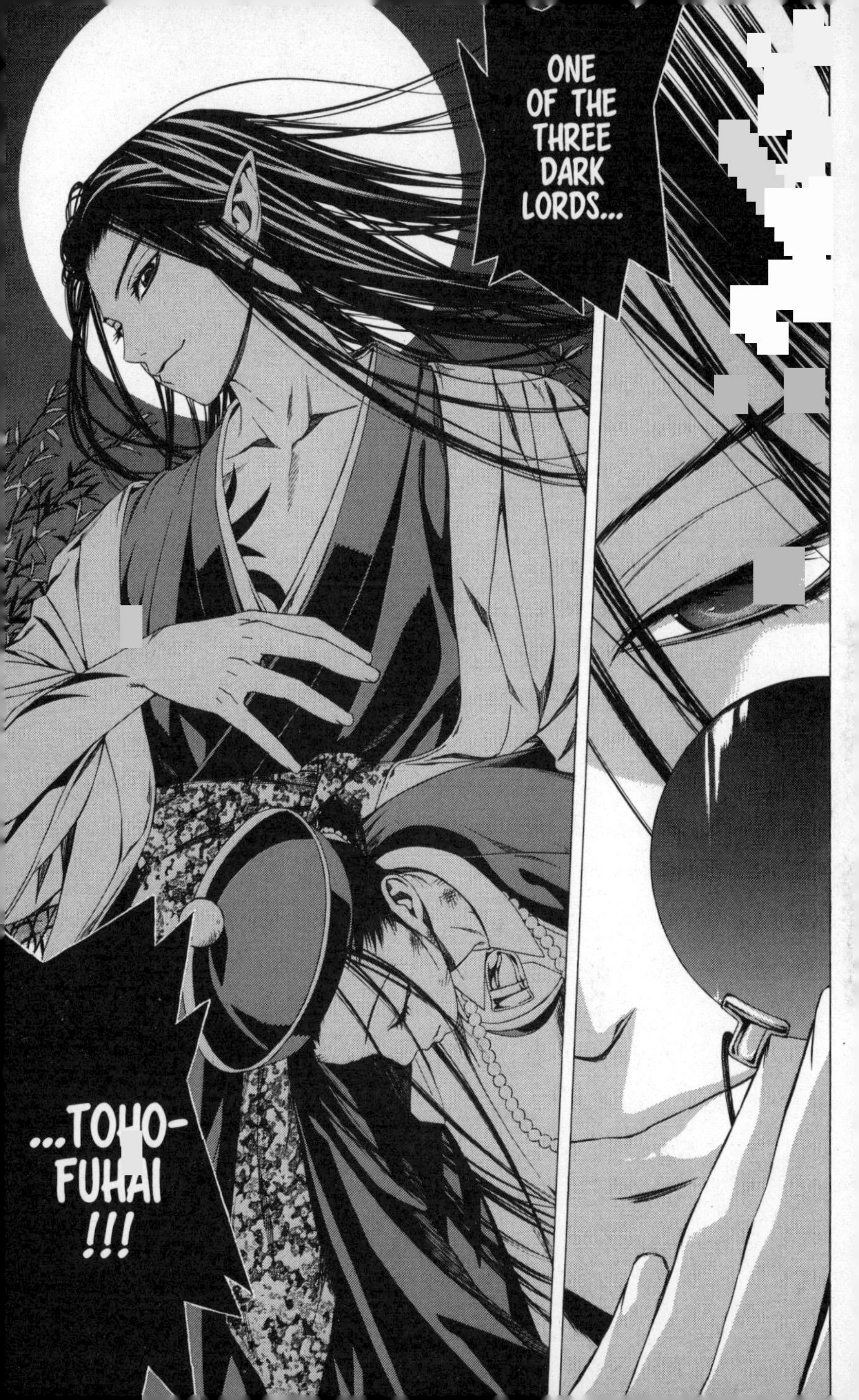
ONE OF THE THREE DARK LORDS...
...TOHO-FUHAI!!!

37: Reunion

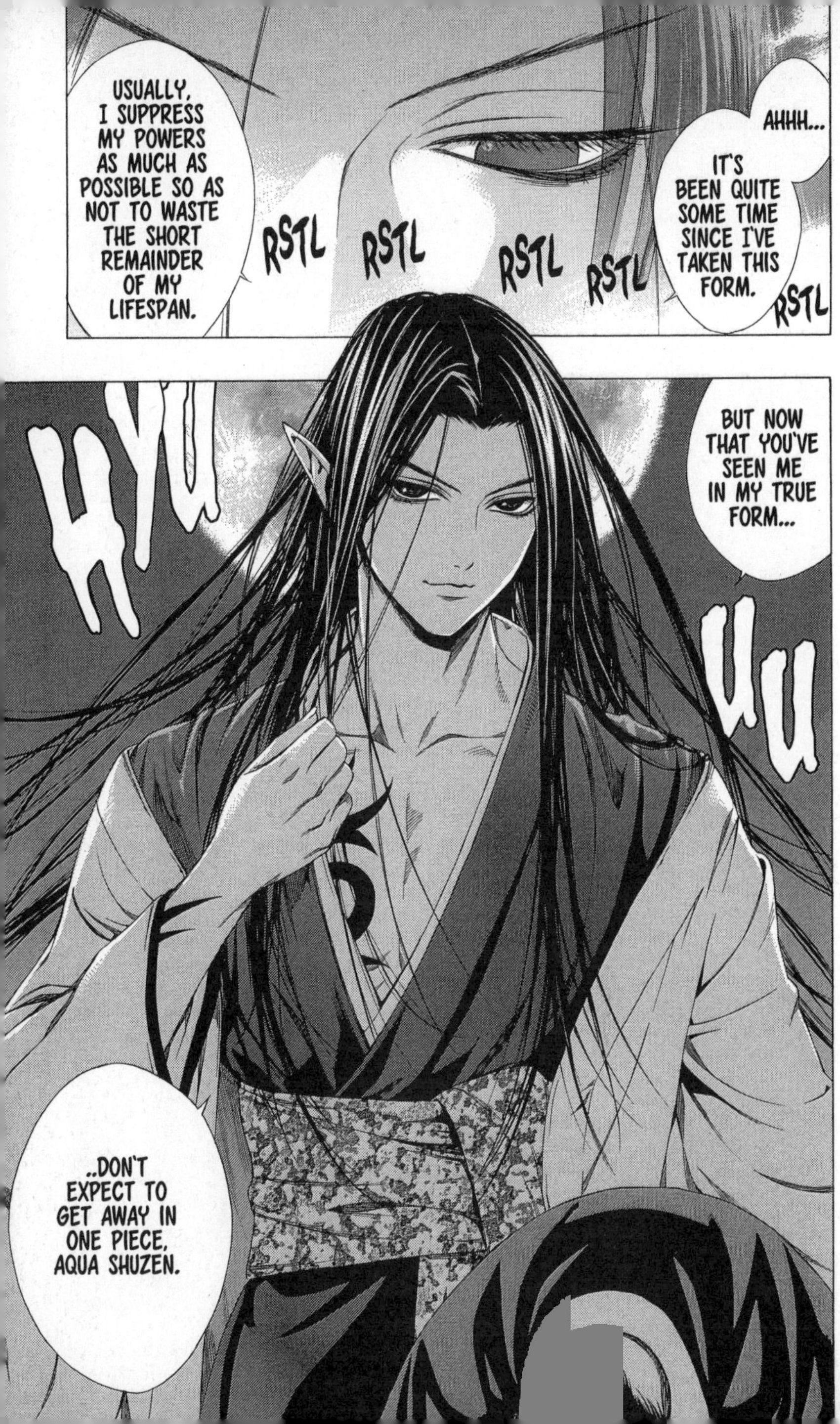
AHHH...
IT'S BEEN QUITE SOME TIME SINCE I'VE TAKEN THIS FORM.
RSTL
RSTL
RSTL
RSTL
RSTL
USUALLY, I SUPPRESS MY POWERS AS MUCH AS POSSIBLE SO AS NOT TO WASTE THE SHORT REMAINDER OF MY LIFESPAN.
BUT NOW THAT YOU'VE SEEN ME IN MY TRUE FORM...
HYU
UU
..DON'T EXPECT TO GET AWAY IN ONE PIECE, AQUA SHUZEN.

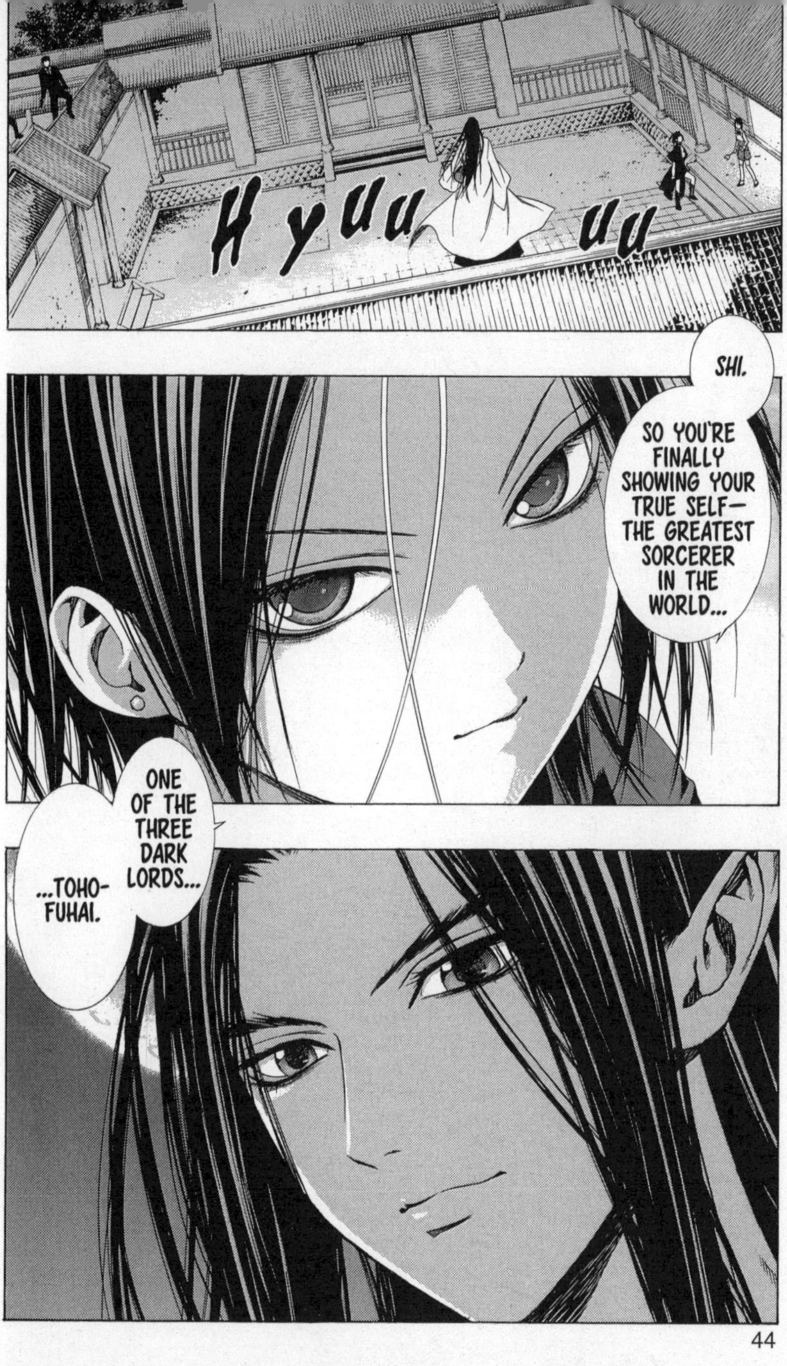
HYUUUUU
SHI.
SO YOU'RE FINALLY SHOWING YOUR TRUE SELF— THE GREATEST SORCERER IN THE WORLD...
ONE OF THE THREE DARK LORDS...
...TOHO-FUHAI.

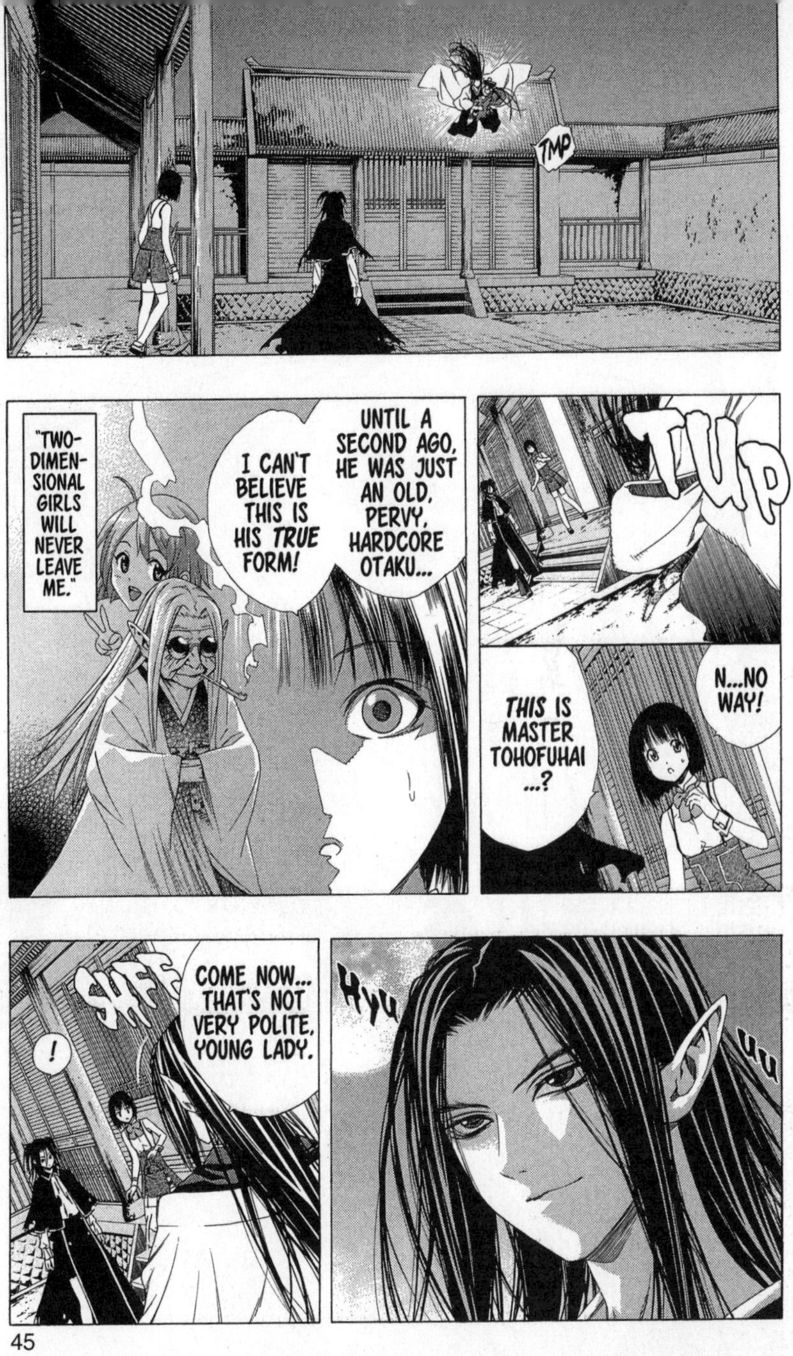
TMP
TUP
N...NO WAY!
THIS IS MASTER TOHOFUHAI ...?
UNTIL A SECOND AGO, HE WAS JUST AN OLD, PERVY, HARDCORE OTAKU...
I CAN'T BELIEVE THIS IS HIS TRUE FORM!
"TWO-DIMENSIONAL GIRLS WILL NEVER LEAVE ME."
HYUUU
SHFF
COME NOW... THAT'S NOT VERY POLITE, YOUNG LADY.
!

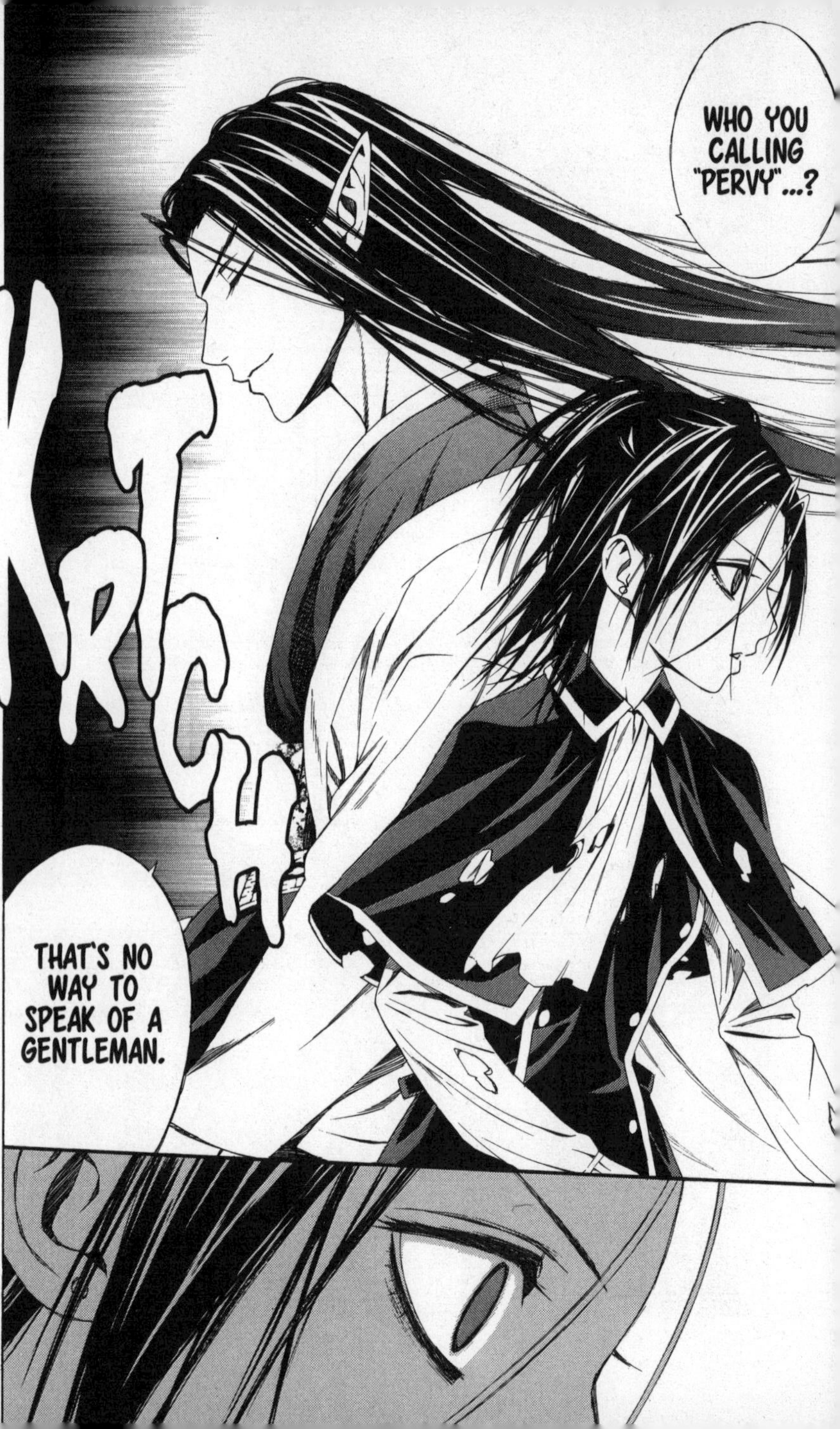
WHO YOU CALLING "PERVY"...?
KRTCH
THAT'S NO WAY TO SPEAK OF A GENTLEMAN.

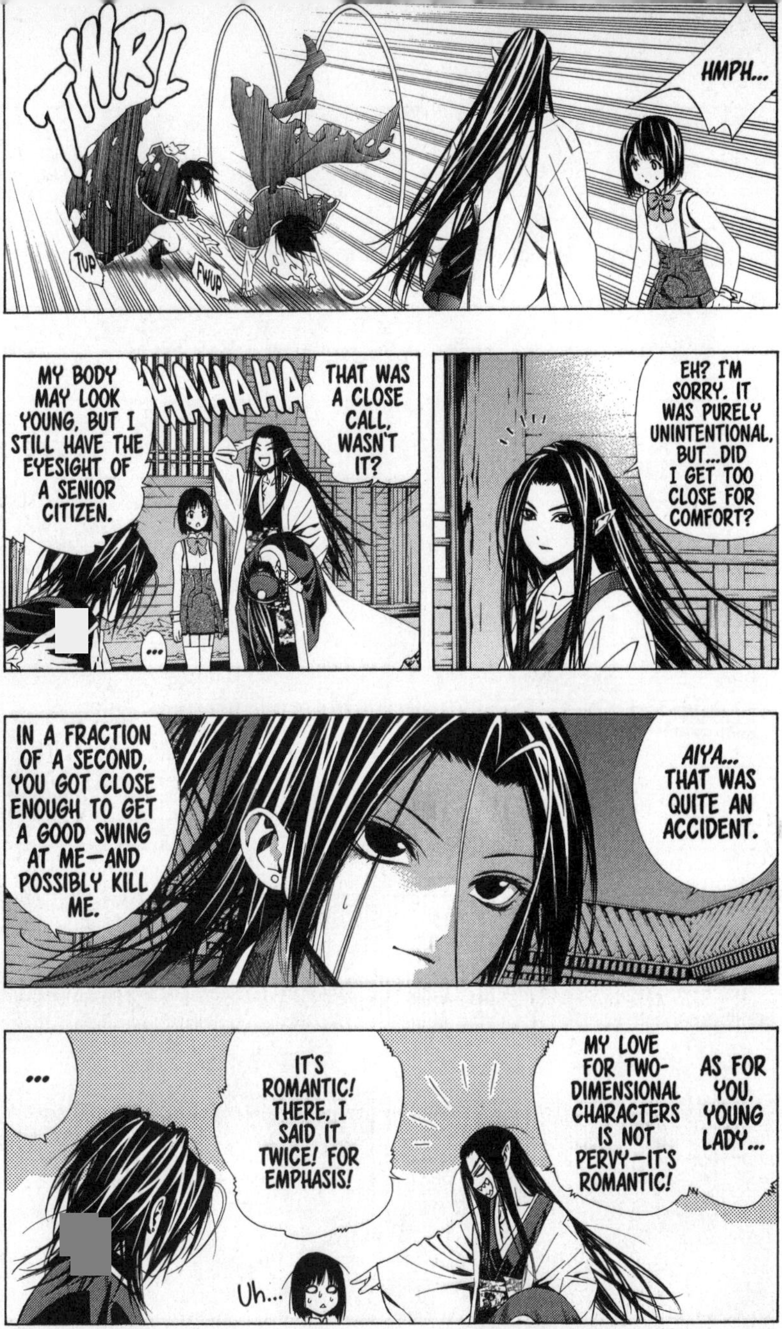
HMPH...
TWRL
TUP
FWUP
EH? I'M SORRY. IT WAS PURELY UNINTENTIONAL, BUT...DID I GET TOO CLOSE FOR COMFORT?
THAT WAS A CLOSE CALL, WASN'T IT?
HAHAHA
MY BODY MAY LOOK YOUNG, BUT I STILL HAVE THE EYESIGHT OF A SENIOR CITIZEN.
...
AIYA... THAT WAS QUITE AN ACCIDENT.
IN A FRACTION OF A SECOND, YOU GOT CLOSE ENOUGH TO GET A GOOD SWING AT ME—AND POSSIBLY KILL ME.
AS FOR YOU, YOUNG LADY...
MY LOVE FOR TWO-DIMENSIONAL CHARACTERS IS NOT PERVY—IT'S ROMANTIC!
IT'S ROMANTIC! THERE, I SAID IT TWICE! FOR EMPHASIS!
...
Uh...

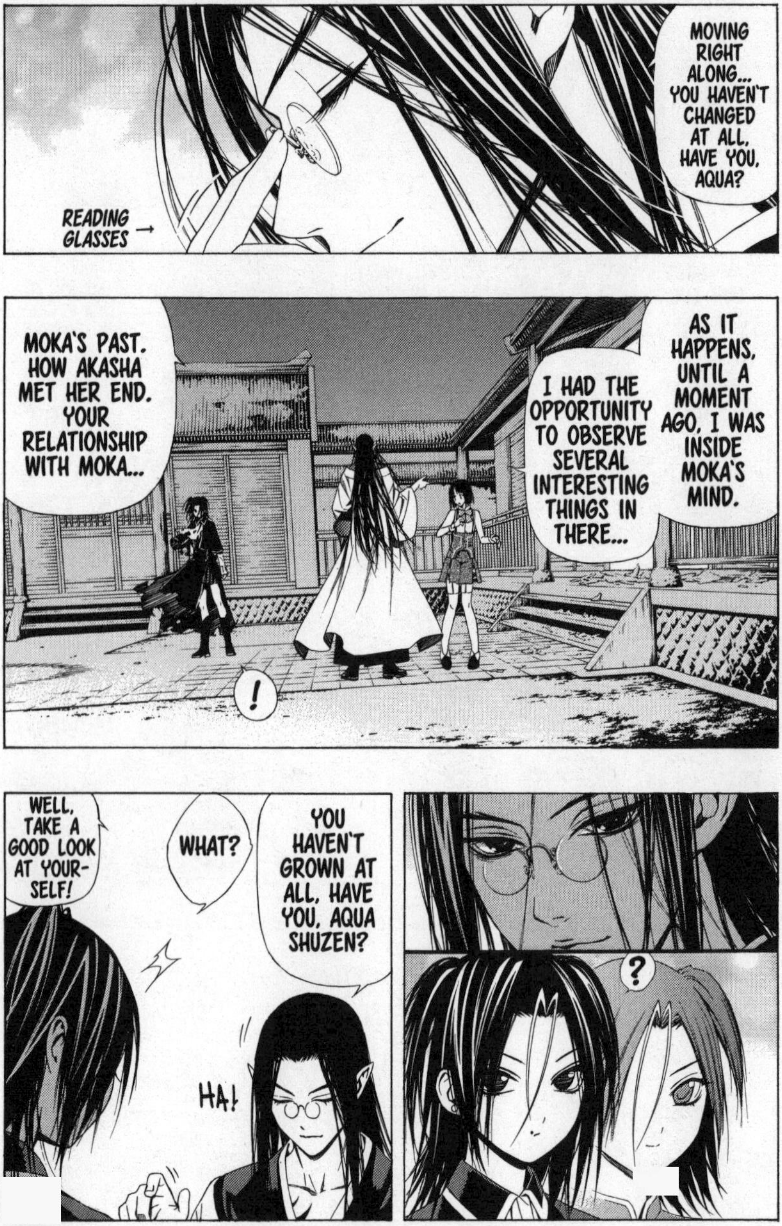
MOVING RIGHT ALONG... YOU HAVEN'T CHANGED AT ALL, HAVE YOU, AQUA?
READING GLASSES →
AS IT HAPPENS, UNTIL A MOMENT AGO, I WAS INSIDE MOKA'S MIND.
I HAD THE OPPORTUNITY TO OBSERVE SEVERAL INTERESTING THINGS IN THERE...
MOKA'S PAST. HOW AKASHA MET HER END. YOUR RELATIONSHIP WITH MOKA...
!
?
YOU HAVEN'T GROWN AT ALL, HAVE YOU, AQUA SHUZEN?
WHAT?
WELL, TAKE A GOOD LOOK AT YOUR-SELF!
HA!

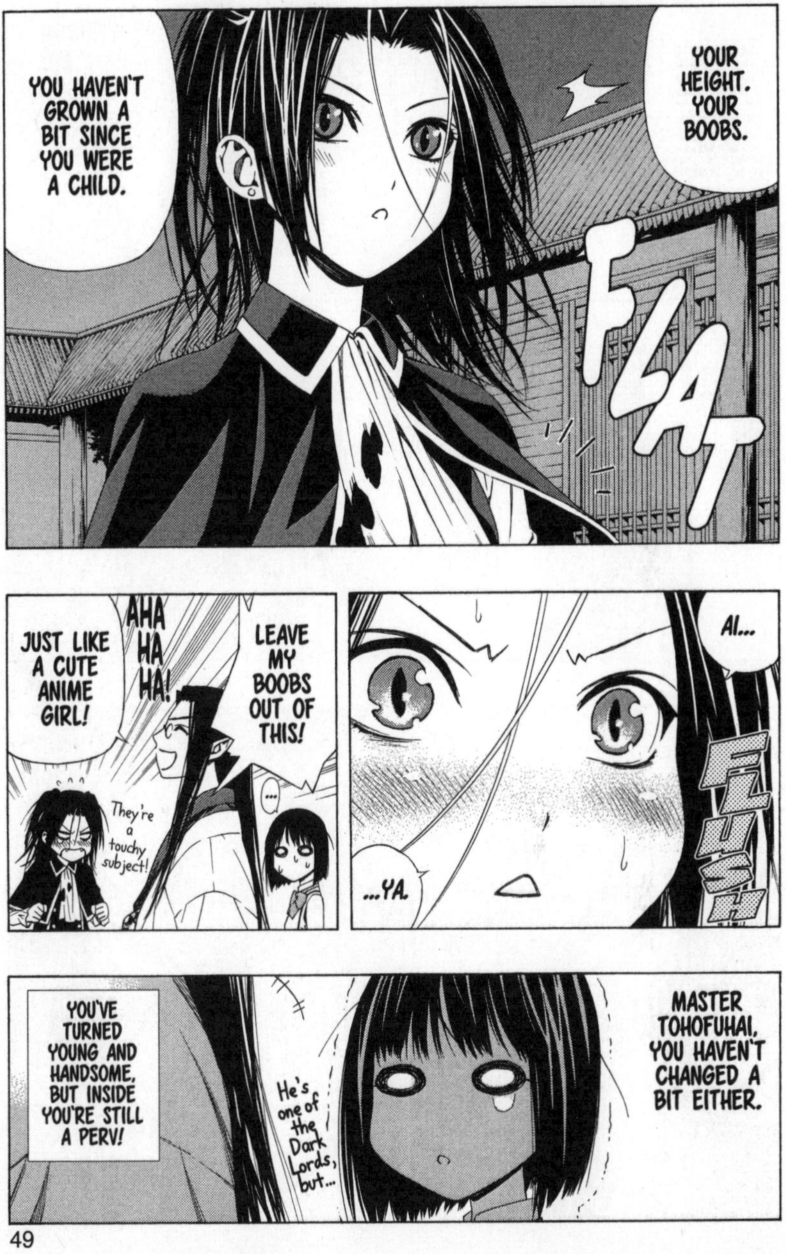
YOUR HEIGHT. YOUR BOOBS.
YOU HAVEN'T GROWN A BIT SINCE YOU WERE A CHILD.
FLAT
AI...
FLUSH
...YA.
LEAVE MY BOOBS OUT OF THIS!
AHA HA HA!
JUST LIKE A CUTE ANIME GIRL!
...
They're a touchy subject!
MASTER TOHOFUHAI, YOU HAVEN'T CHANGED A BIT EITHER.
He's one of the Dark Lords, but...
YOU'VE TURNED YOUNG AND HANDSOME, BUT INSIDE YOU'RE STILL A PERV!

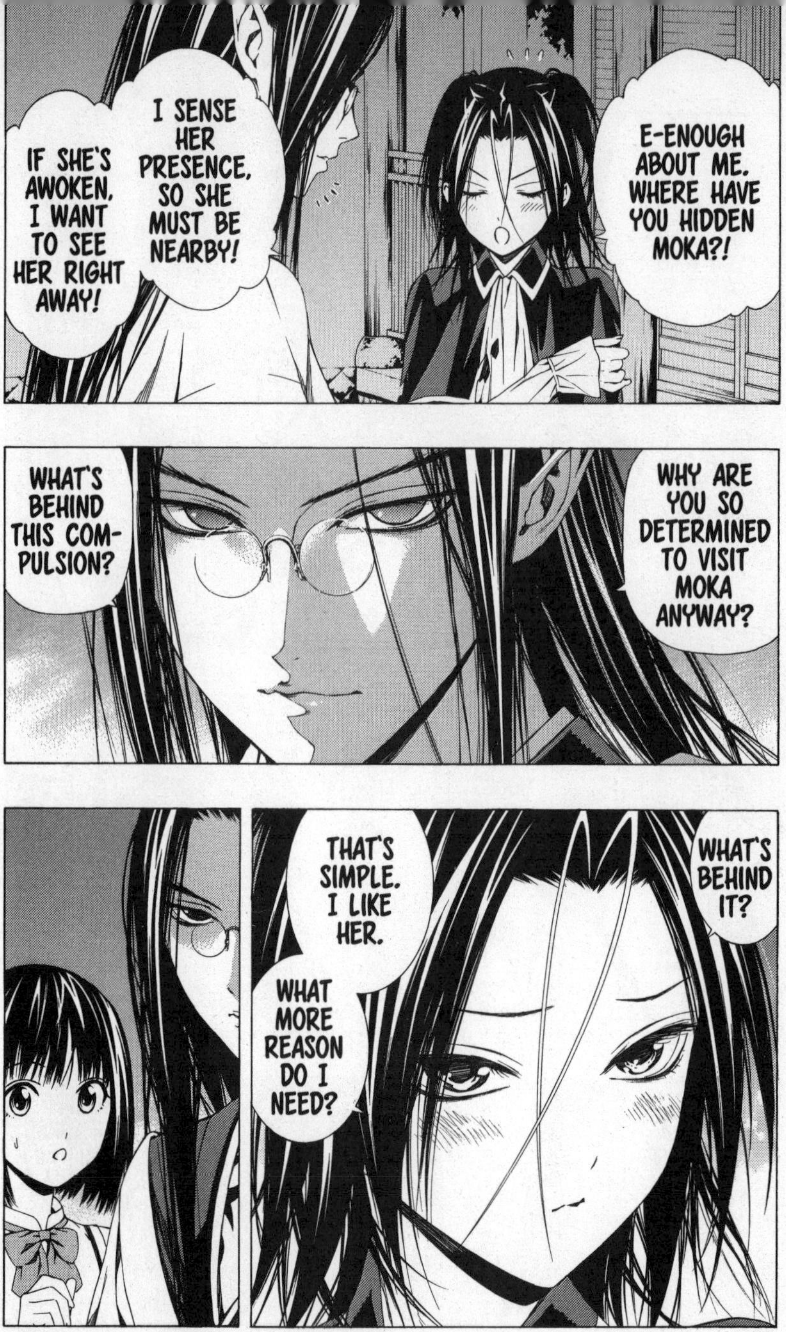
E-ENOUGH ABOUT ME. WHERE HAVE YOU HIDDEN MOKA?!
I SENSE HER PRESENCE, SO SHE MUST BE NEARBY!
IF SHE'S AWOKEN, I WANT TO SEE HER RIGHT AWAY!
WHY ARE YOU SO DETERMINED TO VISIT MOKA ANYWAY?
WHAT'S BEHIND THIS COMPULSION?
WHAT'S BEHIND IT?
THAT'S SIMPLE. I LIKE HER.
WHAT MORE REASON DO I NEED?

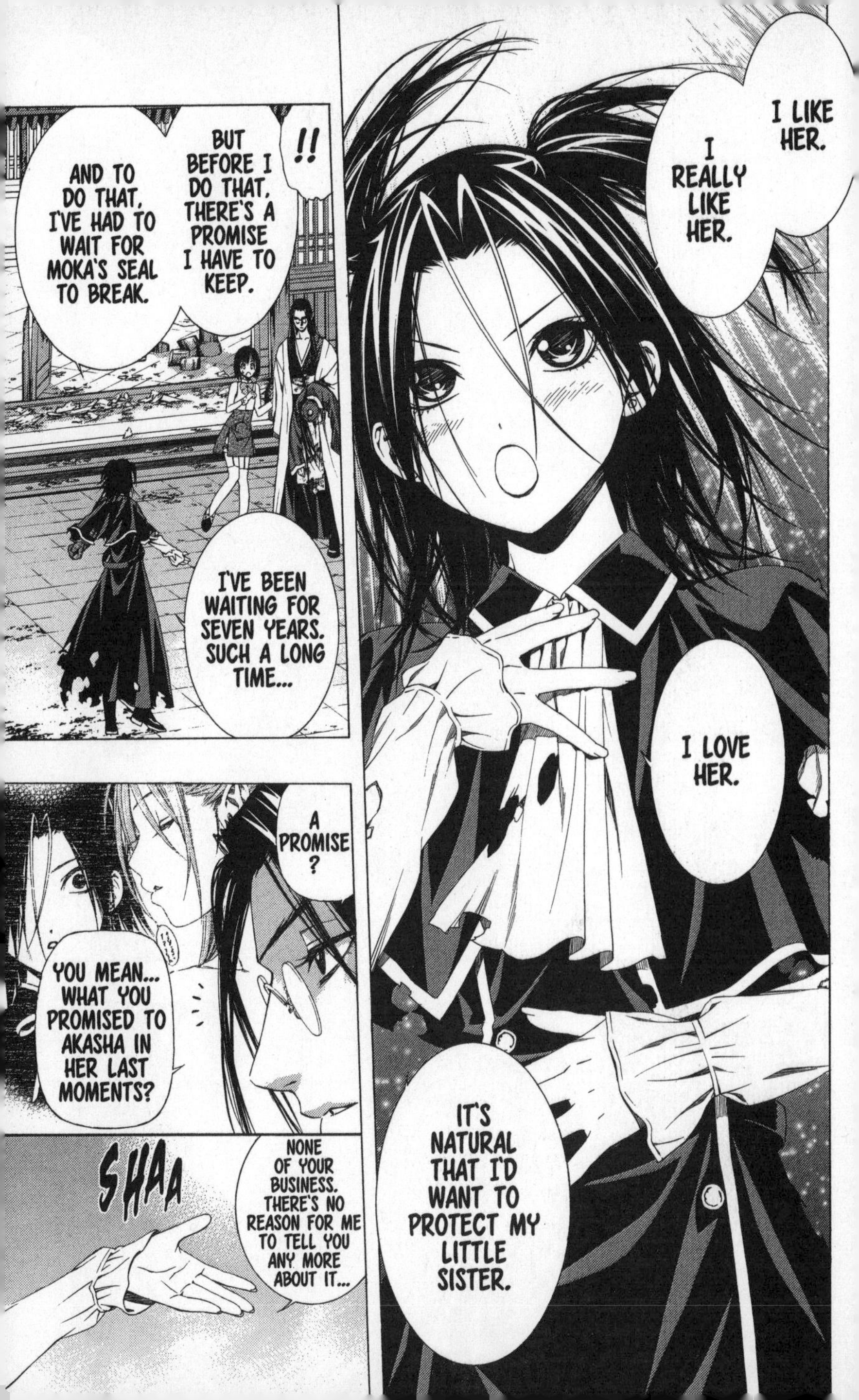
I LIKE HER.
I REALLY LIKE HER.
I LOVE HER.
IT'S NATURAL THAT I'D WANT TO PROTECT MY LITTLE SISTER.
!!
BUT BEFORE I DO THAT, THERE'S A PROMISE I HAVE TO KEEP.
AND TO DO THAT, I'VE HAD TO WAIT FOR MOKA'S SEAL TO BREAK.
I'VE BEEN WAITING FOR SEVEN YEARS. SUCH A LONG TIME...
A PROMISE?
YOU MEAN... WHAT YOU PROMISED TO AKASHA IN HER LAST MOMENTS?
NONE OF YOUR BUSINESS. THERE'S NO REASON FOR ME TO TELL YOU ANY MORE ABOUT IT...
SHAA

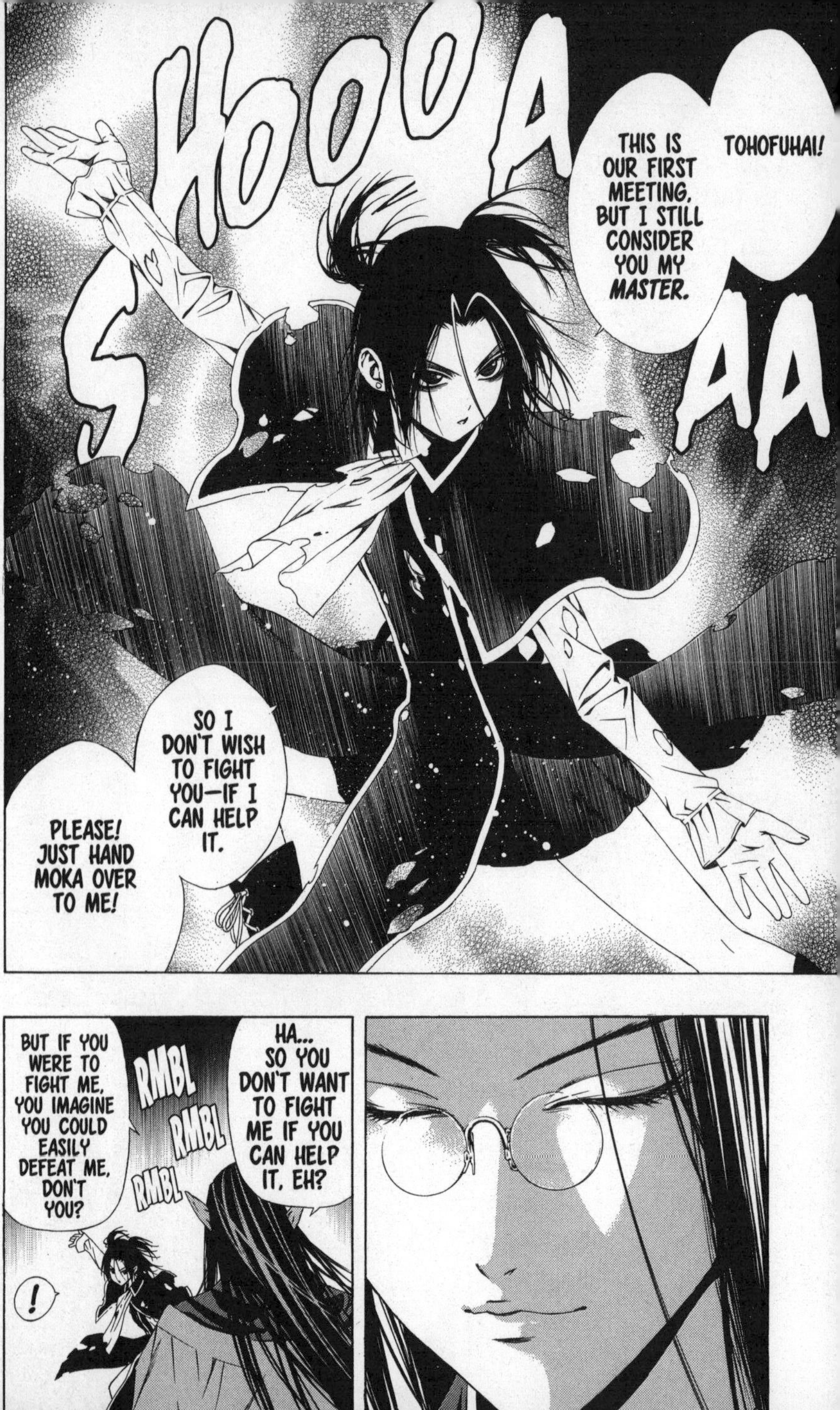
TOHOFUHAI!
THIS IS OUR FIRST MEETING, BUT I STILL CONSIDER YOU MY *MASTER*.
SHOOOAAA
SO I DON'T WISH TO FIGHT YOU—IF I CAN HELP IT.
PLEASE! JUST HAND MOKA OVER TO ME!
HA... SO YOU DON'T WANT TO FIGHT ME IF YOU CAN HELP IT, EH?
RMBL RMBL RMBL
BUT IF YOU WERE TO FIGHT ME, YOU IMAGINE YOU COULD EASILY DEFEAT ME, DON'T YOU?
!

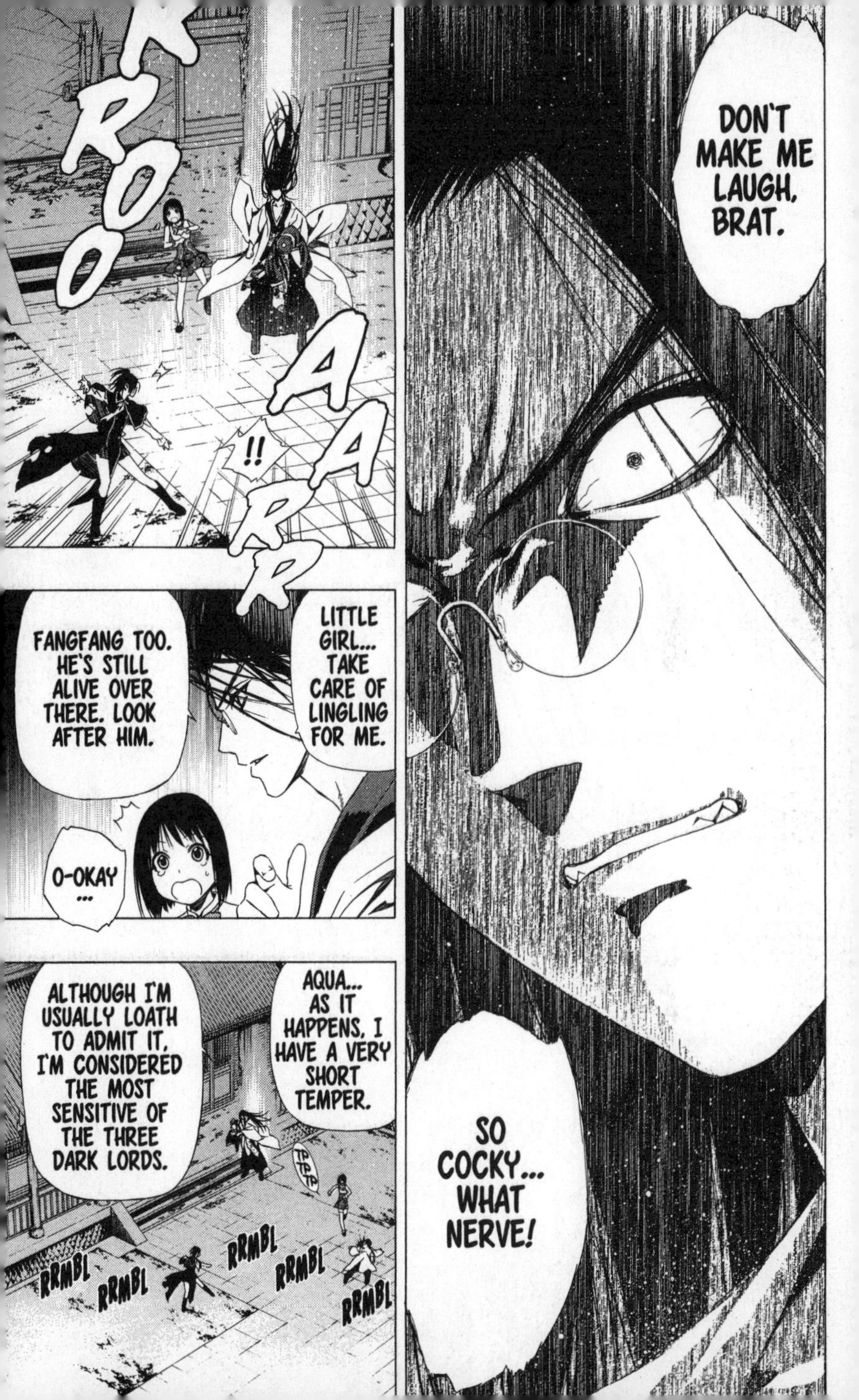
DON'T MAKE ME LAUGH, BRAT.
SO COCKY... WHAT NERVE!
KROOAARR
!!
LITTLE GIRL... TAKE CARE OF LINGLING FOR ME.
FANGFANG TOO. HE'S STILL ALIVE OVER THERE. LOOK AFTER HIM.
O-OKAY...
AQUA... AS IT HAPPENS, I HAVE A VERY SHORT TEMPER.
ALTHOUGH I'M USUALLY LOATH TO ADMIT IT, I'M CONSIDERED THE MOST SENSITIVE OF THE THREE DARK LORDS.
TP TP TP
RRMBL
RRMBL
RRMBL
RRMBL
RRMBL

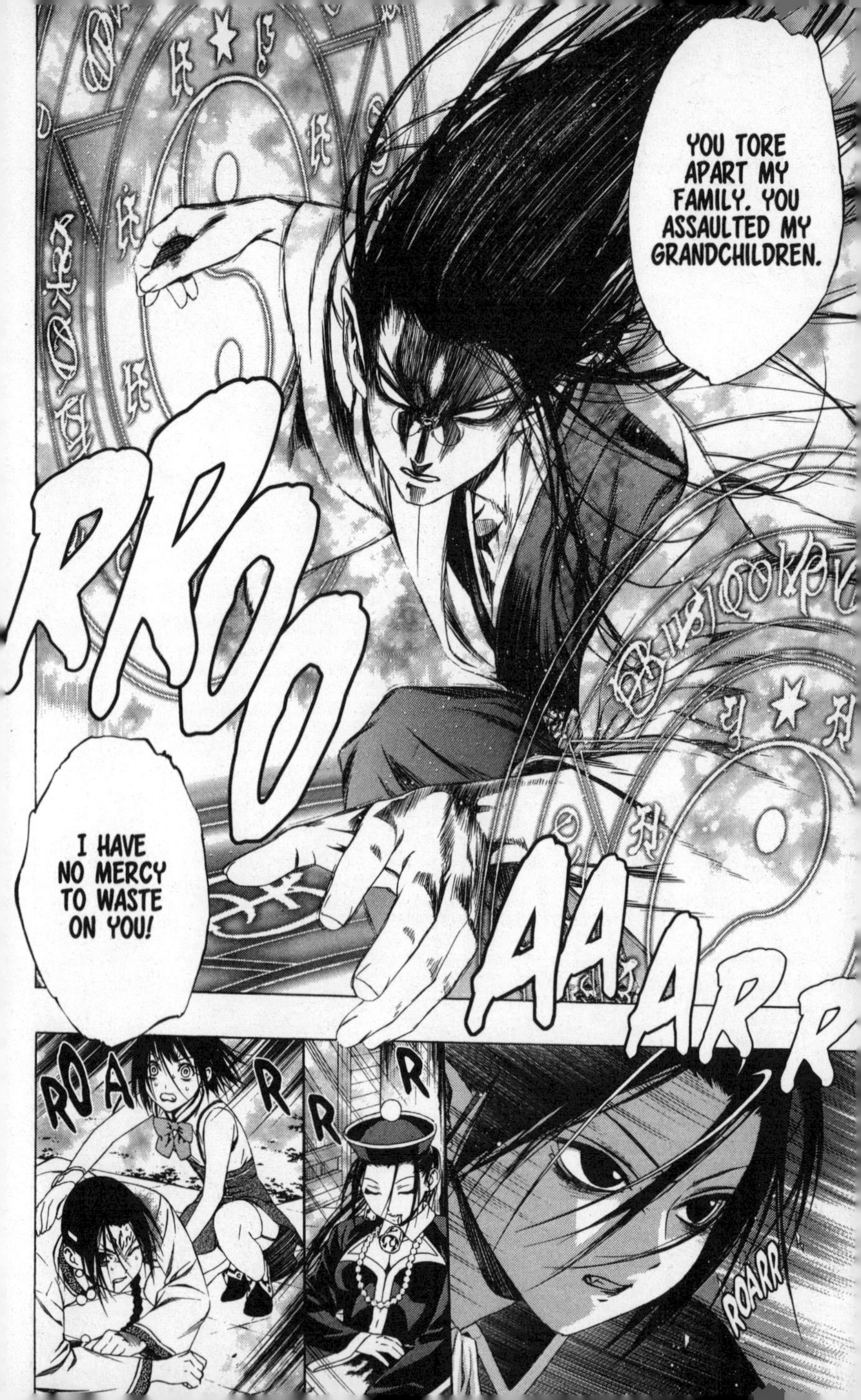

YOU TORE APART MY FAMILY. YOU ASSAULTED MY GRANDCHILDREN.
RROOOAAAARR
I HAVE NO MERCY TO WASTE ON YOU!
ROARR
ROA R R

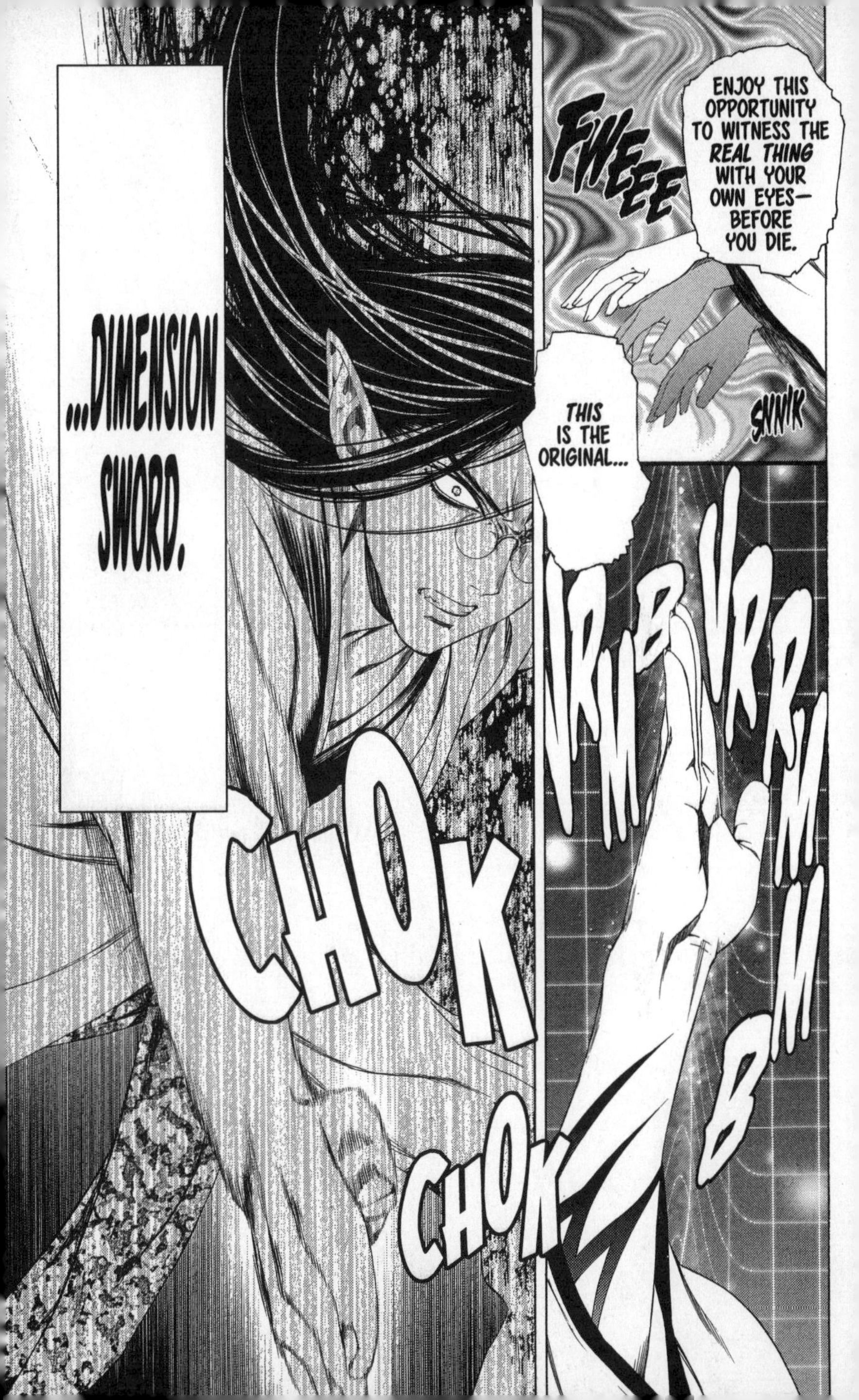
ENJOY THIS OPPORTUNITY TO WITNESS THE REAL THING WITH YOUR OWN EYES—BEFORE YOU DIE.
FWEEE
SNNIK
THIS IS THE ORIGINAL...
VRRM BVRRM BM
CHOK
CHOK
...DIMENSION SWORD.

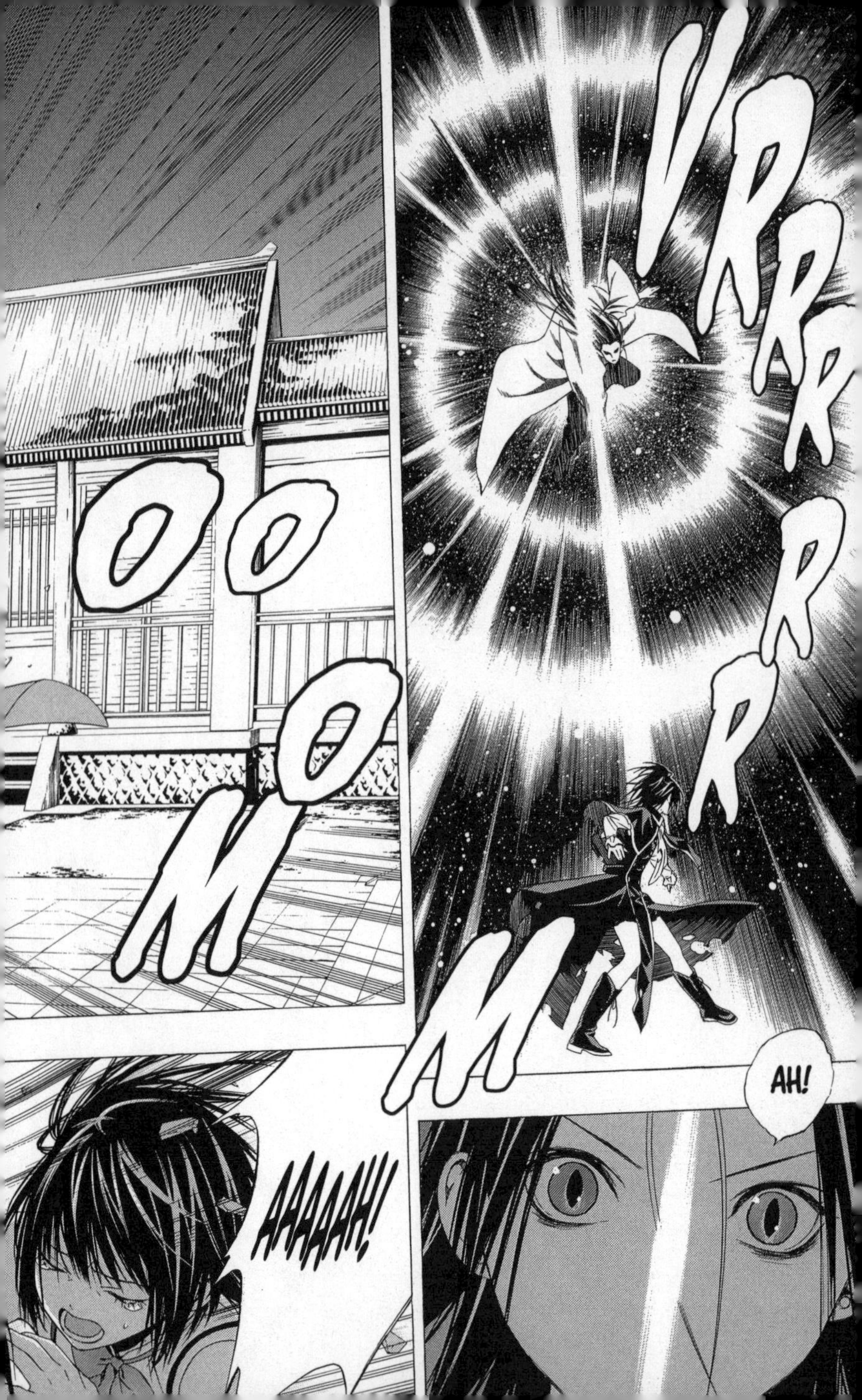

VRRRRR
OOOMM
M
AH!
AAAAAH!

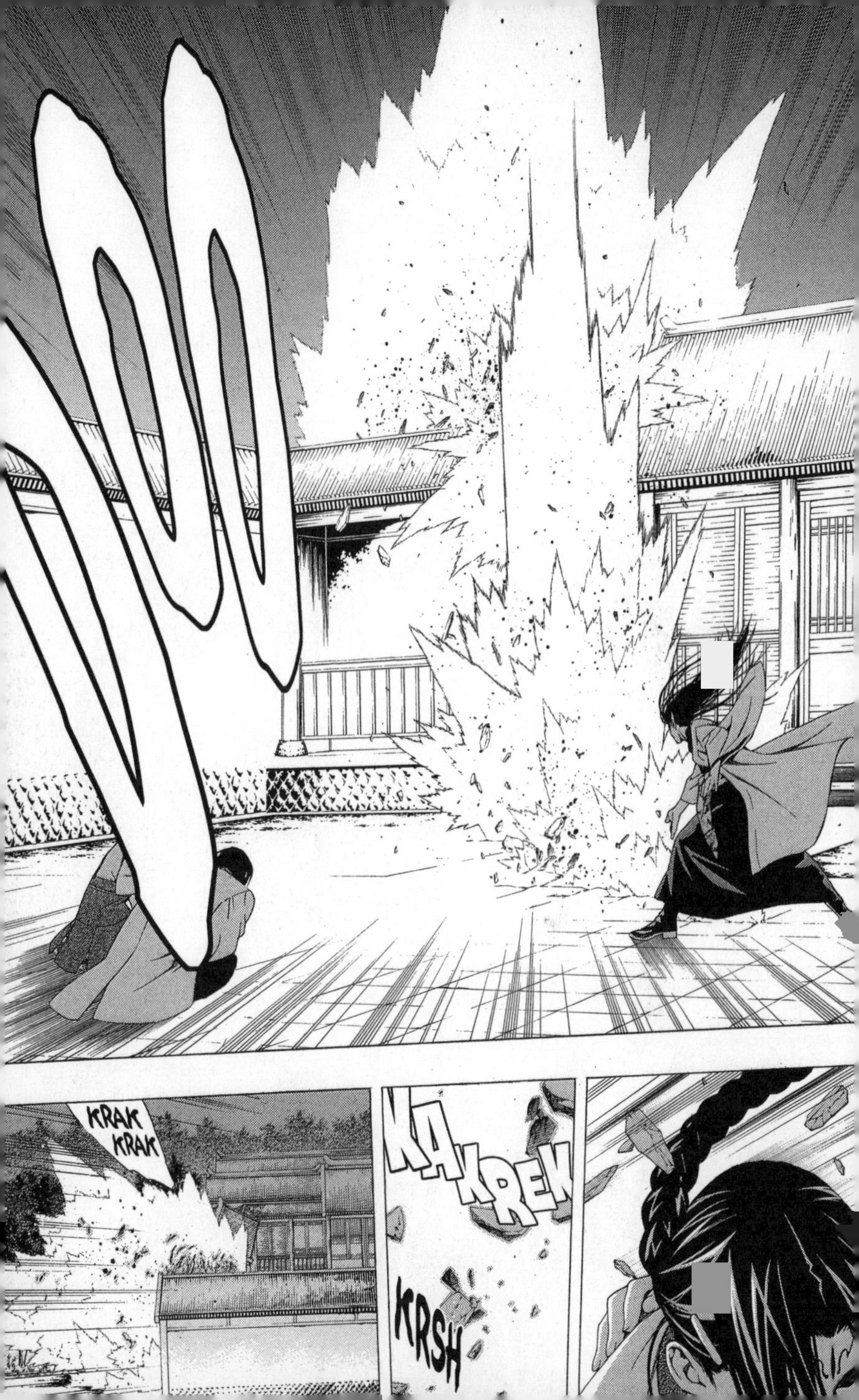
KAKREN
KRSH
KRAK KRAK

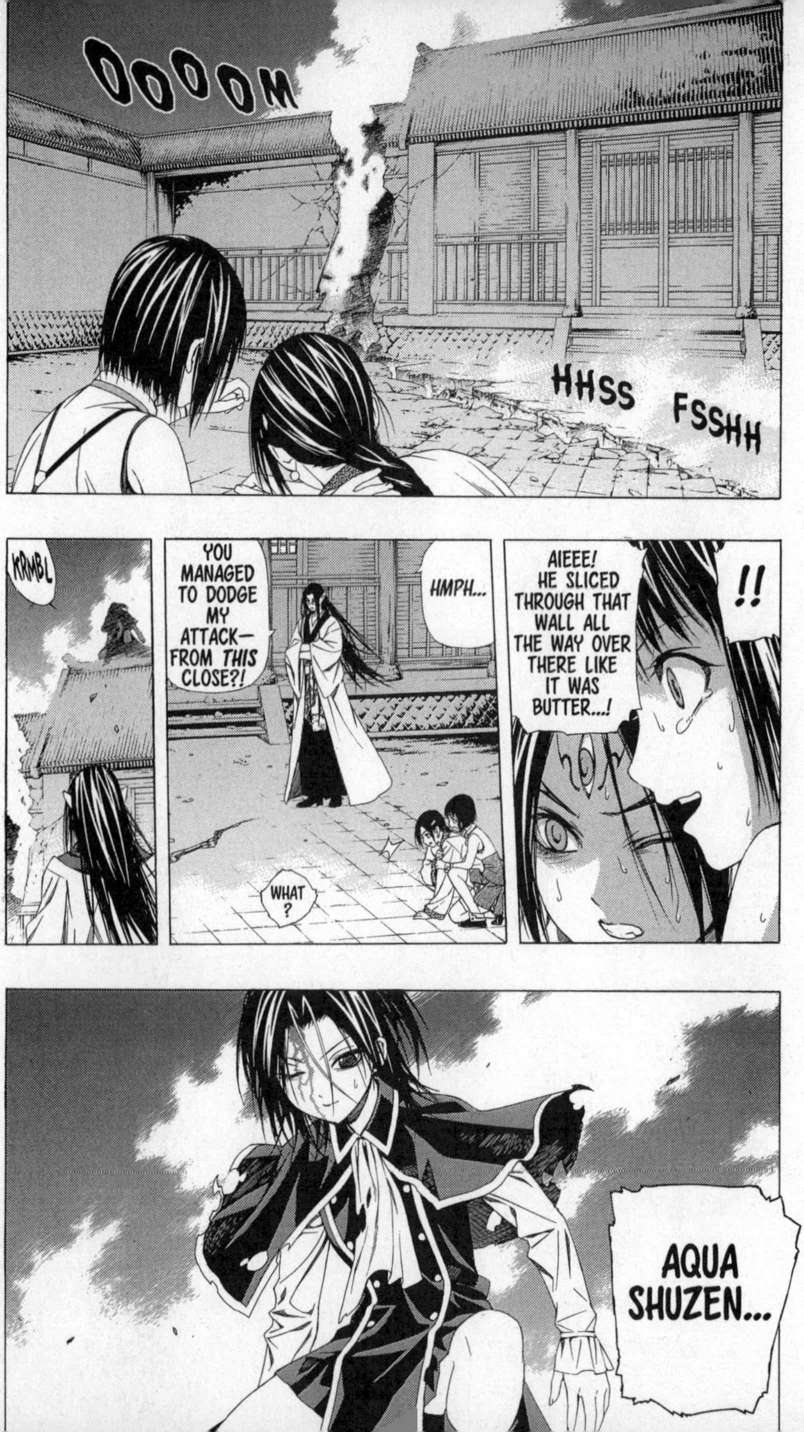
OOOOM
FSSHH
HHSS
!!
AIEEE! HE SLICED THROUGH THAT WALL ALL THE WAY OVER THERE LIKE IT WAS BUTTER...!
HMPH...
YOU MANAGED TO DODGE MY ATTACK—FROM *THIS* CLOSE?!
WHAT?
KRMBL
AQUA SHUZEN...

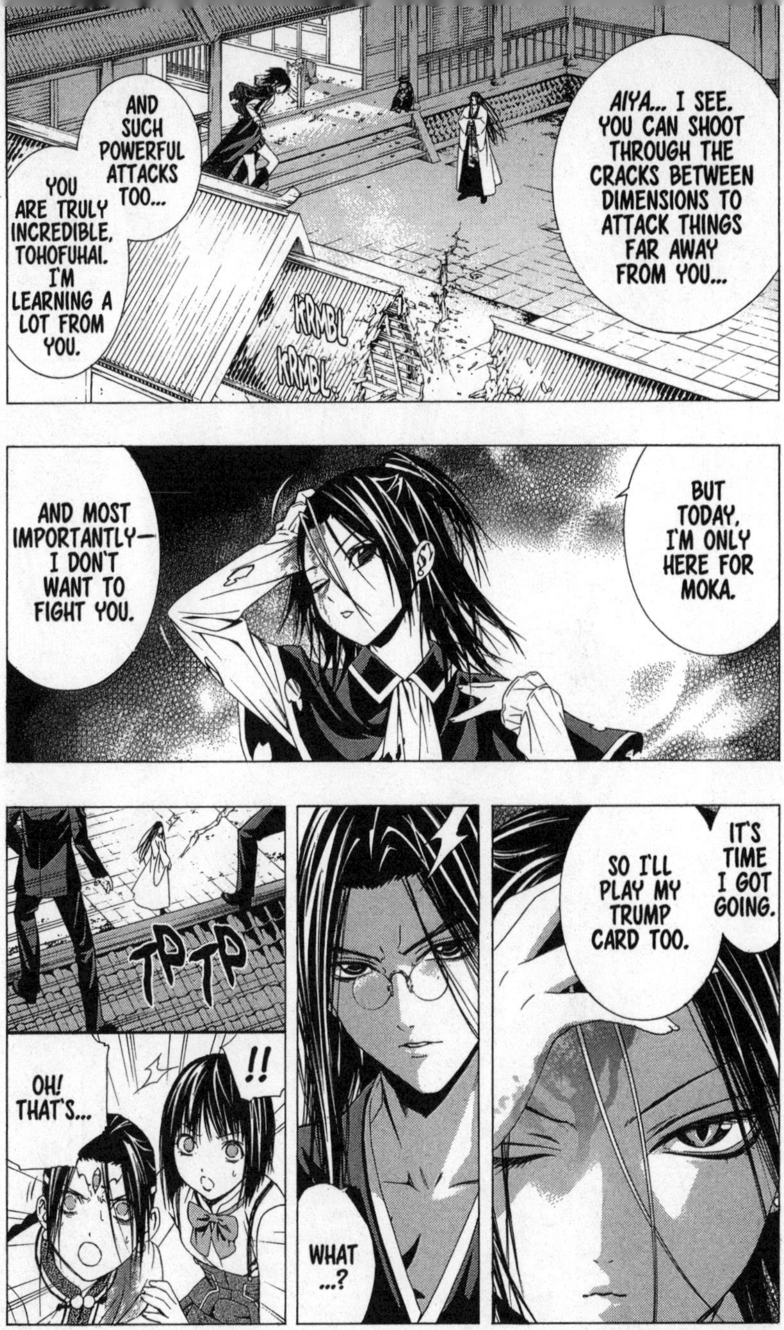
AIYA... I SEE. YOU CAN SHOOT THROUGH THE CRACKS BETWEEN DIMENSIONS TO ATTACK THINGS FAR AWAY FROM YOU...
AND SUCH POWERFUL ATTACKS TOO...
YOU ARE TRULY INCREDIBLE, TOHOFUHAI. I'M LEARNING A LOT FROM YOU.
KRMBL
KRMBL
BUT TODAY, I'M ONLY HERE FOR MOKA.
AND MOST IMPORTANTLY— I DON'T WANT TO FIGHT YOU.
IT'S TIME I GOT GOING.
SO I'LL PLAY MY TRUMP CARD TOO.
WHAT ...?
TPTP
!!
OH! THAT'S...

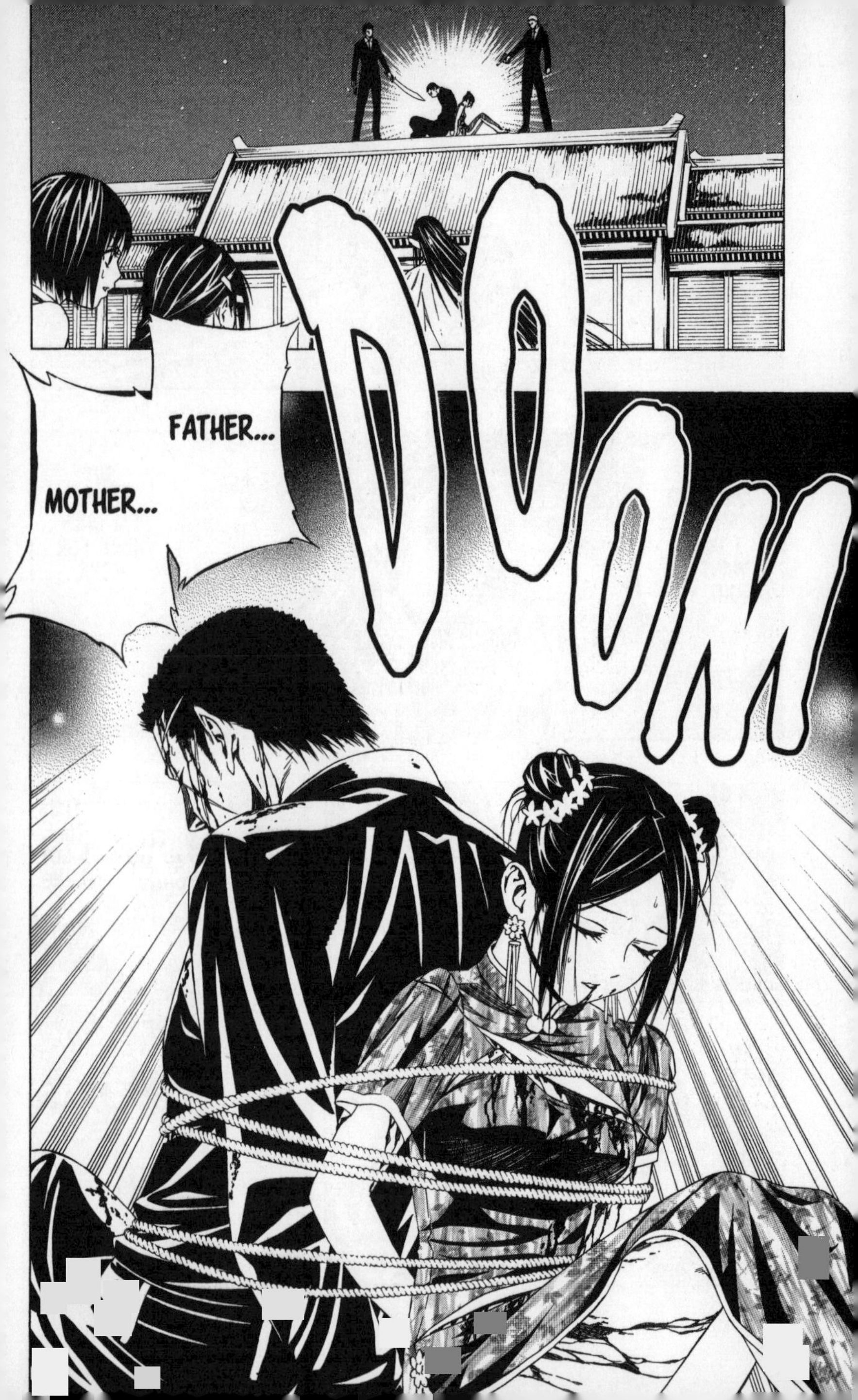
DOOM
FATHER...
MOTHER...

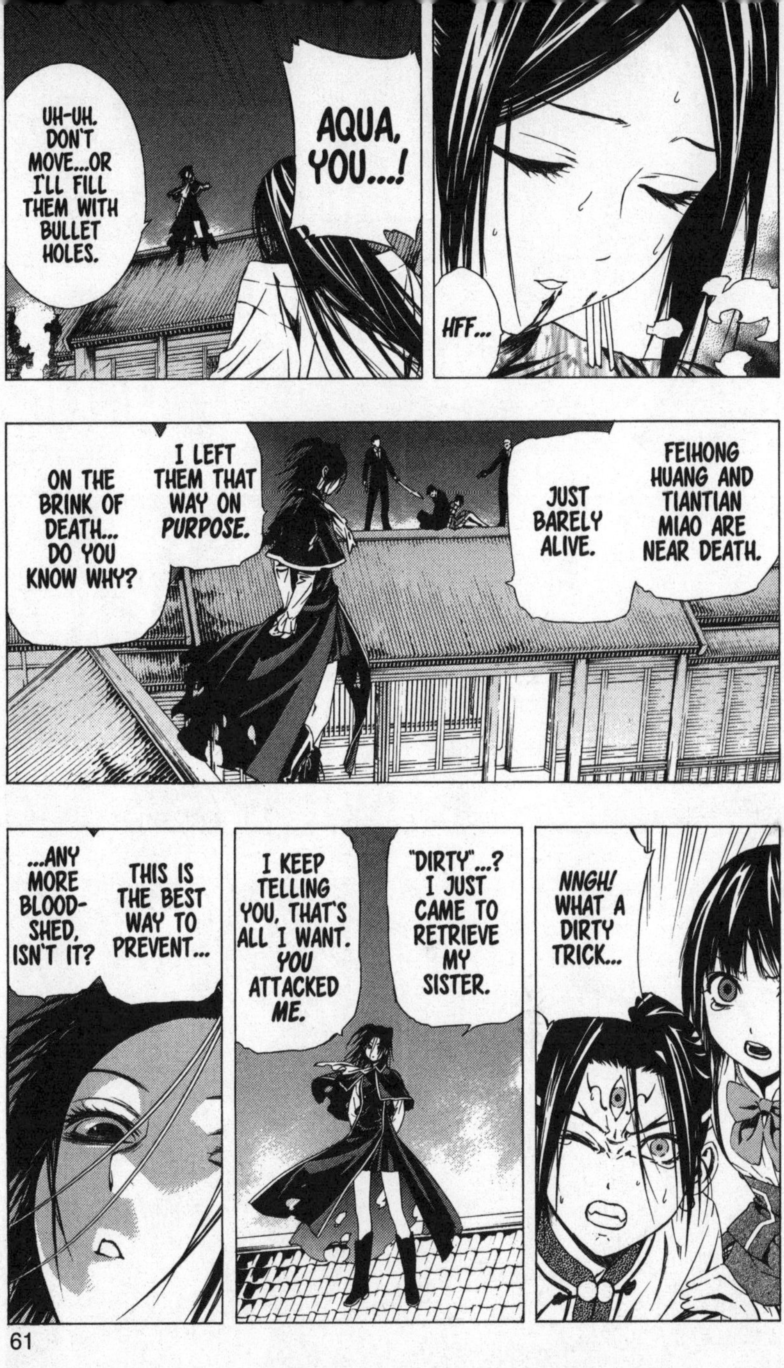
HFF...
AQUA, YOU...!
UH-UH. DON'T MOVE...OR I'LL FILL THEM WITH BULLET HOLES.
FEIHONG HUANG AND TIANTIAN MIAO ARE NEAR DEATH.
JUST BARELY ALIVE.
I LEFT THEM THAT WAY ON *PURPOSE.*
ON THE BRINK OF DEATH... DO YOU KNOW WHY?
NNGH! WHAT A DIRTY TRICK...
"DIRTY"...? I JUST CAME TO RETRIEVE MY SISTER.
I KEEP TELLING YOU, THAT'S ALL I WANT. *YOU* ATTACKED *ME.*
THIS IS THE BEST WAY TO PREVENT...
...ANY MORE BLOOD-SHED, ISN'T IT?

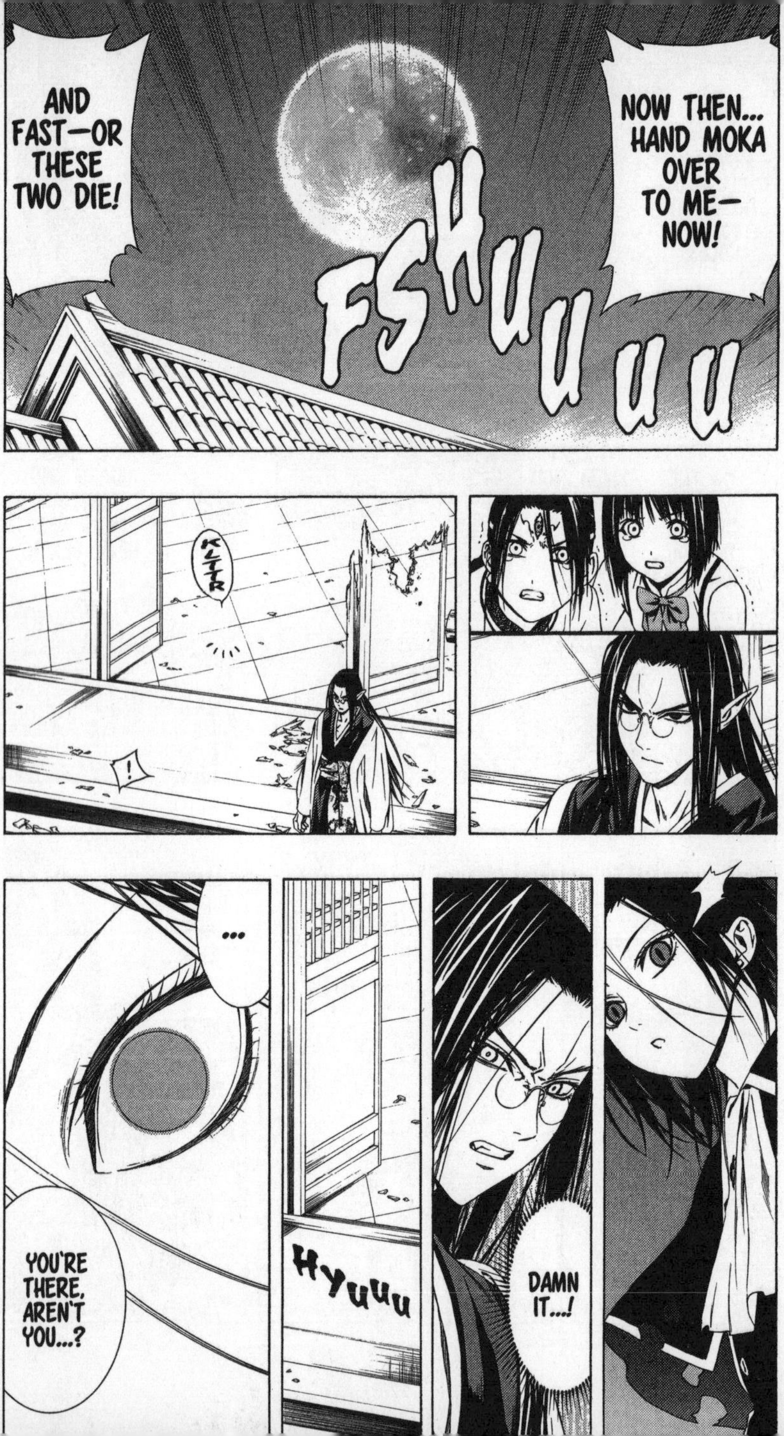
NOW THEN... HAND MOKA OVER TO ME— NOW!
AND FAST—OR THESE TWO DIE!
FSHUUUUU
KLTTR
!
DAMN IT...!
HYUUU
...
YOU'RE THERE, AREN'T YOU...?

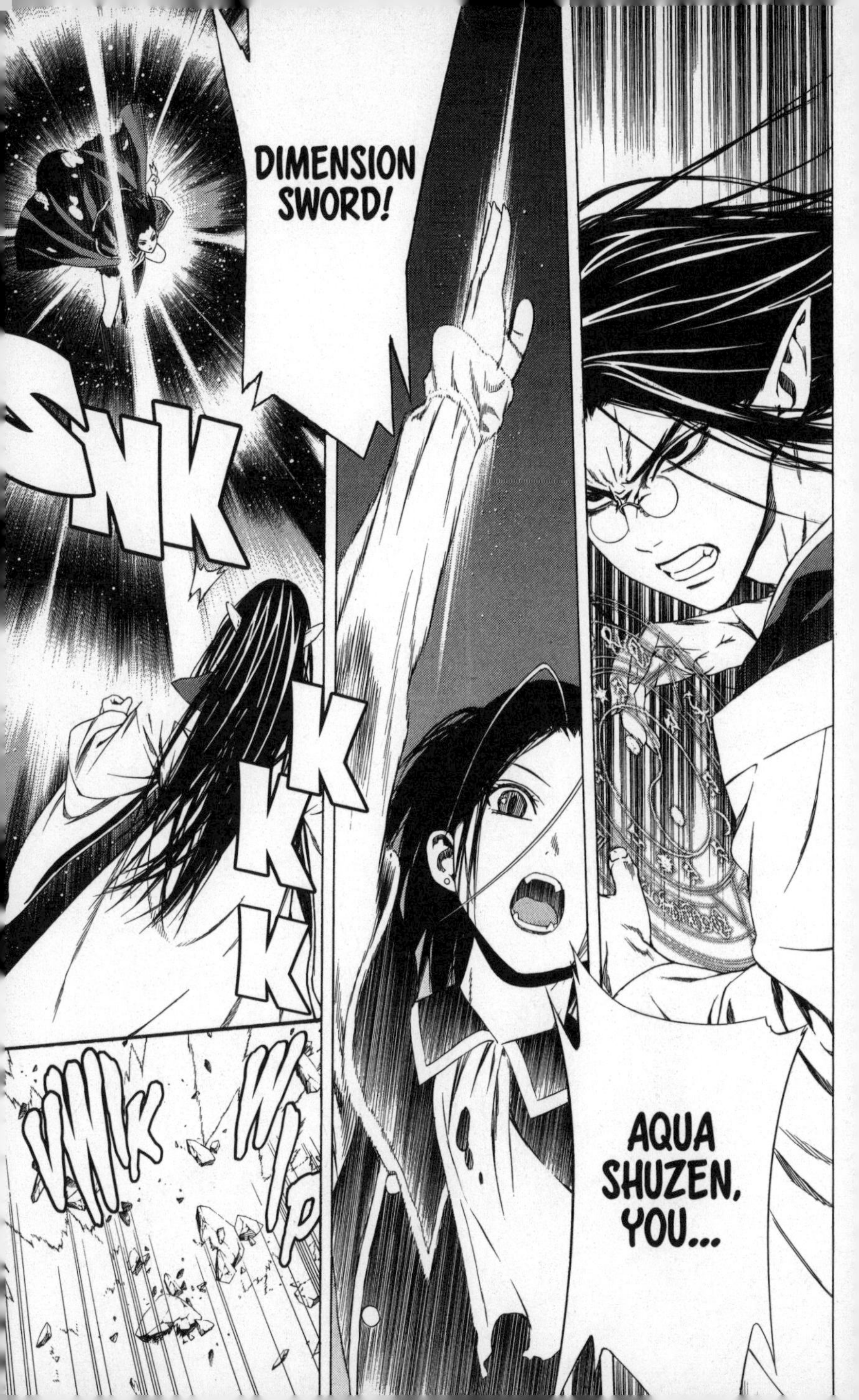
AQUA SHUZEN, YOU...
DIMENSION SWORD!

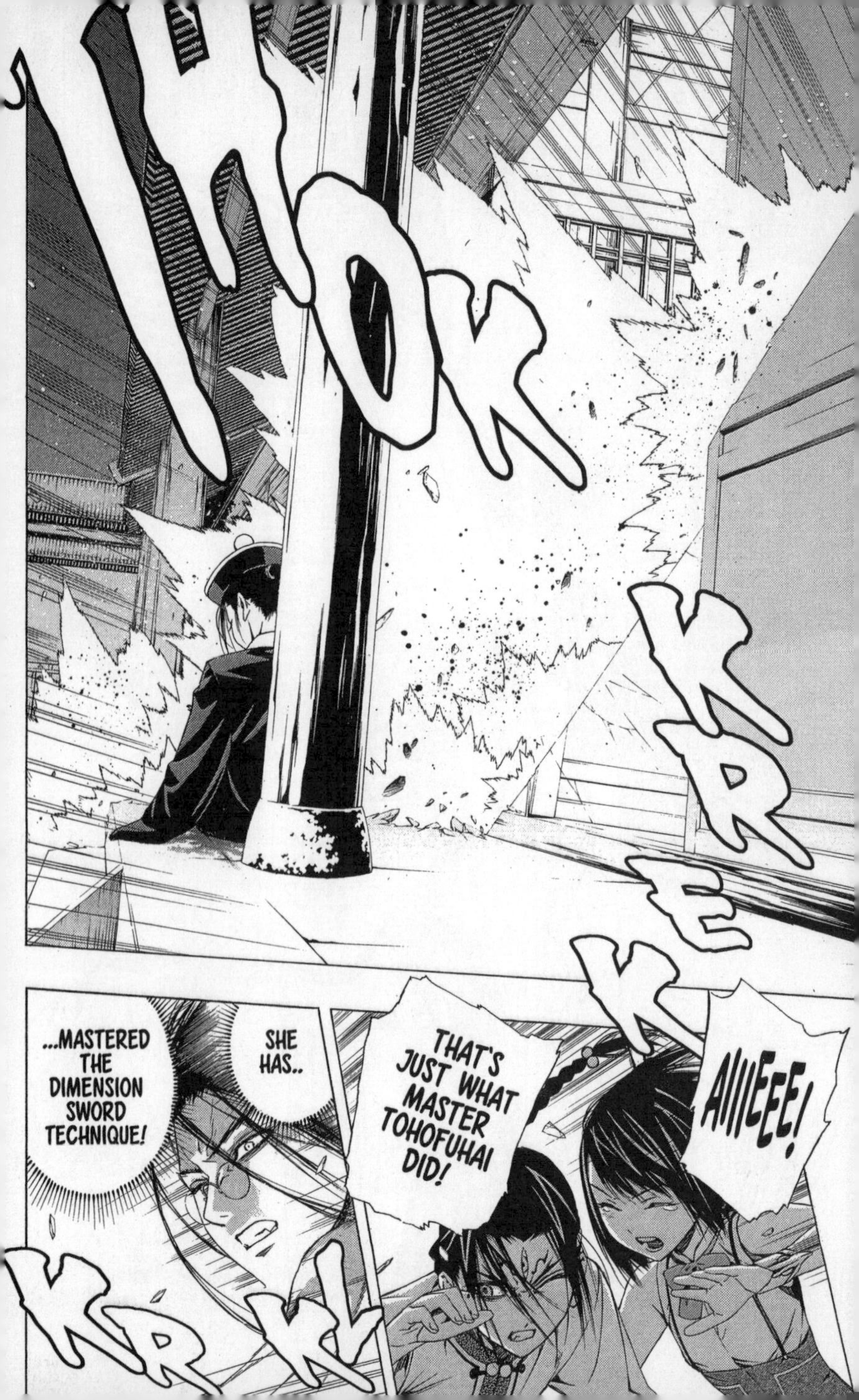
KREEK
AIIIEEE!
THAT'S JUST WHAT MASTER TOHOFUHAI DID!
SHE HAS..
...MASTERED THE DIMENSION SWORD TECHNIQUE!

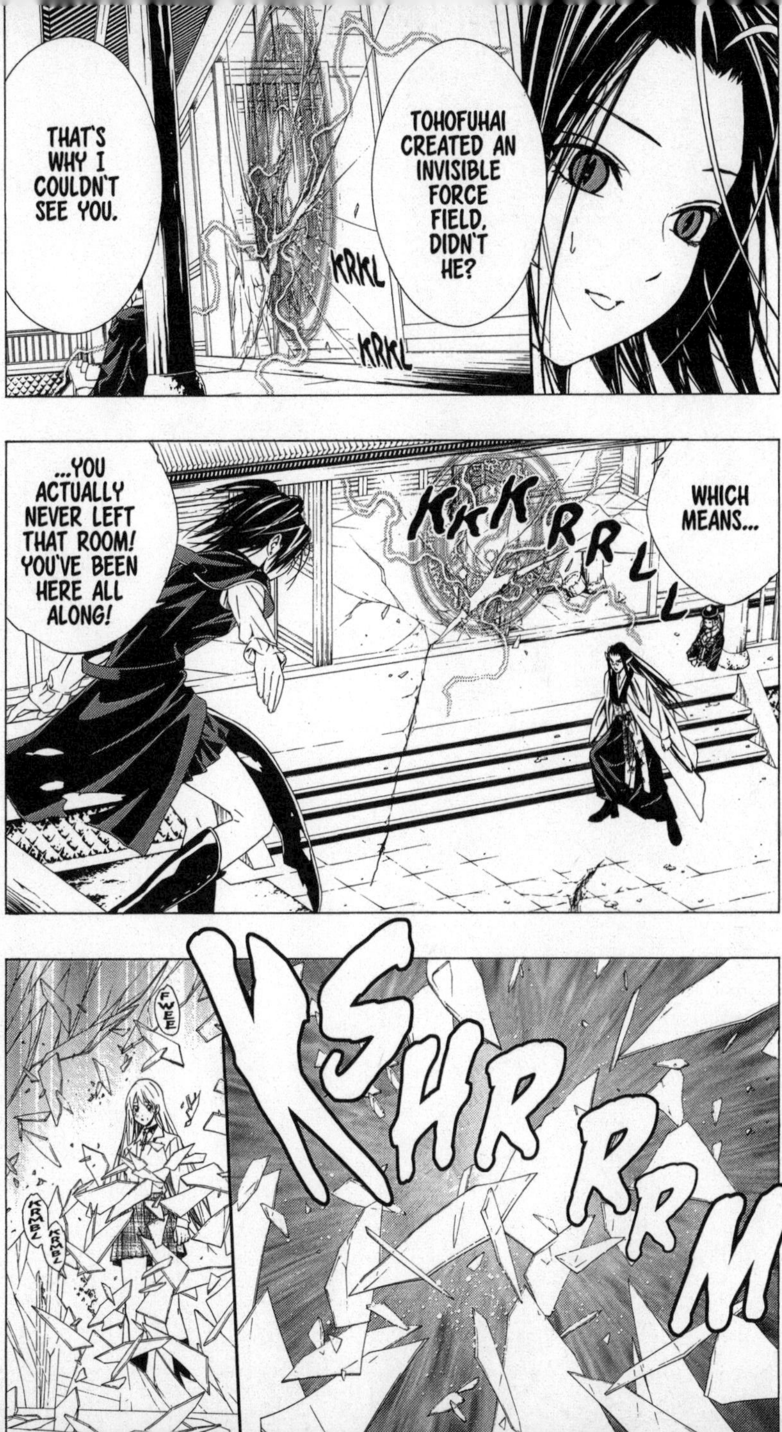
TOHOFUHAI CREATED AN INVISIBLE FORCE FIELD, DIDN'T HE?
KRKL
KRKL
THAT'S WHY I COULDN'T SEE YOU.
WHICH MEANS...
KKK RRLL
...YOU ACTUALLY NEVER LEFT THAT ROOM! YOU'VE BEEN HERE ALL ALONG!
VSHRRRRM
FWEE
KRMBL
KRMBL

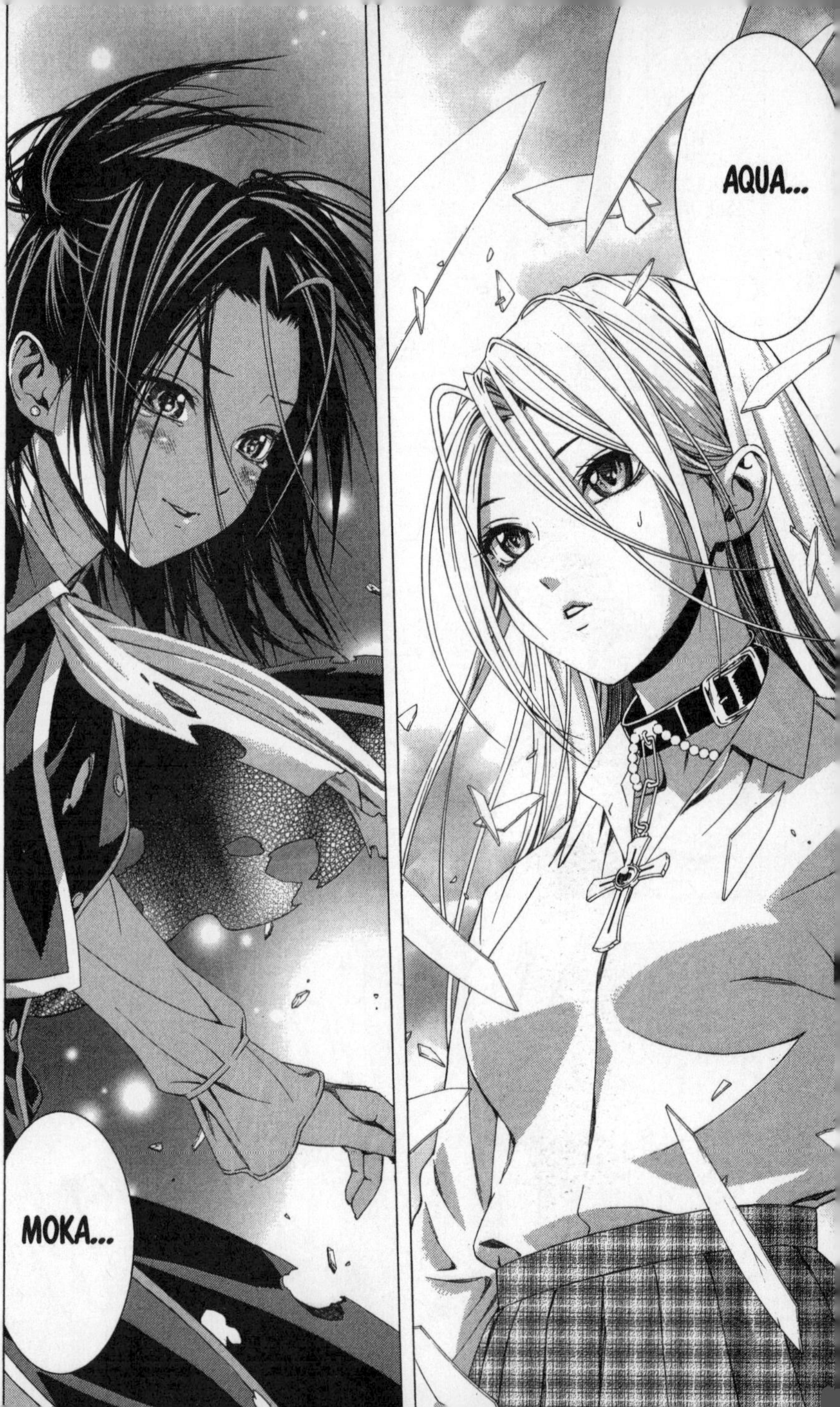
AQUA...
MOKA...

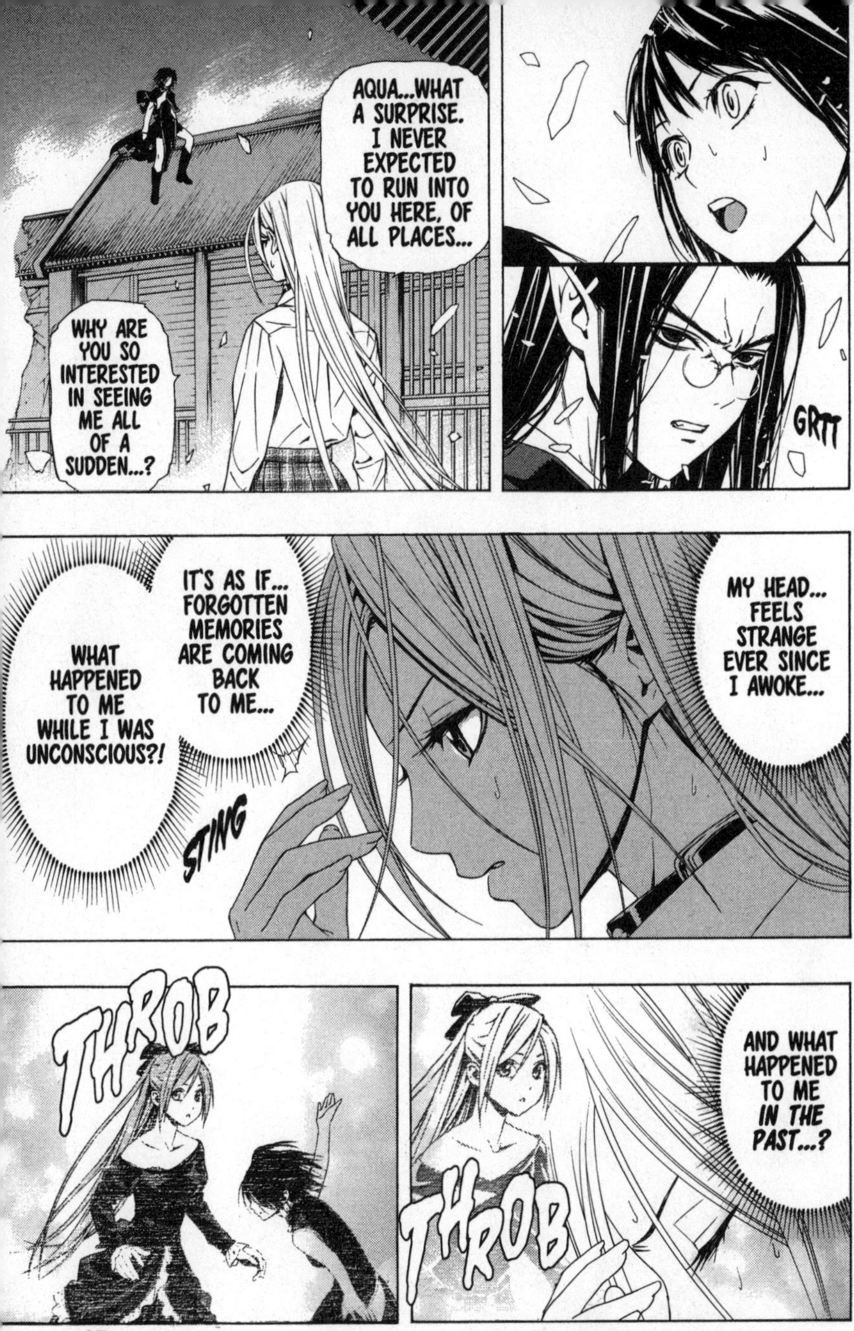
GRTT
AQUA...WHAT A SURPRISE. I NEVER EXPECTED TO RUN INTO YOU HERE, OF ALL PLACES...
WHY ARE YOU SO INTERESTED IN SEEING ME ALL OF A SUDDEN...?
MY HEAD... FEELS STRANGE EVER SINCE I AWOKE...
IT'S AS IF... FORGOTTEN MEMORIES ARE COMING BACK TO ME...
WHAT HAPPENED TO ME WHILE I WAS UNCONSCIOUS?!
STING
AND WHAT HAPPENED TO ME IN THE PAST...?
THROB
THROB

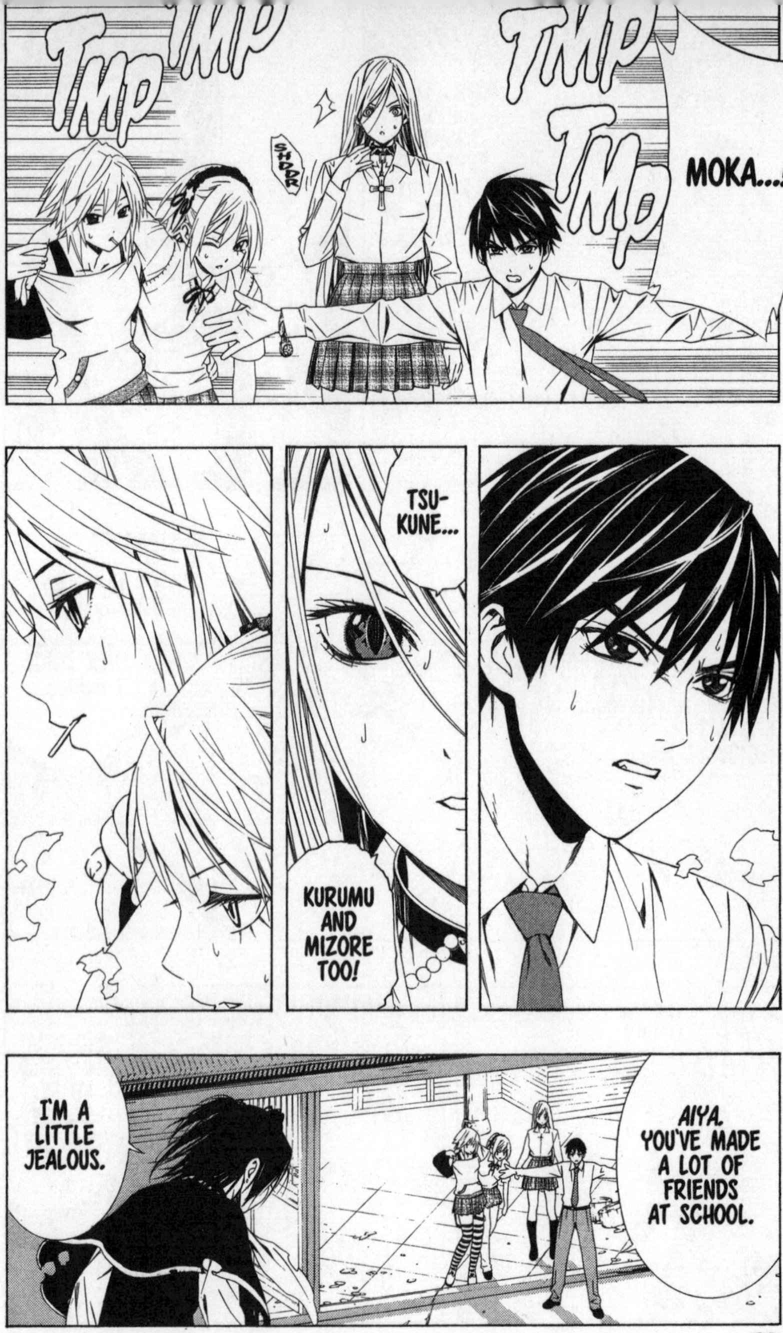
MOKA...!
TMP
TMP
SHDDR
TMP
TMP
TSU-KUNE...
KURUMU AND MIZORE TOO!
AIYA. YOU'VE MADE A LOT OF FRIENDS AT SCHOOL.
I'M A LITTLE JEALOUS.

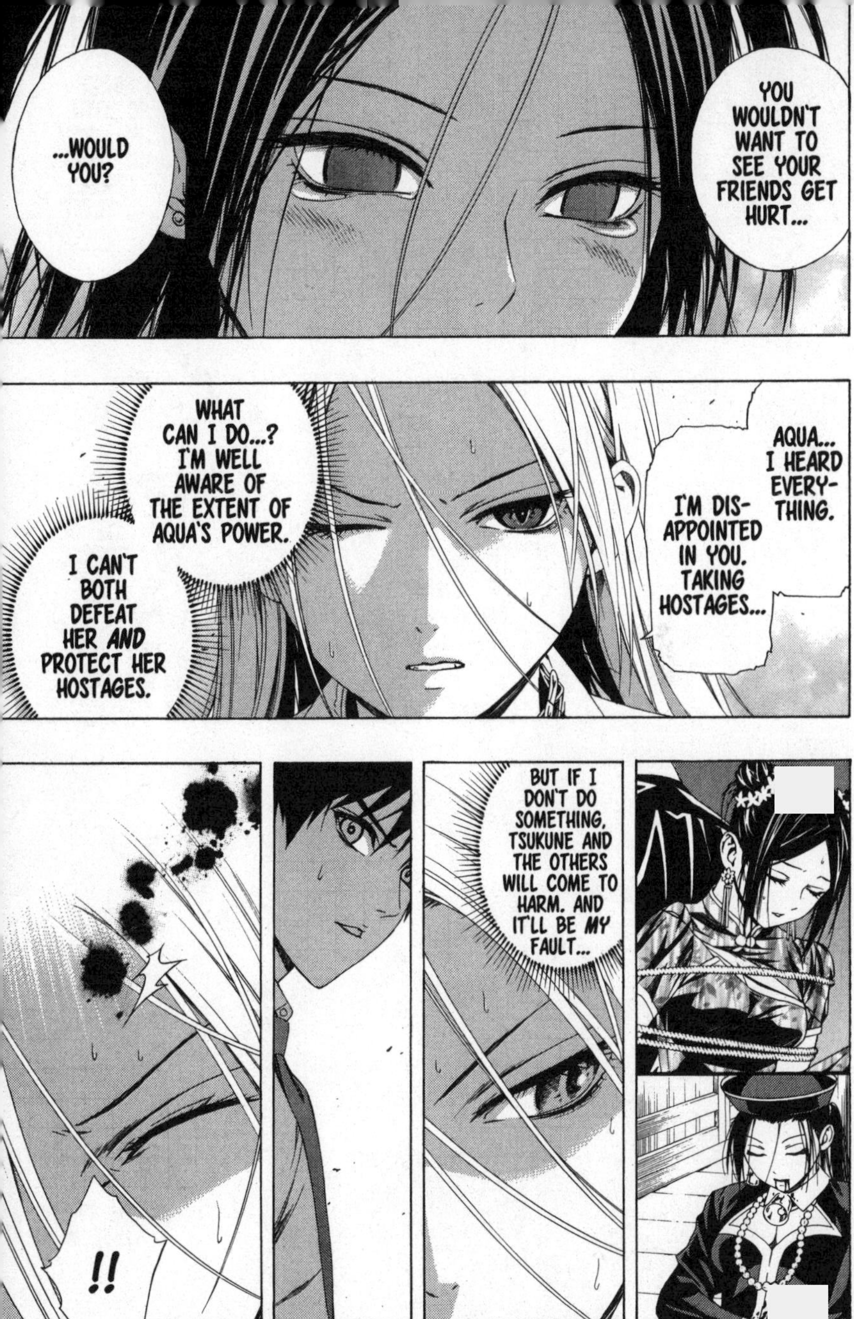
YOU WOULDN'T WANT TO SEE YOUR FRIENDS GET HURT...
...WOULD YOU?
AQUA... I HEARD EVERY-THING.
I'M DIS-APPOINTED IN YOU. TAKING HOSTAGES...
WHAT CAN I DO...? I'M WELL AWARE OF THE EXTENT OF AQUA'S POWER.
I CAN'T BOTH DEFEAT HER *AND* PROTECT HER HOSTAGES.
BUT IF I DON'T DO SOMETHING, TSUKUNE AND THE OTHERS WILL COME TO HARM. AND IT'LL BE *MY* FAULT...
!!

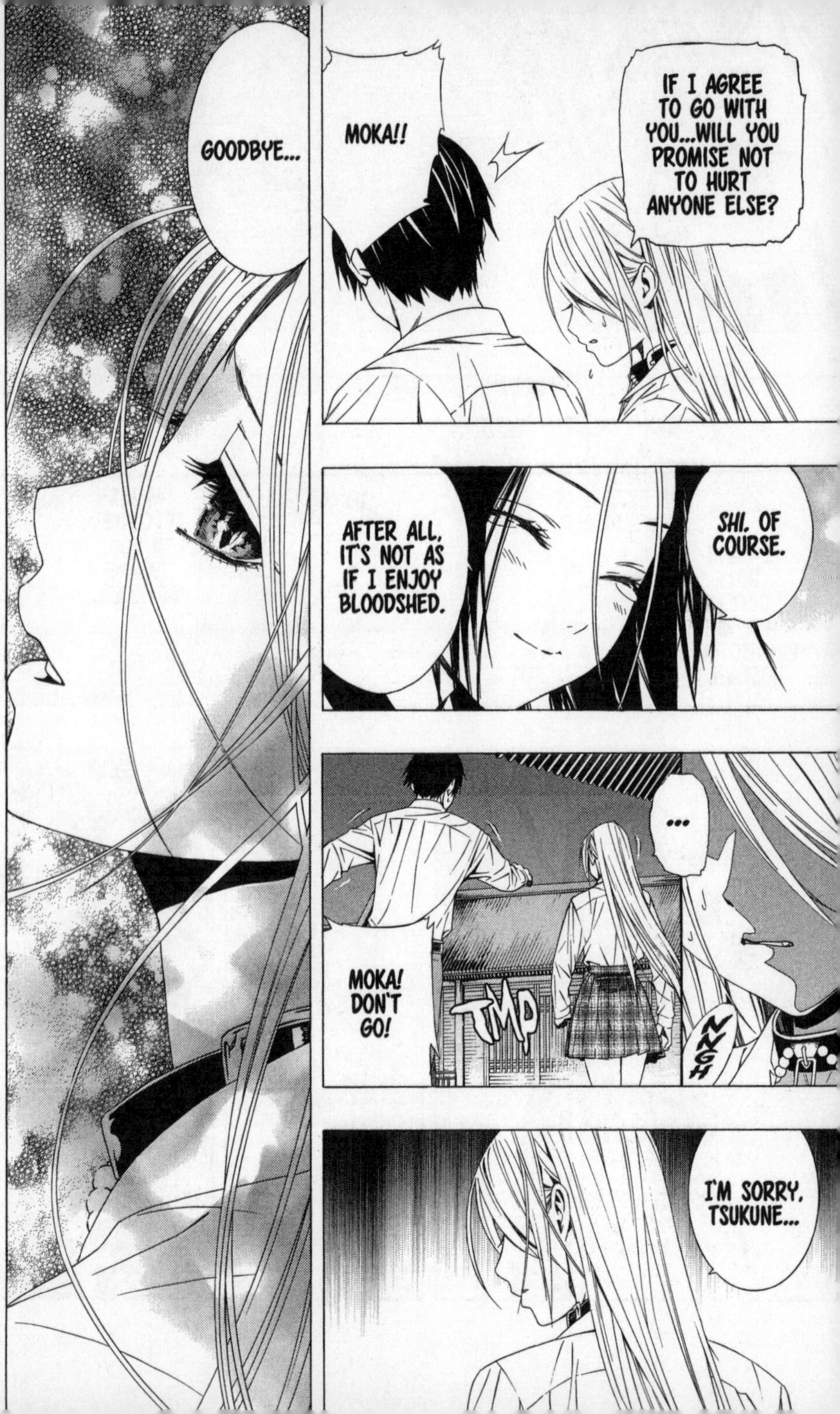
IF I AGREE TO GO WITH YOU...WILL YOU PROMISE NOT TO HURT ANYONE ELSE?
MOKA!!
SHI. OF COURSE.
AFTER ALL, IT'S NOT AS IF I ENJOY BLOODSHED.
...
NNGH
MOKA! DON'T GO!
TMP
I'M SORRY, TSUKUNE...
GOODBYE...

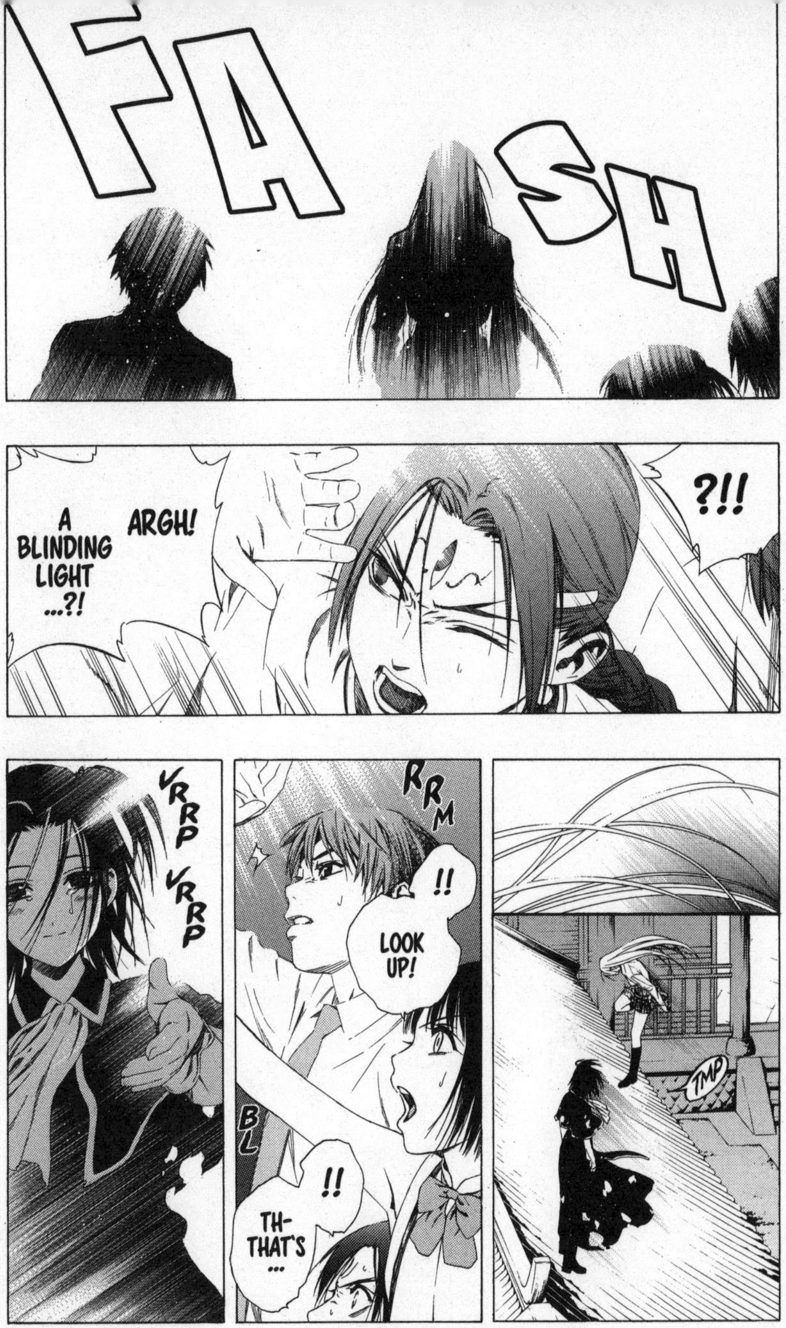
FASH
?!!
ARGH!
A BLINDING LIGHT ...?!
TMP
RRM
!!
LOOK UP!
BL
!!
TH- THAT'S ...
VRRP VRRP

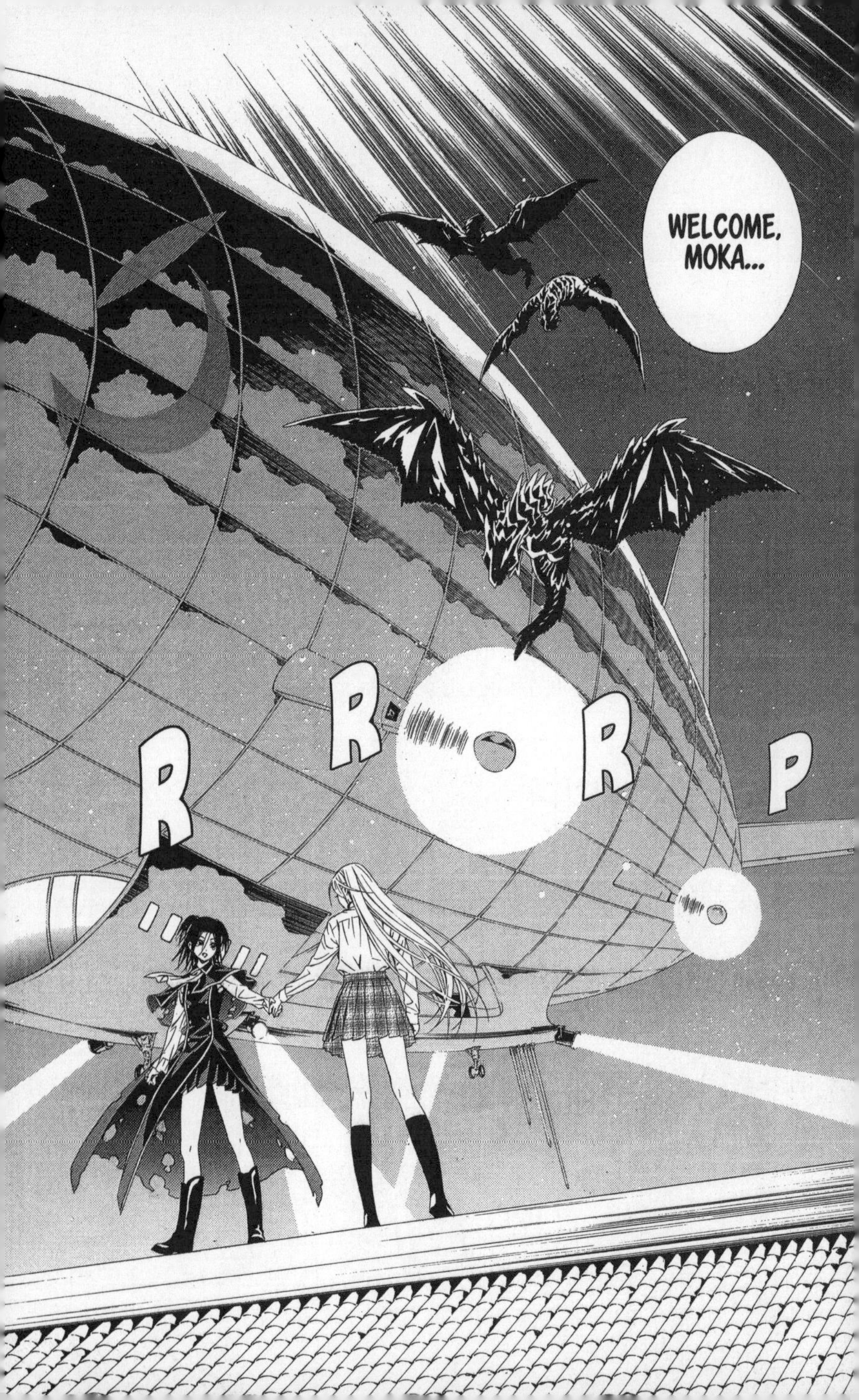
WELCOME, MOKA...
RRORP

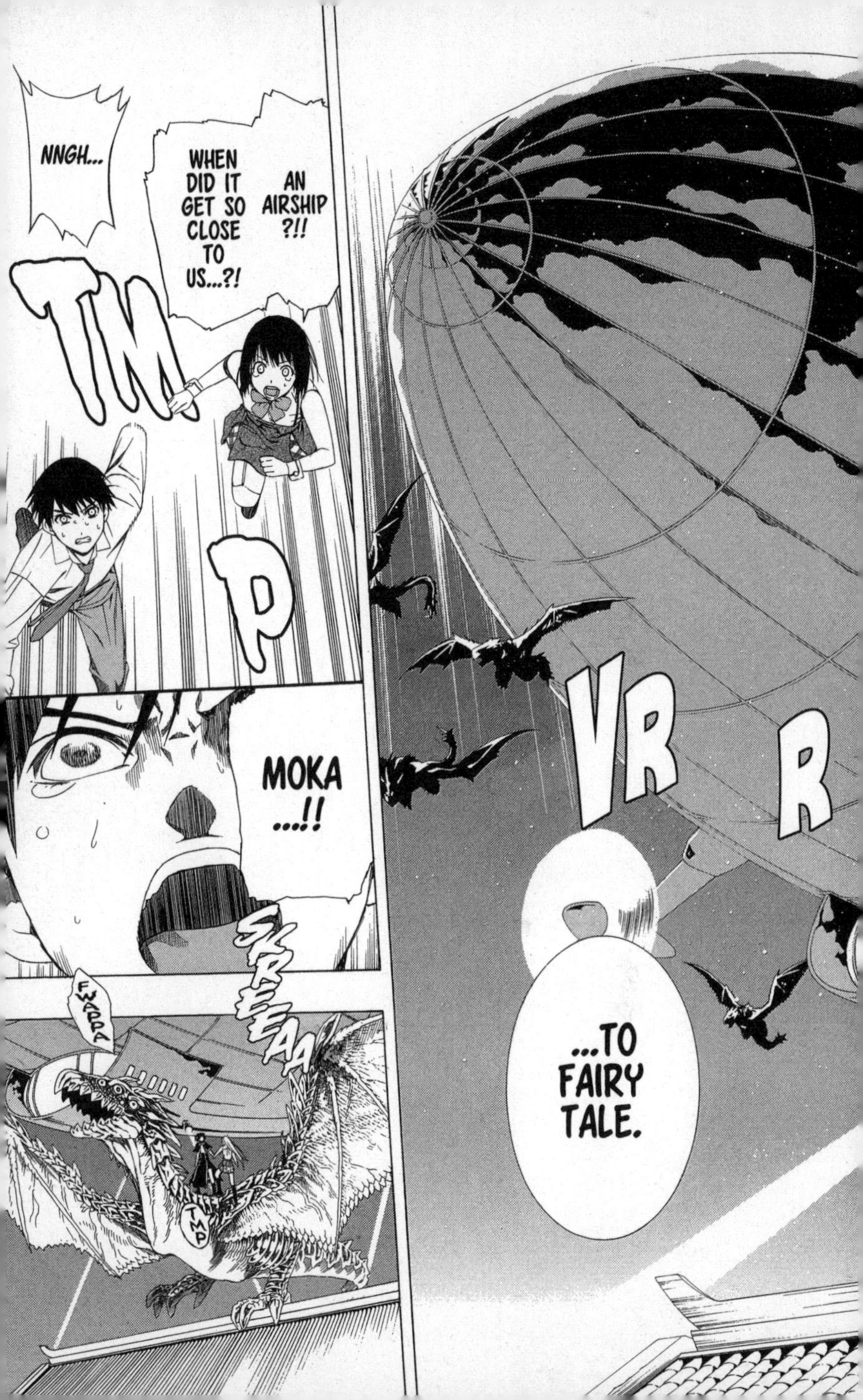
VR R
...TO FAIRY TALE.
AN AIRSHIP ?!!
WHEN DID IT GET SO CLOSE TO US...?!
NNGH...
TMP
MOKA ...!!
SKREEAA
FWAPPA
TMP

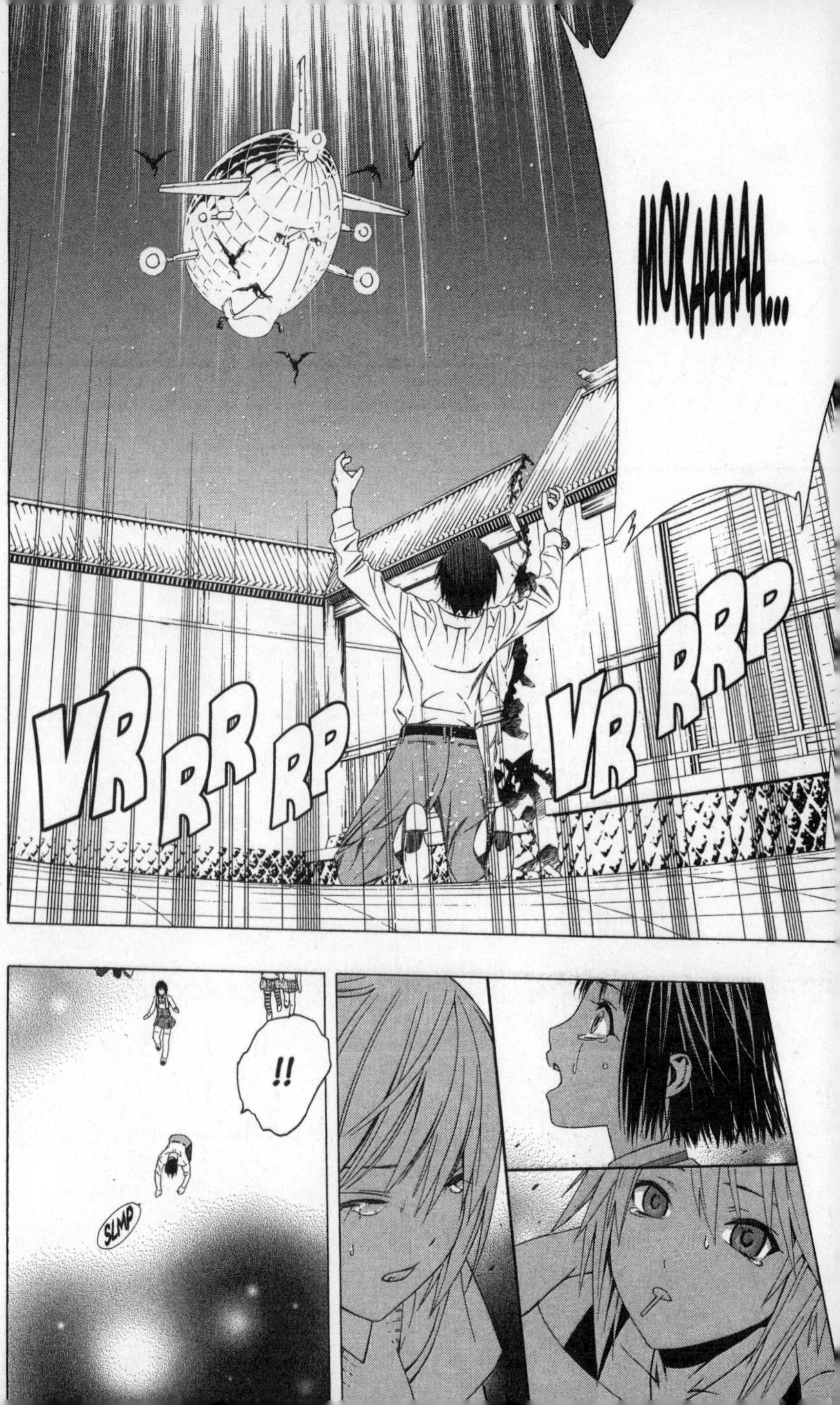
MOKAAAA...
VRRRP
VRRRRP
!!
SLMP

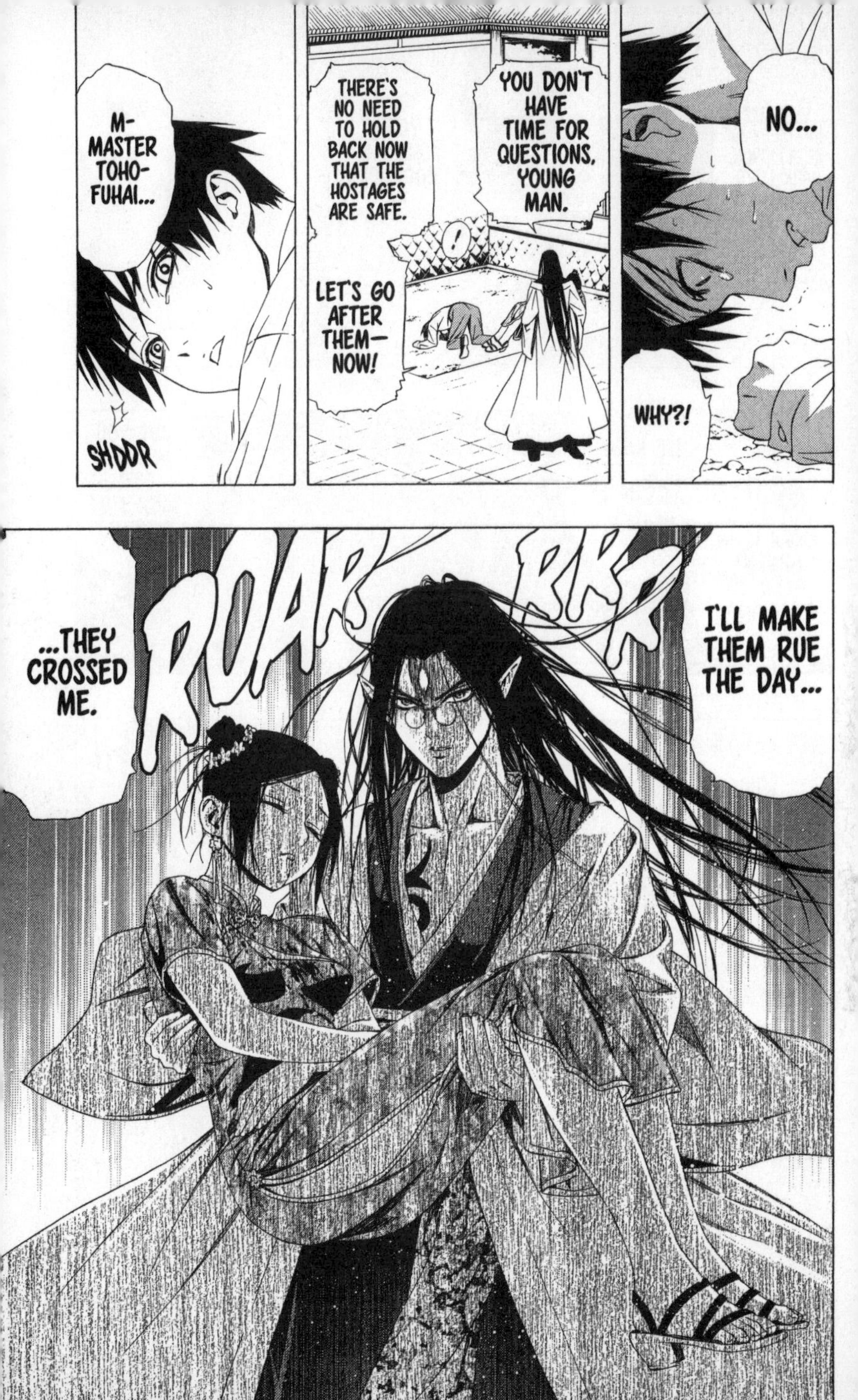
NO...
WHY?!
YOU DON'T HAVE TIME FOR QUESTIONS, YOUNG MAN.
THERE'S NO NEED TO HOLD BACK NOW THAT THE HOSTAGES ARE SAFE.
!
LET'S GO AFTER THEM—NOW!
M-MASTER TOHO-FUHAI...
SHDDR
I'LL MAKE THEM RUE THE DAY...
ROAR
RR
...THEY CROSSED ME.

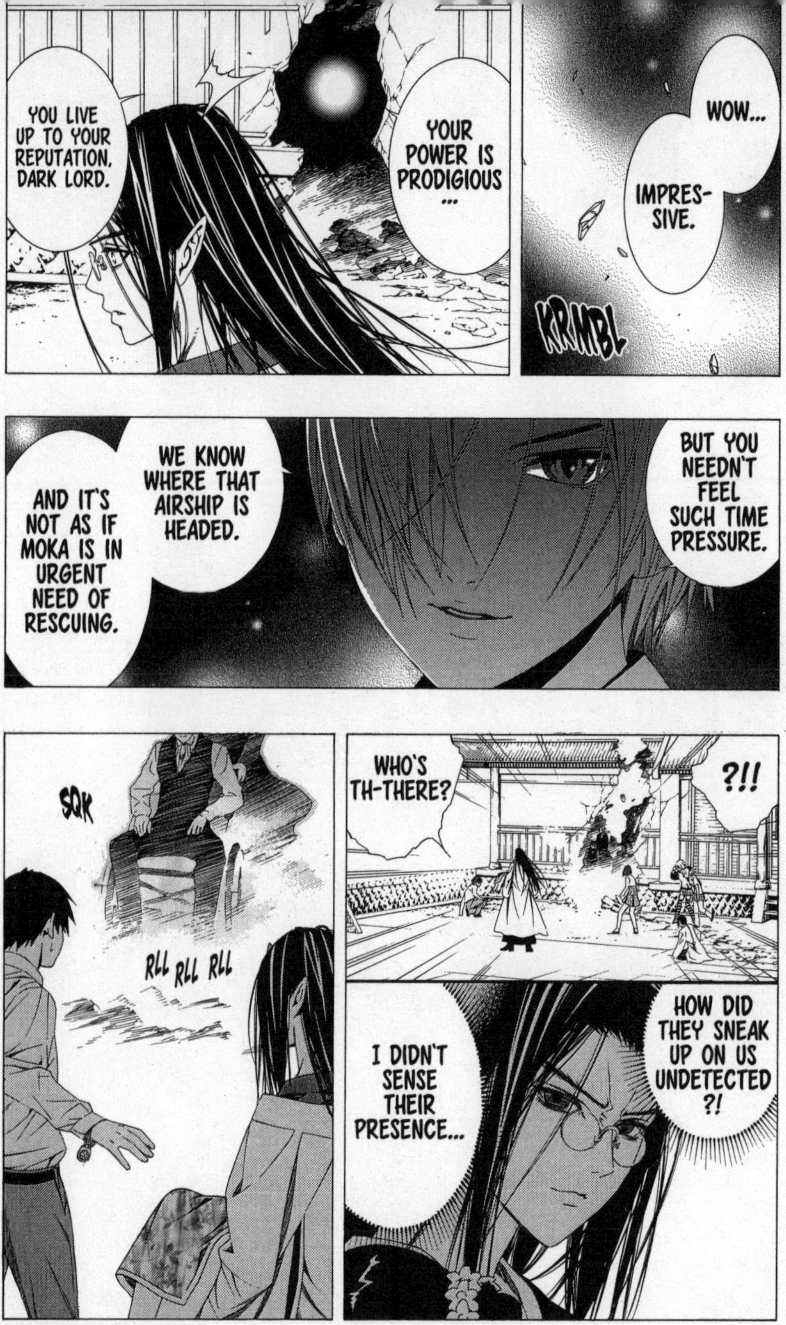
WOW...
IMPRESSIVE.
KRMBL
YOUR POWER IS PRODIGIOUS...
YOU LIVE UP TO YOUR REPUTATION, DARK LORD.
BUT YOU NEEDN'T FEEL SUCH TIME PRESSURE.
WE KNOW WHERE THAT AIRSHIP IS HEADED.
AND IT'S NOT AS IF MOKA IS IN URGENT NEED OF RESCUING.
?!!
WHO'S TH-THERE?
HOW DID THEY SNEAK UP ON US UNDETECTED?!
I DIDN'T SENSE THEIR PRESENCE...
SQK
RLL RLL RLL

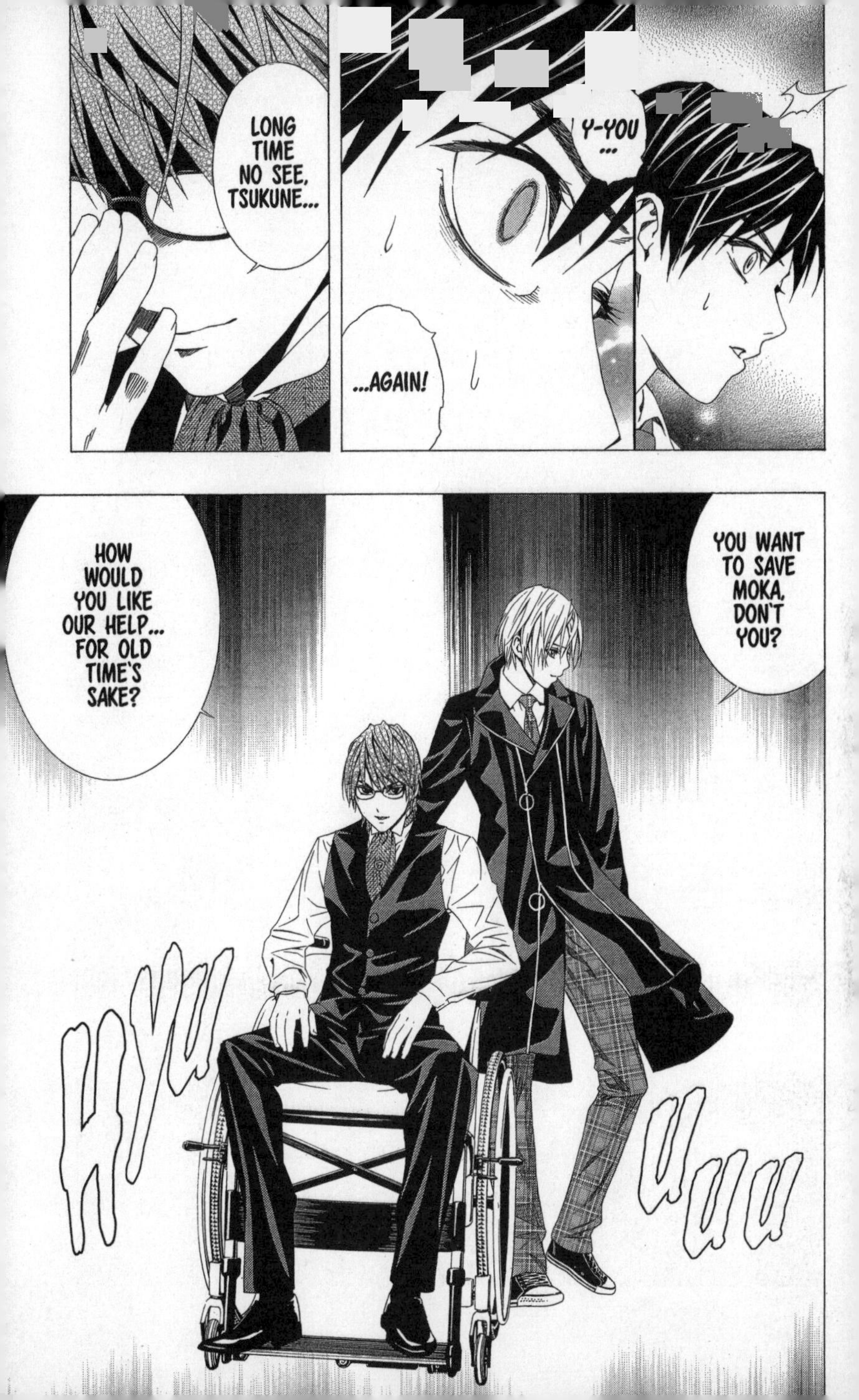
Y-YOU ...
...AGAIN!
LONG TIME NO SEE, TSUKUNE...
YOU WANT TO SAVE MOKA, DON'T YOU?
HOW WOULD YOU LIKE OUR HELP... FOR OLD TIME'S SAKE?
HYUU
UUU

38: Alliance

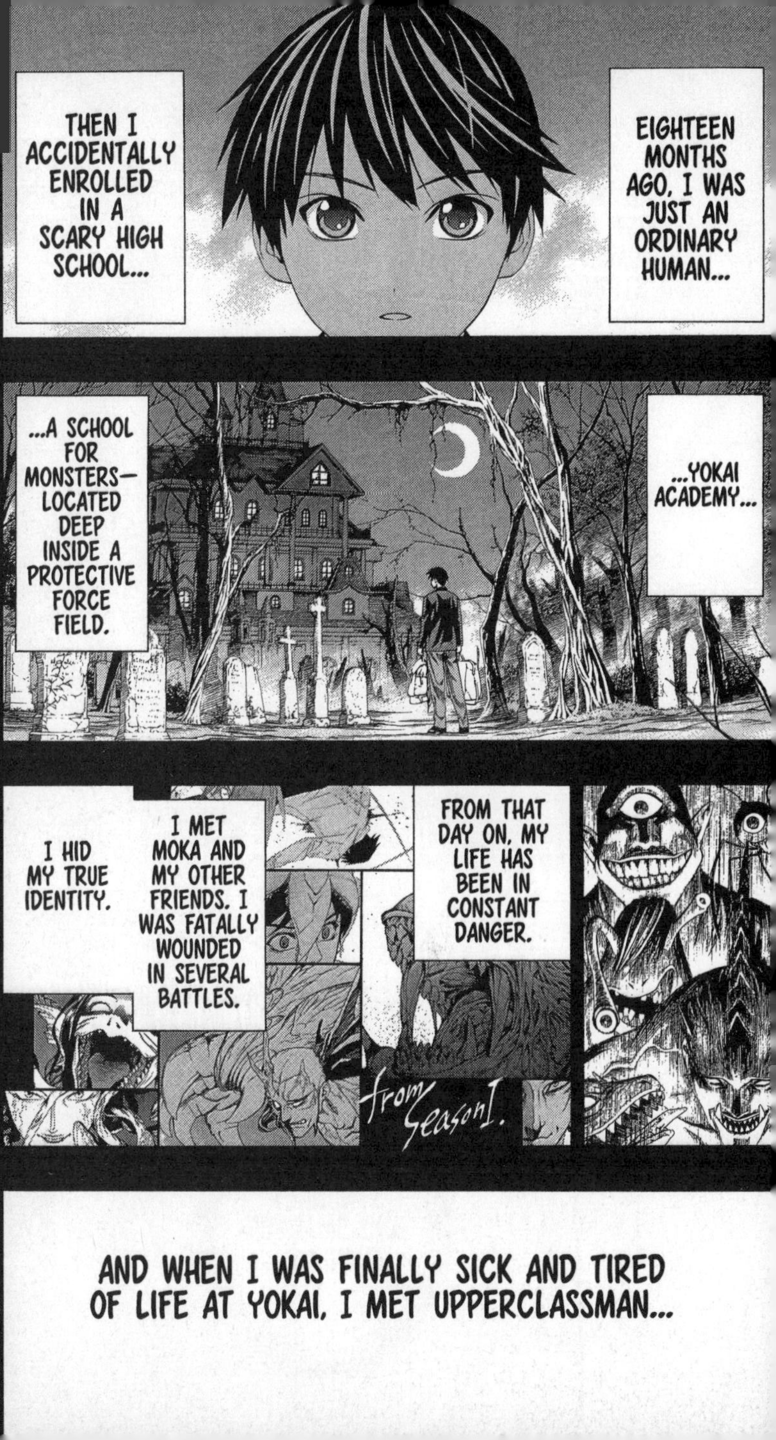
EIGHTEEN MONTHS AGO, I WAS JUST AN ORDINARY HUMAN...
THEN I ACCIDENTALLY ENROLLED IN A SCARY HIGH SCHOOL...
...YOKAI ACADEMY...
...A SCHOOL FOR MONSTERS—LOCATED DEEP INSIDE A PROTECTIVE FORCE FIELD.
FROM THAT DAY ON, MY LIFE HAS BEEN IN CONSTANT DANGER.
from Season I.
I MET MOKA AND MY OTHER FRIENDS. I WAS FATALLY WOUNDED IN SEVERAL BATTLES.
I HID MY TRUE IDENTITY.
AND WHEN I WAS FINALLY SICK AND TIRED OF LIFE AT YOKAI, I MET UPPERCLASSMAN...

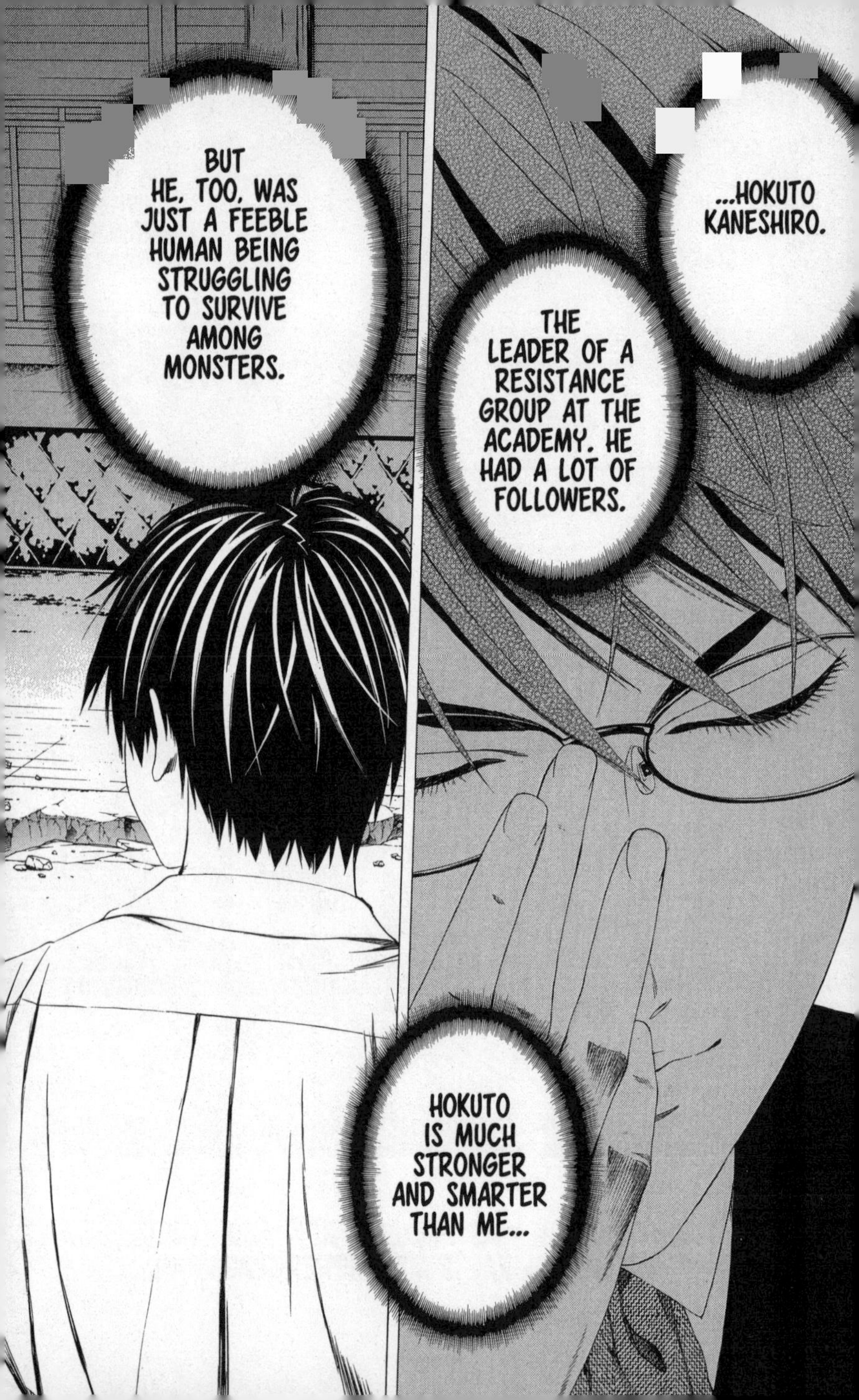

...HOKUTO KANESHIRO.
THE LEADER OF A RESISTANCE GROUP AT THE ACADEMY. HE HAD A LOT OF FOLLOWERS.
HOKUTO IS MUCH STRONGER AND SMARTER THAN ME...
BUT HE, TOO, WAS JUST A FEEBLE HUMAN BEING STRUGGLING TO SURVIVE AMONG MONSTERS.

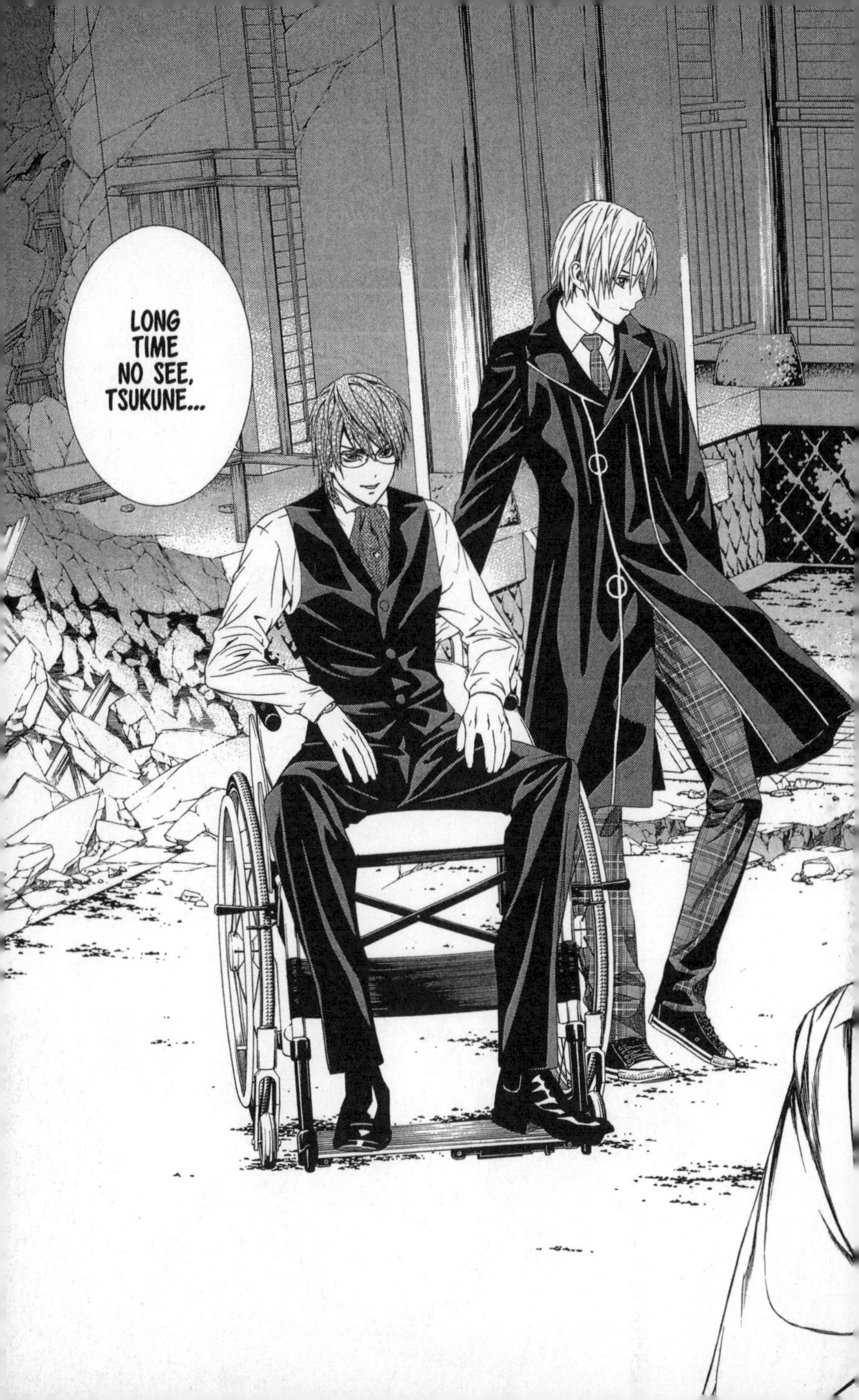
LONG TIME NO SEE, TSUKUNE...

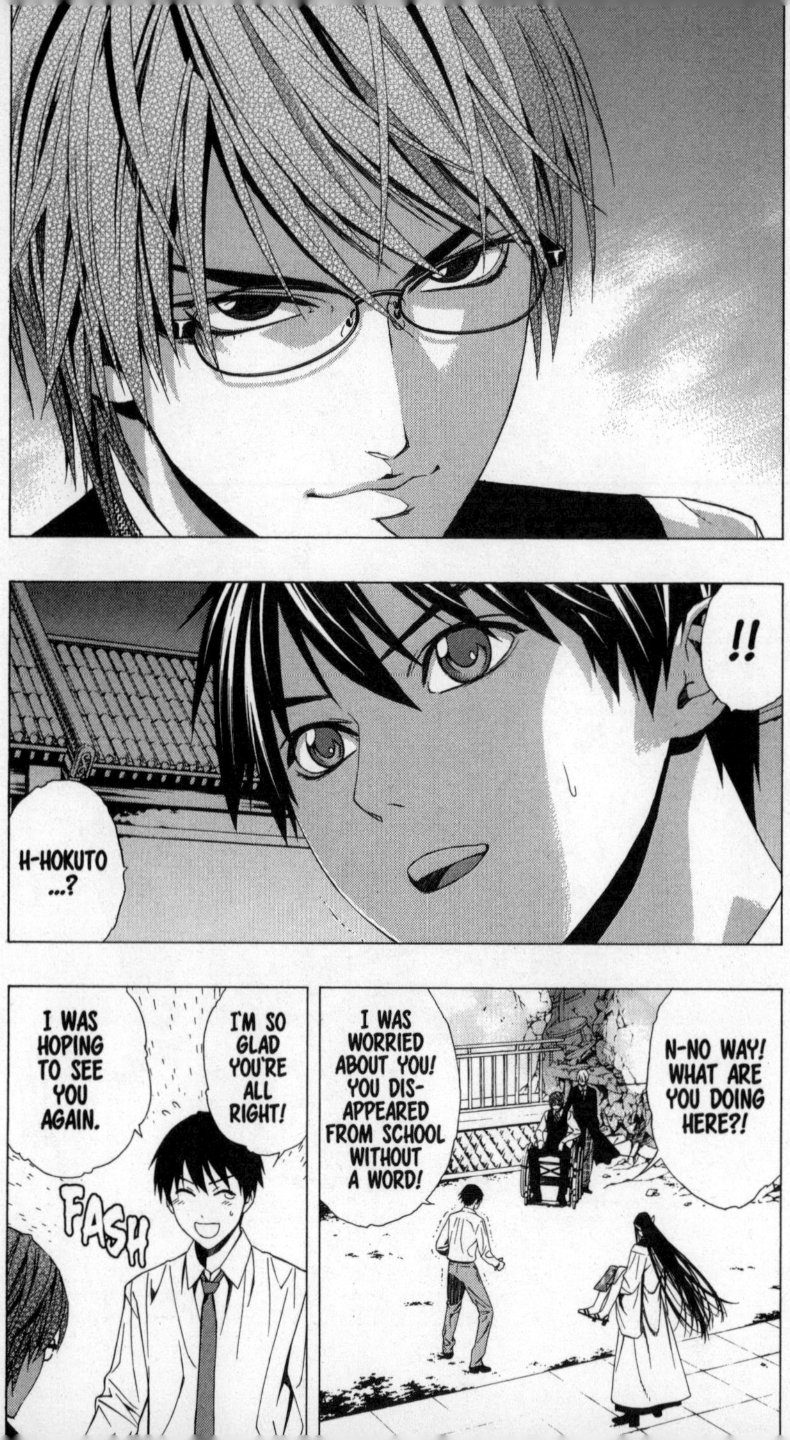
!!
H-HOKUTO ...?
N-NO WAY! WHAT ARE YOU DOING HERE?!
I WAS WORRIED ABOUT YOU! YOU DIS-APPEARED FROM SCHOOL WITHOUT A WORD!
I'M SO GLAD YOU'RE ALL RIGHT!
I WAS HOPING TO SEE YOU AGAIN.
FASH

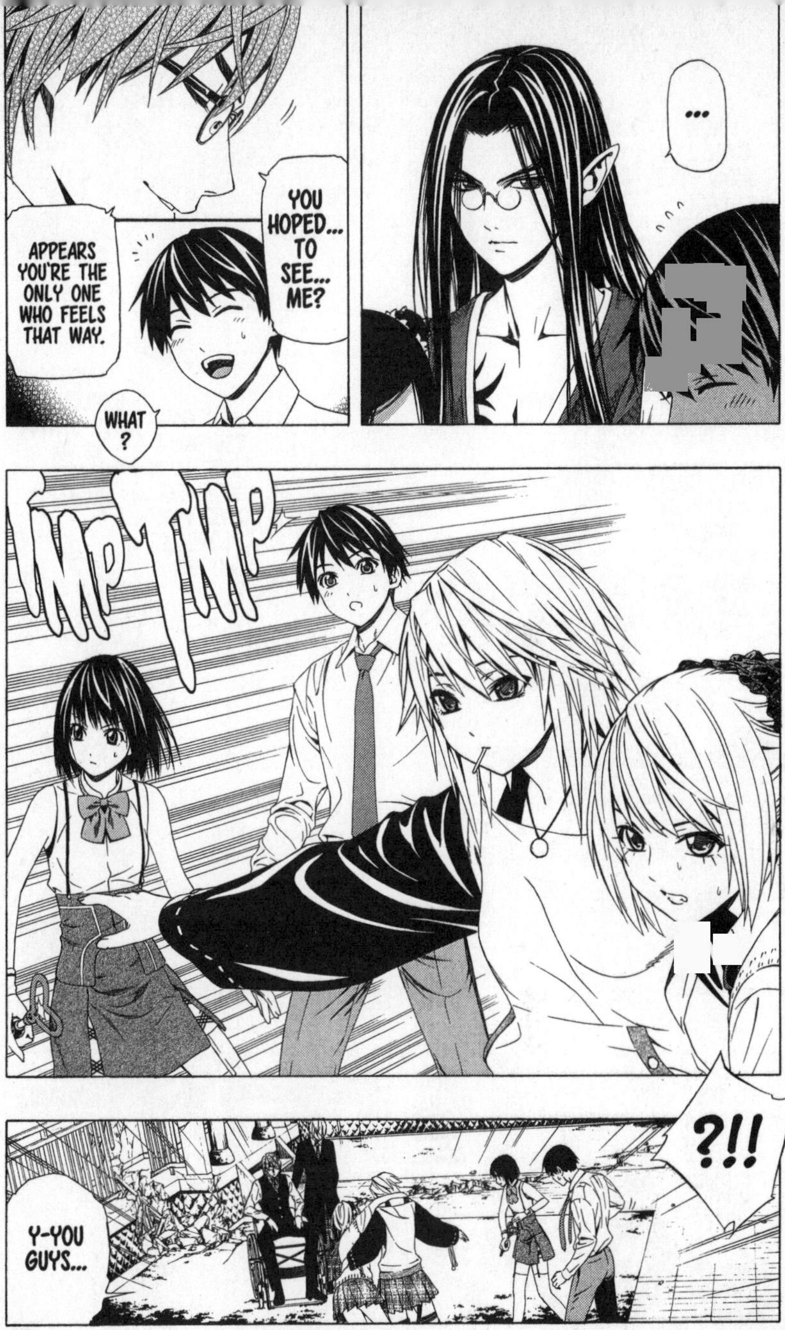
...
YOU HOPED... TO SEE... ME?
APPEARS YOU'RE THE ONLY ONE WHO FEELS THAT WAY.
WHAT?
MP TMP
?!!
Y-YOU GUYS...

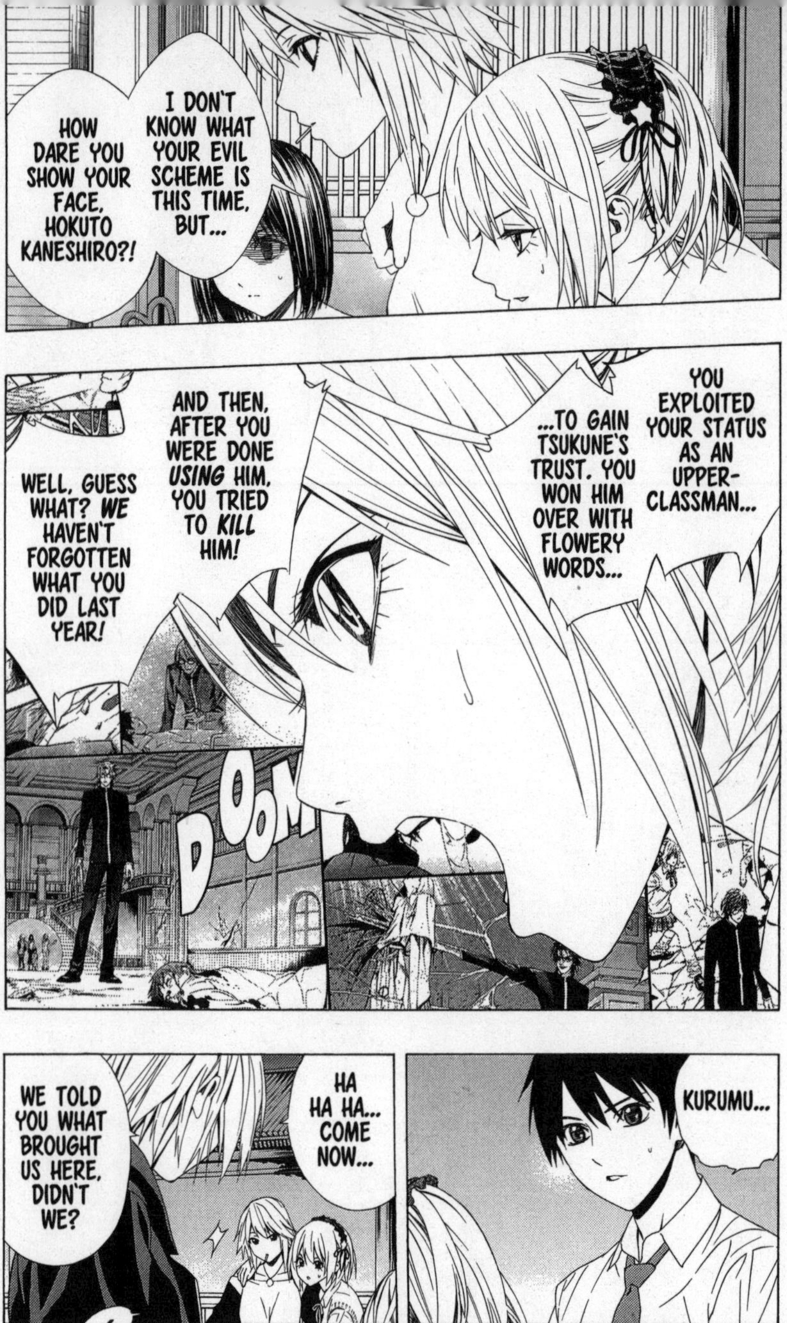
I DON'T KNOW WHAT YOUR EVIL SCHEME IS THIS TIME, BUT...
HOW DARE YOU SHOW YOUR FACE, HOKUTO KANESHIRO?!
YOU EXPLOITED YOUR STATUS AS AN UPPER-CLASSMAN...
...TO GAIN TSUKUNE'S TRUST. YOU WON HIM OVER WITH FLOWERY WORDS...
AND THEN, AFTER YOU WERE DONE *USING* HIM, YOU TRIED TO *KILL* HIM!
WELL, GUESS WHAT? *WE* HAVEN'T FORGOTTEN WHAT YOU DID LAST YEAR!
DOOM
KURUMU...
HA HA HA... COME NOW...
WE TOLD YOU WHAT BROUGHT US HERE, DIDN'T WE?
!

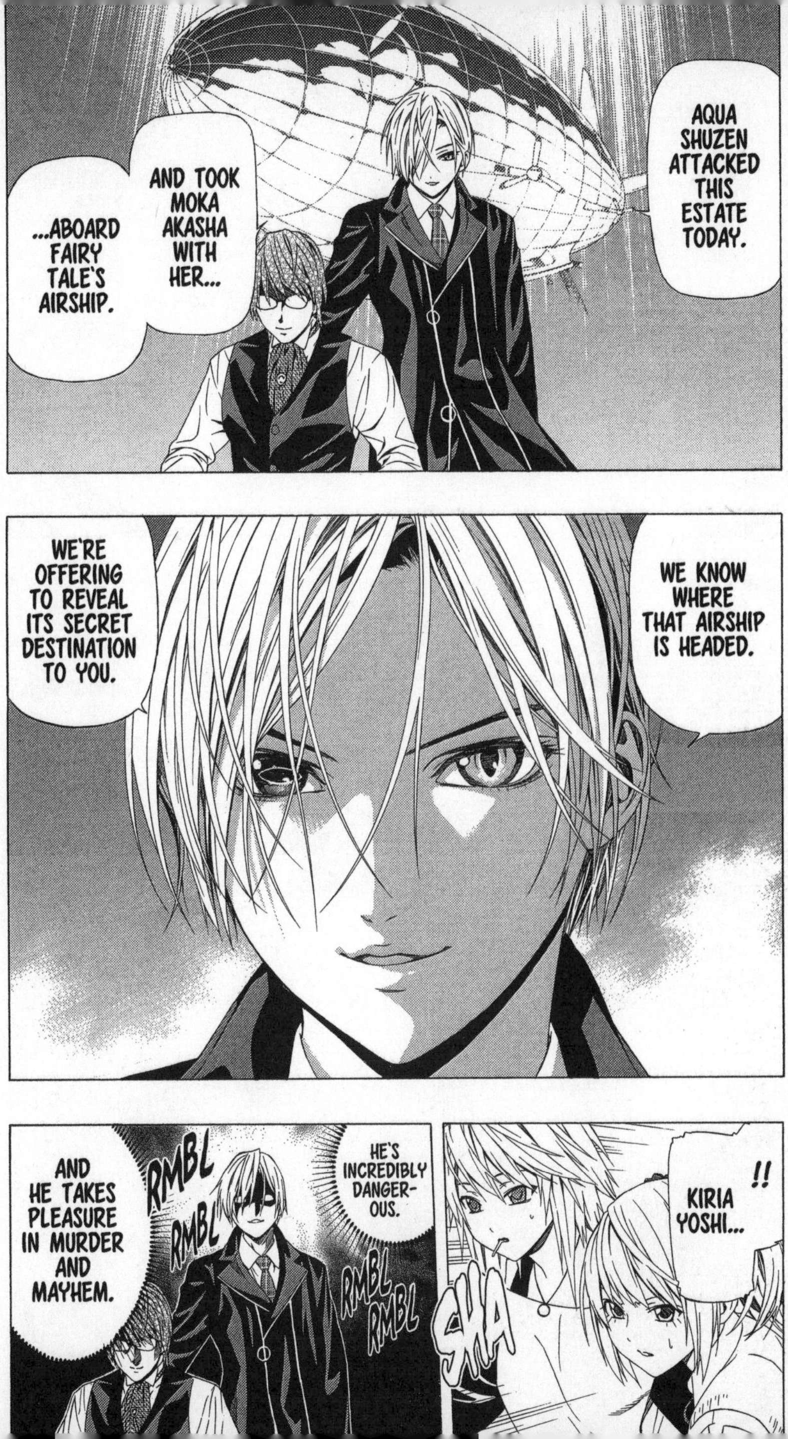

AQUA SHUZEN ATTACKED THIS ESTATE TODAY.
AND TOOK MOKA AKASHA WITH HER...
...ABOARD FAIRY TALE'S AIRSHIP.
WE KNOW WHERE THAT AIRSHIP IS HEADED.
WE'RE OFFERING TO REVEAL ITS SECRET DESTINATION TO YOU.
!!
KIRIA YOSHI...
SHA
HE'S INCREDIBLY DANGER-OUS.
AND HE TAKES PLEASURE IN MURDER AND MAYHEM.
RMBL RMBL
RMBL RMBL

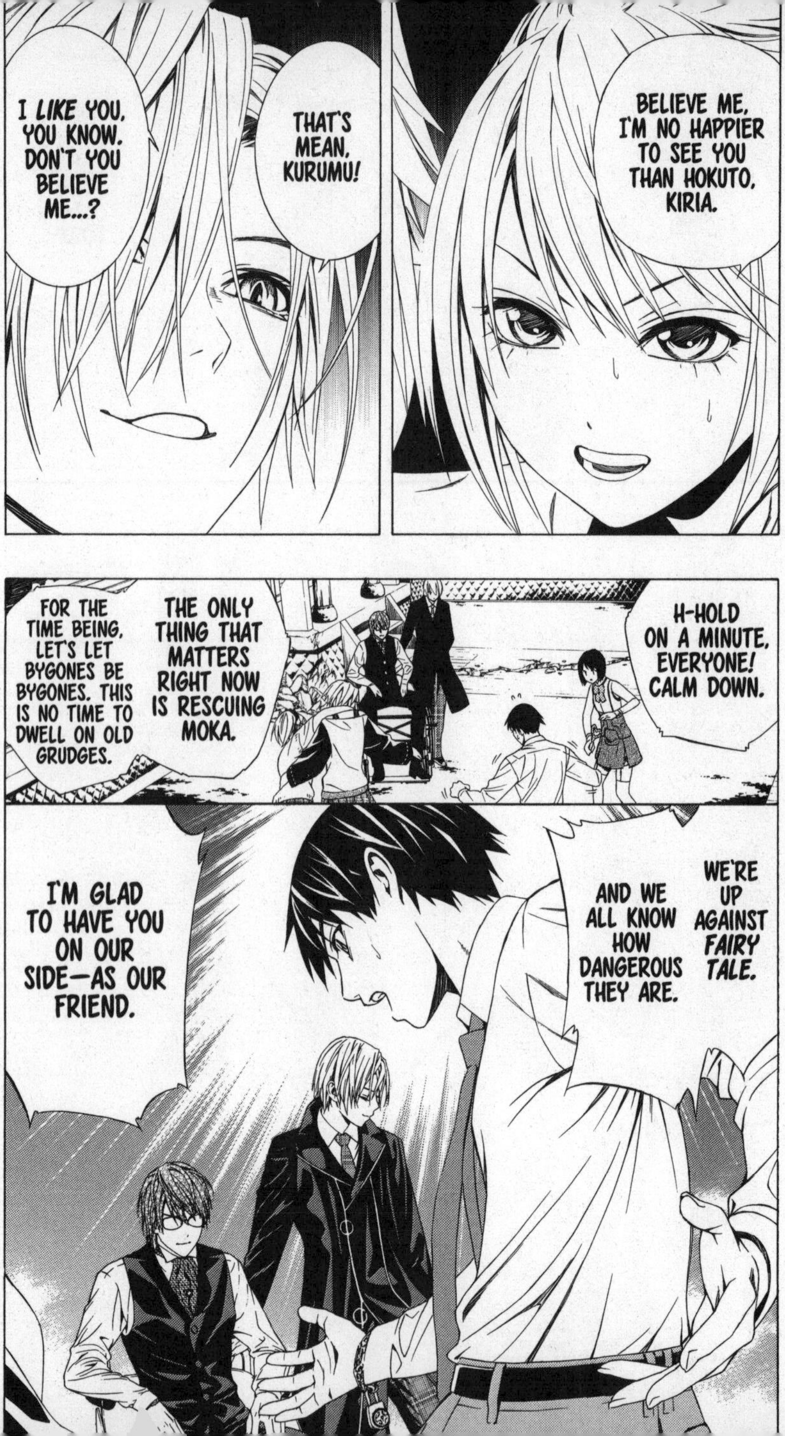
BELIEVE ME, I'M NO HAPPIER TO SEE YOU THAN HOKUTO, KIRIA.
THAT'S MEAN, KURUMU!
I *LIKE* YOU, YOU KNOW. DON'T YOU BELIEVE ME...?
H-HOLD ON A MINUTE, EVERYONE! CALM DOWN.
THE ONLY THING THAT MATTERS RIGHT NOW IS RESCUING MOKA.
FOR THE TIME BEING, LET'S LET BYGONES BE BYGONES. THIS IS NO TIME TO DWELL ON OLD GRUDGES.
WE'RE UP AGAINST *FAIRY TALE*.
AND WE ALL KNOW HOW DANGEROUS THEY ARE.
I'M GLAD TO HAVE YOU ON OUR SIDE—AS OUR FRIEND.

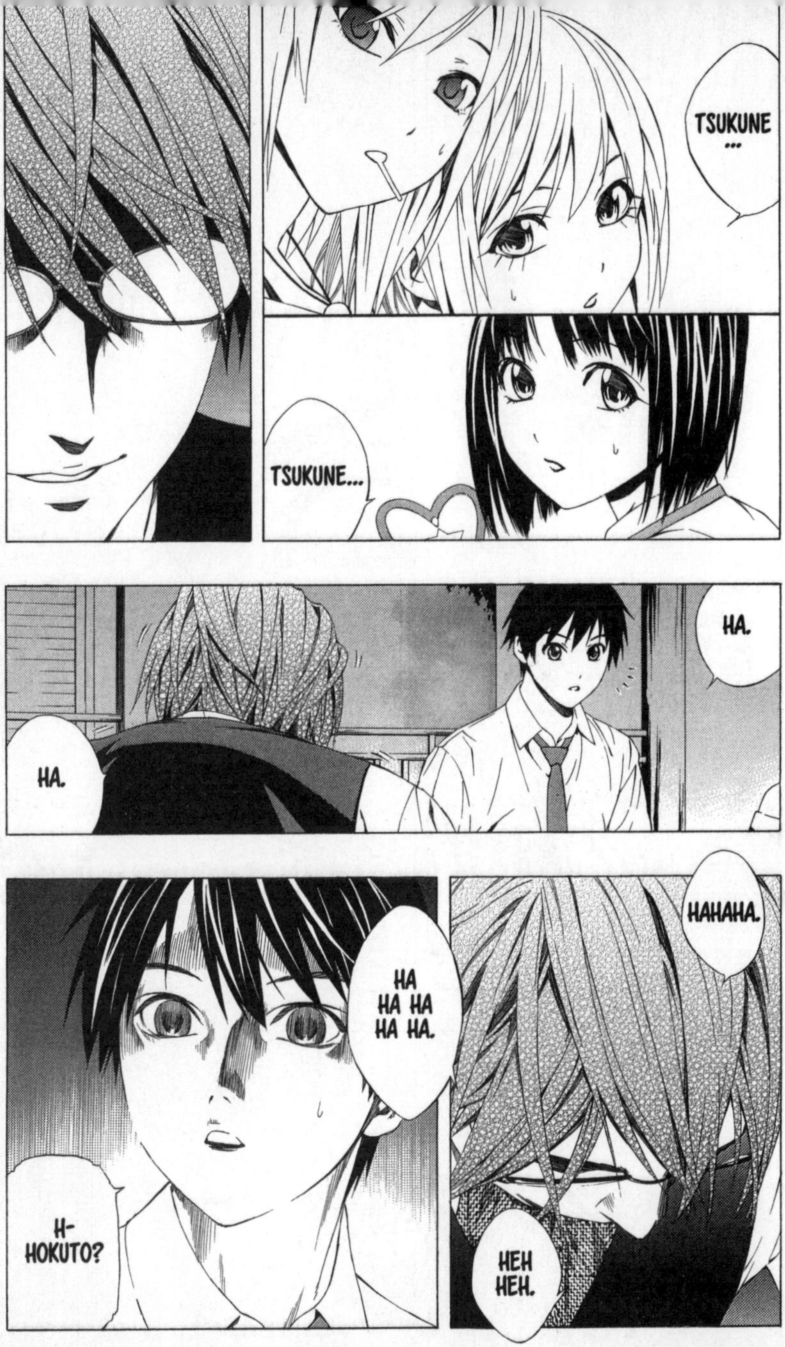
TSUKUNE ...
TSUKUNE...
HA.
HA.
HAHAHA.
HEH HEH.
HA HA HA HA HA.
H-HOKUTO?

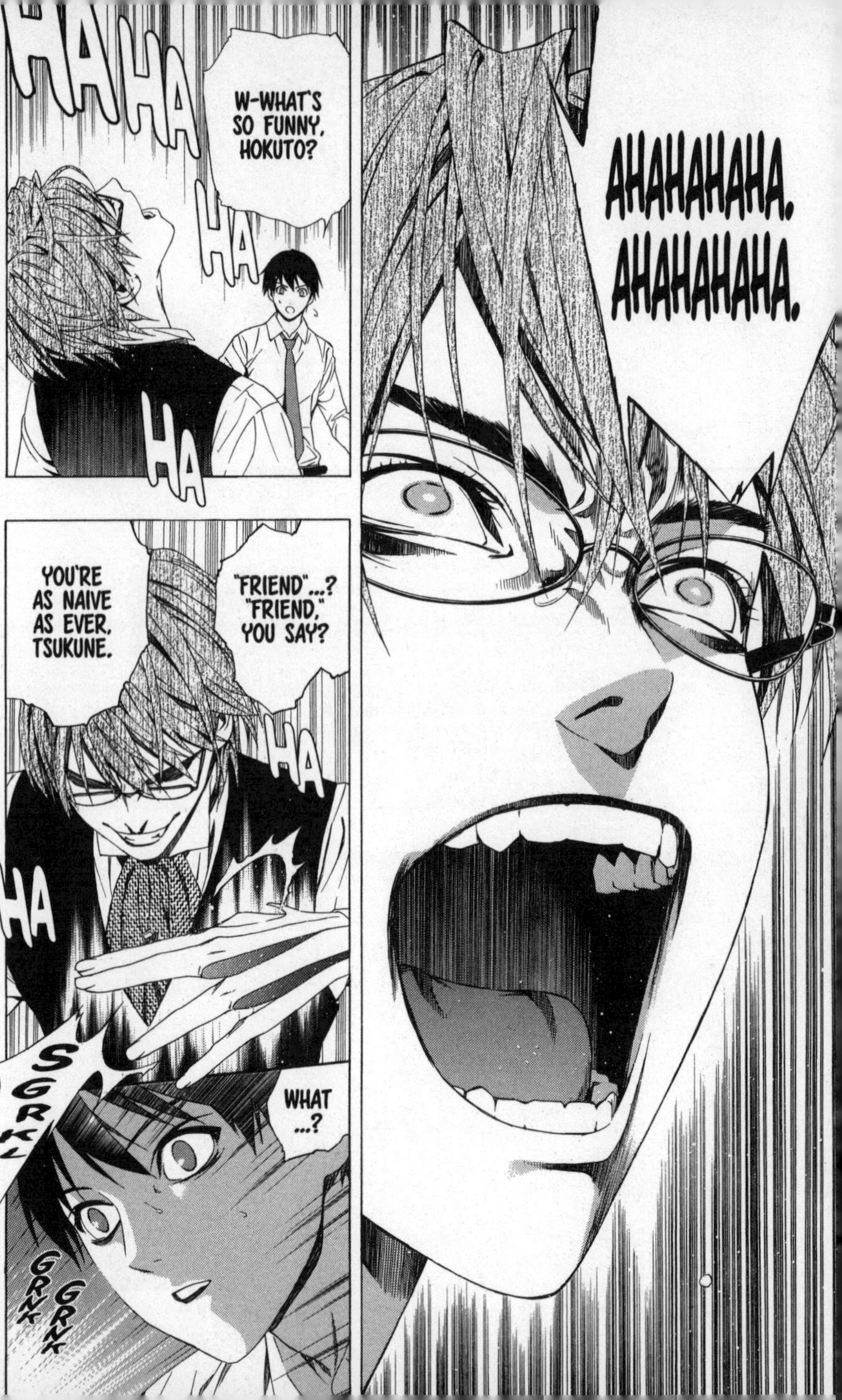
AHAHAHAHA.
AHAHAHAHA.
HAHA
W-WHAT'S SO FUNNY, HOKUTO?
HA
HA
HA
"FRIEND"...? "FRIEND," YOU SAY?
YOU'RE AS NAIVE AS EVER, TSUKUNE.
HA
HA
SGRK
WHAT ...?
GRNK GRNK

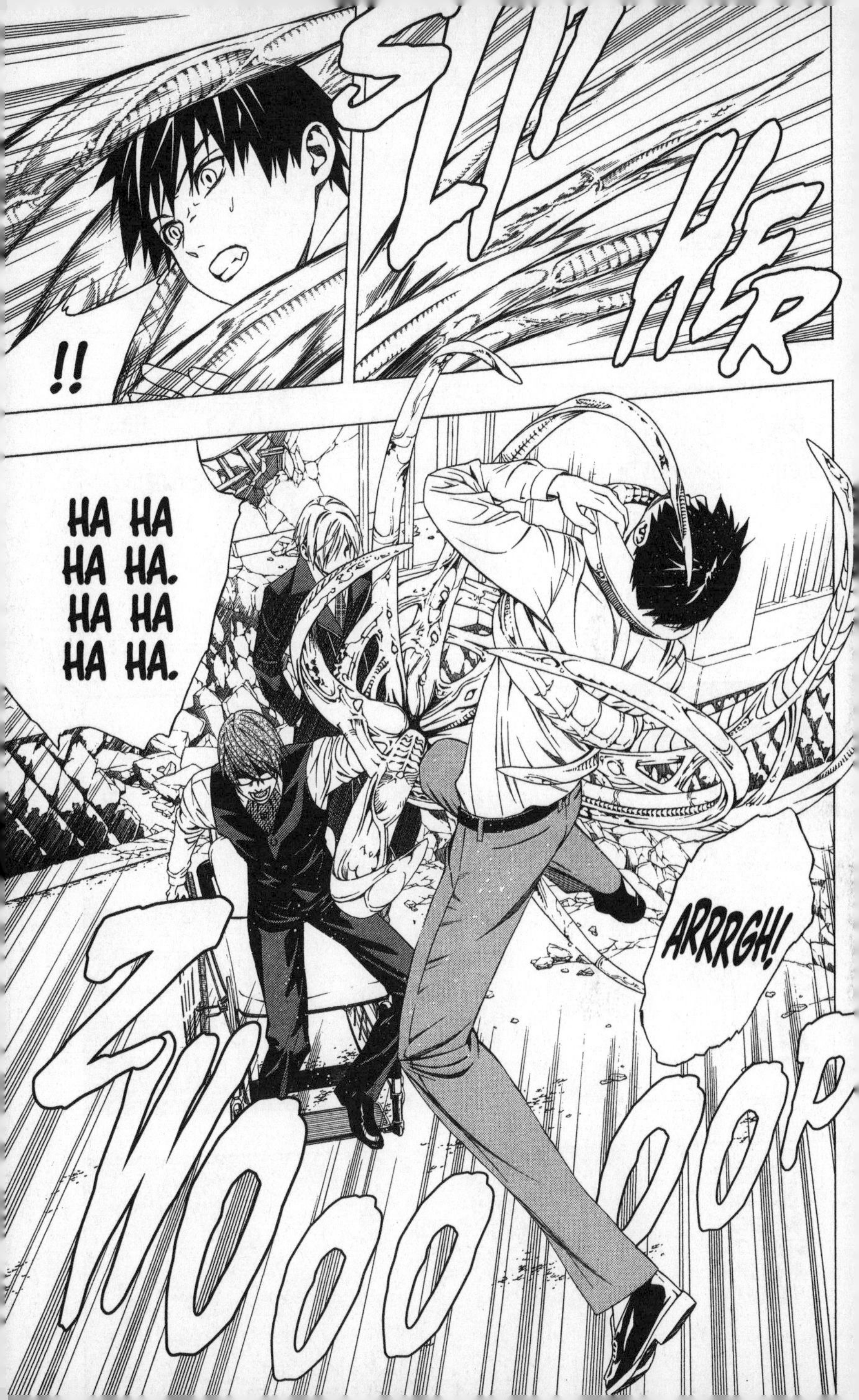
SLITHER
!!
ARRRGH!
HA HA HA HA. HA HA HA HA.
ZWOOOOOOOP

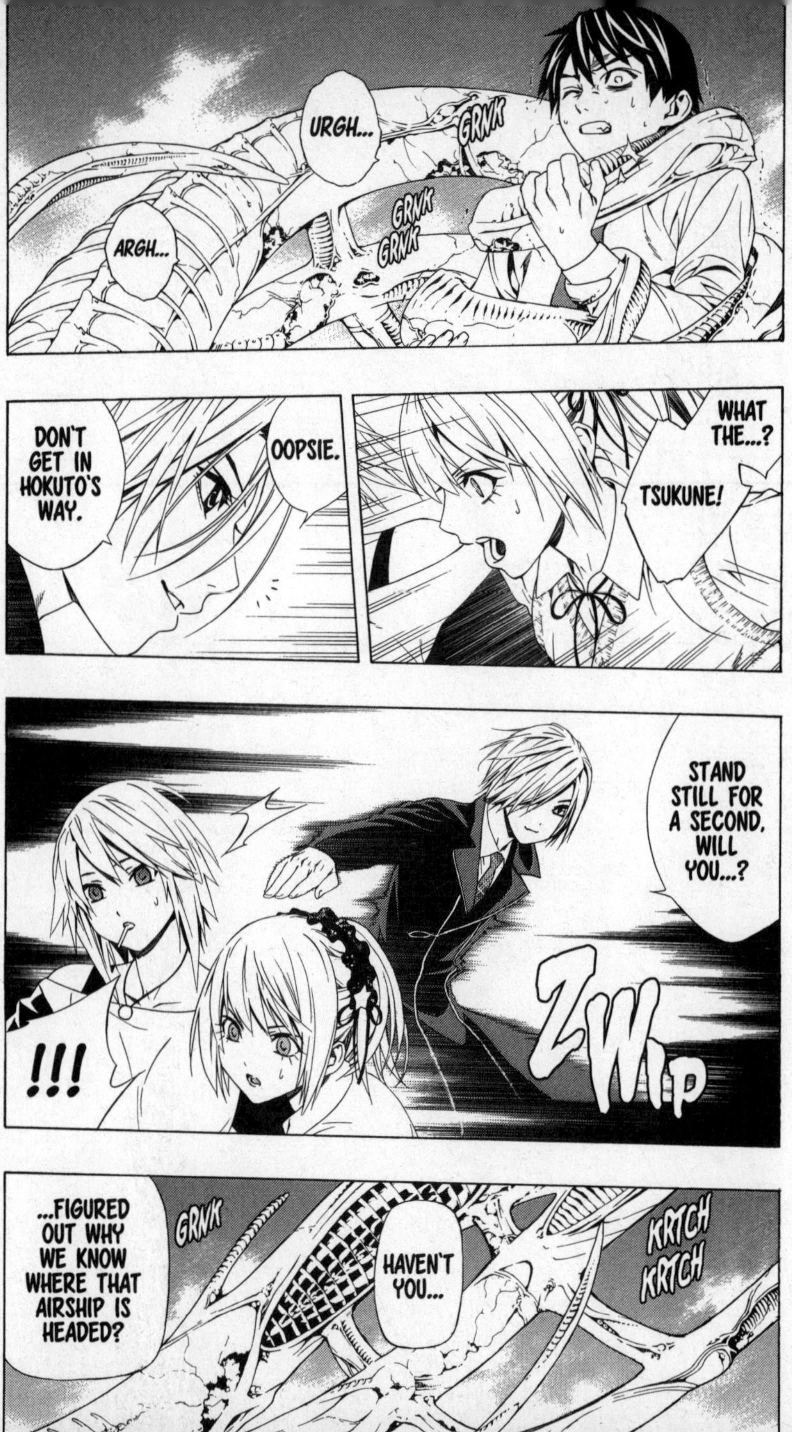
GRNK
URGH...
GRNK GRNK
ARGH...
WHAT THE...?
TSUKUNE!
OOPSIE.
DON'T GET IN HOKUTO'S WAY.
STAND STILL FOR A SECOND, WILL YOU...?
ZWIP
!!!
KRTCH KRTCH
HAVEN'T YOU...
GRNK
...FIGURED OUT WHY WE KNOW WHERE THAT AIRSHIP IS HEADED?

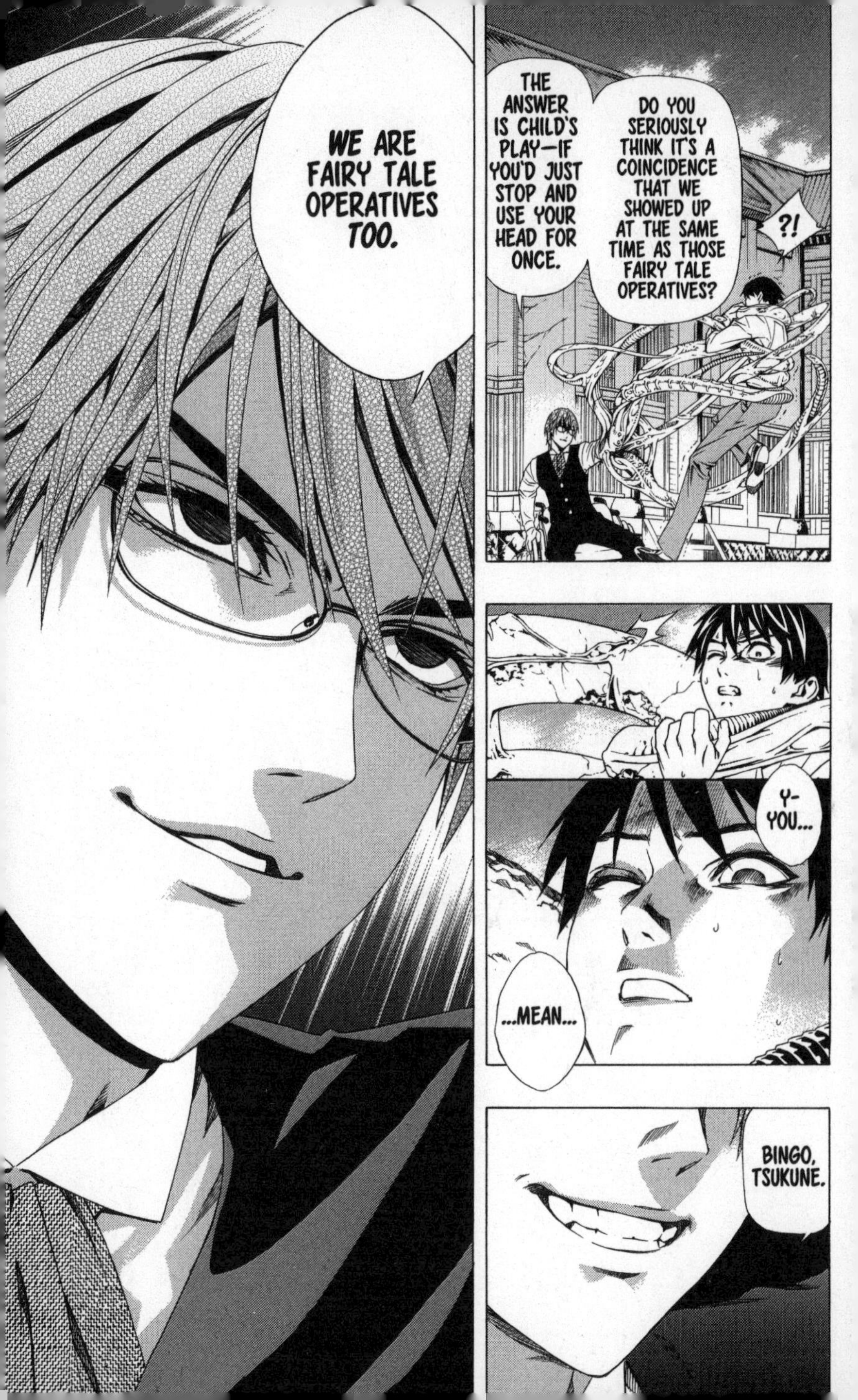
DO YOU SERIOUSLY THINK IT'S A COINCIDENCE THAT WE SHOWED UP AT THE SAME TIME AS THOSE FAIRY TALE OPERATIVES?
THE ANSWER IS CHILD'S PLAY—IF YOU'D JUST STOP AND USE YOUR HEAD FOR ONCE.
?!
Y-YOU...
...MEAN...
BINGO, TSUKUNE.
WE ARE FAIRY TALE OPERATIVES TOO.

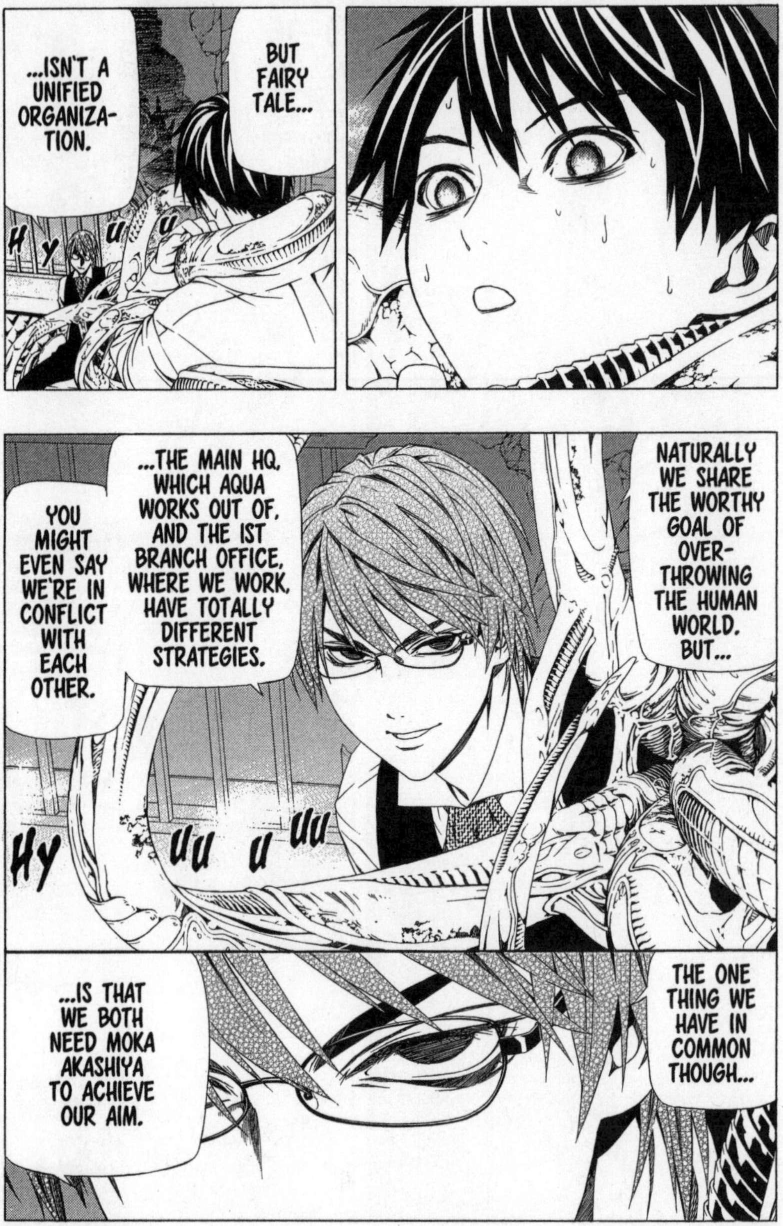
BUT FAIRY TALE...
...ISN'T A UNIFIED ORGANIZA-TION.
HYUU
NATURALLY WE SHARE THE WORTHY GOAL OF OVER-THROWING THE HUMAN WORLD. BUT...
...THE MAIN HQ, WHICH AQUA WORKS OUT OF, AND THE 1ST BRANCH OFFICE, WHERE WE WORK, HAVE TOTALLY DIFFERENT STRATEGIES.
YOU MIGHT EVEN SAY WE'RE IN CONFLICT WITH EACH OTHER.
HYUUUUU
THE ONE THING WE HAVE IN COMMON THOUGH...
...IS THAT WE BOTH NEED MOKA AKASHIYA TO ACHIEVE OUR AIM.

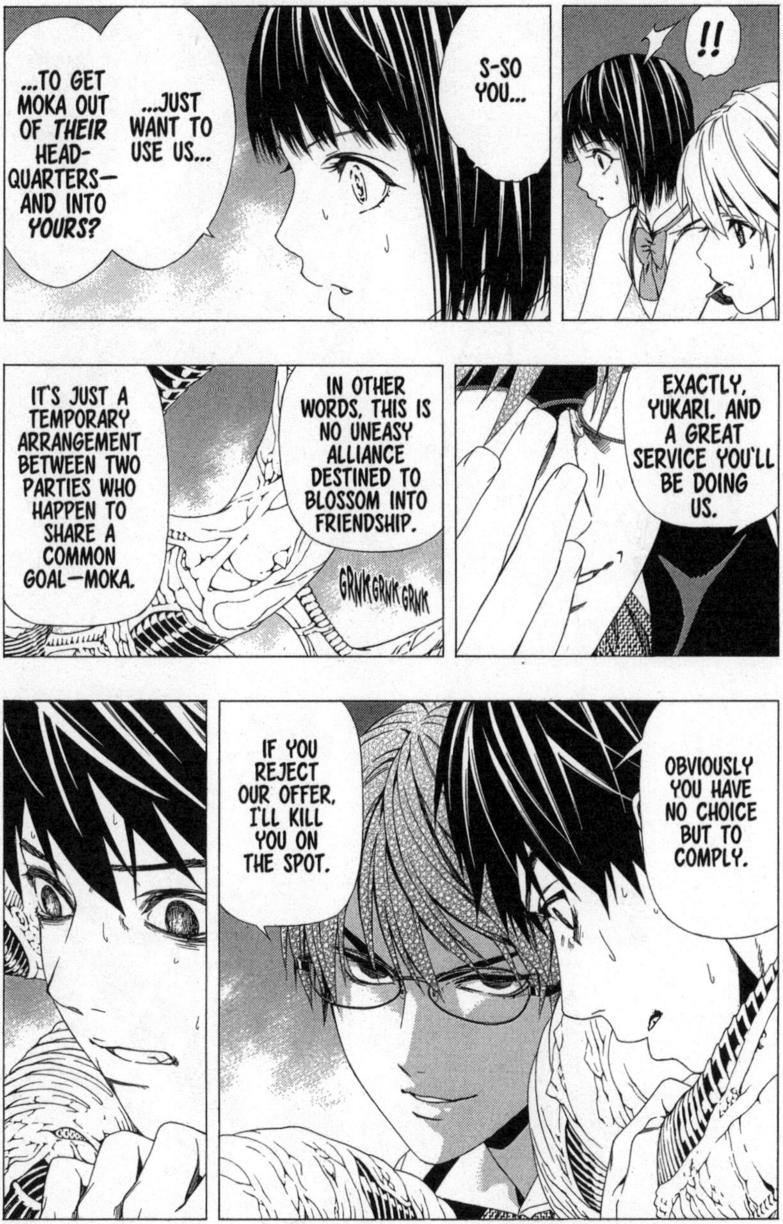
!!
S-SO YOU...
...JUST WANT TO USE US...
...TO GET MOKA OUT OF *THEIR* HEAD-QUARTERS—AND INTO *YOURS?*
EXACTLY, YUKARI. AND A GREAT SERVICE YOU'LL BE DOING US.
IN OTHER WORDS, THIS IS NO UNEASY ALLIANCE DESTINED TO BLOSSOM INTO FRIENDSHIP.
IT'S JUST A TEMPORARY ARRANGEMENT BETWEEN TWO PARTIES WHO HAPPEN TO SHARE A COMMON GOAL—MOKA.
GRNK GRNK GRNK
OBVIOUSLY YOU HAVE NO CHOICE BUT TO COMPLY.
IF YOU REJECT OUR OFFER, I'LL KILL YOU ON THE SPOT.

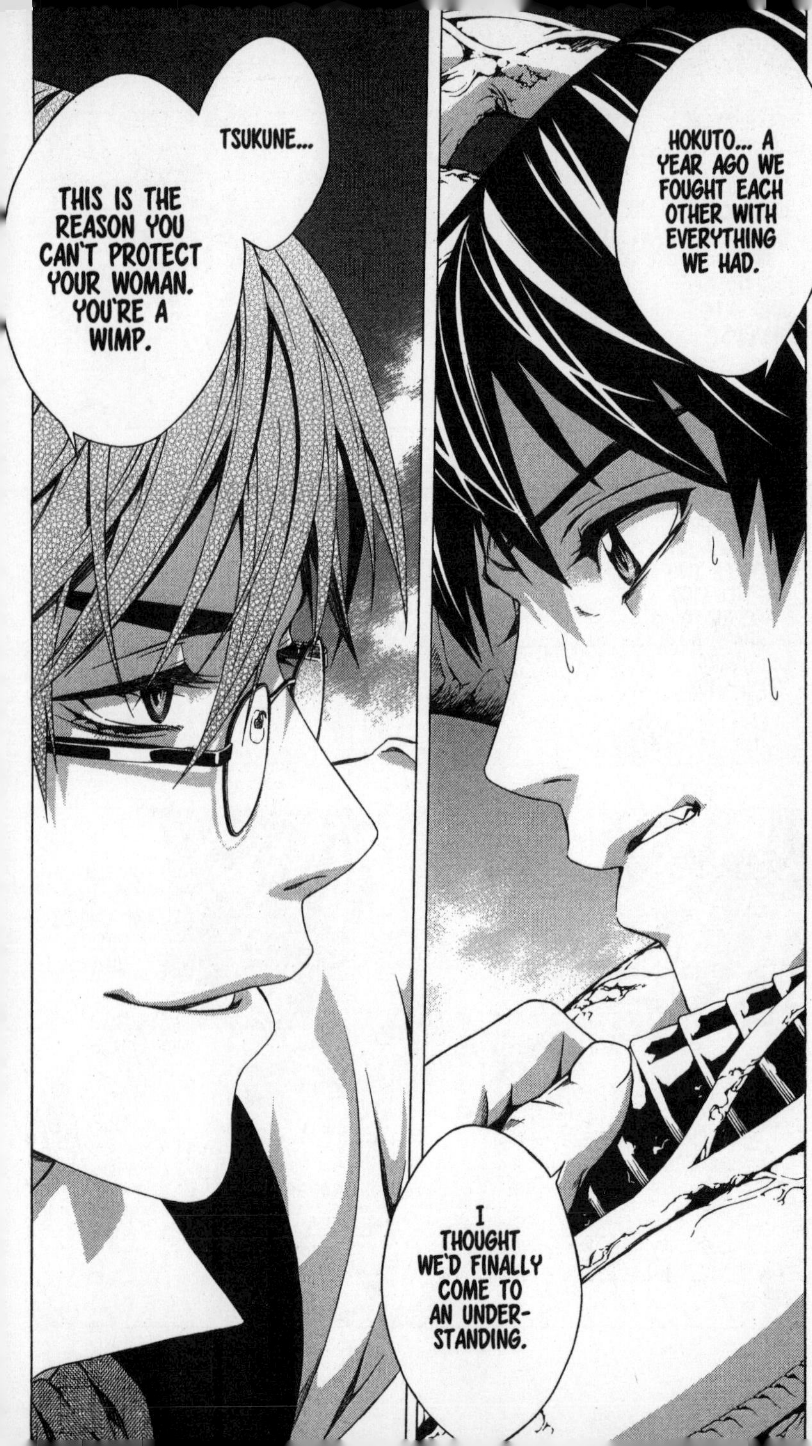
HOKUTO... A YEAR AGO WE FOUGHT EACH OTHER WITH EVERYTHING WE HAD.
I THOUGHT WE'D FINALLY COME TO AN UNDER-STANDING.
TSUKUNE...
THIS IS THE REASON YOU CAN'T PROTECT YOUR WOMAN. YOU'RE A WIMP.

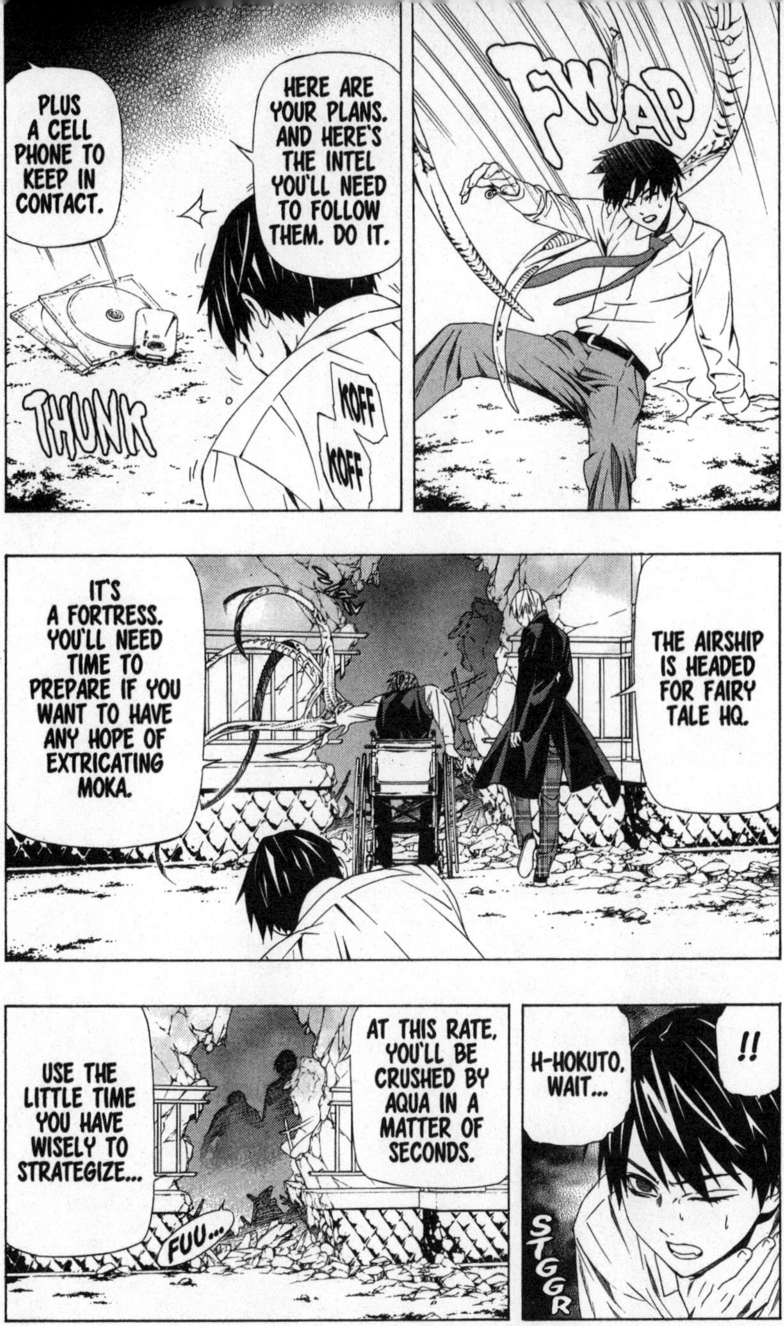
FWAP
HERE ARE YOUR PLANS. AND HERE'S THE INTEL YOU'LL NEED TO FOLLOW THEM. DO IT.
PLUS A CELL PHONE TO KEEP IN CONTACT.
KOFF
KOFF
THUNK
THE AIRSHIP IS HEADED FOR FAIRY TALE HQ.
IT'S A FORTRESS. YOU'LL NEED TIME TO PREPARE IF YOU WANT TO HAVE ANY HOPE OF EXTRICATING MOKA.
!!
H-HOKUTO, WAIT...
STGGR
AT THIS RATE, YOU'LL BE CRUSHED BY AQUA IN A MATTER OF SECONDS.
USE THE LITTLE TIME YOU HAVE WISELY TO STRATEGIZE...
FUU...

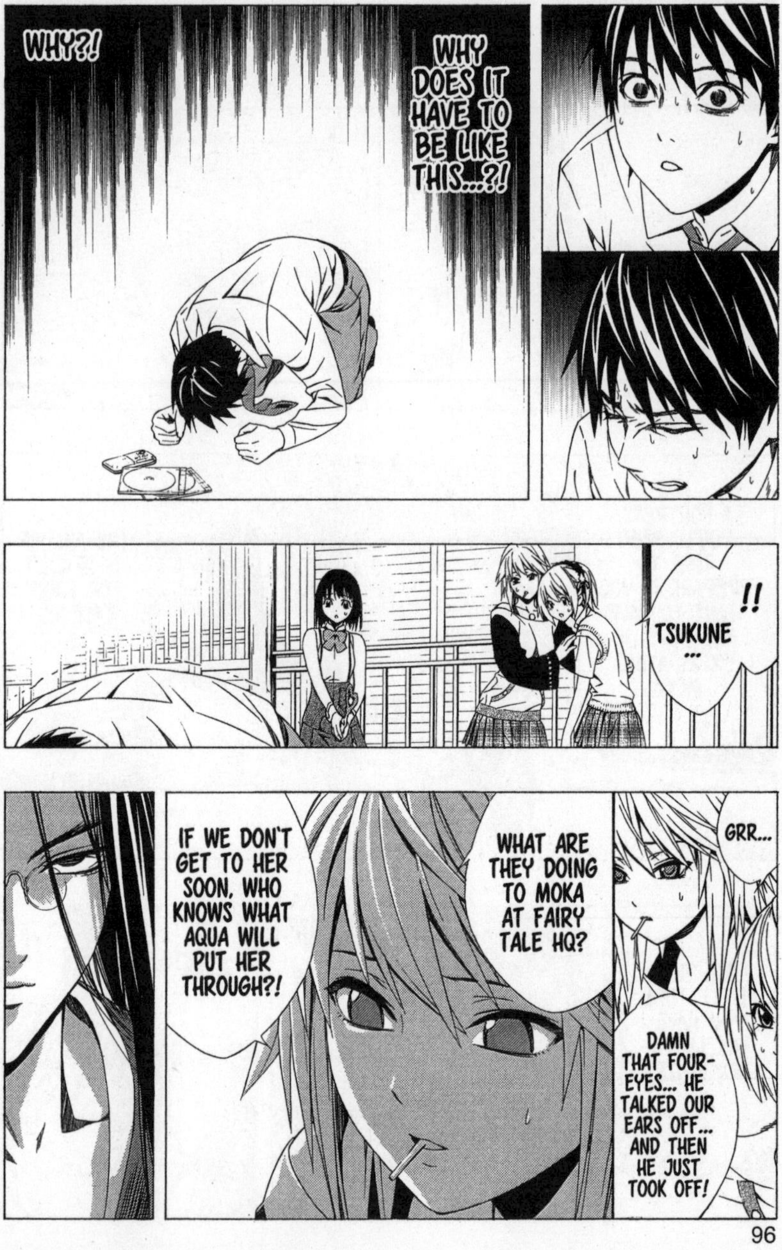
WHY?!
WHY DOES IT HAVE TO BE LIKE THIS...?!
!!
TSUKUNE ...
GRR...
DAMN THAT FOUR-EYES... HE TALKED OUR EARS OFF... AND THEN HE JUST TOOK OFF!
WHAT ARE THEY DOING TO MOKA AT FAIRY TALE HQ?
IF WE DON'T GET TO HER SOON, WHO KNOWS WHAT AQUA WILL PUT HER THROUGH?!

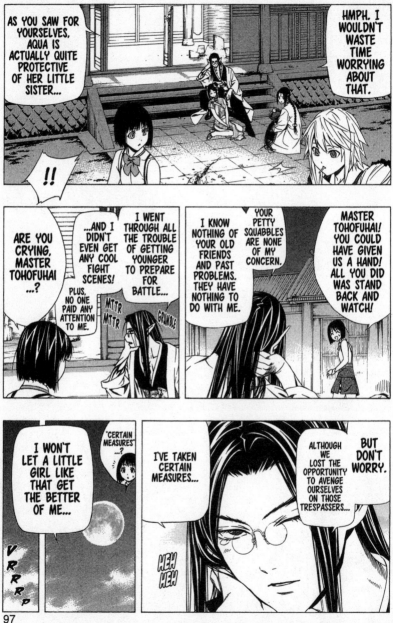

HMPH. I WOULDN'T WASTE TIME WORRYING ABOUT THAT.
AS YOU SAW FOR YOURSELVES, AQUA IS ACTUALLY QUITE PROTECTIVE OF HER LITTLE SISTER...
!!
MASTER TOHOFUHAI! YOU COULD HAVE GIVEN US A HAND! ALL YOU DID WAS STAND BACK AND WATCH!
YOUR PETTY SQUABBLES ARE NONE OF MY CONCERN.
I KNOW NOTHING OF YOUR OLD FRIENDS AND PAST PROBLEMS. THEY HAVE NOTHING TO DO WITH ME.
I WENT THROUGH ALL THE TROUBLE OF GETTING YOUNGER TO PREPARE FOR BATTLE...
...AND I DIDN'T EVEN GET ANY COOL FIGHT SCENES!
GRUMBLE
MTTR MTTR
PLUS, NO ONE PAID ANY ATTENTION TO ME.
ARE YOU CRYING, MASTER TOHOFUHAI ...?
BUT DON'T WORRY.
ALTHOUGH WE LOST THE OPPORTUNITY TO AVENGE OURSELVES ON THOSE TRESPASSERS...
I'VE TAKEN CERTAIN MEASURES...
HEH HEH
"CERTAIN MEASURES" ...?
I WON'T LET A LITTLE GIRL LIKE THAT GET THE BETTER OF ME...
VRRRP

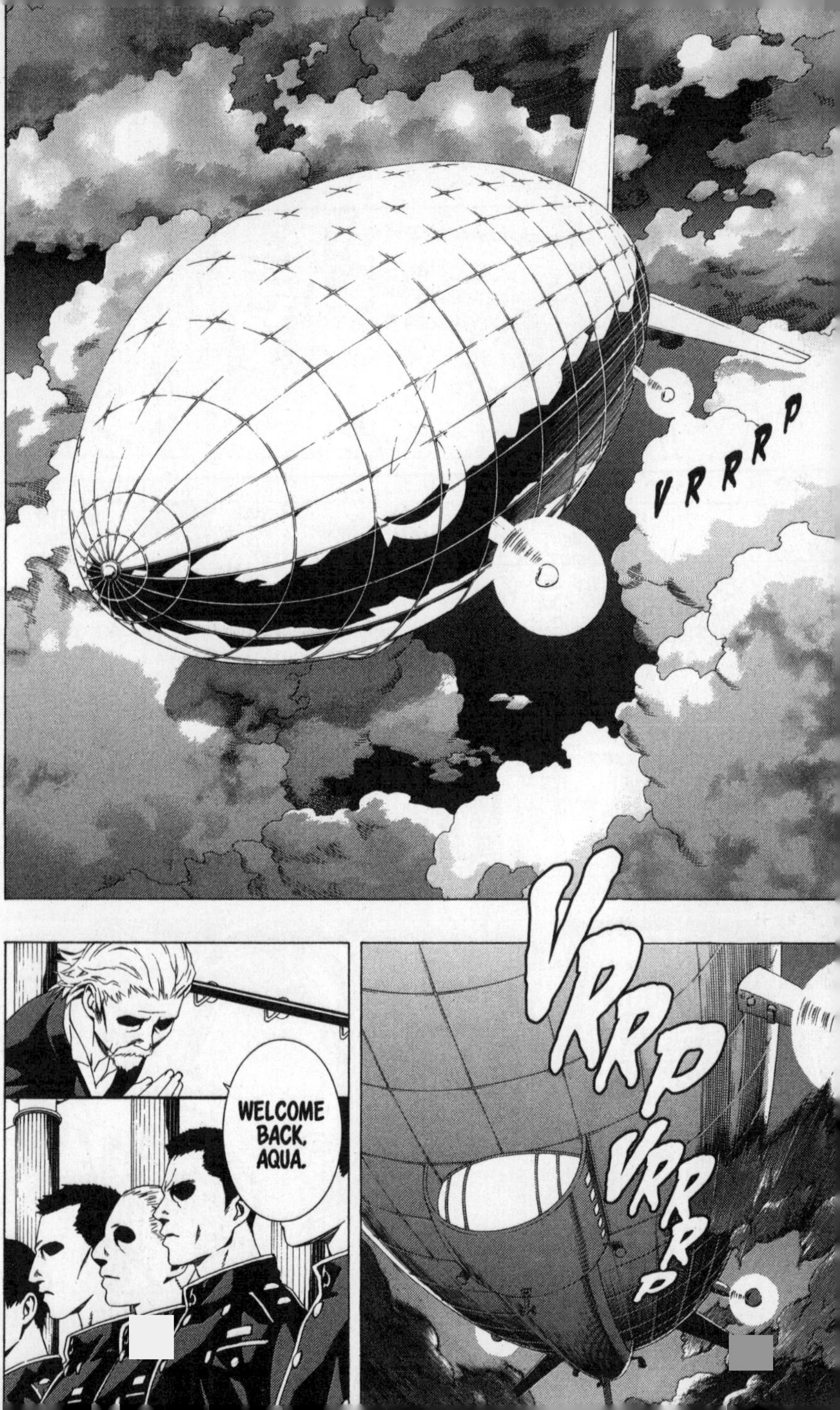
VRRRP
VRRP
VRRRP
WELCOME BACK, AQUA.

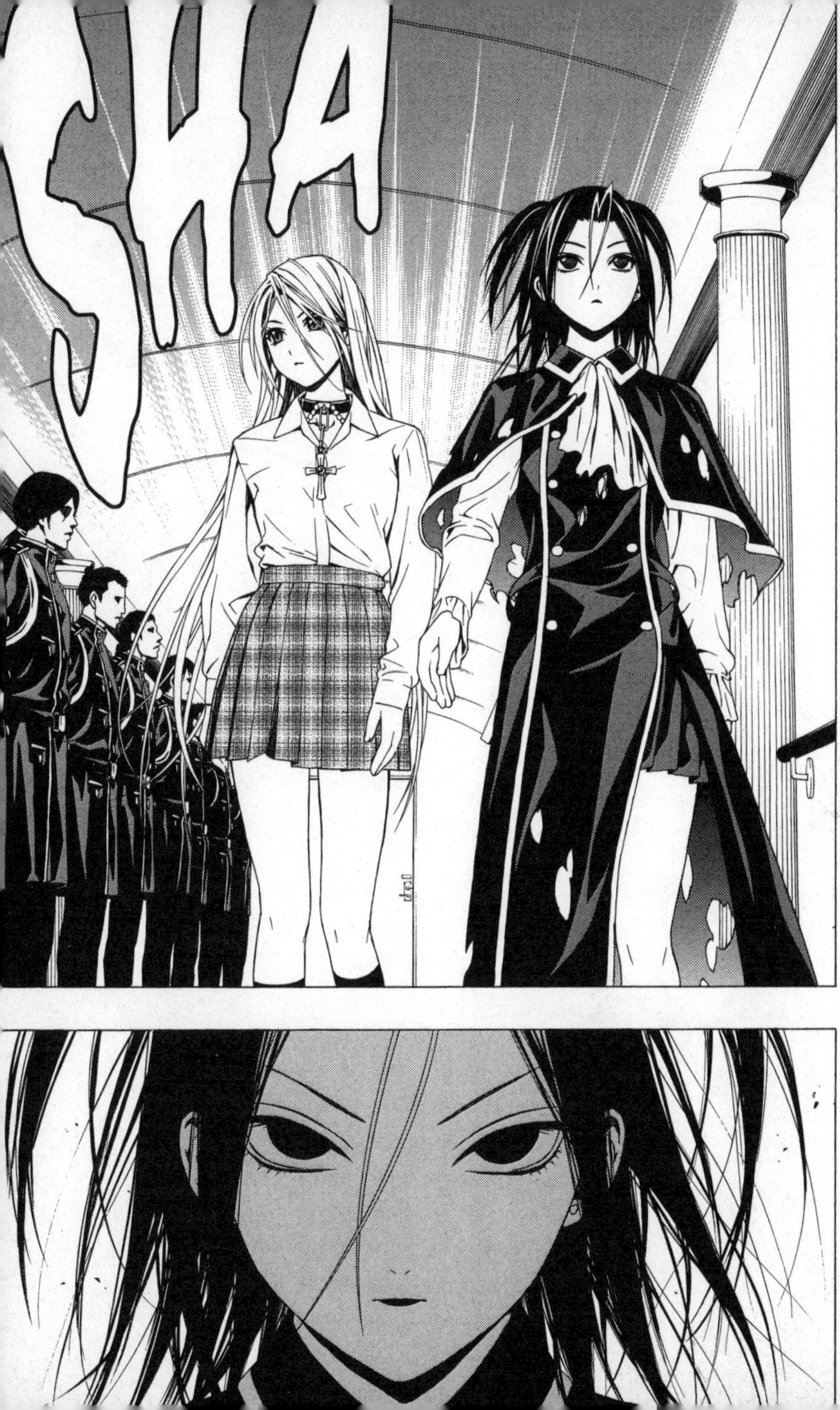
SHA

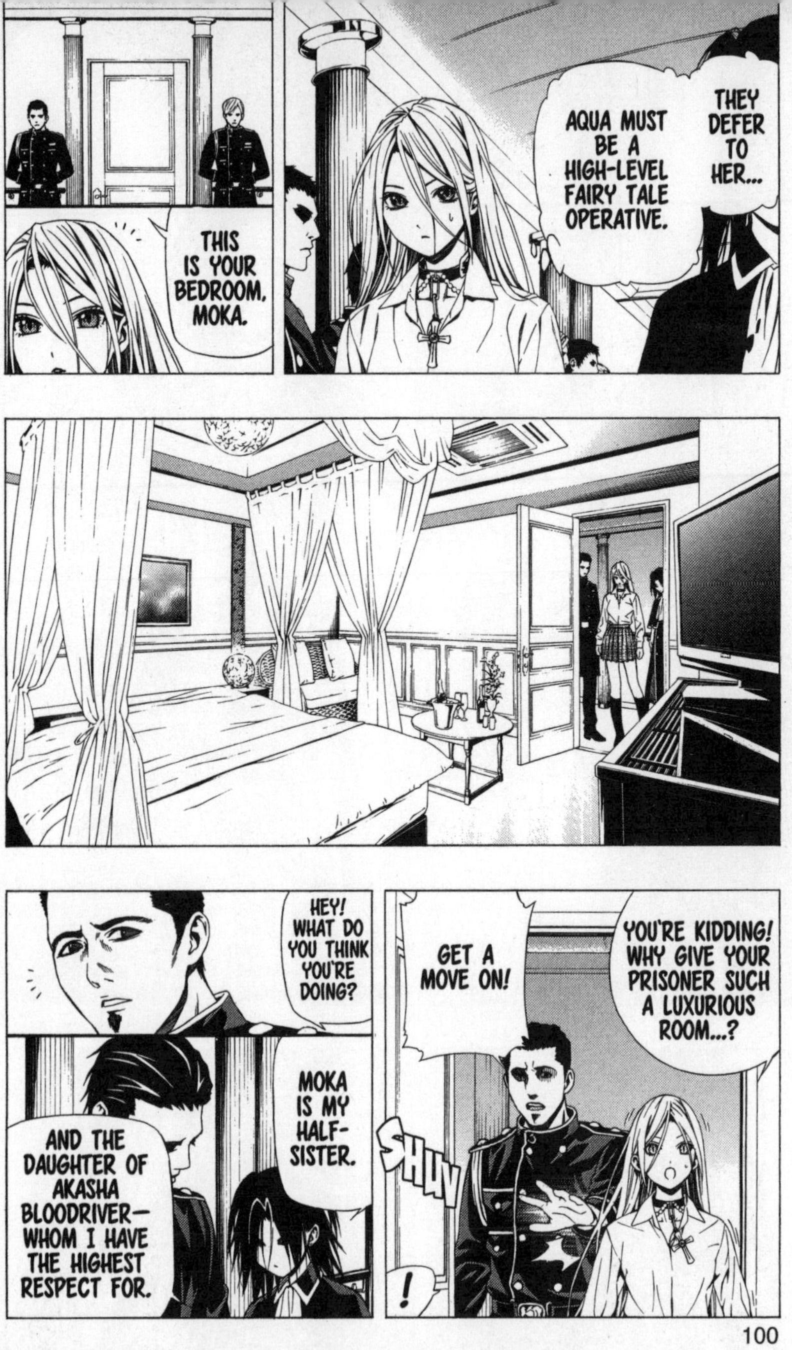
THEY DEFER TO HER...
AQUA MUST BE A HIGH-LEVEL FAIRY TALE OPERATIVE.
THIS IS YOUR BEDROOM, MOKA.
YOU'RE KIDDING! WHY GIVE YOUR PRISONER SUCH A LUXURIOUS ROOM...?
GET A MOVE ON!
SHUV
!
HEY! WHAT DO YOU THINK YOU'RE DOING?
MOKA IS MY HALF-SISTER.
AND THE DAUGHTER OF AKASHA BLOODRIVER—WHOM I HAVE THE HIGHEST RESPECT FOR.

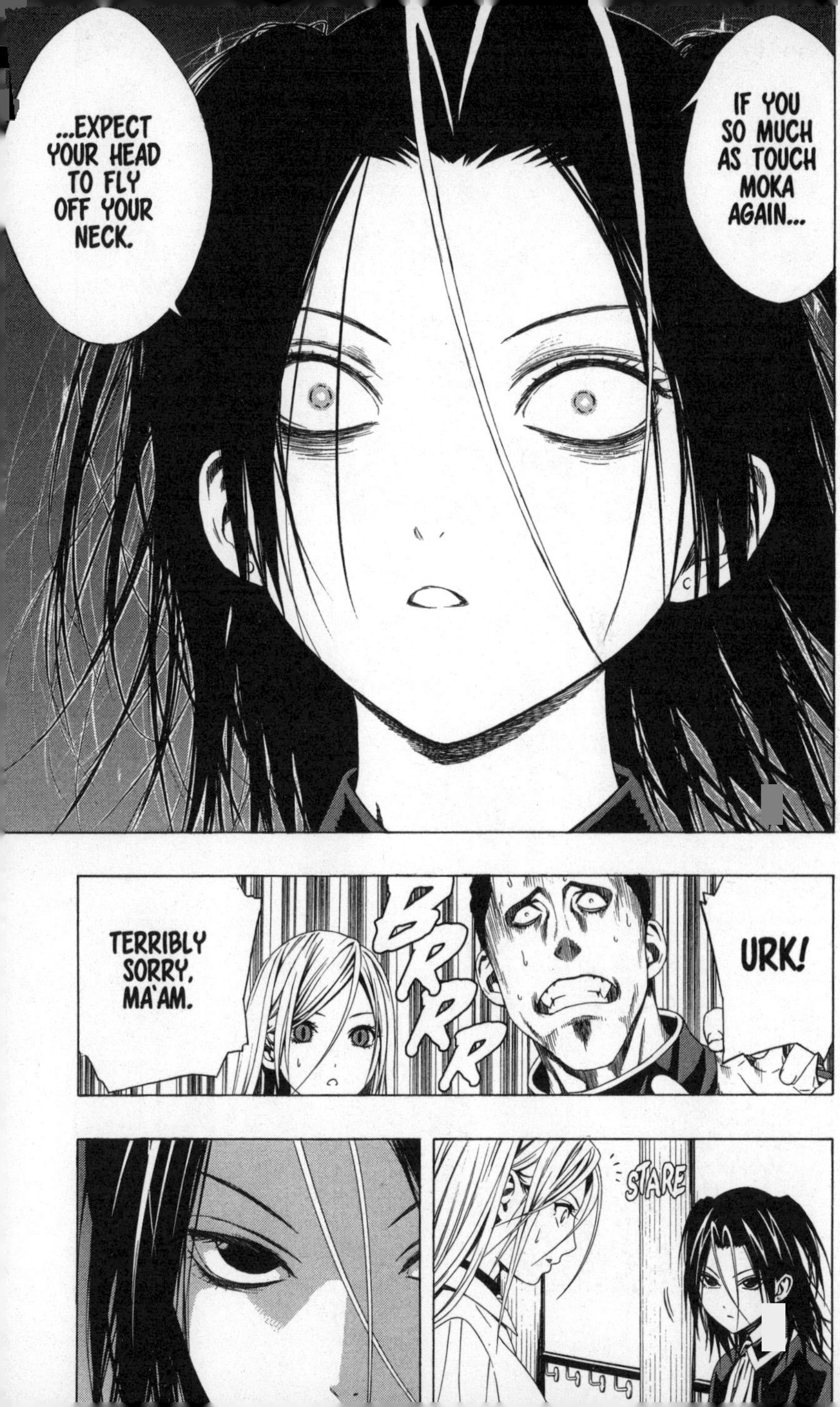
IF YOU SO MUCH AS TOUCH MOKA AGAIN...
...EXPECT YOUR HEAD TO FLY OFF YOUR NECK.
URK!
BRRR
TERRIBLY SORRY, MA'AM.
STARE

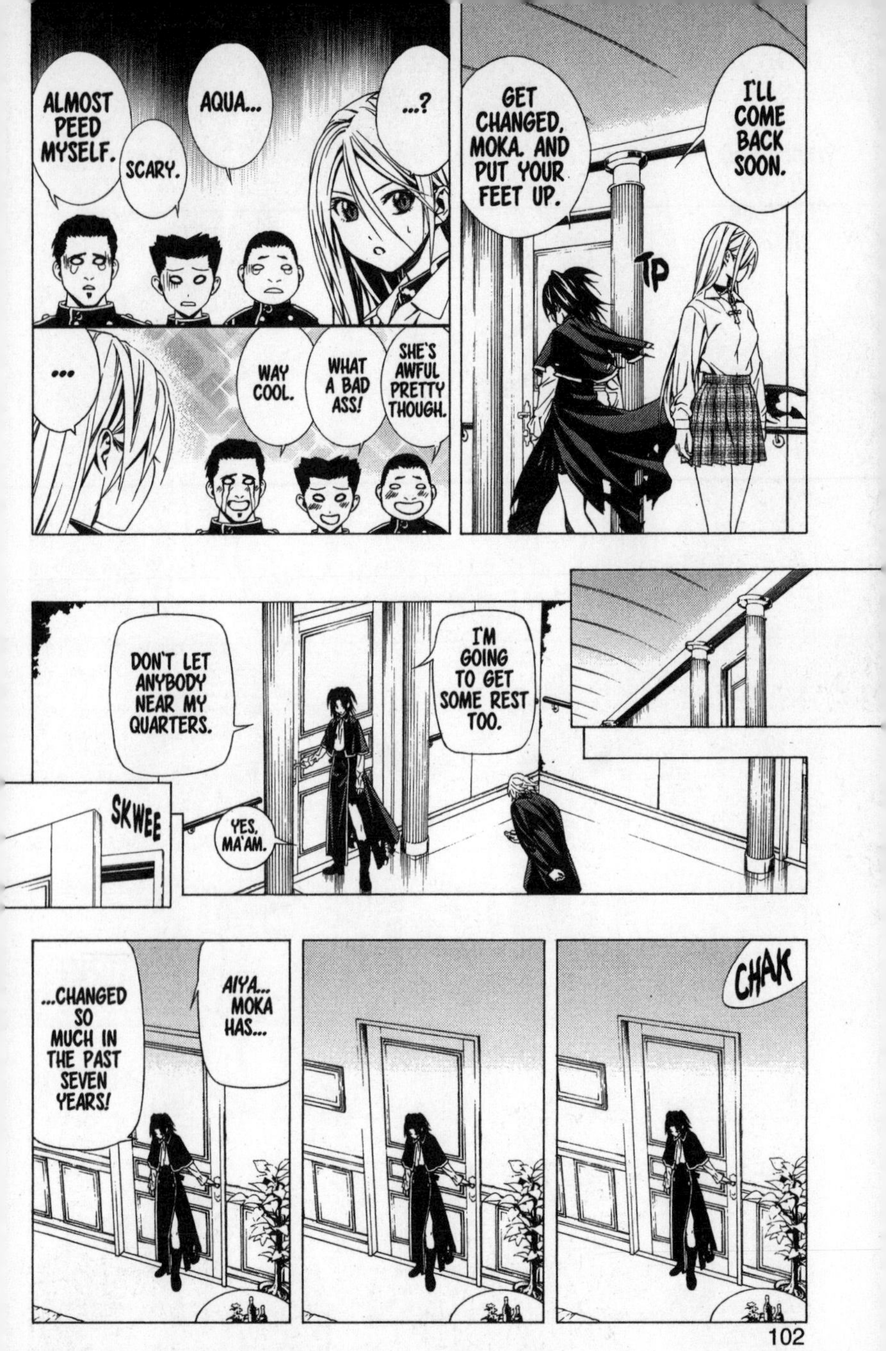
I'LL COME BACK SOON.
GET CHANGED, MOKA. AND PUT YOUR FEET UP.
TP
...?
AQUA...
SCARY.
ALMOST PEED MYSELF.
SHE'S AWFUL PRETTY THOUGH.
WHAT A BAD ASS!
WAY COOL.
...
I'M GOING TO GET SOME REST TOO.
DON'T LET ANYBODY NEAR MY QUARTERS.
YES, MA'AM.
SKWEE
CHAK
AIYA... MOKA HAS...
...CHANGED SO MUCH IN THE PAST SEVEN YEARS!

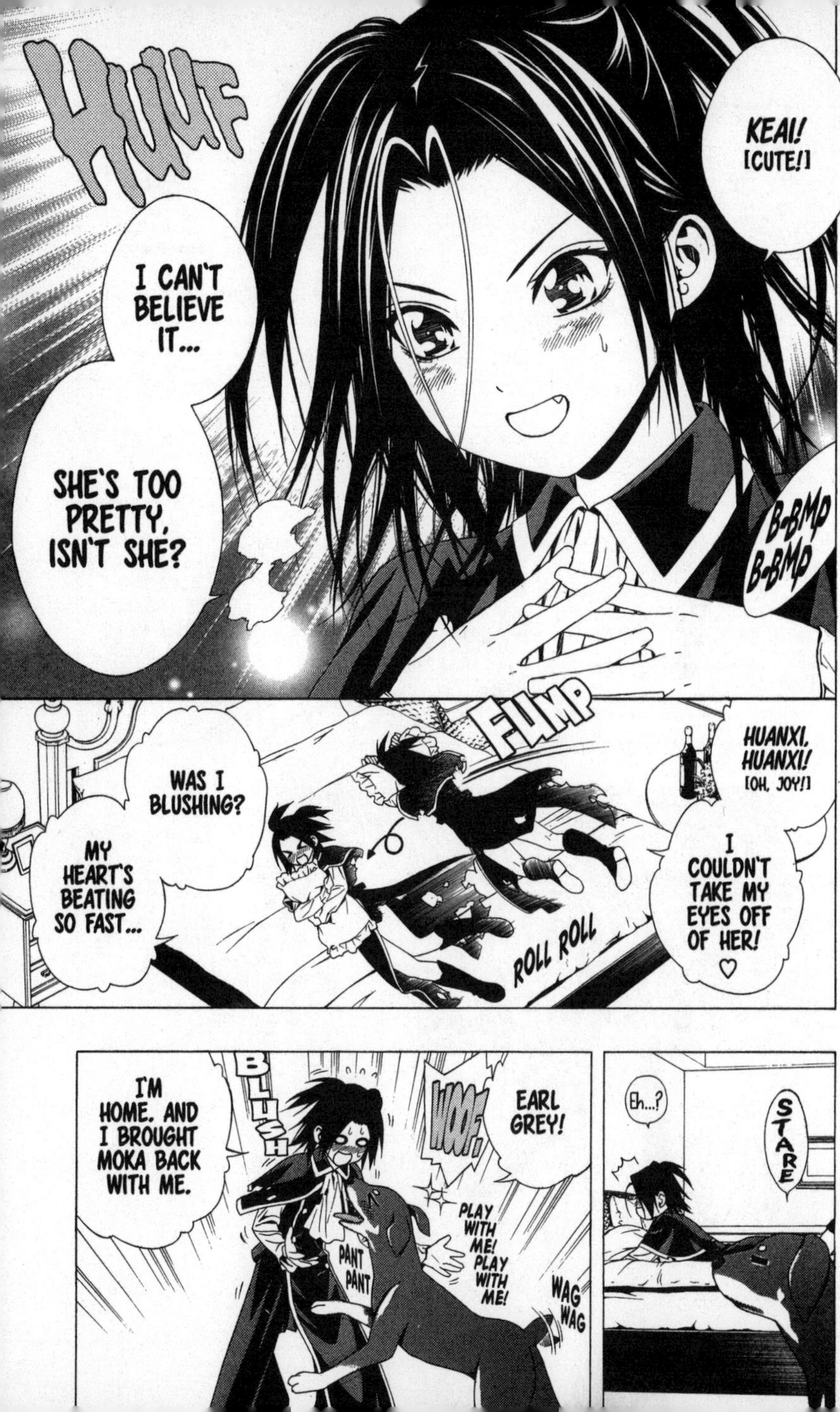
KEAI! [CUTE!]
B-BMP B-BMP
HUFF
I CAN'T BELIEVE IT...
SHE'S TOO PRETTY, ISN'T SHE?
HUANXI, HUANXI! [OH, JOY!]
I COULDN'T TAKE MY EYES OFF OF HER! ♡
FUMP
WAS I BLUSHING?
MY HEART'S BEATING SO FAST...
ROLL ROLL
STARE
Eh...?
EARL GREY!
WOOF!
BLUSH
I'M HOME. AND I BROUGHT MOKA BACK WITH ME.
PLAY WITH ME! PLAY WITH ME!
PANT PANT
WAG WAG

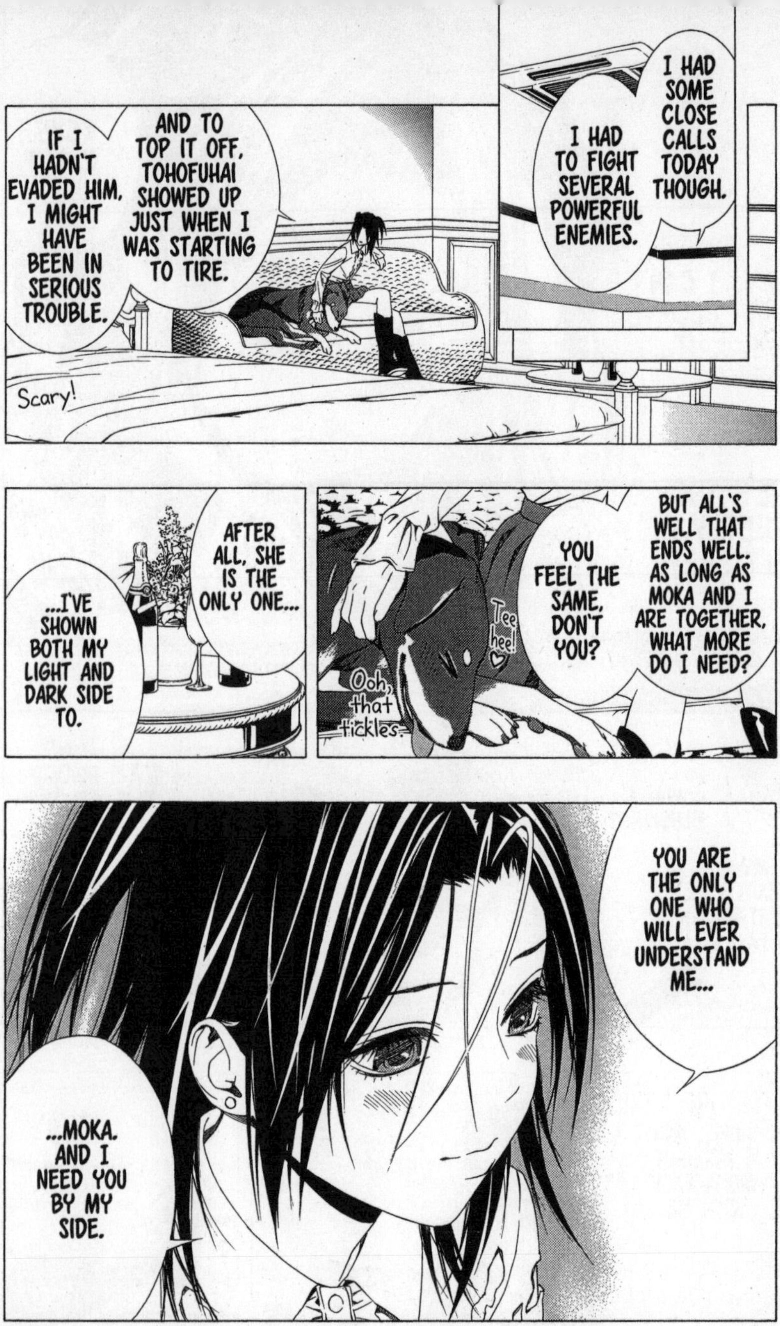
I HAD SOME CLOSE CALLS TODAY THOUGH.
I HAD TO FIGHT SEVERAL POWERFUL ENEMIES.
AND TO TOP IT OFF, TOHOFUHAI SHOWED UP JUST WHEN I WAS STARTING TO TIRE.
IF I HADN'T EVADED HIM, I MIGHT HAVE BEEN IN SERIOUS TROUBLE.
Scary!
BUT ALL'S WELL THAT ENDS WELL. AS LONG AS MOKA AND I ARE TOGETHER, WHAT MORE DO I NEED?
YOU FEEL THE SAME, DON'T YOU?
Tee hee! ♡
Ooh, that tickles.
AFTER ALL, SHE IS THE ONLY ONE...
...I'VE SHOWN BOTH MY LIGHT AND DARK SIDE TO.
YOU ARE THE ONLY ONE WHO WILL EVER UNDERSTAND ME...
...MOKA. AND I NEED YOU BY MY SIDE.

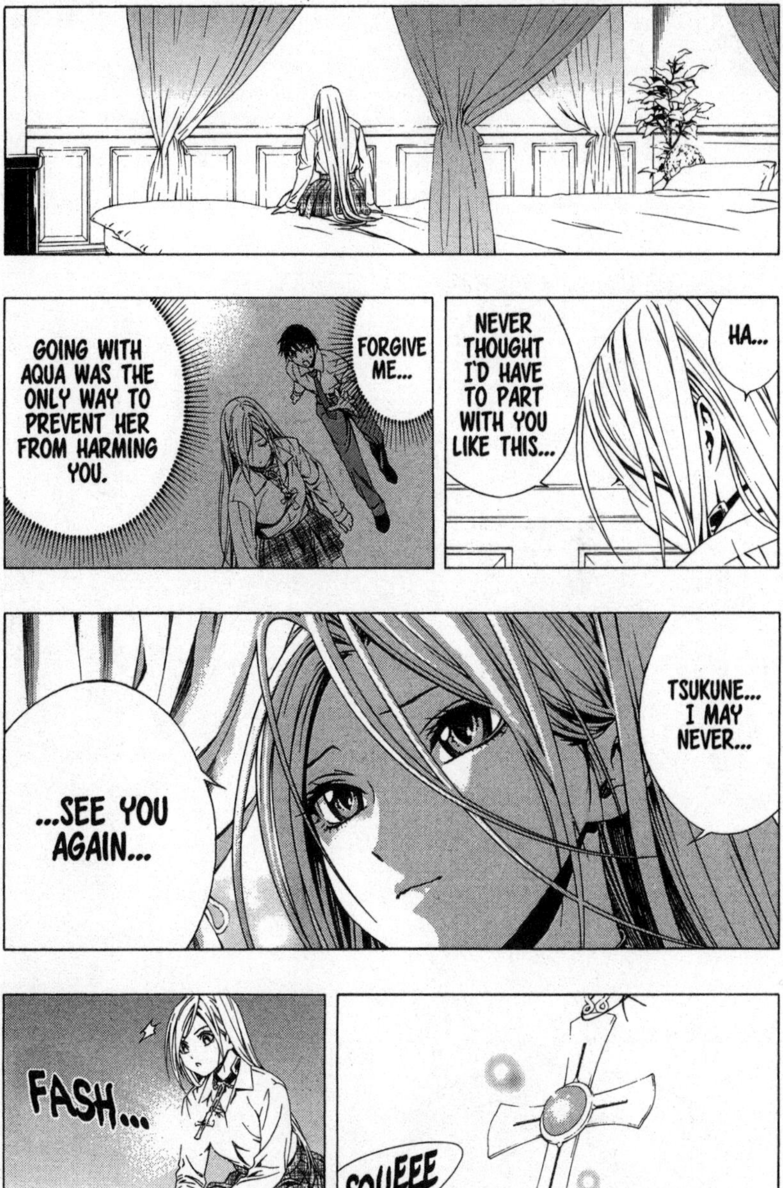
HA...
NEVER THOUGHT I'D HAVE TO PART WITH YOU LIKE THIS...
FORGIVE ME...
GOING WITH AQUA WAS THE ONLY WAY TO PREVENT HER FROM HARMING YOU.
TSUKUNE... I MAY NEVER...
...SEE YOU AGAIN...
SQUEEE
FASH...

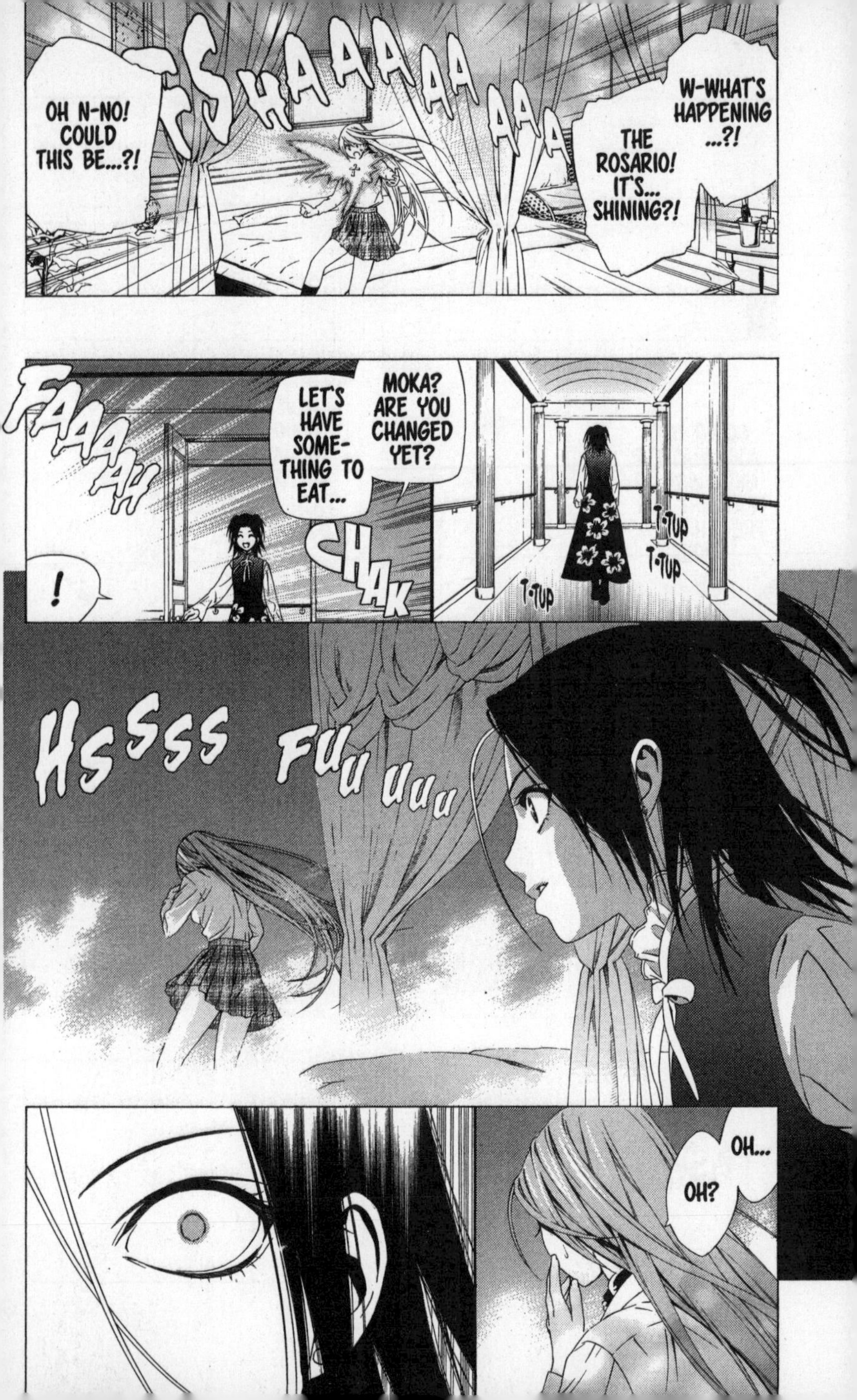
W-WHAT'S HAPPENING ...?!
THE ROSARIO! IT'S... SHINING?!
SHAAAAAAAAAA
OH N-NO! COULD THIS BE...?!
T-TUP
T-TUP
T-TUP
MOKA? ARE YOU CHANGED YET?
LET'S HAVE SOME-THING TO EAT...
CHAK
FAAAAH
!
FUuuuu
HSSSS
OH...
OH?

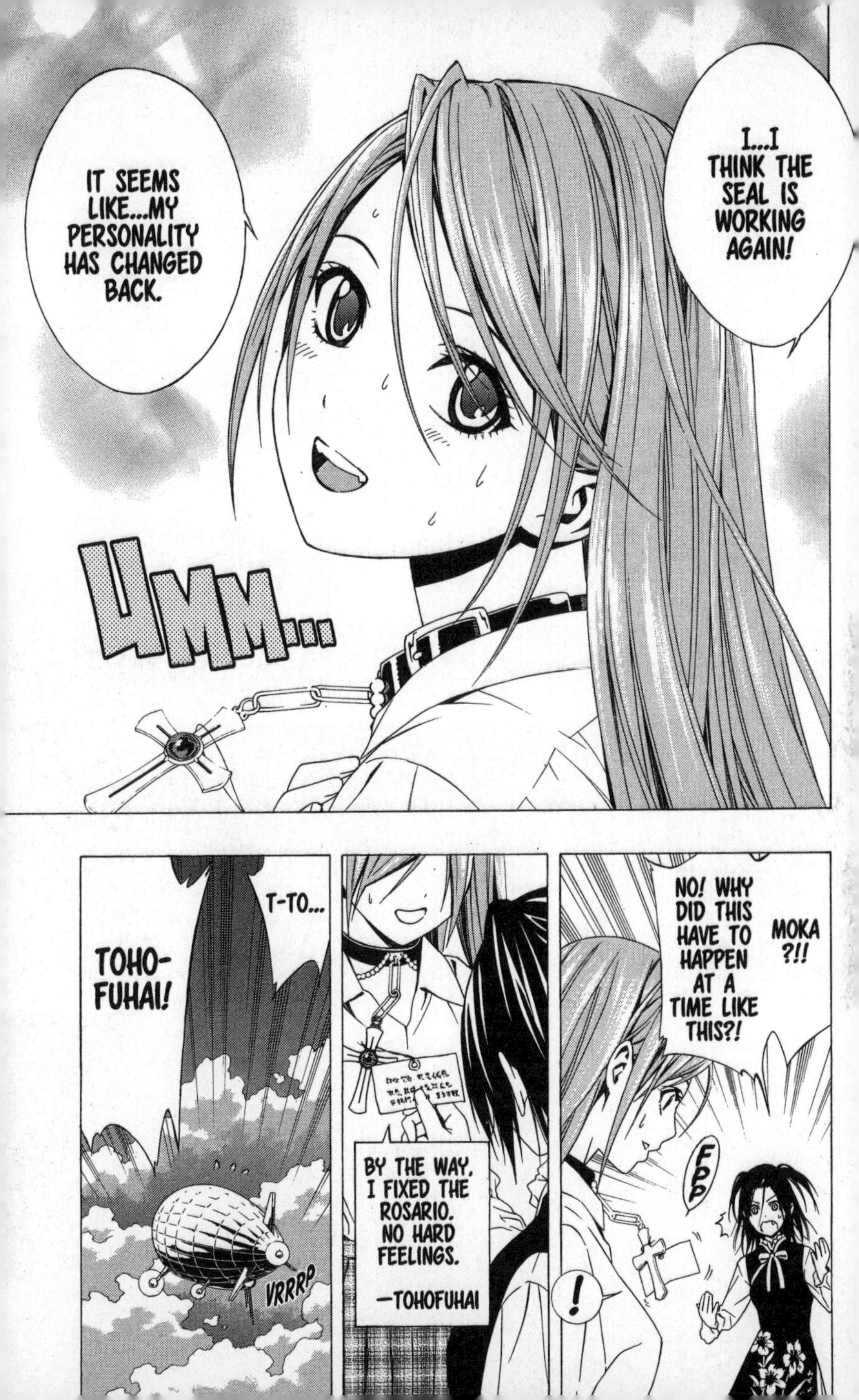
I...I THINK THE SEAL IS WORKING AGAIN!
IT SEEMS LIKE...MY PERSONALITY HAS CHANGED BACK.
UMM...
MOKA ?!!
NO! WHY DID THIS HAVE TO HAPPEN AT A TIME LIKE THIS?!
FPP
!
BY THE WAY, I FIXED THE ROSARIO. NO HARD FEELINGS. —TOHOFUHAI
T-TO...
TOHO-FUHAI!
VRRRP

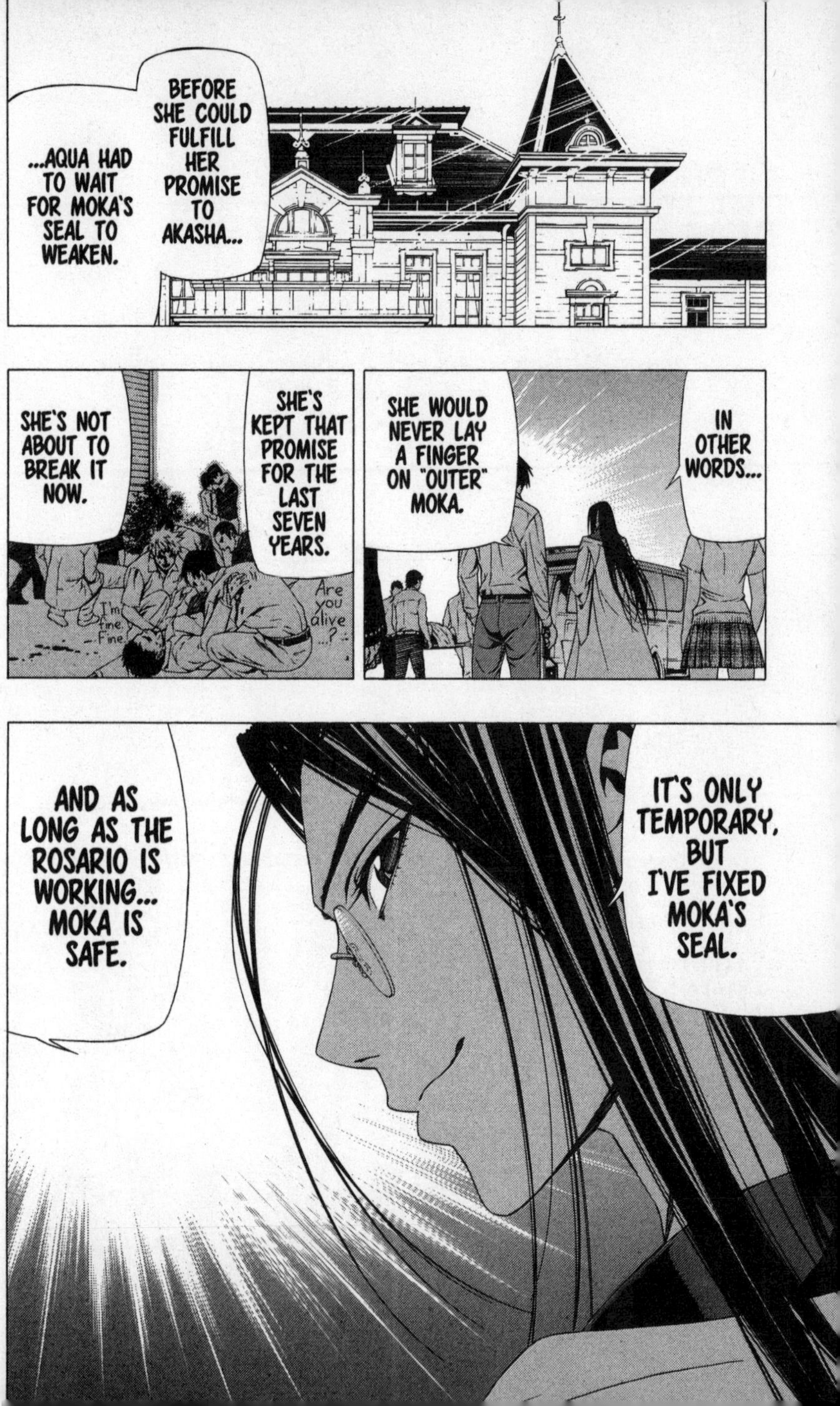
BEFORE SHE COULD FULFILL HER PROMISE TO AKASHA...
...AQUA HAD TO WAIT FOR MOKA'S SEAL TO WEAKEN.
IN OTHER WORDS...
SHE WOULD NEVER LAY A FINGER ON "OUTER" MOKA.
SHE'S KEPT THAT PROMISE FOR THE LAST SEVEN YEARS.
SHE'S NOT ABOUT TO BREAK IT NOW.
Are you alive...?
I'm fine. Fine.
IT'S ONLY TEMPORARY, BUT I'VE FIXED MOKA'S SEAL.
AND AS LONG AS THE ROSARIO IS WORKING... MOKA IS SAFE.

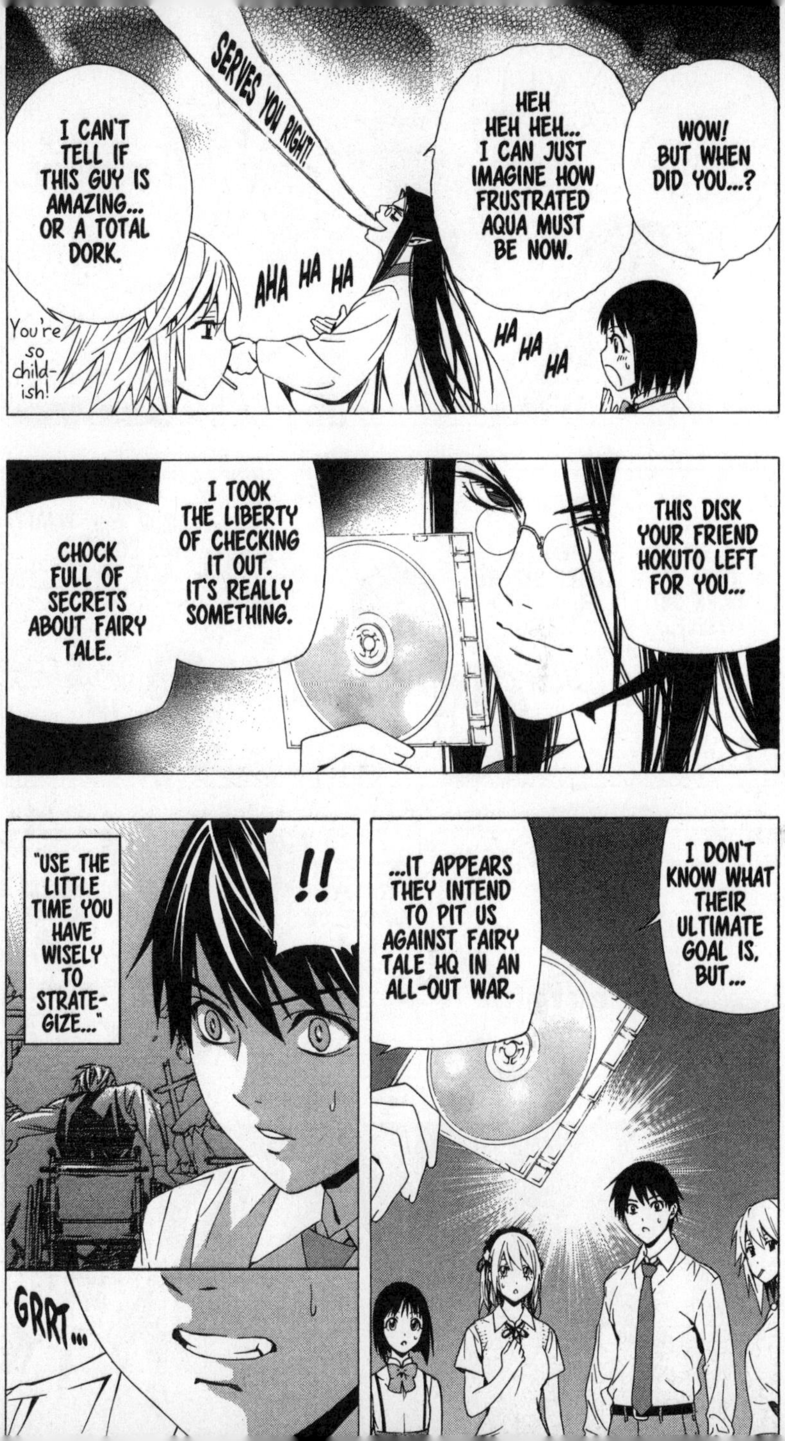
WOW! BUT WHEN DID YOU...?
HEH HEH HEH... I CAN JUST IMAGINE HOW FRUSTRATED AQUA MUST BE NOW.
SERVES YOU RIGHT!
HA HA HA
AHA HA HA
I CAN'T TELL IF THIS GUY IS AMAZING... OR A TOTAL DORK.
You're so child-ish!
THIS DISK YOUR FRIEND HOKUTO LEFT FOR YOU...
I TOOK THE LIBERTY OF CHECKING IT OUT. IT'S REALLY SOMETHING.
CHOCK FULL OF SECRETS ABOUT FAIRY TALE.
I DON'T KNOW WHAT THEIR ULTIMATE GOAL IS, BUT...
...IT APPEARS THEY INTEND TO PIT US AGAINST FAIRY TALE HQ IN AN ALL-OUT WAR.
!!
"USE THE LITTLE TIME YOU HAVE WISELY TO STRATE-GIZE..."
GRRT...

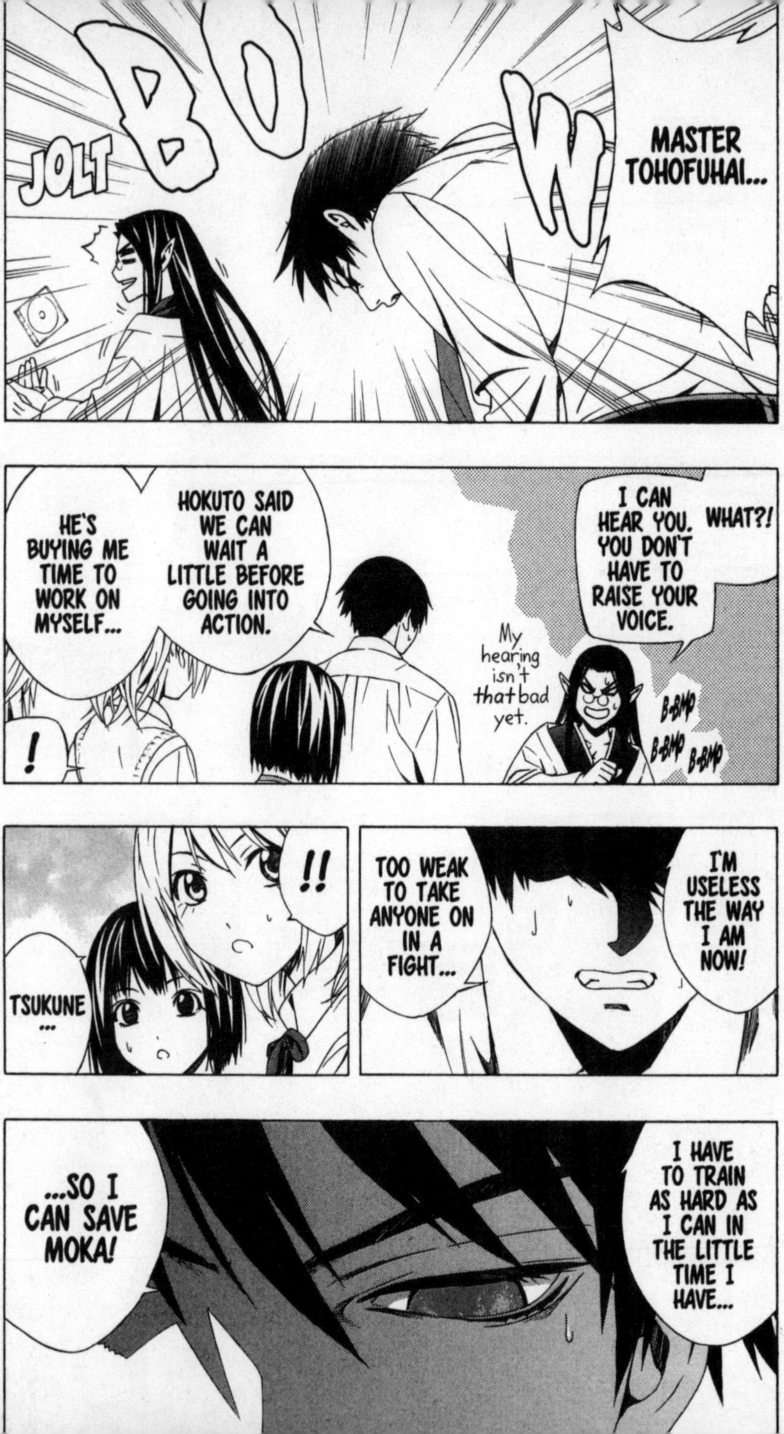
MASTER TOHOFUHAI...
BOW
JOLT
WHAT?!
I CAN HEAR YOU. YOU DON'T HAVE TO RAISE YOUR VOICE.
My hearing isn't that bad yet.
B-BMP B-BMP B-BMP
HOKUTO SAID WE CAN WAIT A LITTLE BEFORE GOING INTO ACTION.
HE'S BUYING ME TIME TO WORK ON MYSELF...
!
I'M USELESS THE WAY I AM NOW!
TOO WEAK TO TAKE ANYONE ON IN A FIGHT...
!!
TSUKUNE...
I HAVE TO TRAIN AS HARD AS I CAN IN THE LITTLE TIME I HAVE...
...SO I CAN SAVE MOKA!

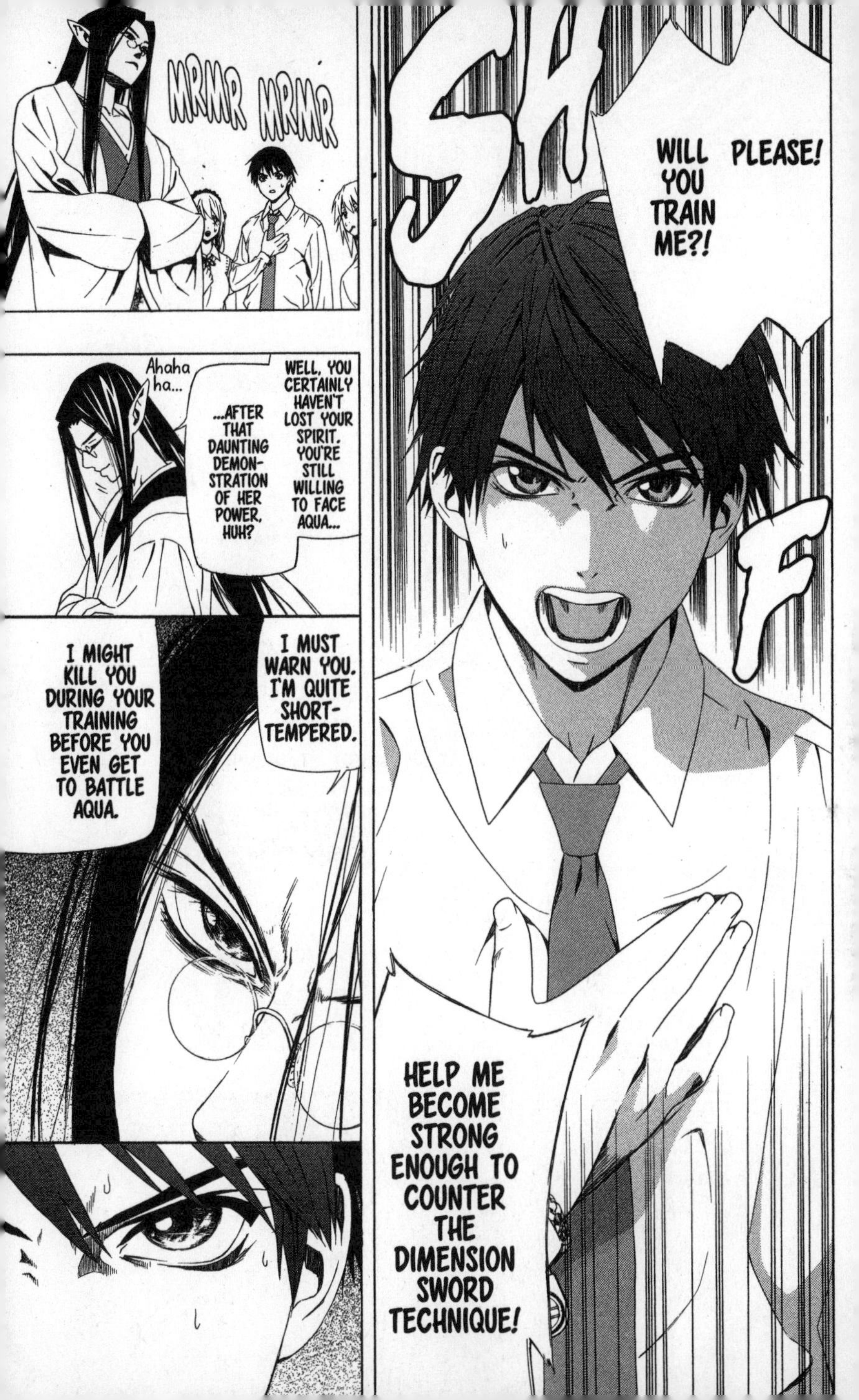
SHF
PLEASE! WILL YOU TRAIN ME?!
HELP ME BECOME STRONG ENOUGH TO COUNTER THE DIMENSION SWORD TECHNIQUE!
MRMR MRMR
WELL, YOU CERTAINLY HAVEN'T LOST YOUR SPIRIT. YOU'RE STILL WILLING TO FACE AQUA...
...AFTER THAT DAUNTING DEMON-STRATION OF HER POWER, HUH?
Ahaha ha...
I MUST WARN YOU. I'M QUITE SHORT-TEMPERED.
I MIGHT KILL YOU DURING YOUR TRAINING BEFORE YOU EVEN GET TO BATTLE AQUA.

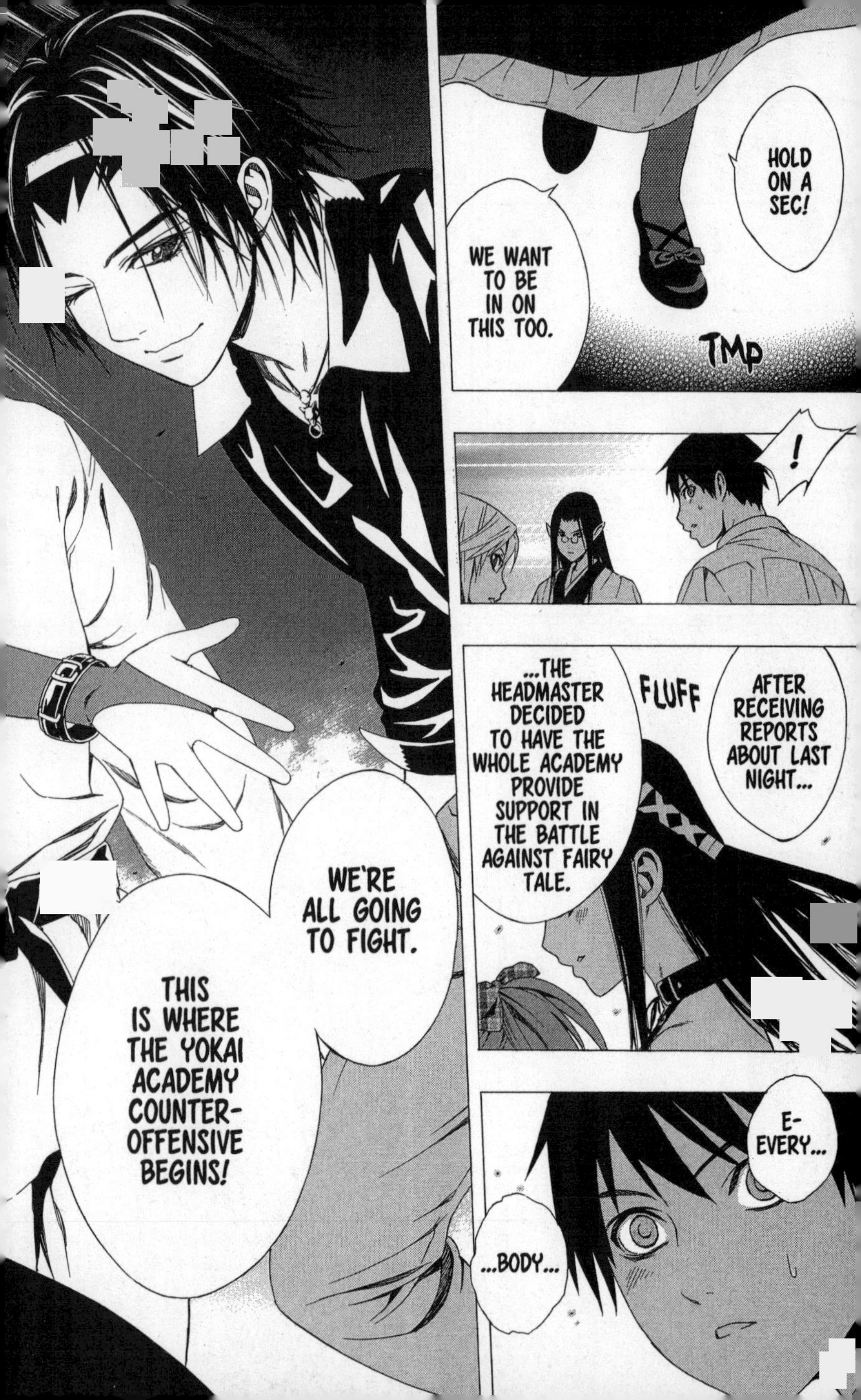
HOLD ON A SEC!
WE WANT TO BE IN ON THIS TOO.
TMP
!
AFTER RECEIVING REPORTS ABOUT LAST NIGHT...
FLUFF
...THE HEADMASTER DECIDED TO HAVE THE WHOLE ACADEMY PROVIDE SUPPORT IN THE BATTLE AGAINST FAIRY TALE.
E-EVERY...
...BODY...
WE'RE ALL GOING TO FIGHT.
THIS IS WHERE THE YOKAI ACADEMY COUNTER-OFFENSIVE BEGINS!

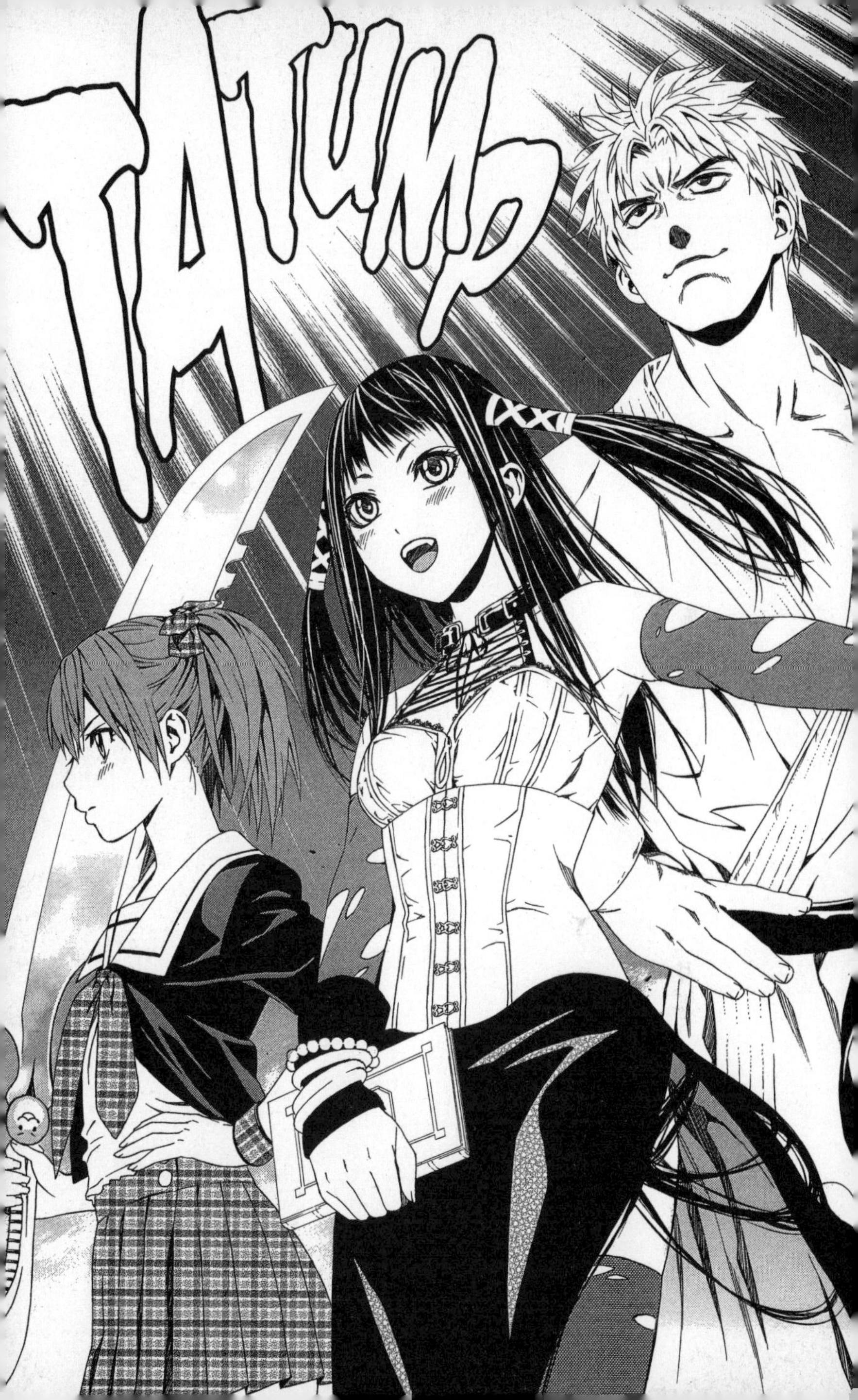
TATUMP

39: Scenes #1

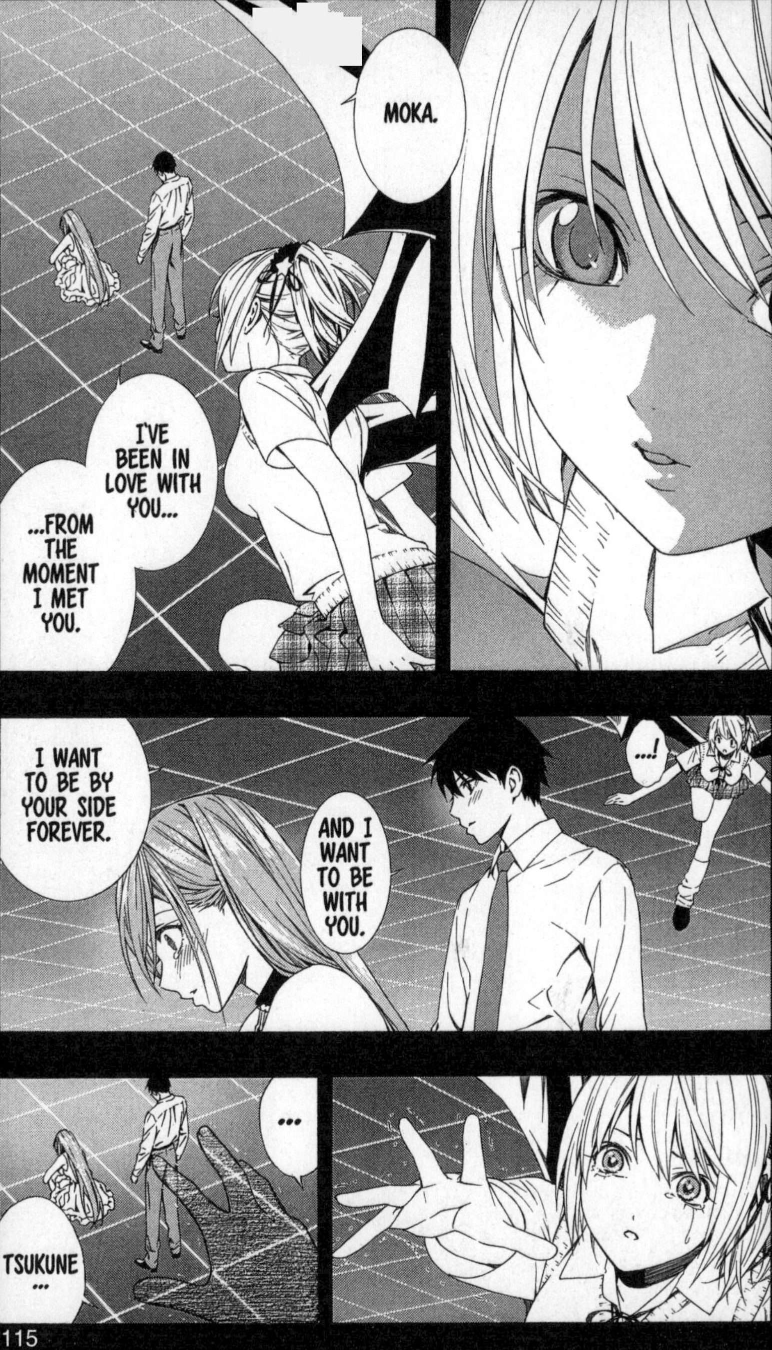
MOKA.
I'VE BEEN IN LOVE WITH YOU...
...FROM THE MOMENT I MET YOU.
...!
I WANT TO BE BY YOUR SIDE FOREVER.
AND I WANT TO BE WITH YOU.
...
TSUKUNE...

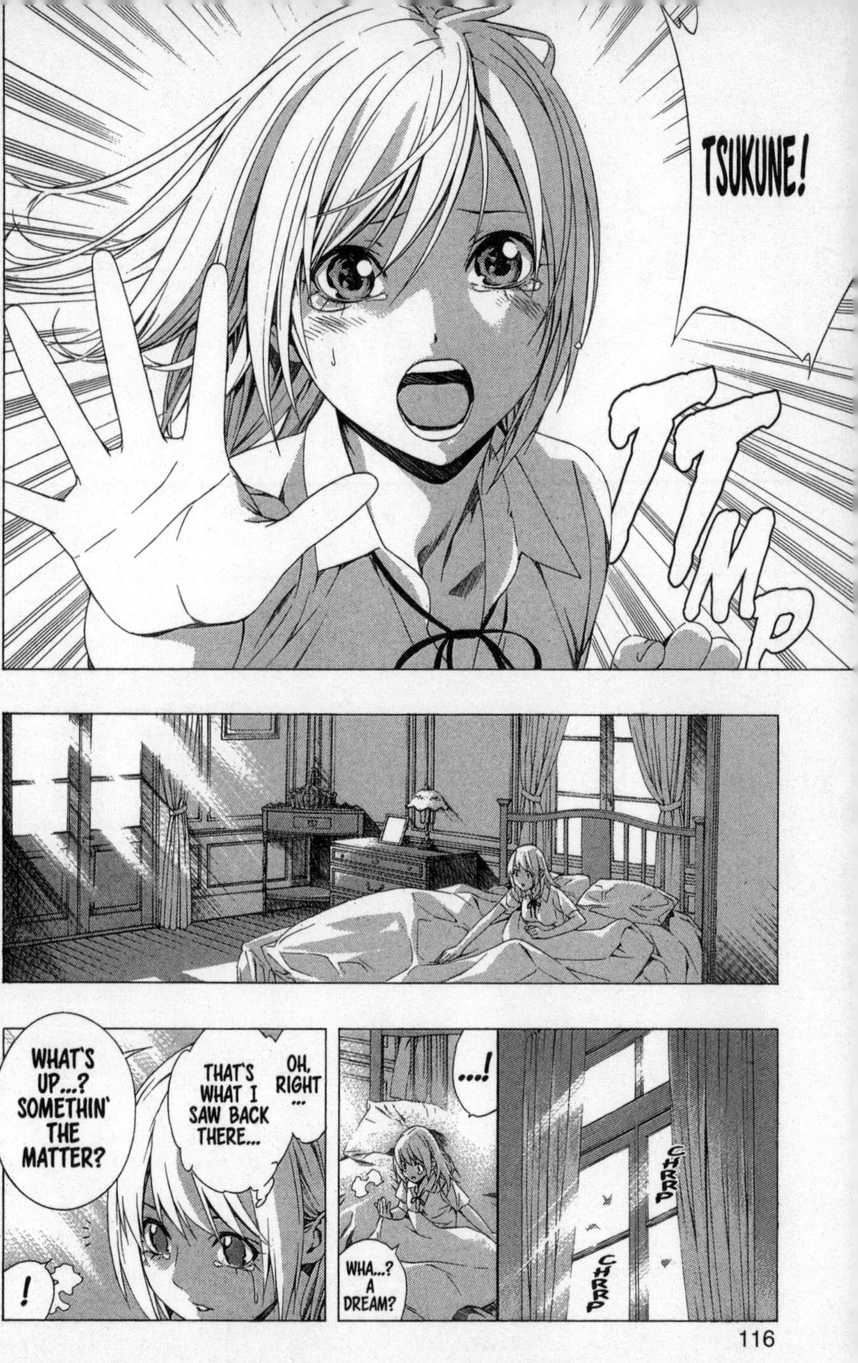
TSUKUNE!
...!
CHRRP
CHRRP
WHA...? A DREAM?
OH, RIGHT ...
THAT'S WHAT I SAW BACK THERE...
WHAT'S UP...? SOMETHIN' THE MATTER?
!

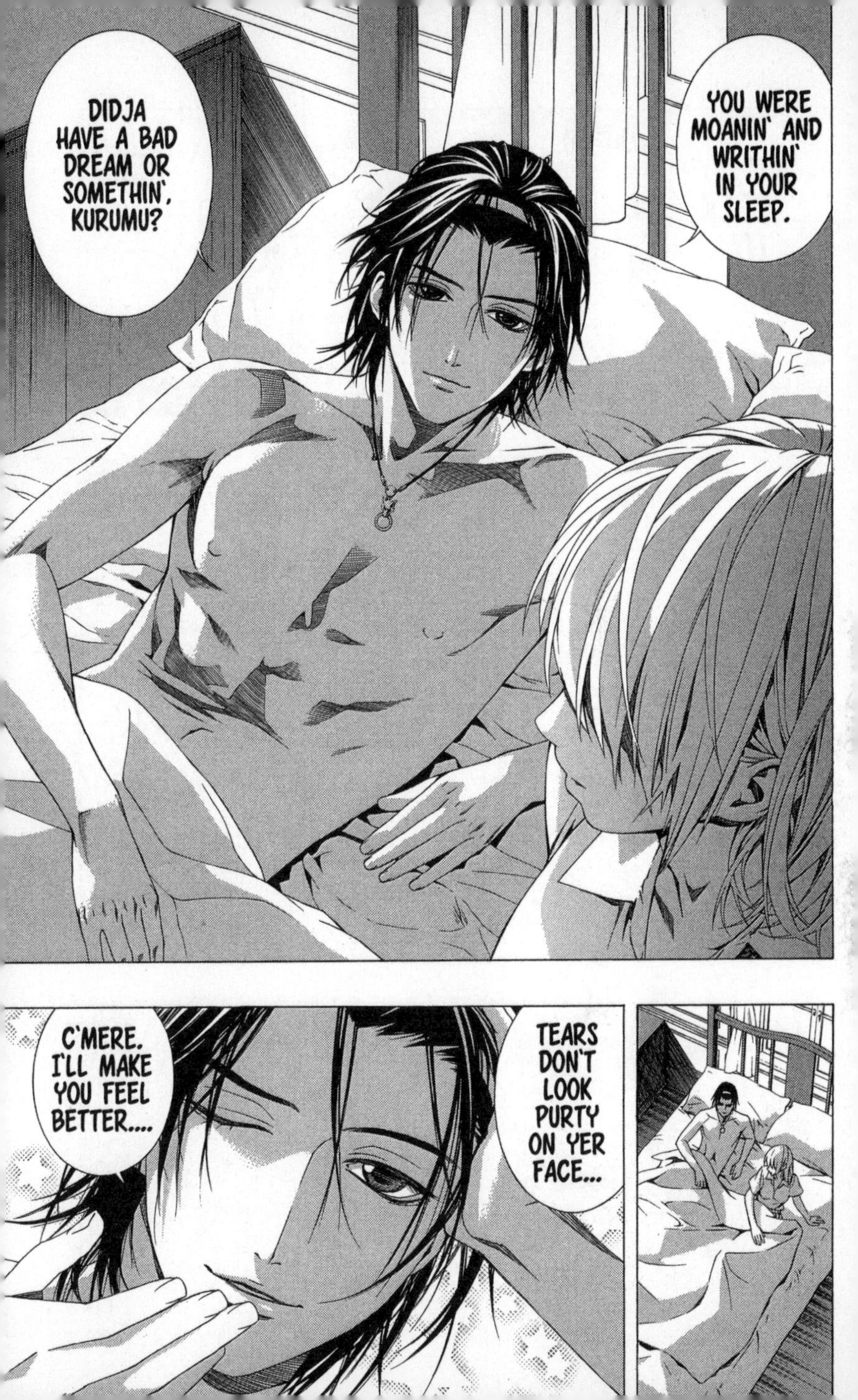
YOU WERE MOANIN' AND WRITHIN' IN YOUR SLEEP.
DIDJA HAVE A BAD DREAM OR SOMETHIN', KURUMU?
TEARS DON'T LOOK PURTY ON YER FACE...
C'MERE. I'LL MAKE YOU FEEL BETTER....

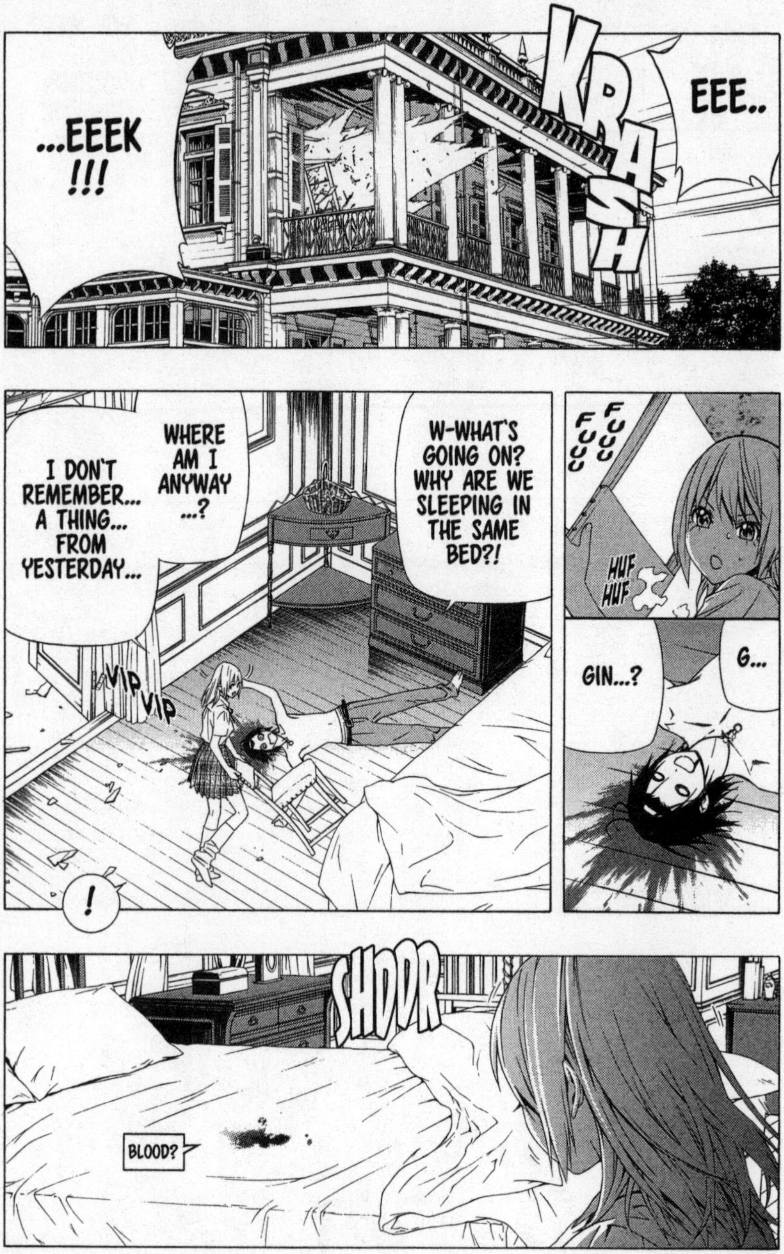
EEE..
KRASH
...EEEK !!!
FUUUU FUUU
HUF HUF
G...
GIN...?
W-WHAT'S GOING ON? WHY ARE WE SLEEPING IN THE SAME BED?!
WHERE AM I ANYWAY ...?
I DON'T REMEMBER... A THING... FROM YESTERDAY...
VIP VIP
!
SHOOR
BLOOD?

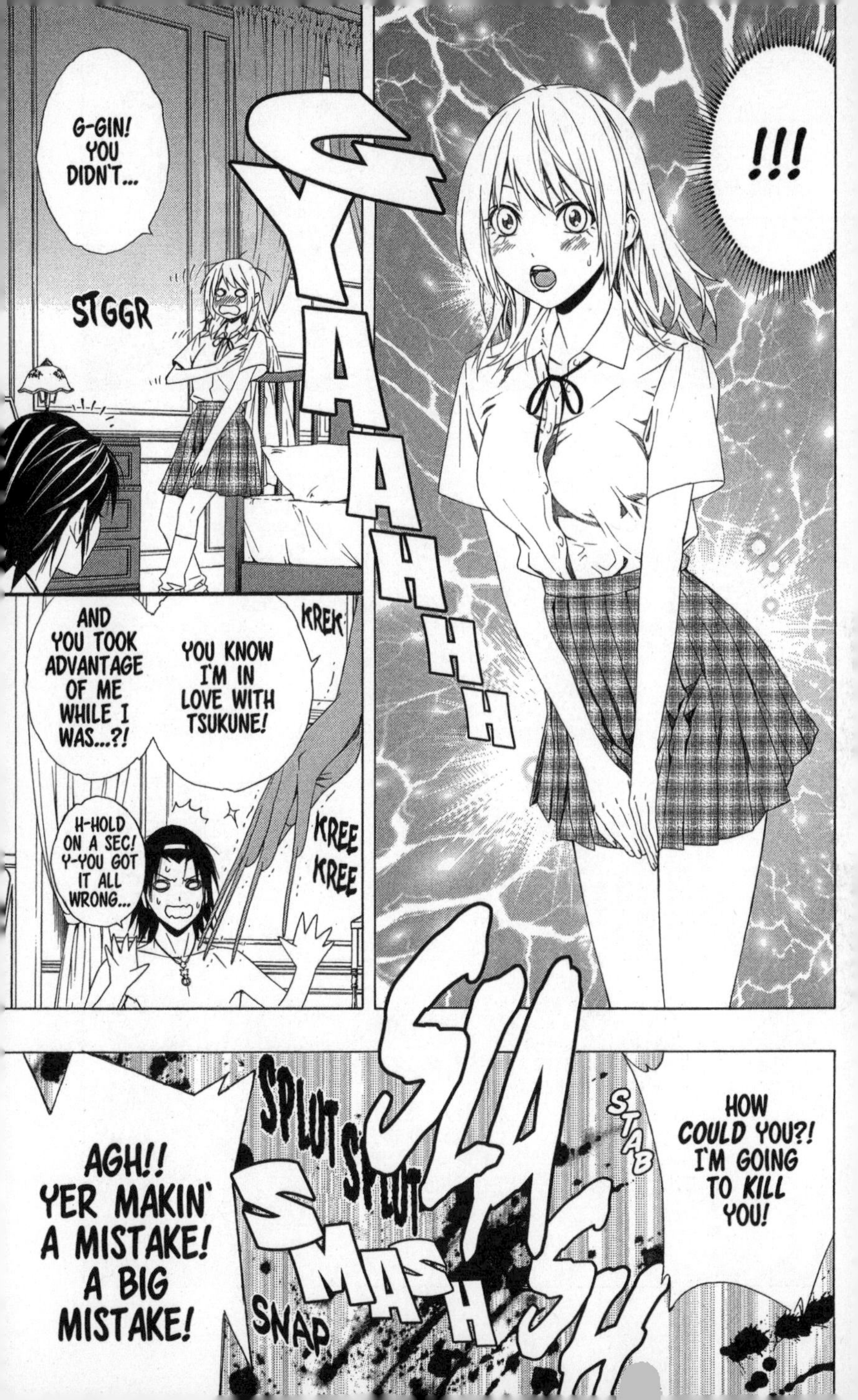
!!!
G-GIN! YOU DIDN'T...
STGGR
GYAAHHHH
YOU KNOW I'M IN LOVE WITH TSUKUNE!
AND YOU TOOK ADVANTAGE OF ME WHILE I WAS...?!
KREK
KREE KREE
H-HOLD ON A SEC! Y-YOU GOT IT ALL WRONG...
HOW COULD YOU?! I'M GOING TO KILL YOU!
STAB
SLASH
SPLUT SPLUT
SMASH
SNAP
AGH!! YER MAKIN' A MISTAKE! A BIG MISTAKE!

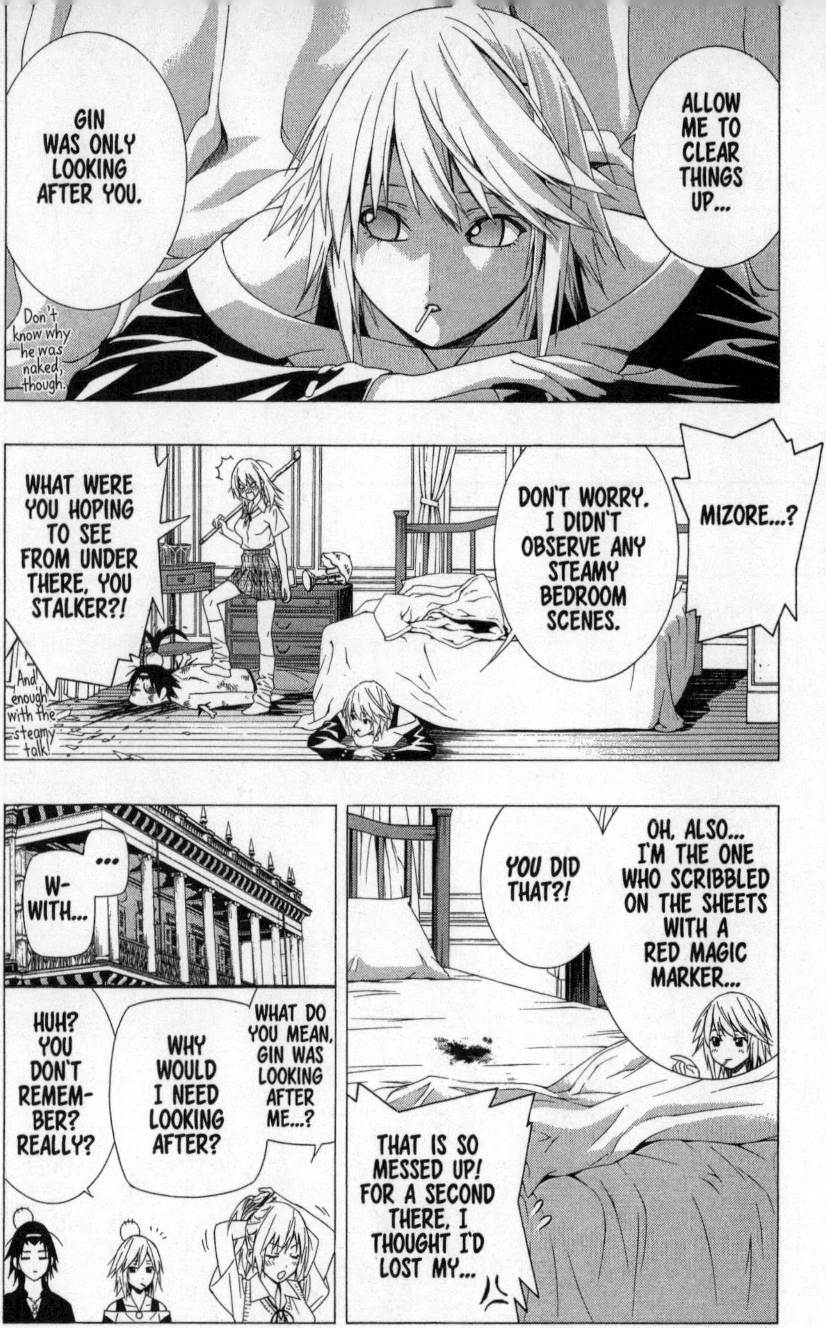
ALLOW ME TO CLEAR THINGS UP...
GIN WAS ONLY LOOKING AFTER YOU.
Don't know why he was naked, though.
MIZORE...?
DON'T WORRY. I DIDN'T OBSERVE ANY STEAMY BEDROOM SCENES.
WHAT WERE YOU HOPING TO SEE FROM UNDER THERE, YOU STALKER?!
And enough with the steamy talk!
OH, ALSO... I'M THE ONE WHO SCRIBBLED ON THE SHEETS WITH A RED MAGIC MARKER...
YOU DID THAT?!
THAT IS SO MESSED UP! FOR A SECOND THERE, I THOUGHT I'D LOST MY...
...
W-WITH...
WHAT DO YOU MEAN, GIN WAS LOOKING AFTER ME...?
WHY WOULD I NEED LOOKING AFTER?
HUH? YOU DON'T REMEMBER? REALLY?

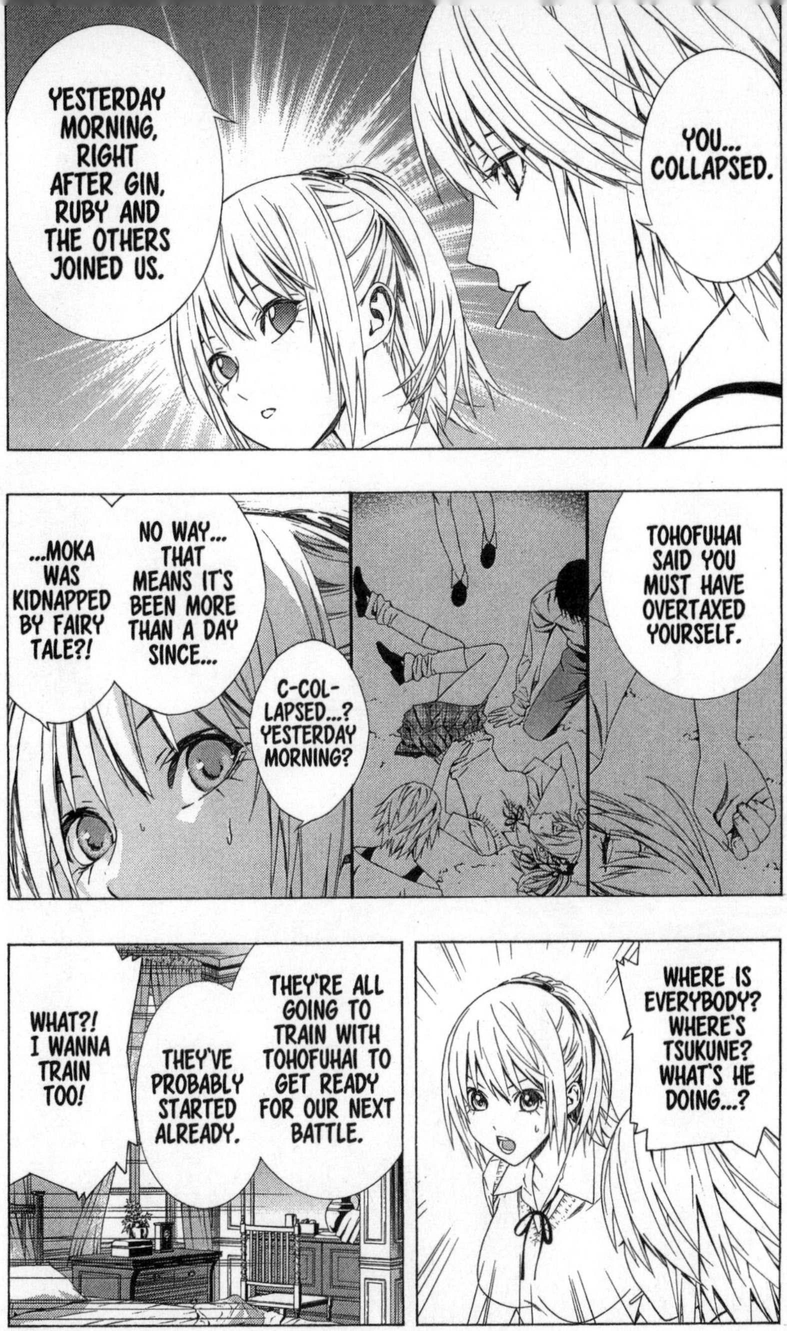
YOU... COLLAPSED.
YESTERDAY MORNING, RIGHT AFTER GIN, RUBY AND THE OTHERS JOINED US.
TOHOFUHAI SAID YOU MUST HAVE OVERTAXED YOURSELF.
C-COLLAPSED...? YESTERDAY MORNING?
NO WAY... THAT MEANS IT'S BEEN MORE THAN A DAY SINCE...
...MOKA WAS KIDNAPPED BY FAIRY TALE?!
WHERE IS EVERYBODY? WHERE'S TSUKUNE? WHAT'S HE DOING...?
THEY'RE ALL GOING TO TRAIN WITH TOHOFUHAI TO GET READY FOR OUR NEXT BATTLE.
THEY'VE PROBABLY STARTED ALREADY.
WHAT?! I WANNA TRAIN TOO!

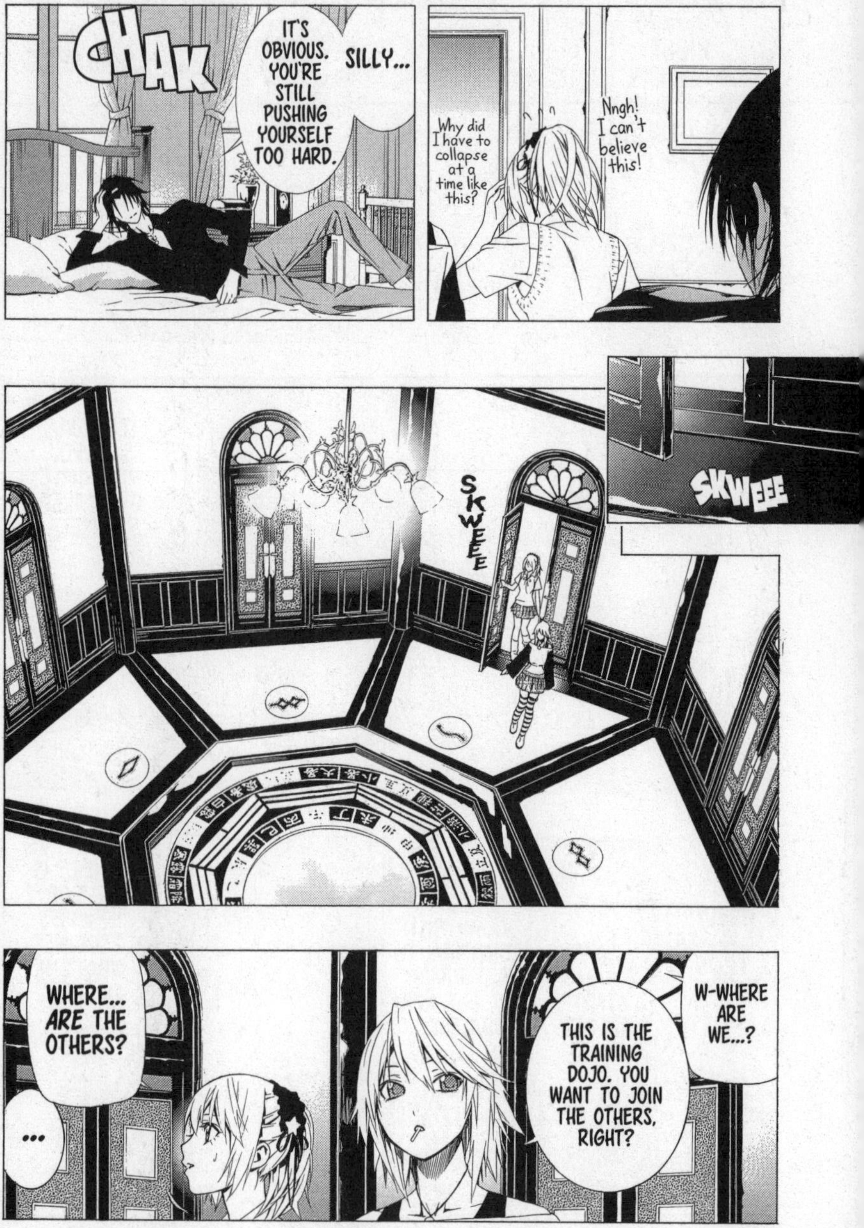

Nngh! I can't believe this!
Why did I have to collapse at a time like this?
SILLY...
IT'S OBVIOUS. YOU'RE STILL PUSHING YOURSELF TOO HARD.
CHAK
SKWEEE
SKWEEE
W-WHERE ARE WE...?
THIS IS THE TRAINING DOJO. YOU WANT TO JOIN THE OTHERS, RIGHT?
WHERE... ARE THE OTHERS?
...

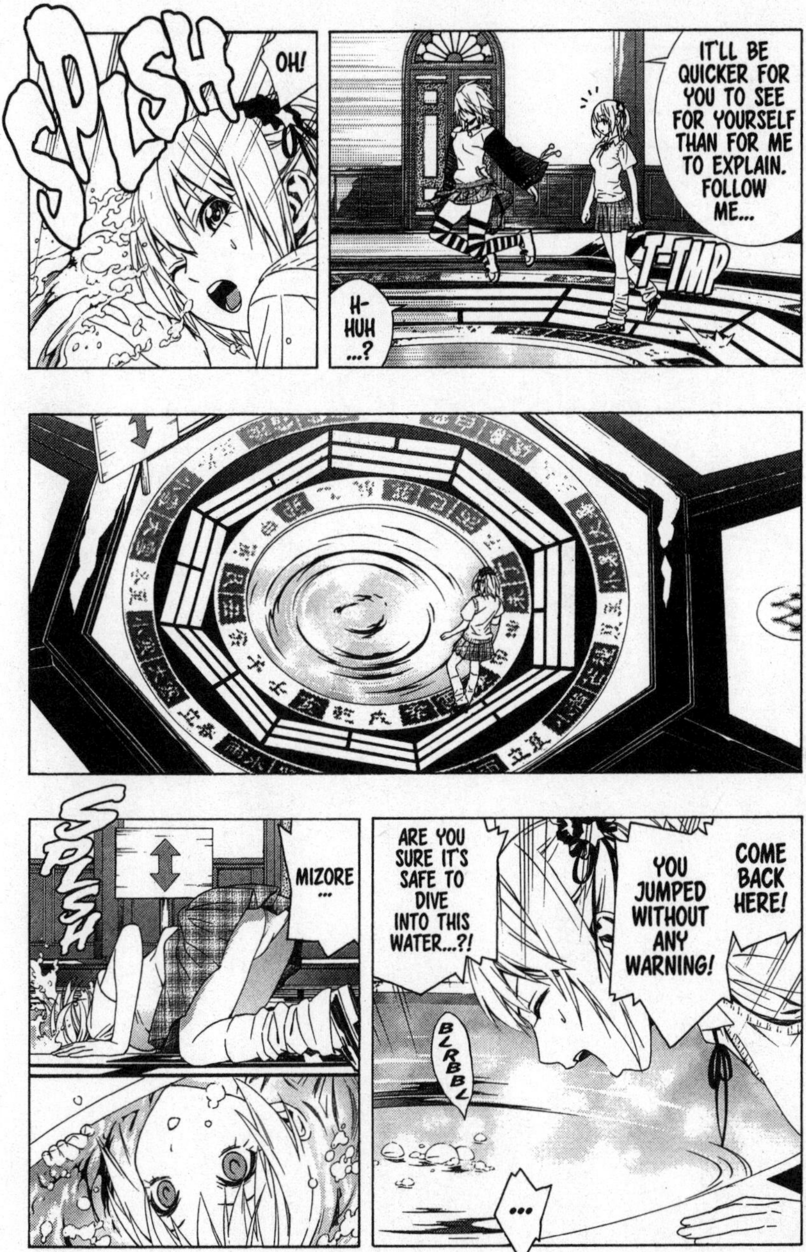
IT'LL BE QUICKER FOR YOU TO SEE FOR YOURSELF THAN FOR ME TO EXPLAIN. FOLLOW ME...
T-TMP
H-HUH ...?
OH!
SPLSH
COME BACK HERE!
YOU JUMPED WITHOUT ANY WARNING!
ARE YOU SURE IT'S SAFE TO DIVE INTO THIS WATER...?!
BLRBBL
...
MIZORE ...
SPLSH

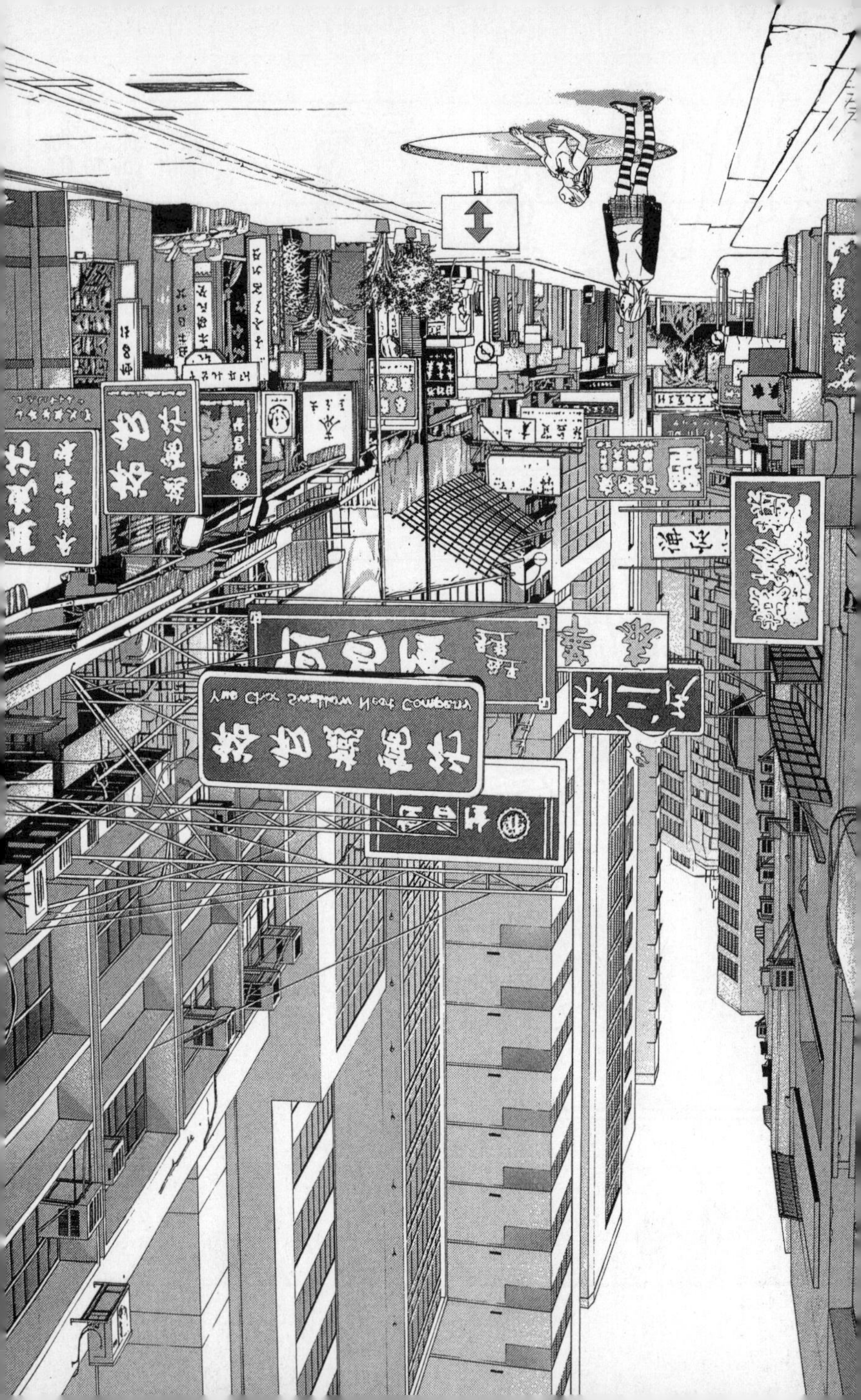

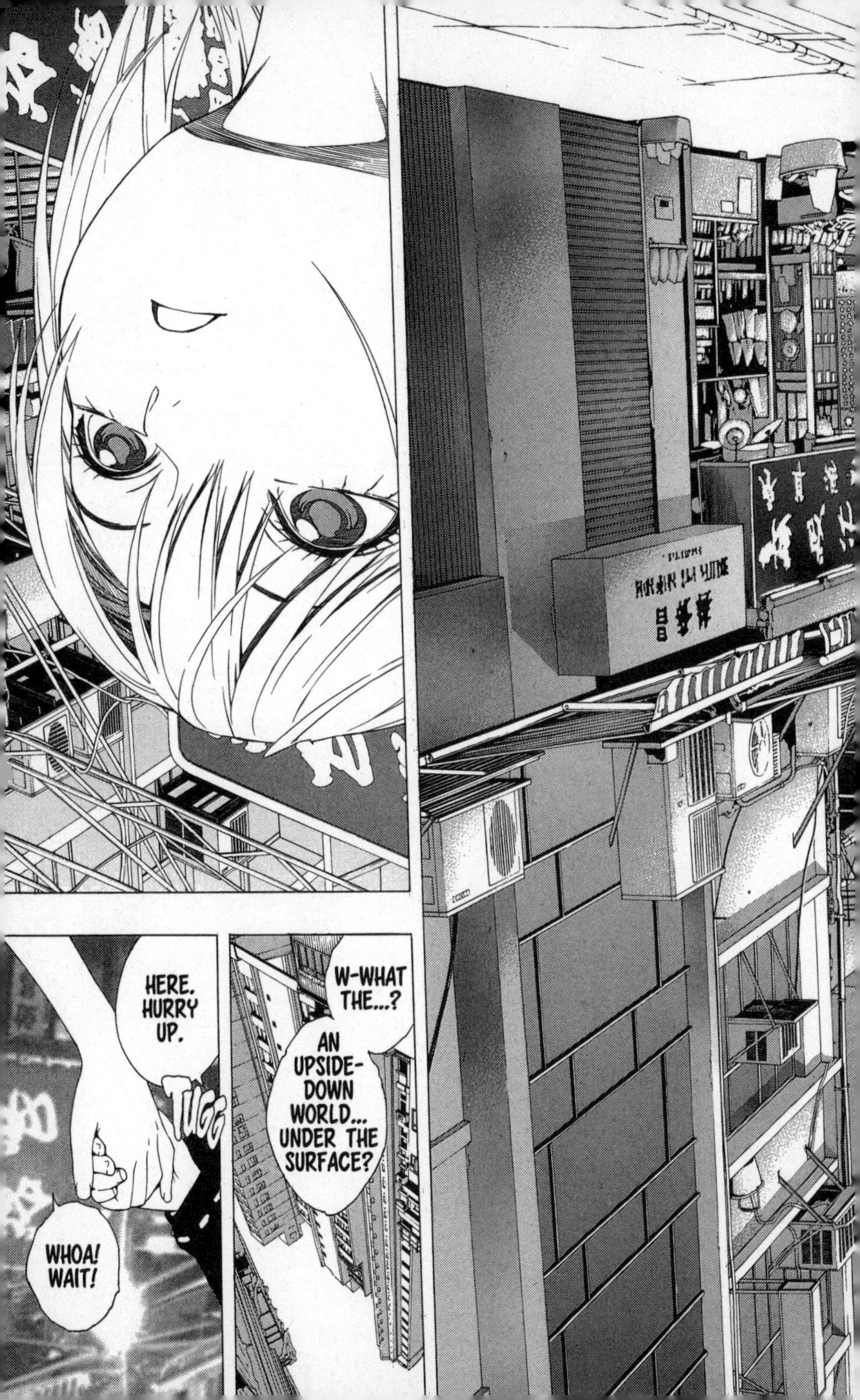
W-WHAT THE...?
AN UPSIDE-DOWN WORLD... UNDER THE SURFACE?
HERE. HURRY UP.
TUGG
WHOA! WAIT!

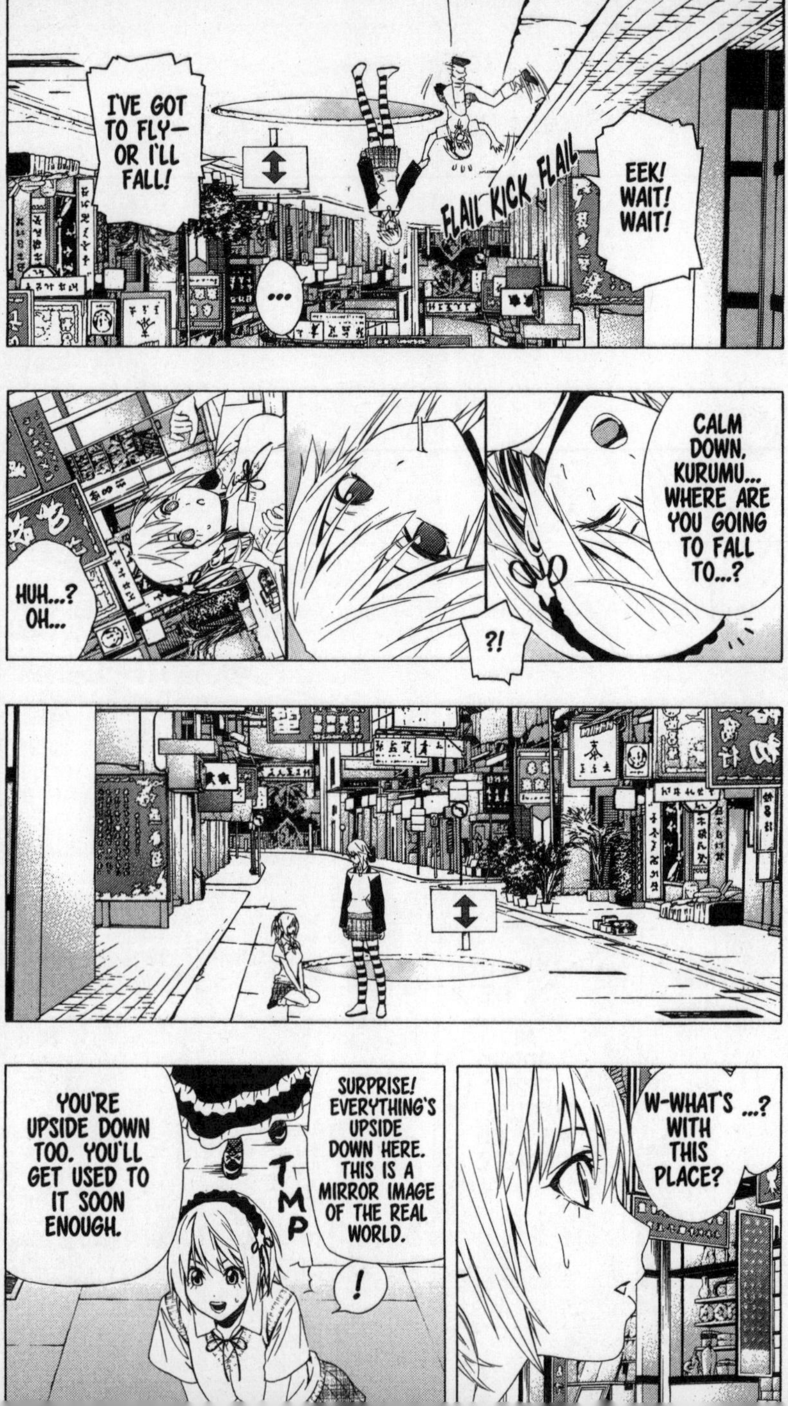
EEK! WAIT! WAIT!
FLAIL KICK FLAIL
I'VE GOT TO FLY— OR I'LL FALL!
...
CALM DOWN, KURUMU... WHERE ARE YOU GOING TO FALL TO...?
?!
HUH...? OH...
W-WHAT'S ...? WITH THIS PLACE?
SURPRISE! EVERYTHING'S UPSIDE DOWN HERE. THIS IS A MIRROR IMAGE OF THE REAL WORLD.
YOU'RE UPSIDE DOWN TOO. YOU'LL GET USED TO IT SOON ENOUGH.
TMP
!

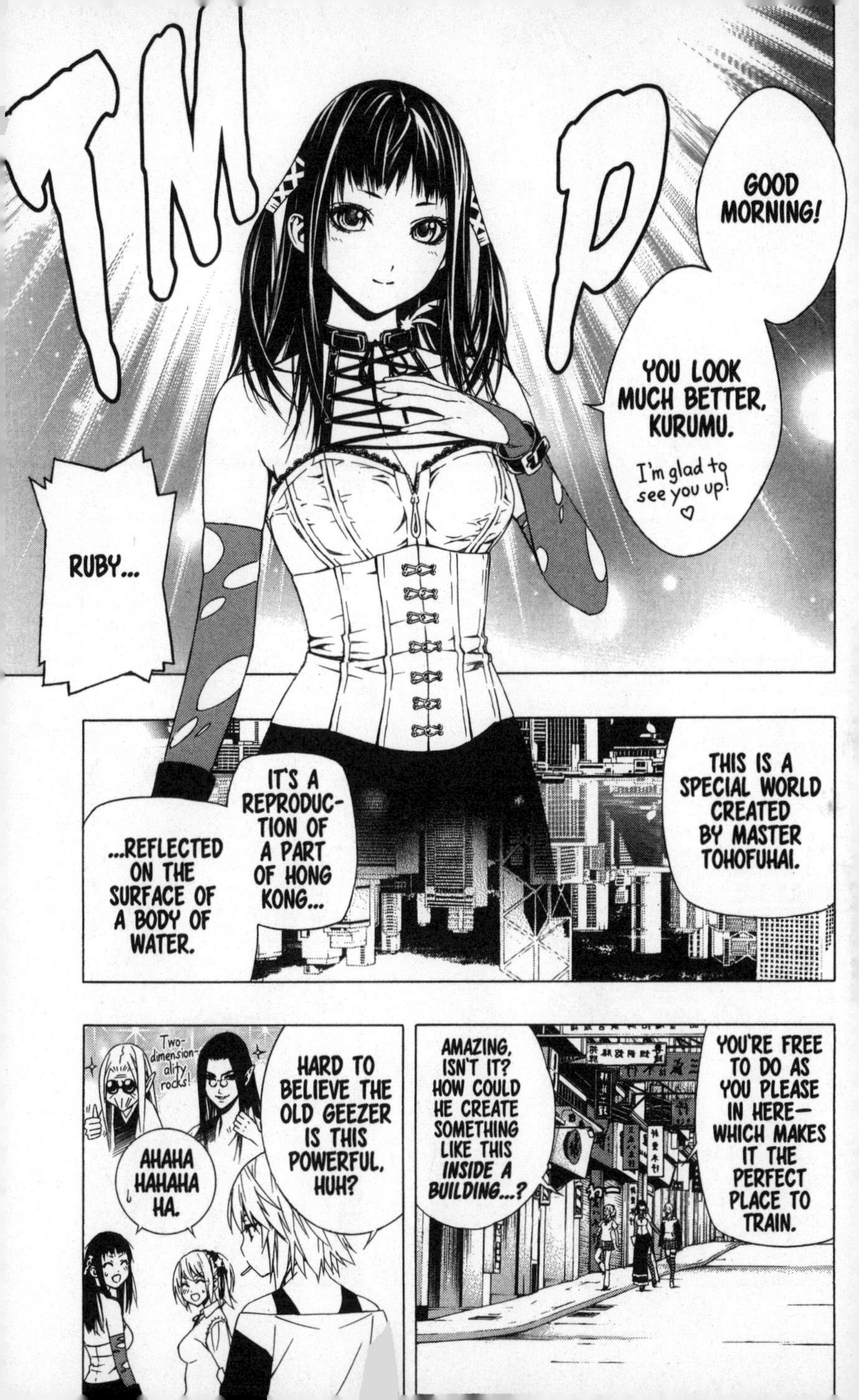
TMP
GOOD MORNING!
YOU LOOK MUCH BETTER, KURUMU.
I'm glad to see you up! ♡
RUBY...
THIS IS A SPECIAL WORLD CREATED BY MASTER TOHOFUHAI.
IT'S A REPRODUCTION OF A PART OF HONG KONG...
...REFLECTED ON THE SURFACE OF A BODY OF WATER.
YOU'RE FREE TO DO AS YOU PLEASE IN HERE— WHICH MAKES IT THE PERFECT PLACE TO TRAIN.
AMAZING, ISN'T IT? HOW COULD HE CREATE SOMETHING LIKE THIS *INSIDE A BUILDING...?*
HARD TO BELIEVE THE OLD GEEZER IS THIS POWERFUL, HUH?
Two-dimensionality rocks!
AHAHA HAHAHA HA.

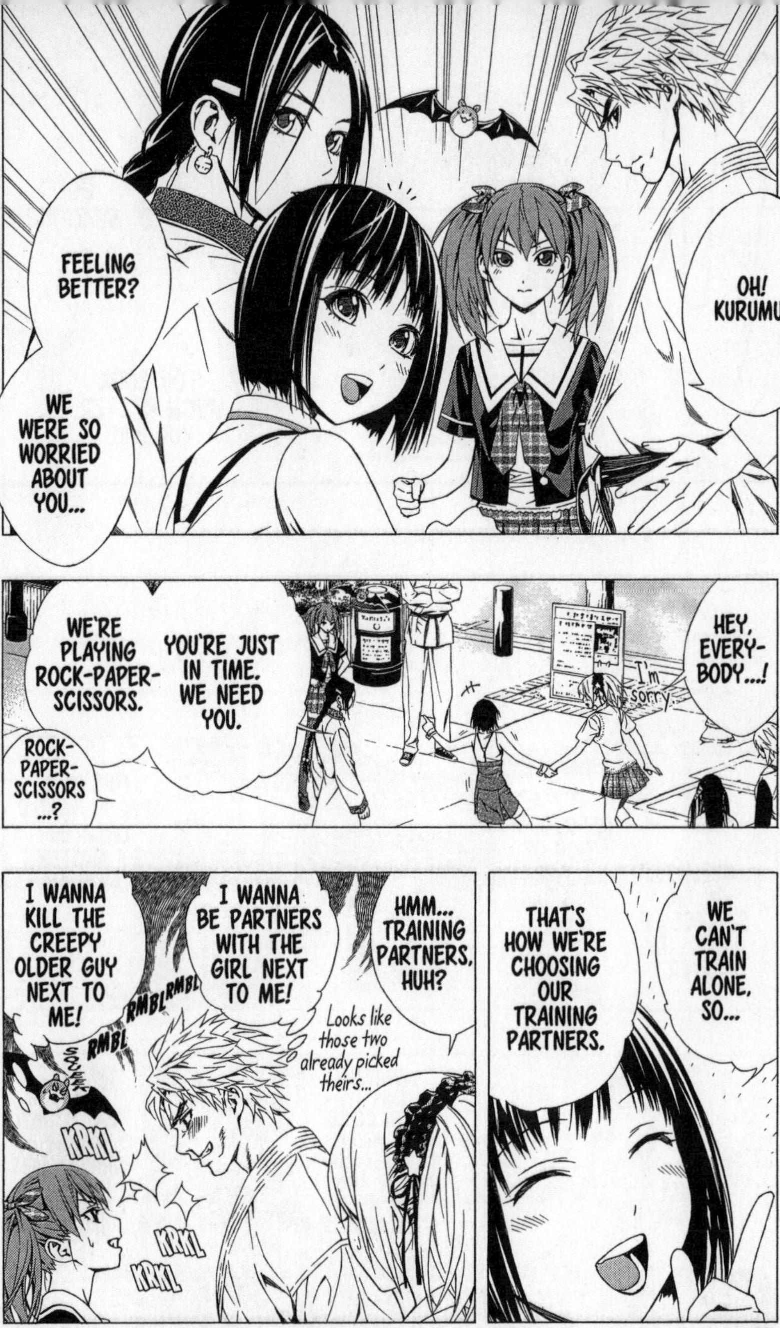
OH! KURUMU!
FEELING BETTER?
WE WERE SO WORRIED ABOUT YOU...
HEY, EVERY-BODY...!
I'm sorry.
YOU'RE JUST IN TIME. WE NEED YOU.
WE'RE PLAYING ROCK-PAPER-SCISSORS.
ROCK-PAPER-SCISSORS...?
WE CAN'T TRAIN ALONE, SO...
THAT'S HOW WE'RE CHOOSING OUR TRAINING PARTNERS.
HMM... TRAINING PARTNERS, HUH?
I WANNA BE PARTNERS WITH THE GIRL NEXT TO ME!
Looks like those two already picked theirs...
I WANNA KILL THE CREEPY OLDER GUY NEXT TO ME!
RMBL RMBL
RMBL
SQUEAK
KRKL
KRKL
KRKL

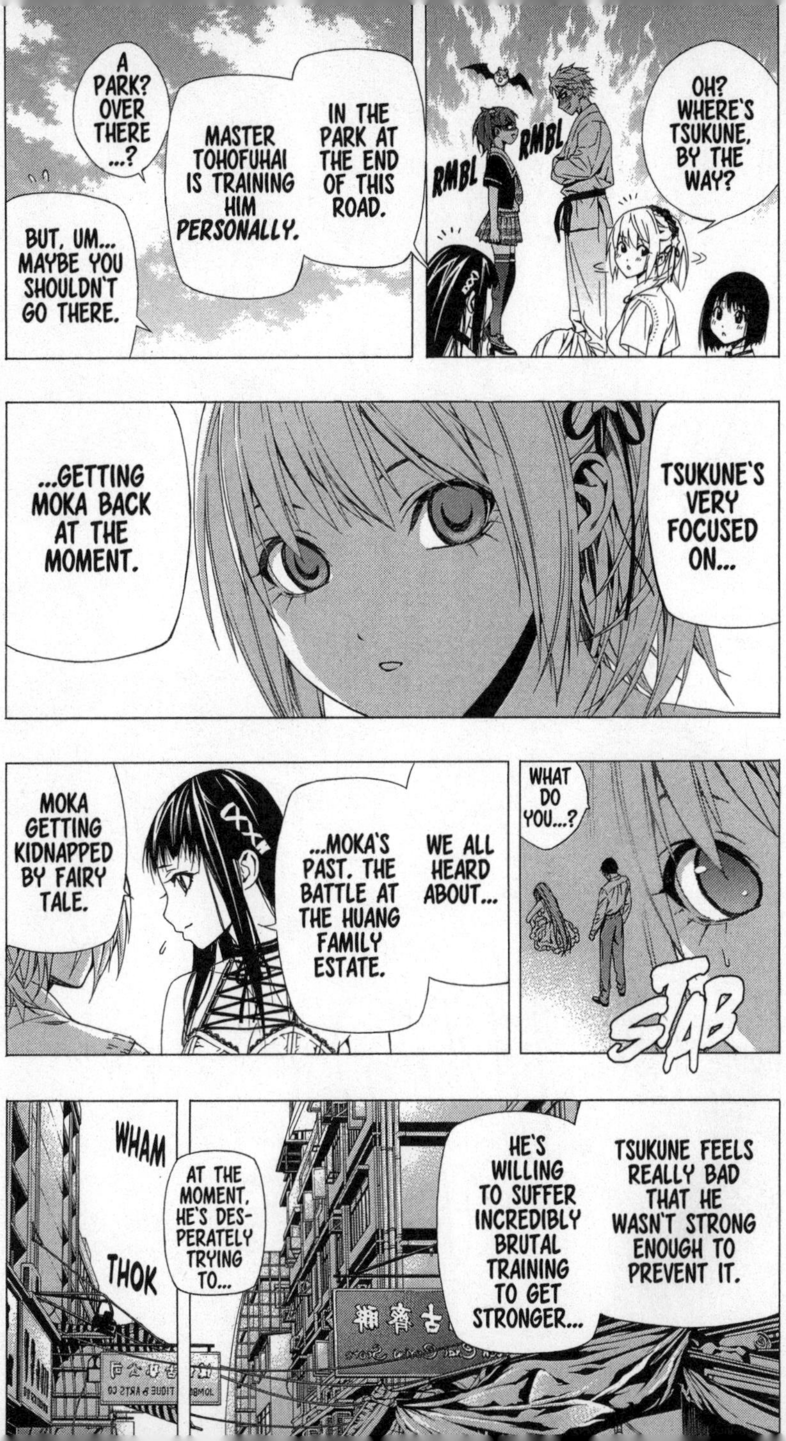
OH? WHERE'S TSUKUNE, BY THE WAY?
RMBL
RMBL
IN THE PARK AT THE END OF THIS ROAD.
MASTER TOHOFUHAI IS TRAINING HIM PERSONALLY.
A PARK? OVER THERE ...?
BUT, UM... MAYBE YOU SHOULDN'T GO THERE.
TSUKUNE'S VERY FOCUSED ON...
...GETTING MOKA BACK AT THE MOMENT.
WHAT DO YOU...?
STAB
WE ALL HEARD ABOUT...
...MOKA'S PAST. THE BATTLE AT THE HUANG FAMILY ESTATE.
MOKA GETTING KIDNAPPED BY FAIRY TALE.
TSUKUNE FEELS REALLY BAD THAT HE WASN'T STRONG ENOUGH TO PREVENT IT.
HE'S WILLING TO SUFFER INCREDIBLY BRUTAL TRAINING TO GET STRONGER...
AT THE MOMENT, HE'S DES-PERATELY TRYING TO...
WHAM
THOK

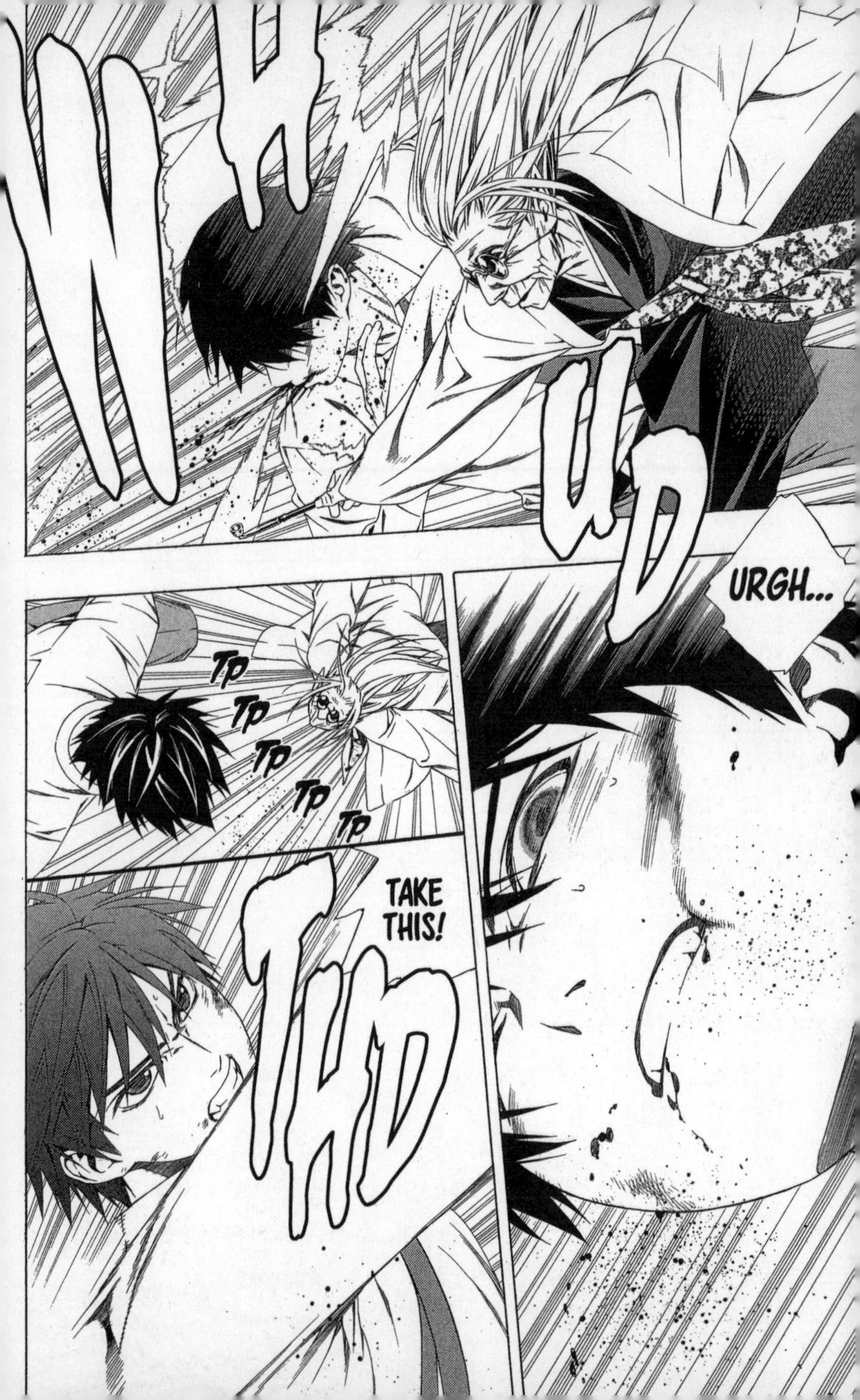
URGH...
Tp
Tp
Tp
Tp
Tp
TAKE THIS!
THD

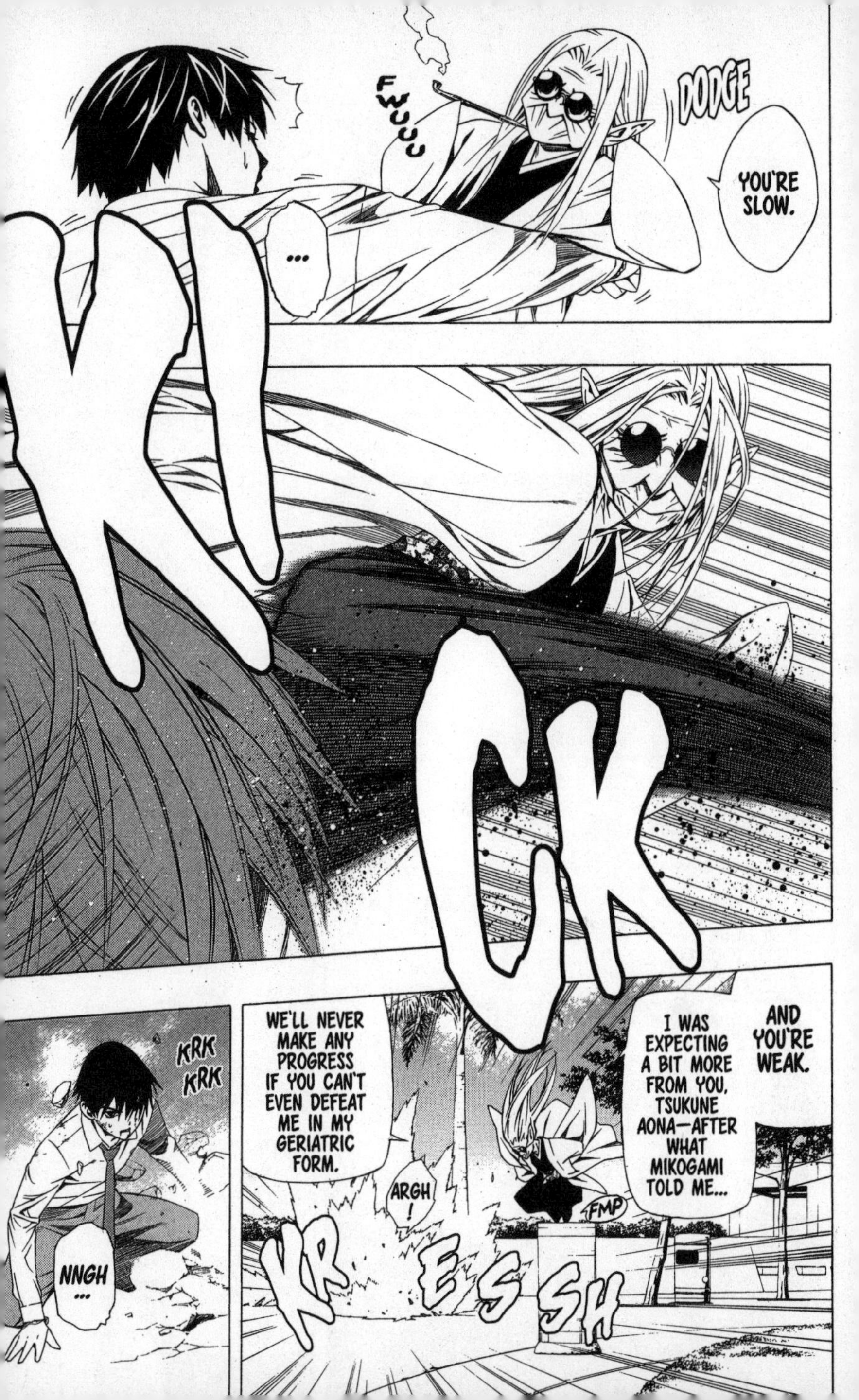
DODGE
YOU'RE SLOW.
FWUUU
...
CK
AND YOU'RE WEAK.
I WAS EXPECTING A BIT MORE FROM YOU, TSUKUNE AONA—AFTER WHAT MIKOGAMI TOLD ME...
FMP
WE'LL NEVER MAKE ANY PROGRESS IF YOU CAN'T EVEN DEFEAT ME IN MY GERIATRIC FORM.
ARGH!
KRESSH
KRK KRK
NNGH...

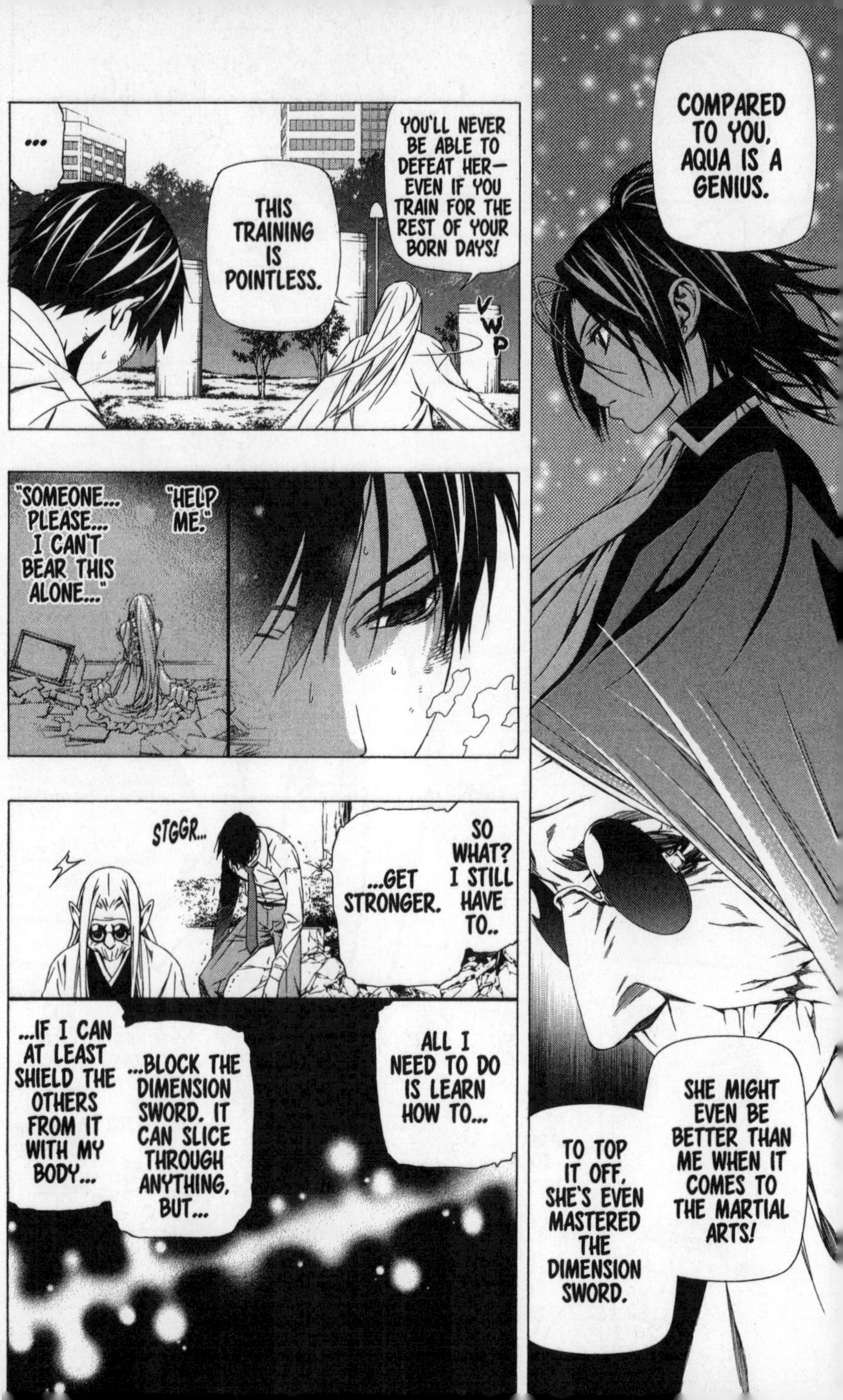
COMPARED TO YOU, AQUA IS A GENIUS.
SHE MIGHT EVEN BE BETTER THAN ME WHEN IT COMES TO THE MARTIAL ARTS!
TO TOP IT OFF, SHE'S EVEN MASTERED THE DIMENSION SWORD.
YOU'LL NEVER BE ABLE TO DEFEAT HER— EVEN IF YOU TRAIN FOR THE REST OF YOUR BORN DAYS!
THIS TRAINING IS POINTLESS.
VWP
...
"HELP ME."
"SOMEONE... PLEASE... I CAN'T BEAR THIS ALONE..."
SO WHAT? I STILL HAVE TO..
...GET STRONGER.
STGGR...
ALL I NEED TO DO IS LEARN HOW TO...
...BLOCK THE DIMENSION SWORD. IT CAN SLICE THROUGH ANYTHING, BUT...
...IF I CAN AT LEAST SHIELD THE OTHERS FROM IT WITH MY BODY...

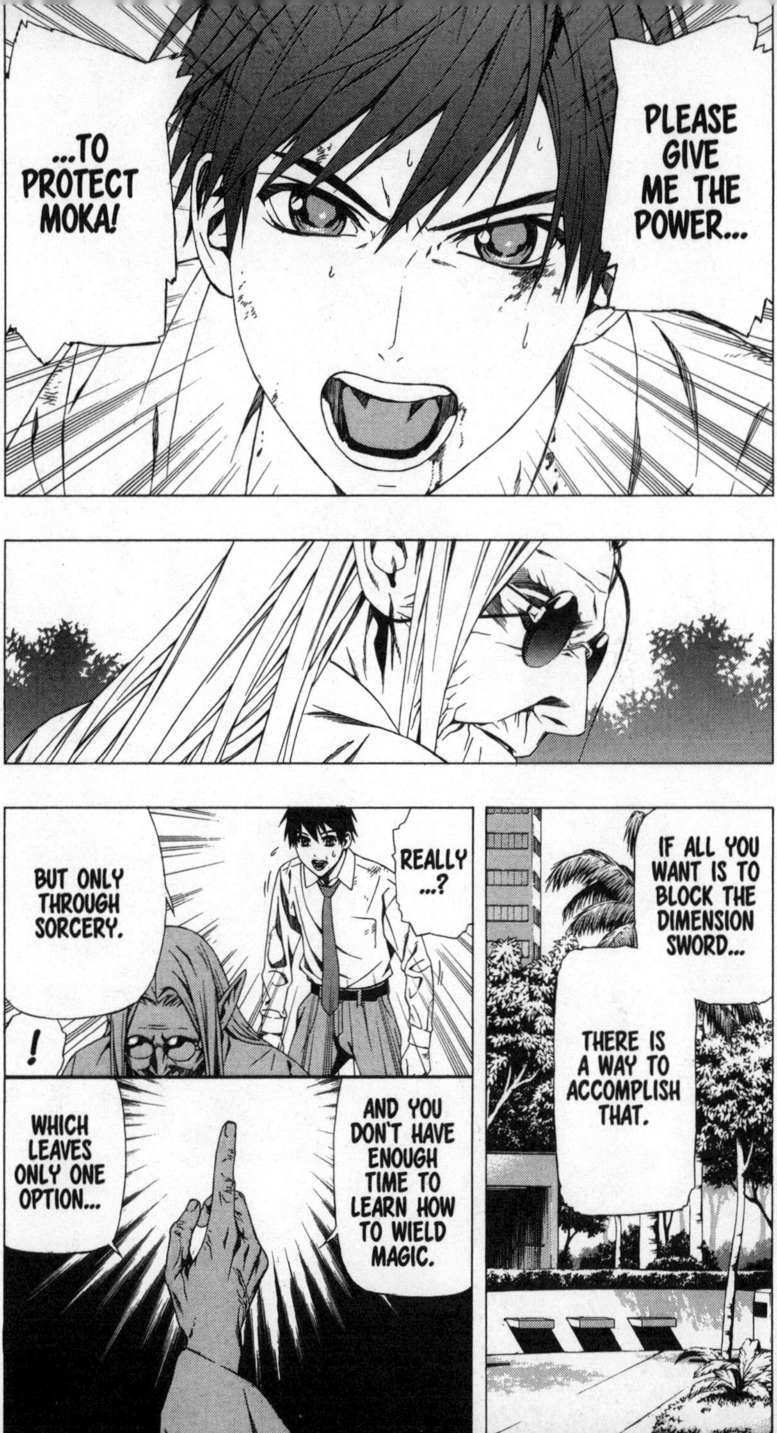
PLEASE GIVE ME THE POWER...
...TO PROTECT MOKA!
IF ALL YOU WANT IS TO BLOCK THE DIMENSION SWORD...
THERE IS A WAY TO ACCOMPLISH THAT.
REALLY ...?
BUT ONLY THROUGH SORCERY.
!
AND YOU DON'T HAVE ENOUGH TIME TO LEARN HOW TO WIELD MAGIC.
WHICH LEAVES ONLY ONE OPTION...

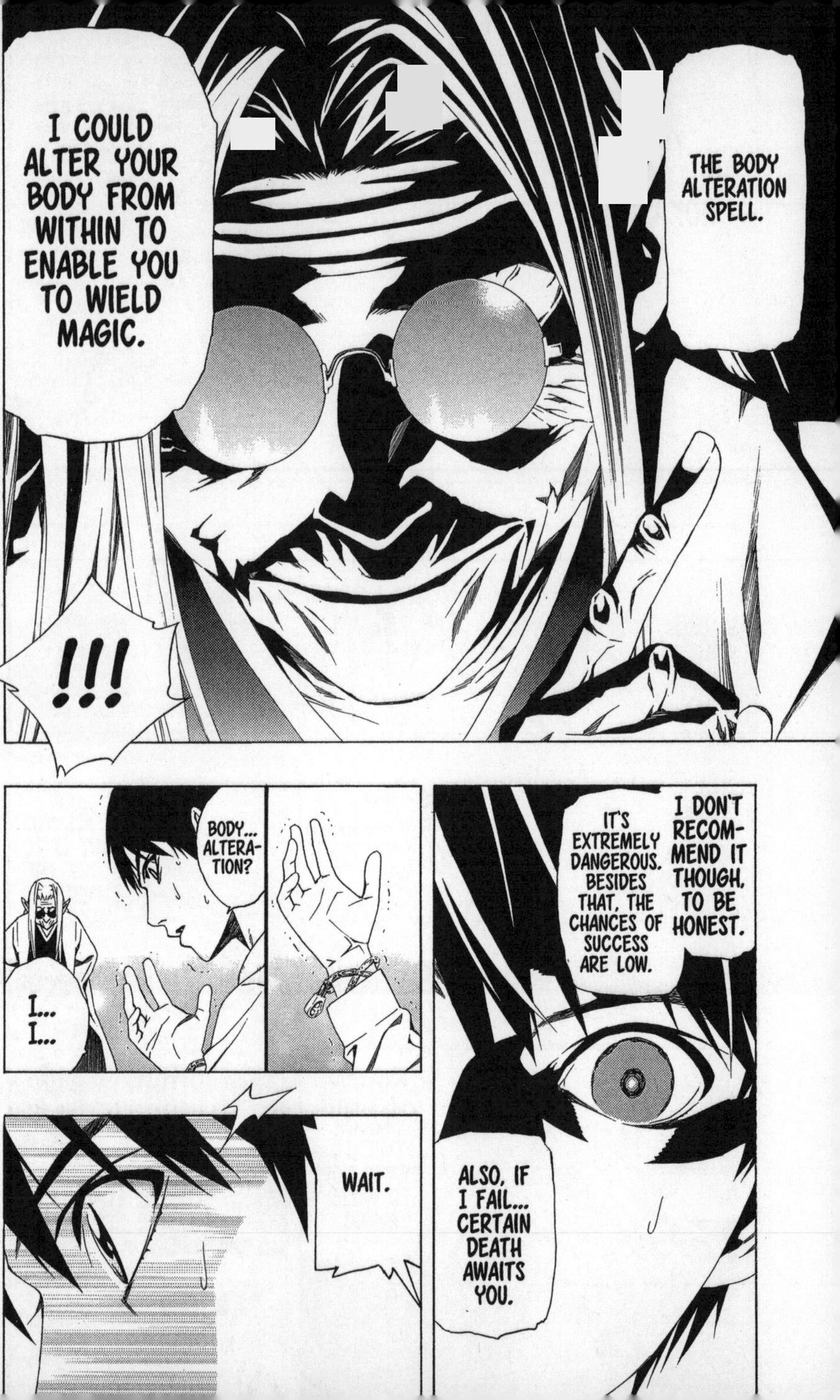
THE BODY ALTERATION SPELL.
I COULD ALTER YOUR BODY FROM WITHIN TO ENABLE YOU TO WIELD MAGIC.
!!!
I DON'T RECOMMEND IT THOUGH, TO BE HONEST.
IT'S EXTREMELY DANGEROUS. BESIDES THAT, THE CHANCES OF SUCCESS ARE LOW.
ALSO, IF I FAIL... CERTAIN DEATH AWAITS YOU.
BODY... ALTERATION?
I... I...
WAIT.

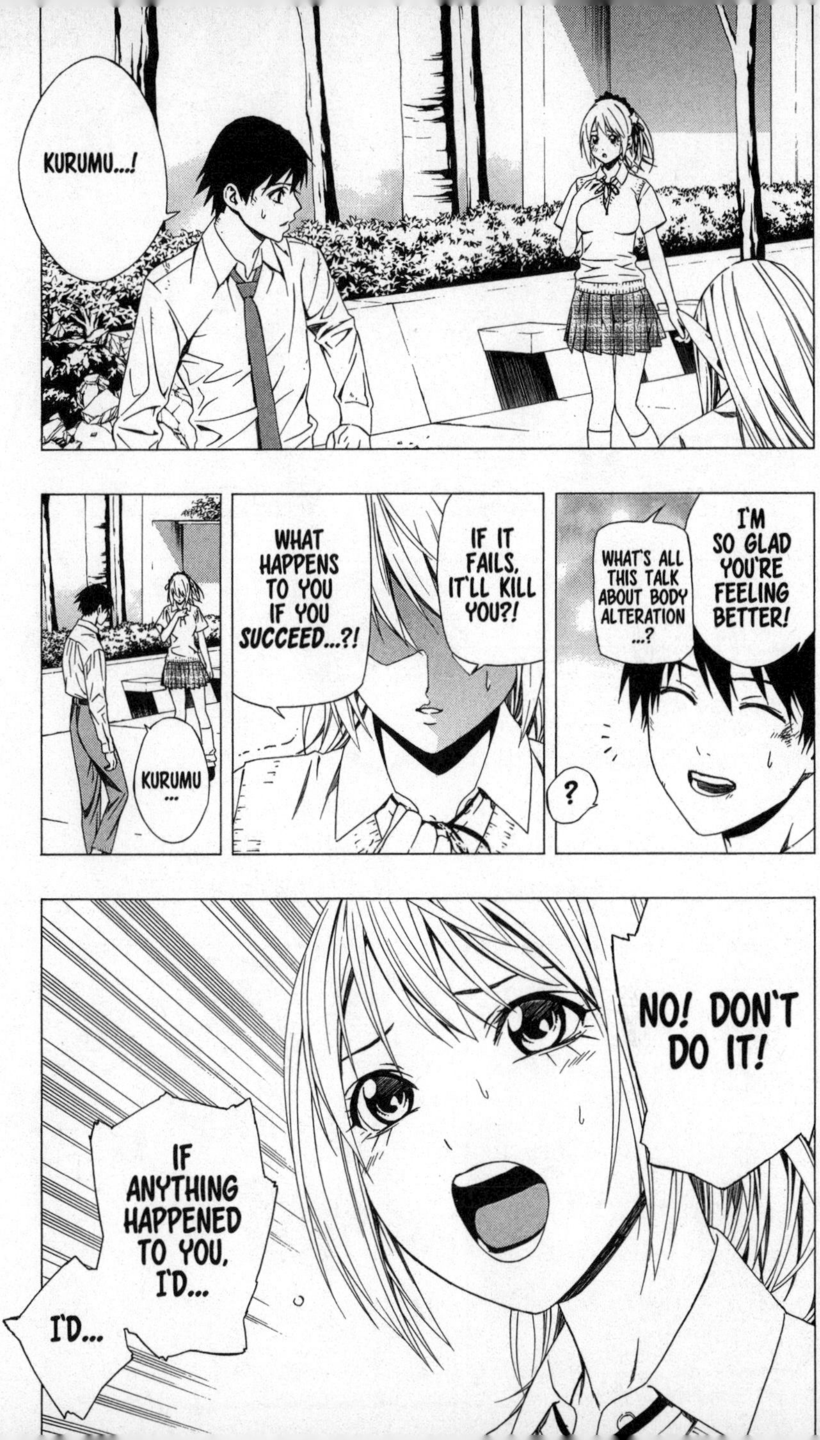
KURUMU...!
I'M SO GLAD YOU'RE FEELING BETTER!
WHAT'S ALL THIS TALK ABOUT BODY ALTERATION ...?
?
IF IT FAILS, IT'LL KILL YOU?!
WHAT HAPPENS TO YOU IF YOU *SUCCEED*...?!
KURUMU ...
NO! DON'T DO IT!
IF ANYTHING HAPPENED TO YOU, I'D...
I'D...

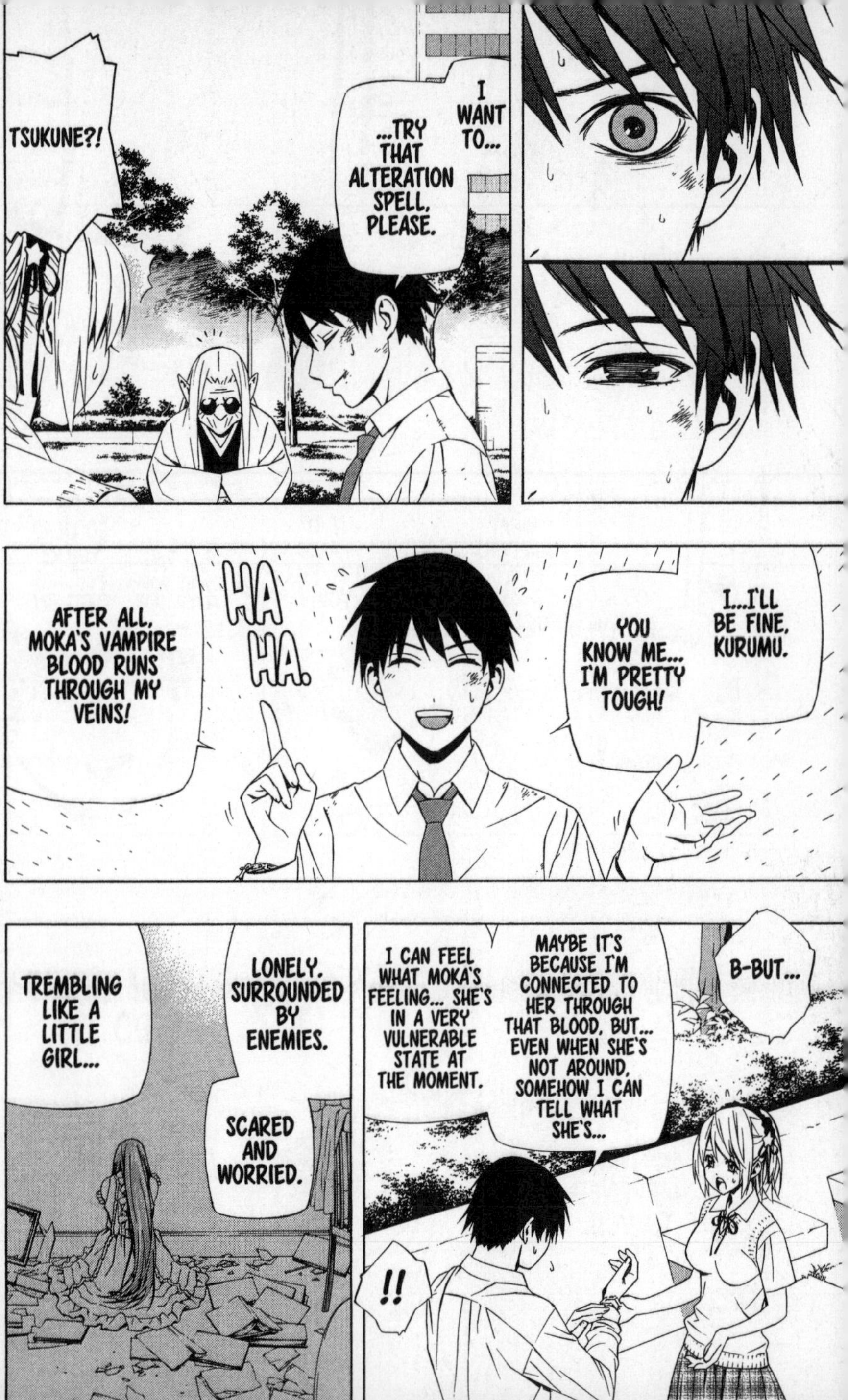
I WANT TO...
...TRY THAT ALTERATION SPELL, PLEASE.
TSUKUNE?!
I...I'LL BE FINE, KURUMU.
YOU KNOW ME... I'M PRETTY TOUGH!
HA HA.
AFTER ALL, MOKA'S VAMPIRE BLOOD RUNS THROUGH MY VEINS!
B-BUT...
MAYBE IT'S BECAUSE I'M CONNECTED TO HER THROUGH THAT BLOOD, BUT... EVEN WHEN SHE'S NOT AROUND, SOMEHOW I CAN TELL WHAT SHE'S...
I CAN FEEL WHAT MOKA'S FEELING... SHE'S IN A VERY VULNERABLE STATE AT THE MOMENT.
!!
LONELY. SURROUNDED BY ENEMIES.
SCARED AND WORRIED.
TREMBLING LIKE A LITTLE GIRL...

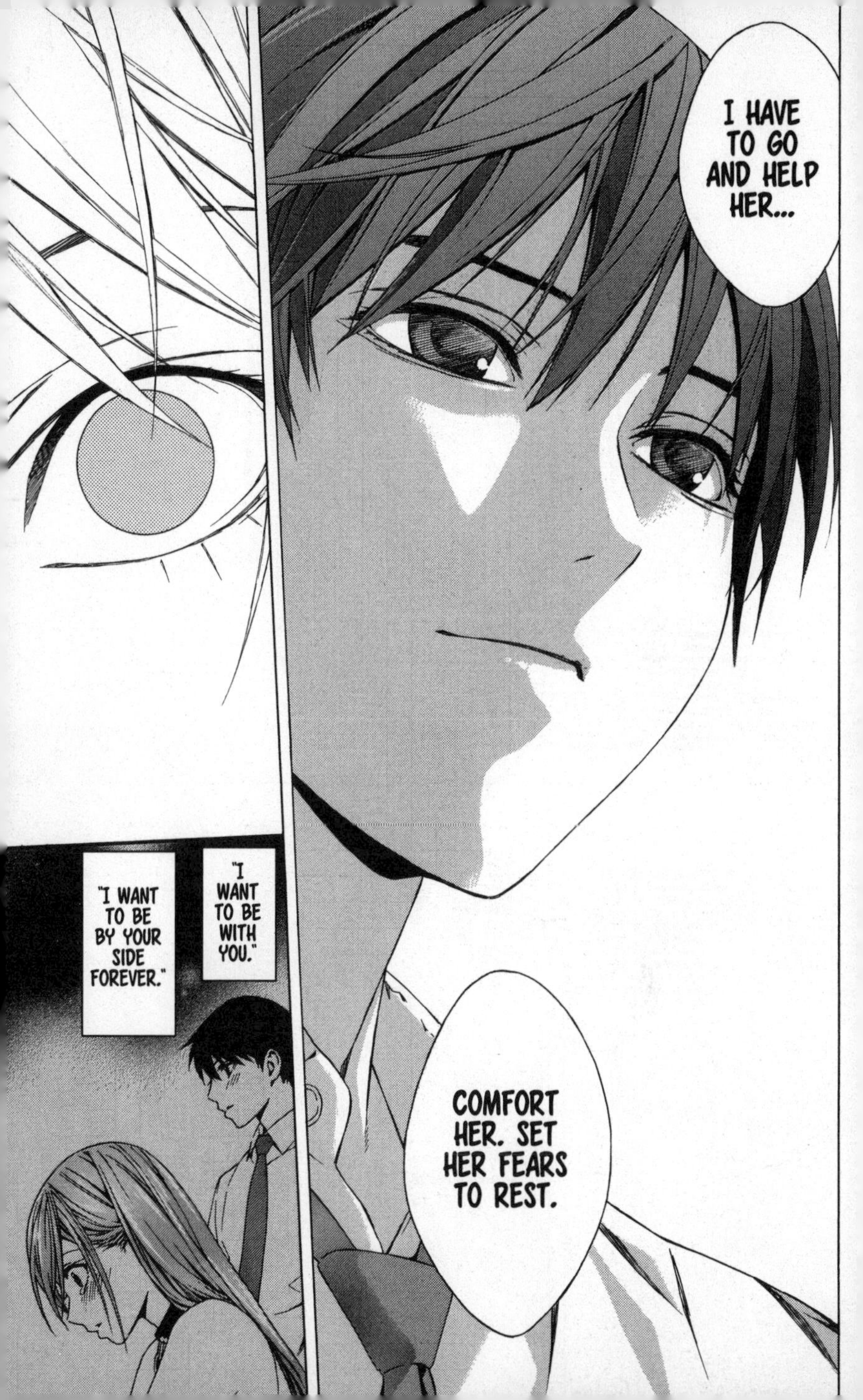
I HAVE TO GO AND HELP HER...
COMFORT HER. SET HER FEARS TO REST.
"I WANT TO BE WITH YOU."
"I WANT TO BE BY YOUR SIDE FOREVER."

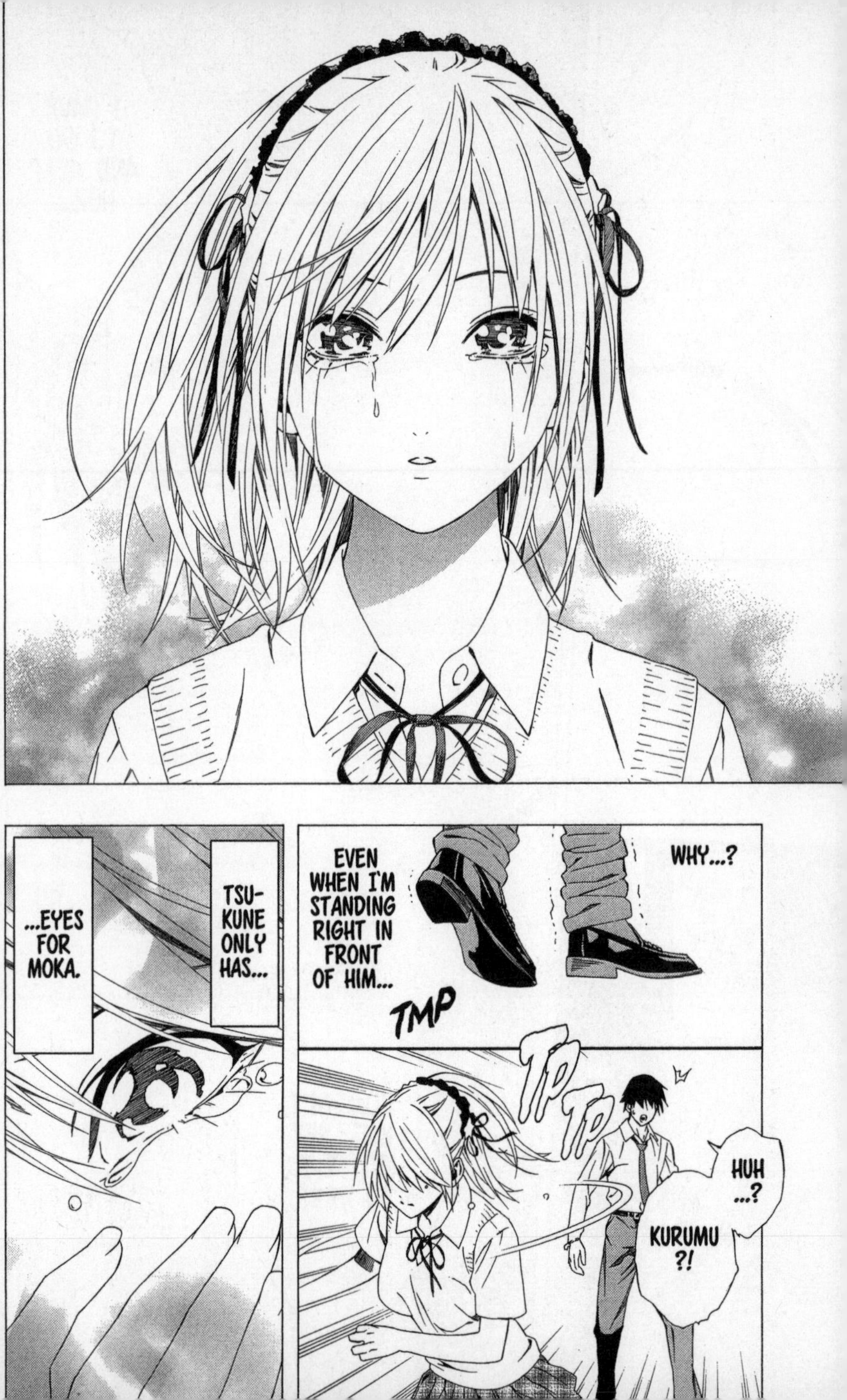
WHY...?
EVEN WHEN I'M STANDING RIGHT IN FRONT OF HIM...
TMP
TP TP
HUH ...?
KURUMU ?!
TSU-KUNE ONLY HAS...
...EYES FOR MOKA.

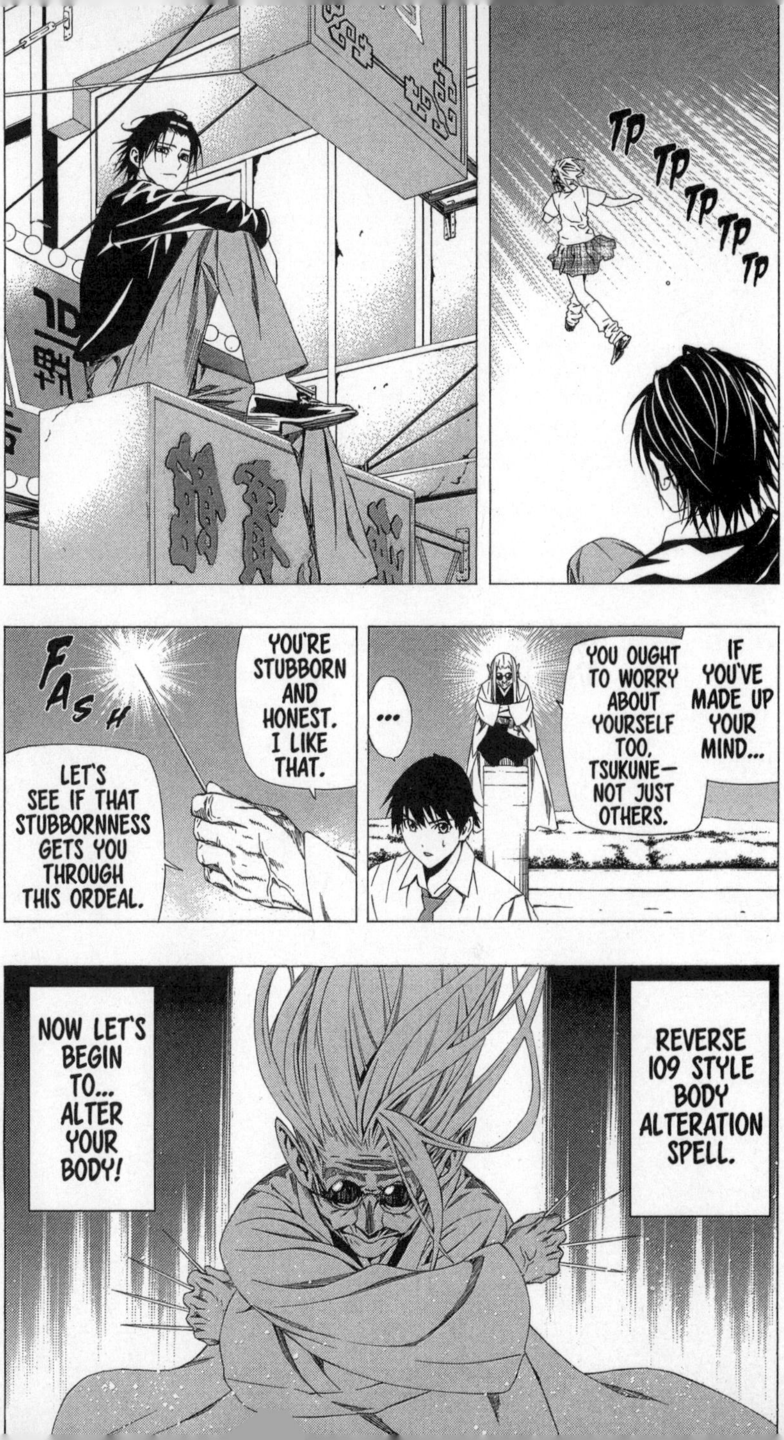
Tp Tp Tp Tp Tp
IF YOU'VE MADE UP YOUR MIND...
YOU OUGHT TO WORRY ABOUT YOURSELF TOO, TSUKUNE— NOT JUST OTHERS.
...
YOU'RE STUBBORN AND HONEST. I LIKE THAT.
FASH
LET'S SEE IF THAT STUBBORNNESS GETS YOU THROUGH THIS ORDEAL.
REVERSE 109 STYLE BODY ALTERATION SPELL.
NOW LET'S BEGIN TO... ALTER YOUR BODY!

40: Scenes #2

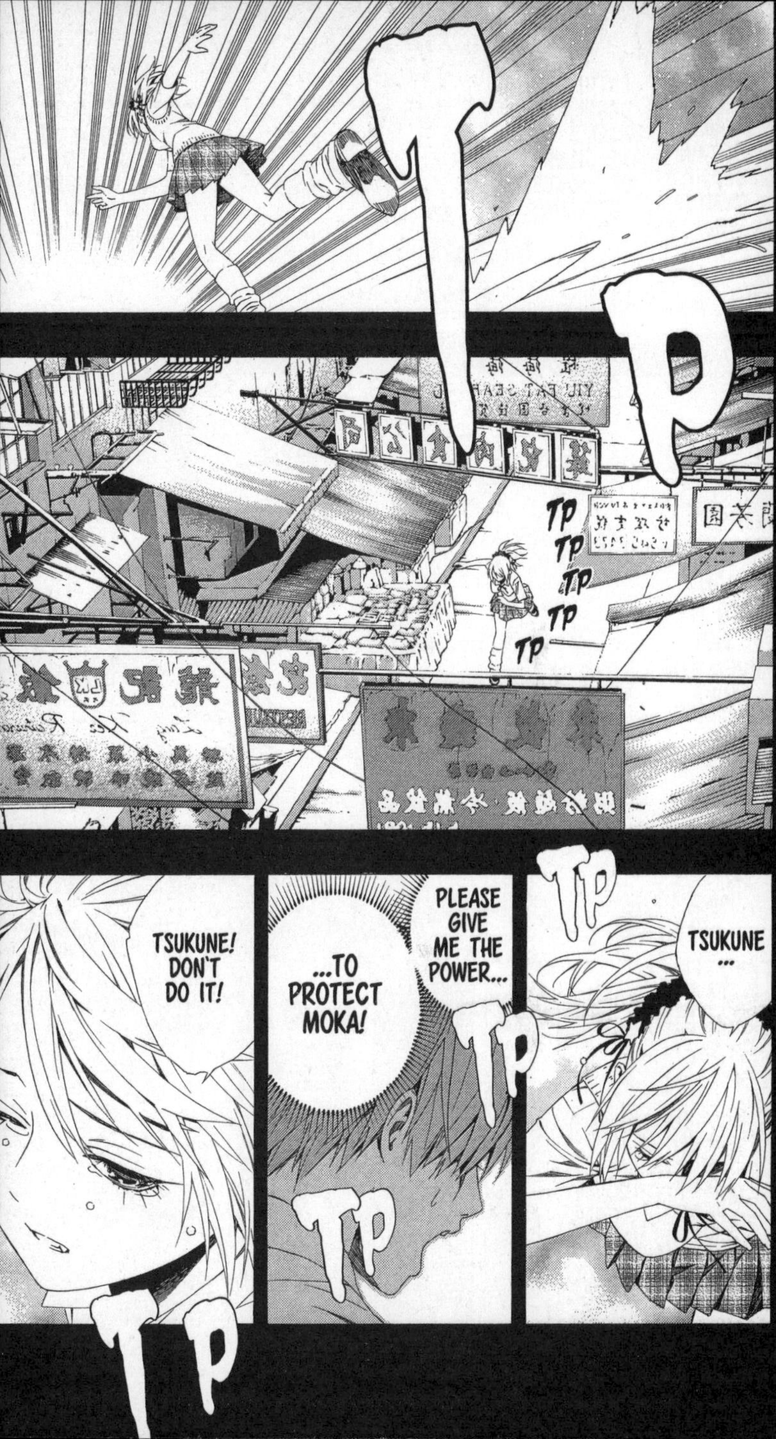
TP
TP
TP
TP
TP
TP
TP
TSUKUNE ...
PLEASE GIVE ME THE POWER...
...TO PROTECT MOKA!
TP
TP
TSUKUNE! DON'T DO IT!
TP

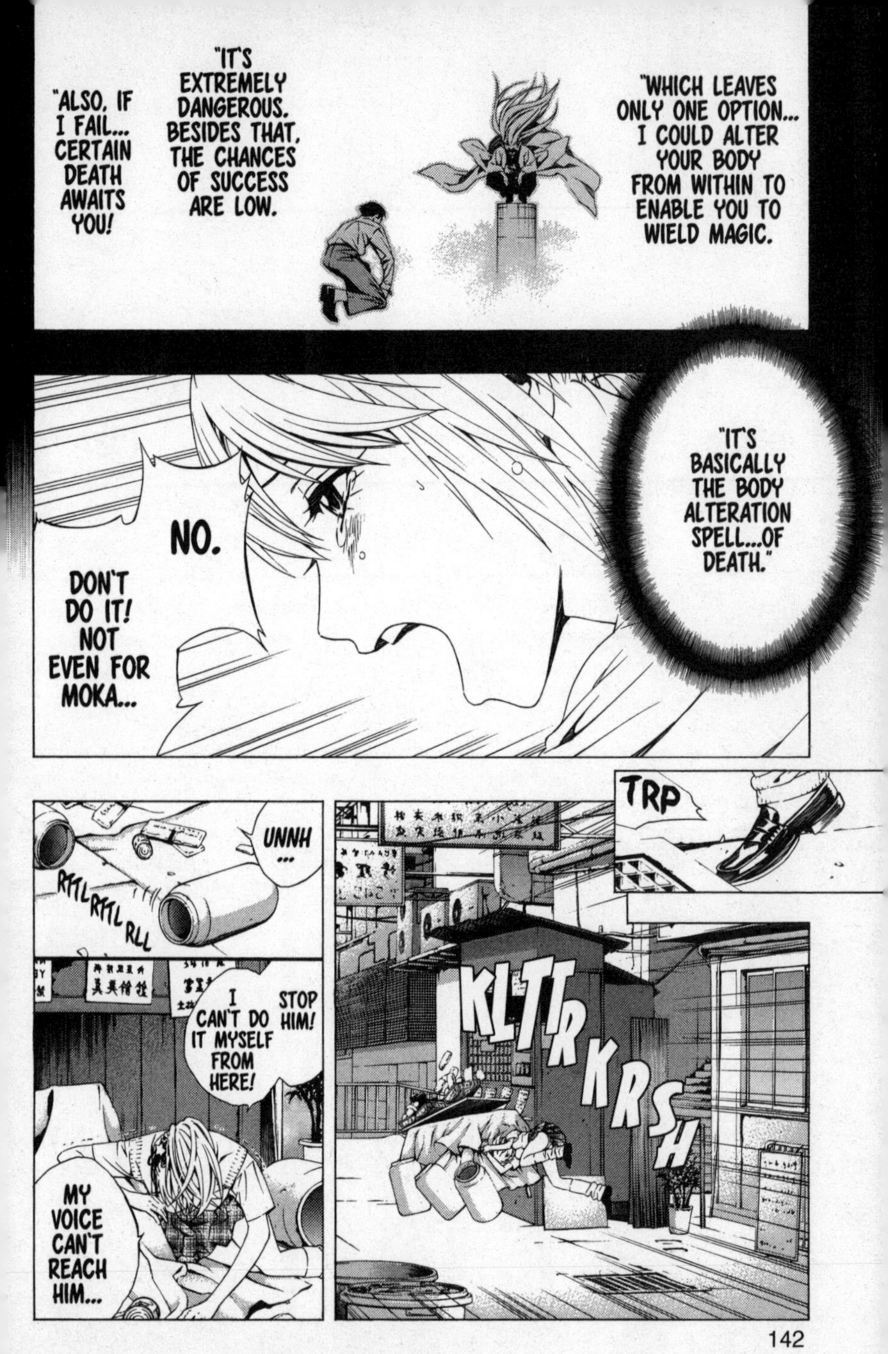
"WHICH LEAVES ONLY ONE OPTION... I COULD ALTER YOUR BODY FROM WITHIN TO ENABLE YOU TO WIELD MAGIC.
"IT'S EXTREMELY DANGEROUS. BESIDES THAT, THE CHANCES OF SUCCESS ARE LOW.
"ALSO, IF I FAIL... CERTAIN DEATH AWAITS YOU!
"IT'S BASICALLY THE BODY ALTERATION SPELL...OF DEATH."
NO.
DON'T DO IT! NOT EVEN FOR MOKA...
TRP
KLTTR KRSH
UNNH...
RTTL RTTL RLL
STOP HIM!
I CAN'T DO IT MYSELF FROM HERE!
MY VOICE CAN'T REACH HIM...

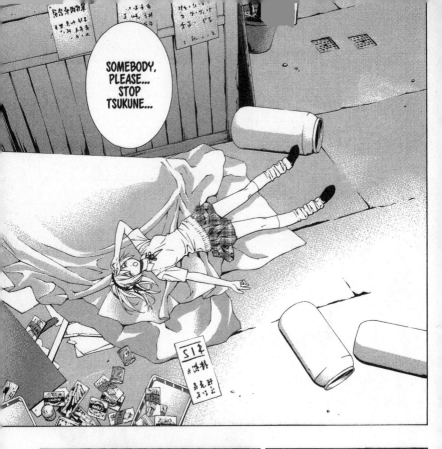

SOMEBODY, PLEASE... STOP TSUKUNE...

RLL RLL RLL

TUP

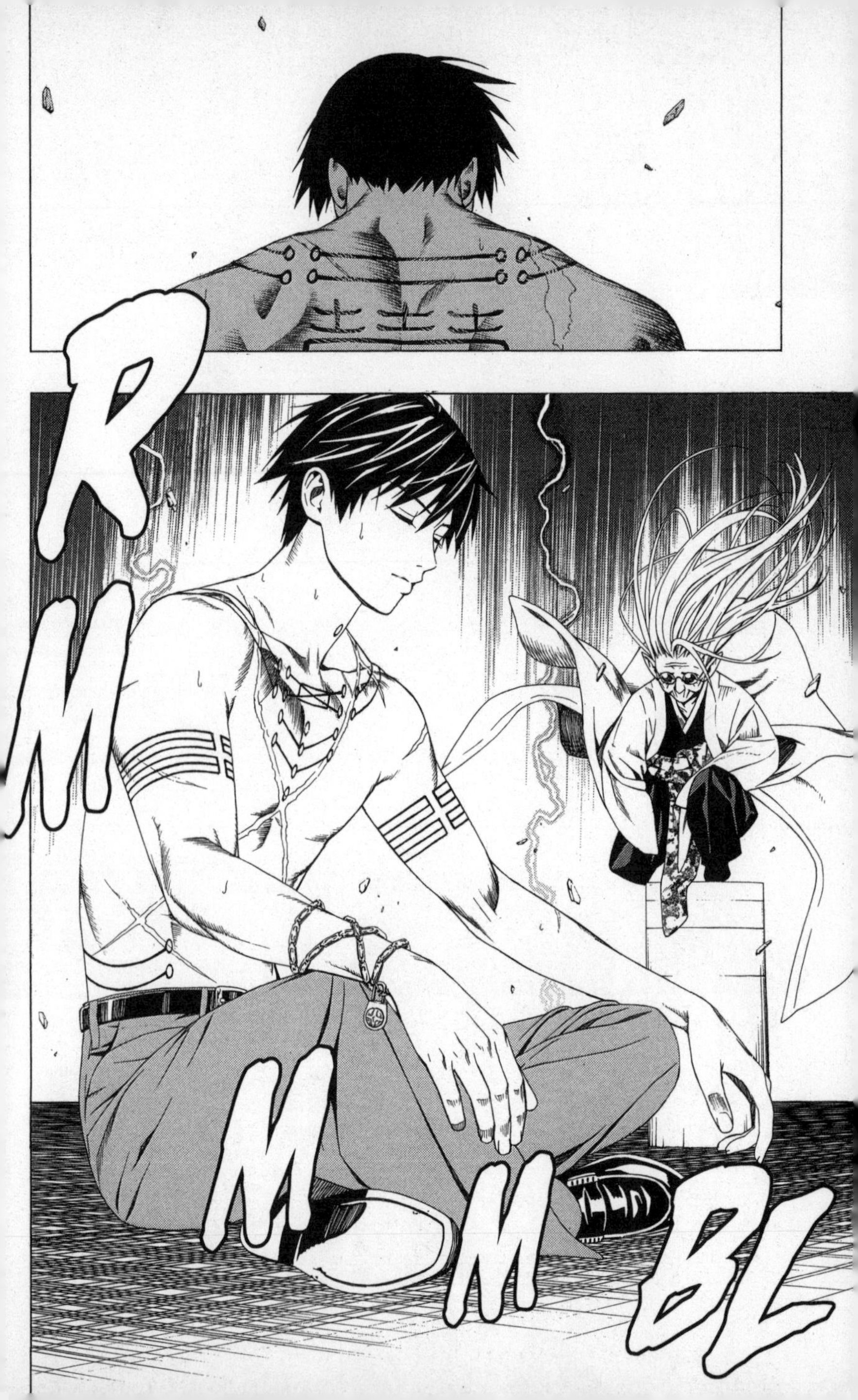
RMMMBL

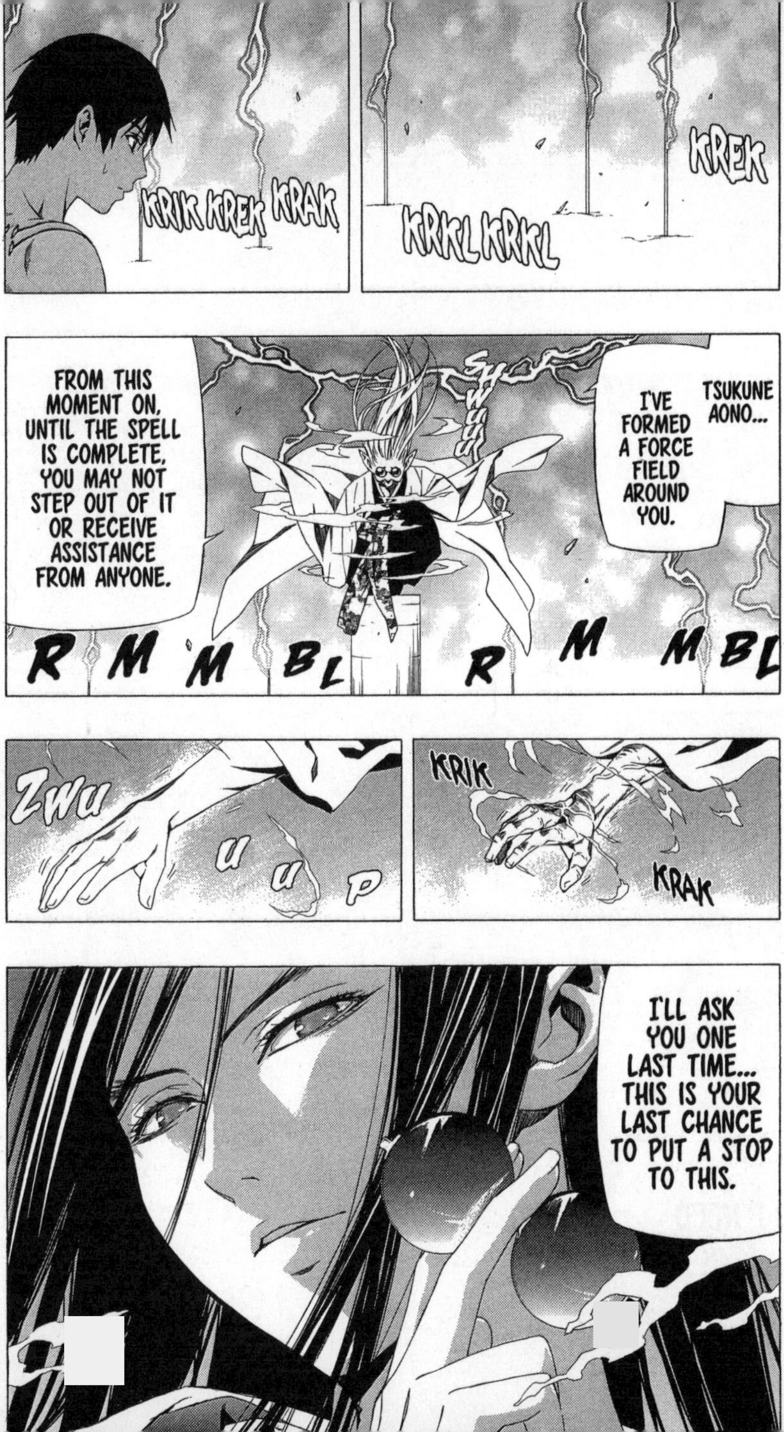
KREK
KRKL KRKL
KRIK KREK KRAK
TSUKUNE AONO...
I'VE FORMED A FORCE FIELD AROUND YOU.
SHWUUU
FROM THIS MOMENT ON, UNTIL THE SPELL IS COMPLETE, YOU MAY NOT STEP OUT OF IT OR RECEIVE ASSISTANCE FROM ANYONE.
RMMBL RMMBL
KRIK
KRAK
ZWUUUP
I'LL ASK YOU ONE LAST TIME... THIS IS YOUR LAST CHANCE TO PUT A STOP TO THIS.

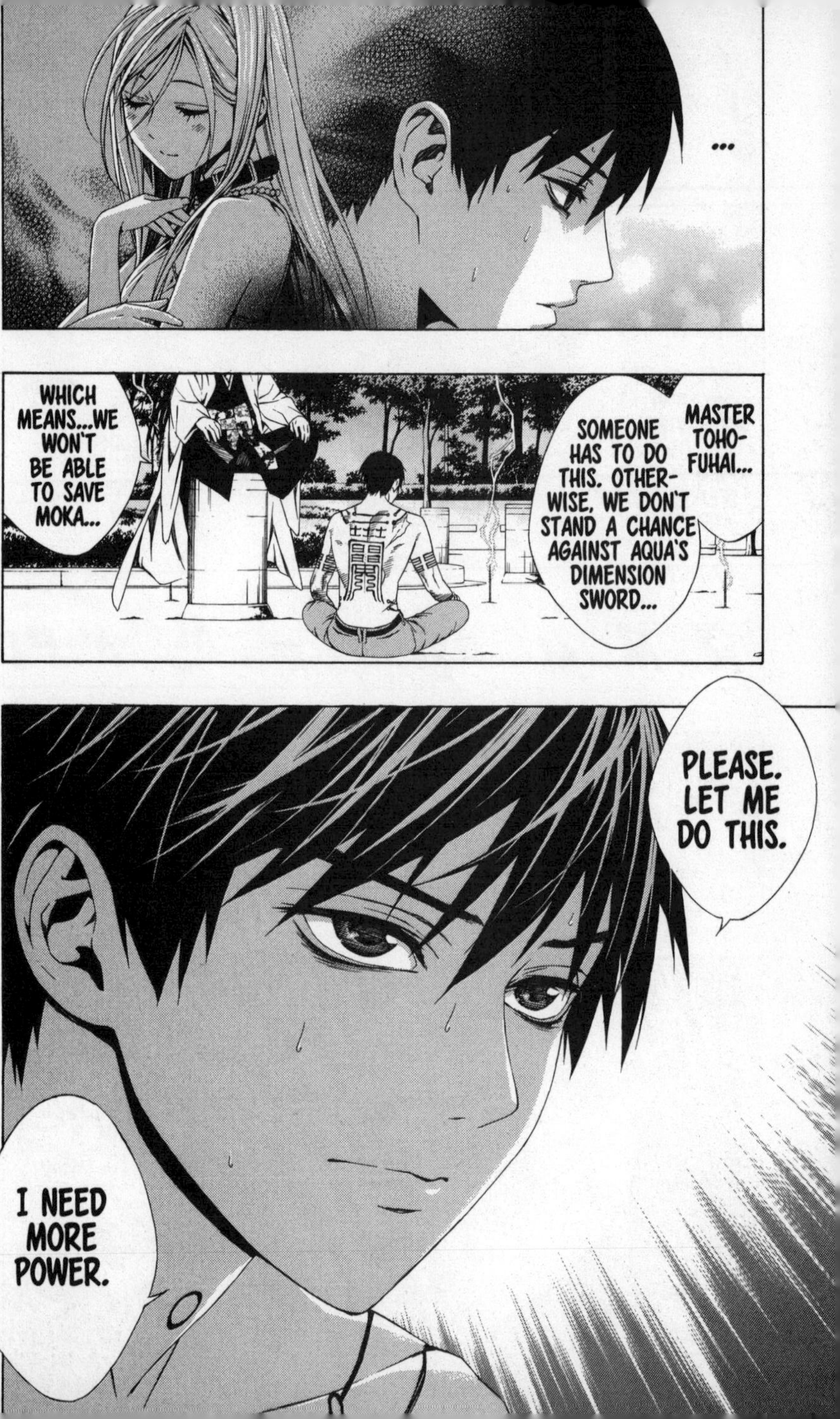
...
MASTER TOHO-FUHAI...
SOMEONE HAS TO DO THIS. OTHERWISE, WE DON'T STAND A CHANCE AGAINST AQUA'S DIMENSION SWORD...
WHICH MEANS...WE WON'T BE ABLE TO SAVE MOKA...
PLEASE. LET ME DO THIS.
I NEED MORE POWER.

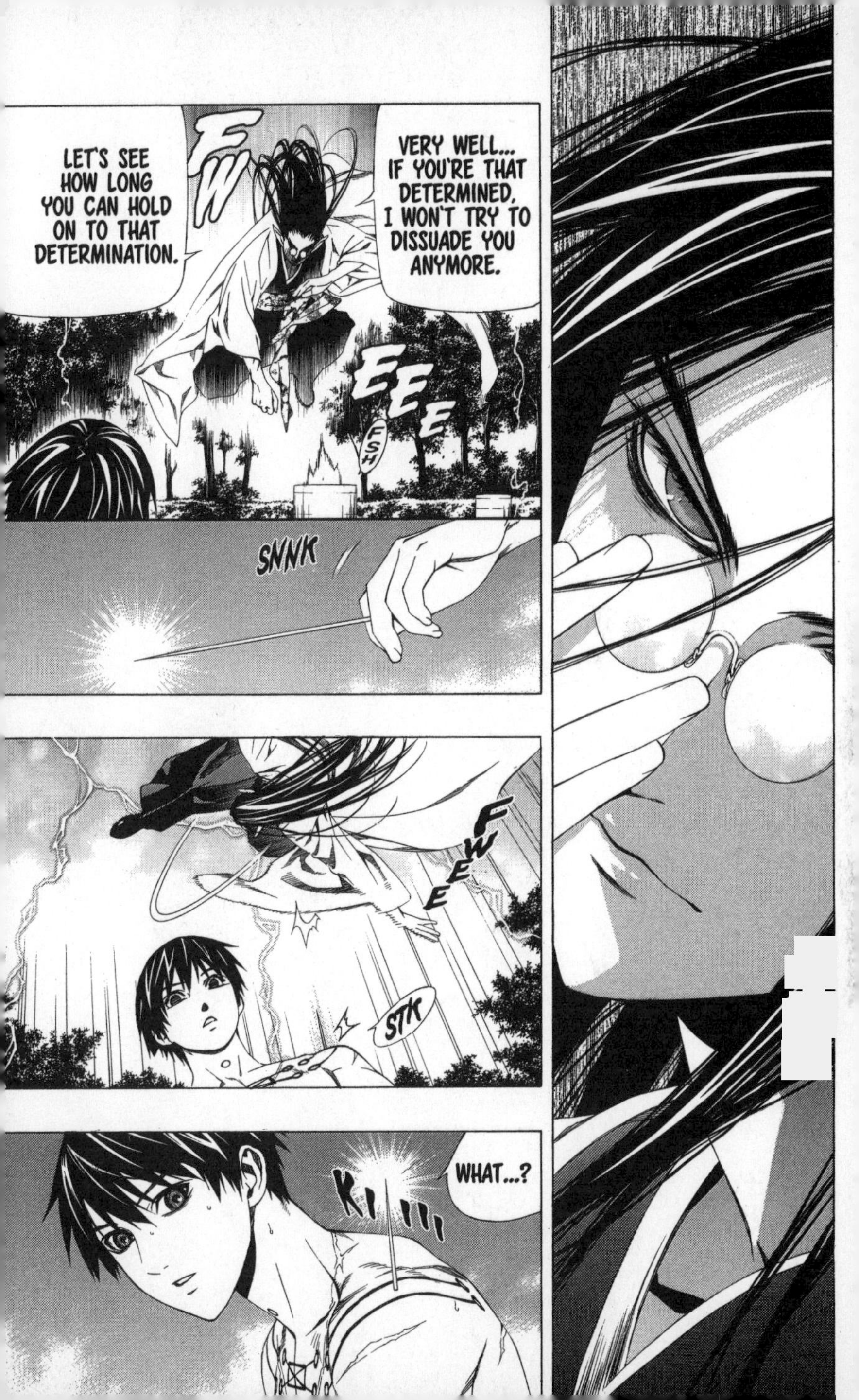
FW
VERY WELL... IF YOU'RE THAT DETERMINED, I WON'T TRY TO DISSUADE YOU ANYMORE.
LET'S SEE HOW LONG YOU CAN HOLD ON TO THAT DETERMINATION.
EEE
FSH
SNNK
FWEEE
STK
WHAT...?
KIIII

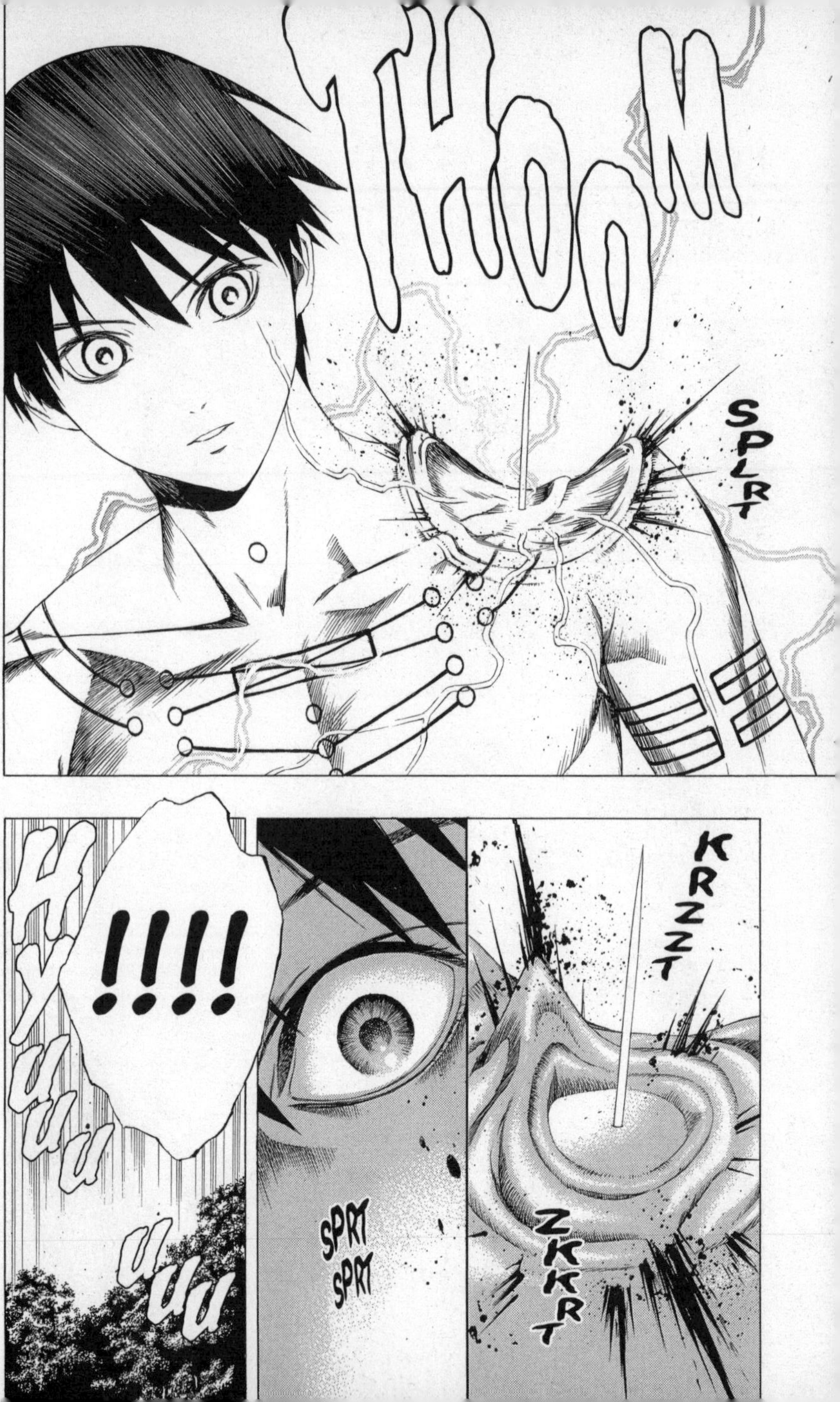
THOOM
SPLRT
KRZZZT
ZKKRT
SPRT
SPRT
!!!!
Hyuuu
uuu

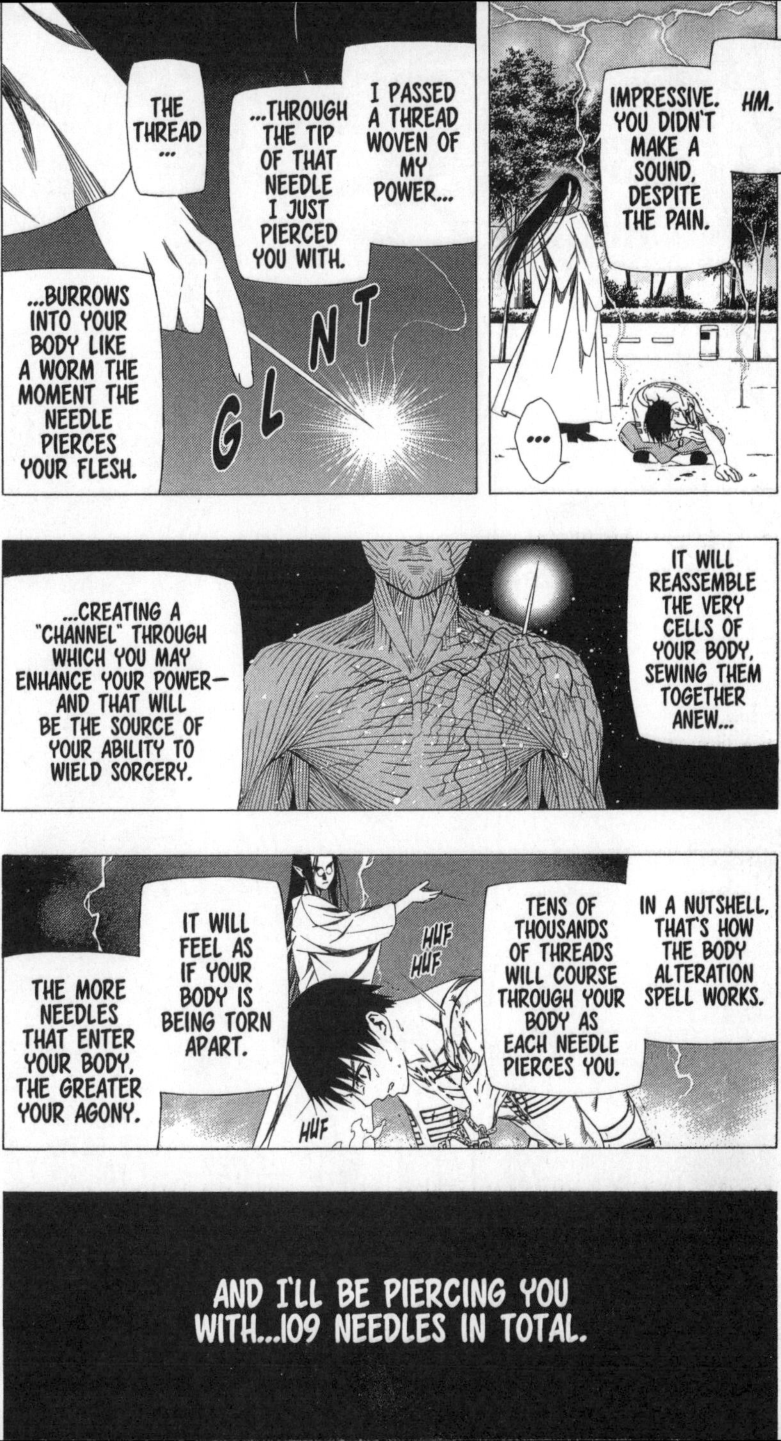
HM.
IMPRESSIVE. YOU DIDN'T MAKE A SOUND, DESPITE THE PAIN.
...
I PASSED A THREAD WOVEN OF MY POWER...
...THROUGH THE TIP OF THAT NEEDLE I JUST PIERCED YOU WITH.
THE THREAD...
GLNT
...BURROWS INTO YOUR BODY LIKE A WORM THE MOMENT THE NEEDLE PIERCES YOUR FLESH.
IT WILL REASSEMBLE THE VERY CELLS OF YOUR BODY, SEWING THEM TOGETHER ANEW...
...CREATING A "CHANNEL" THROUGH WHICH YOU MAY ENHANCE YOUR POWER—AND THAT WILL BE THE SOURCE OF YOUR ABILITY TO WIELD SORCERY.
IN A NUTSHELL, THAT'S HOW THE BODY ALTERATION SPELL WORKS.
TENS OF THOUSANDS OF THREADS WILL COURSE THROUGH YOUR BODY AS EACH NEEDLE PIERCES YOU.
HUF HUF
IT WILL FEEL AS IF YOUR BODY IS BEING TORN APART.
THE MORE NEEDLES THAT ENTER YOUR BODY, THE GREATER YOUR AGONY.
HUF
AND I'LL BE PIERCING YOU WITH...109 NEEDLES IN TOTAL.

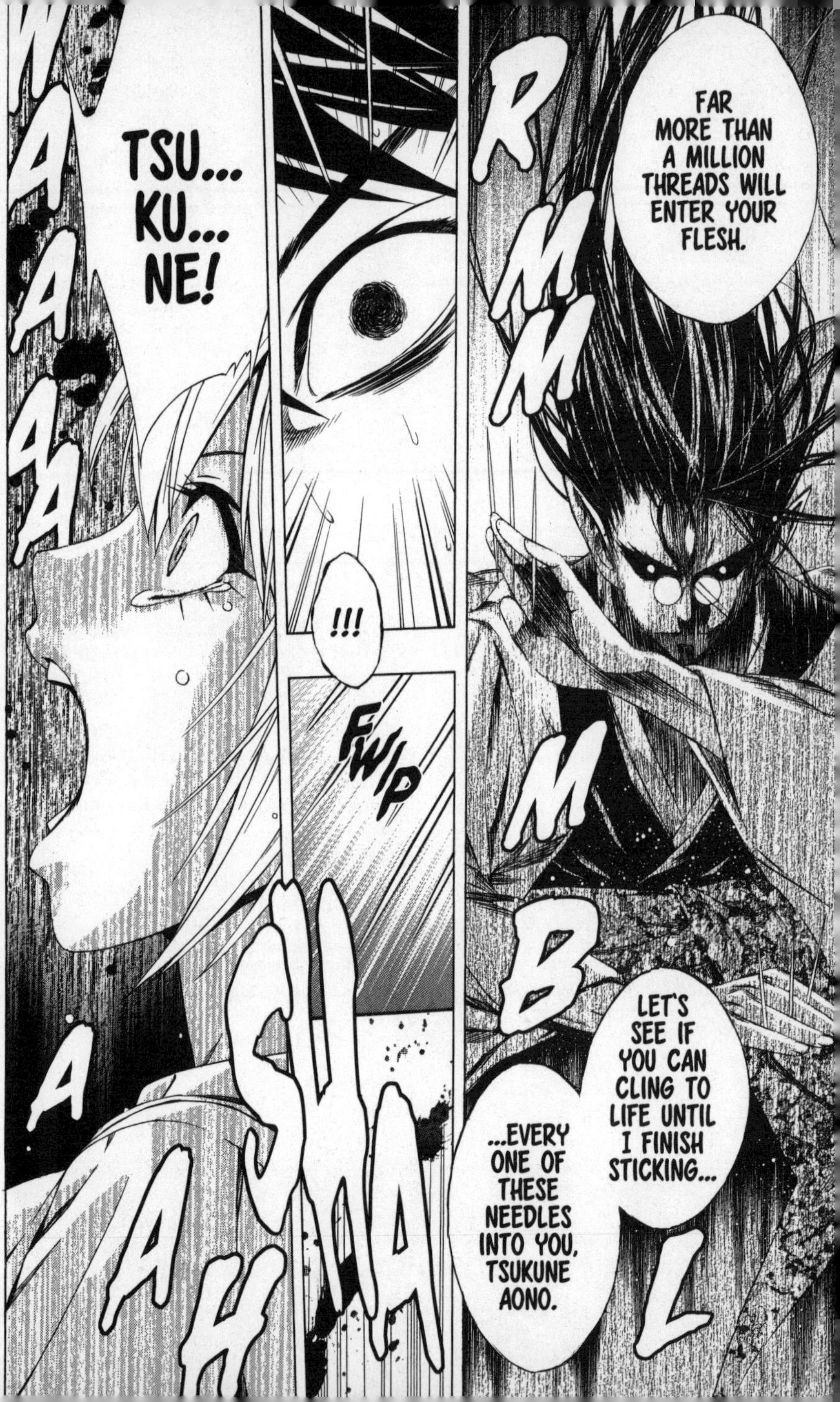
FAR MORE THAN A MILLION THREADS WILL ENTER YOUR FLESH.
RMMMBL
LET'S SEE IF YOU CAN CLING TO LIFE UNTIL I FINISH STICKING...
...EVERY ONE OF THESE NEEDLES INTO YOU, TSUKUNE AONO.
!!!
FWIP
SHAA
TSU... KU... NE!
WAAAAAAAH

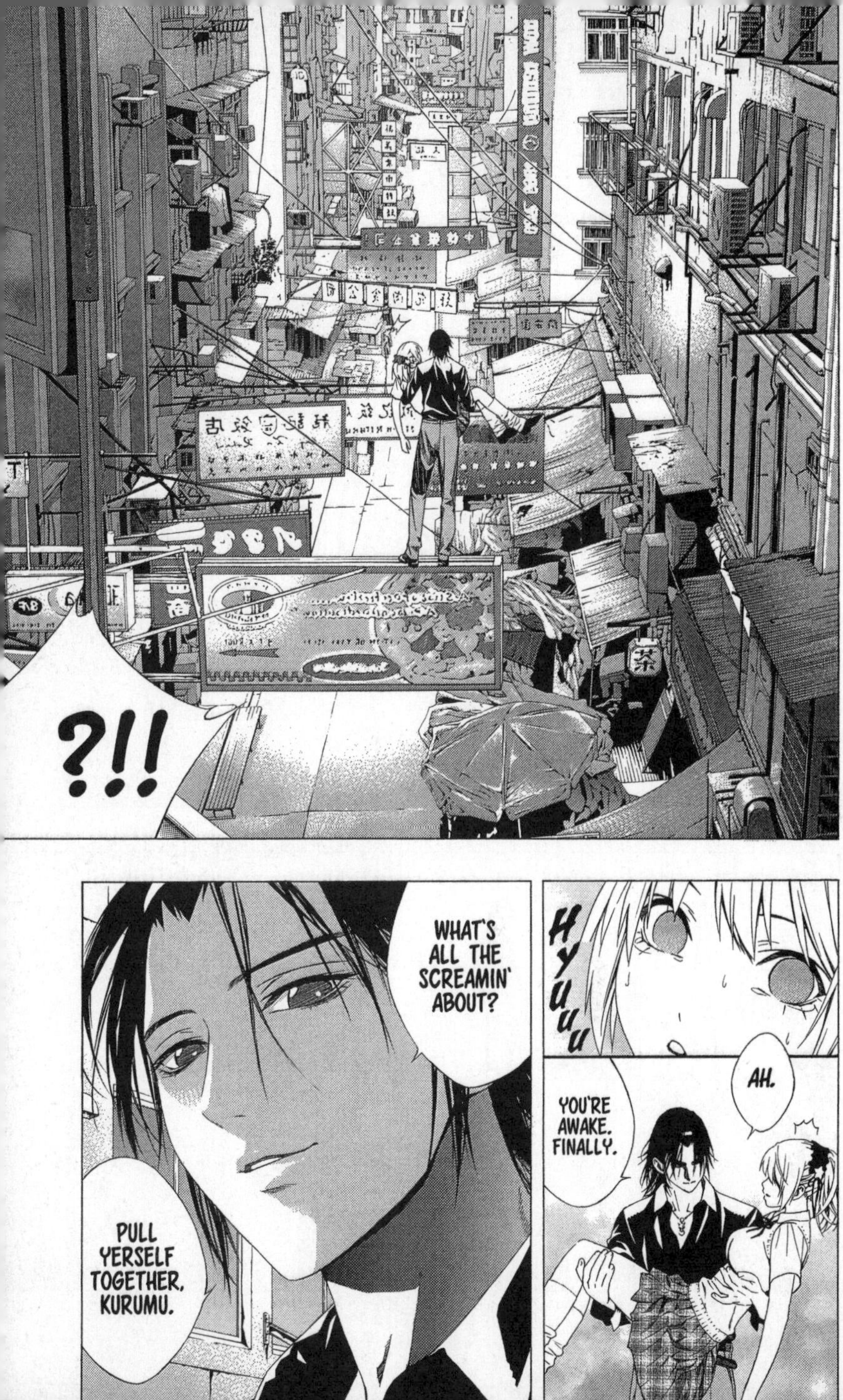

?!!
HYUUU
AH.
YOU'RE AWAKE, FINALLY.
WHAT'S ALL THE SCREAMIN' ABOUT?
PULL YERSELF TOGETHER, KURUMU.

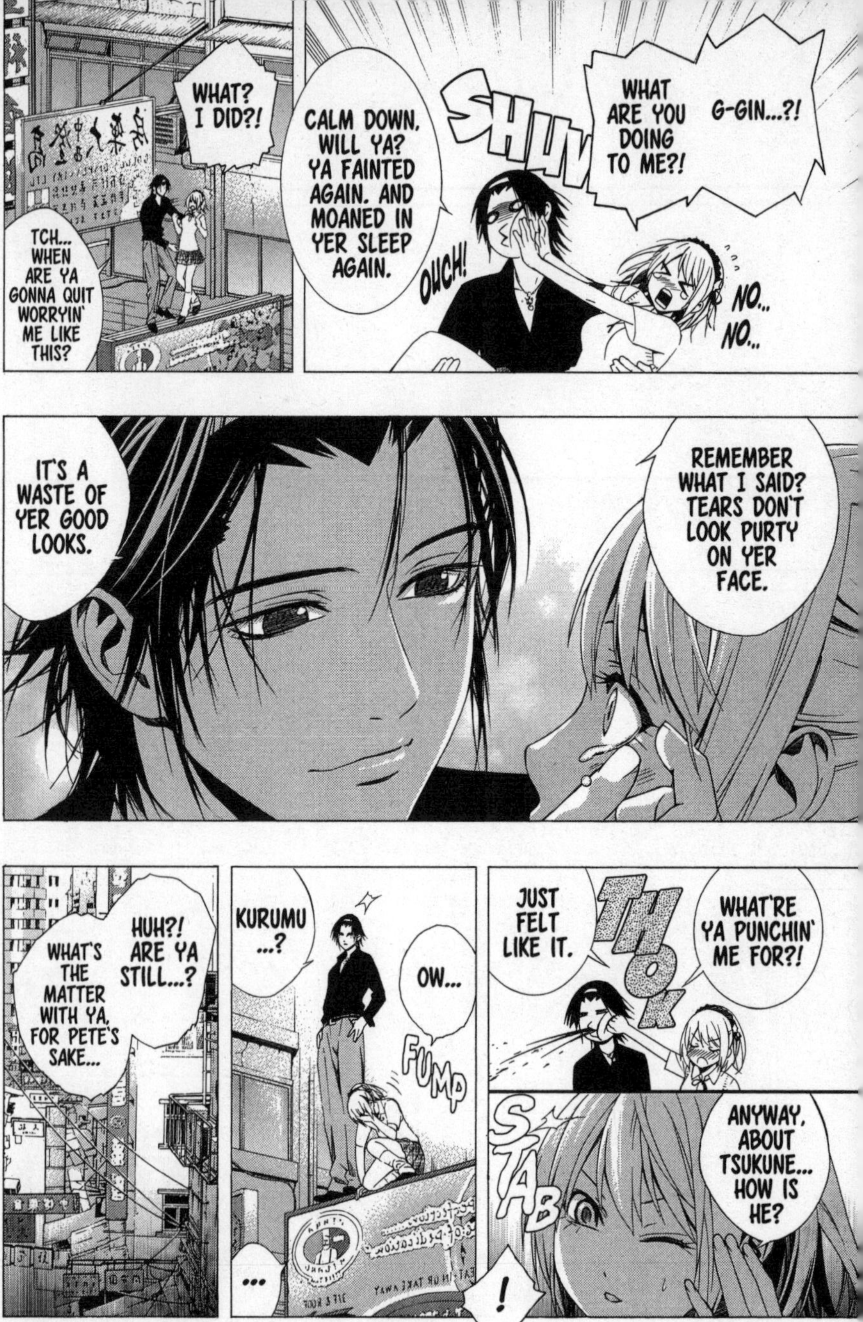
G-GIN...?!
WHAT ARE YOU DOING TO ME?!
SHUV
NO... NO...
OUCH!
CALM DOWN, WILL YA? YA FAINTED AGAIN. AND MOANED IN YER SLEEP AGAIN.
WHAT? I DID?!
TCH... WHEN ARE YA GONNA QUIT WORRYIN' ME LIKE THIS?
REMEMBER WHAT I SAID? TEARS DON'T LOOK PURTY ON YER FACE.
IT'S A WASTE OF YER GOOD LOOKS.
WHAT'RE YA PUNCHIN' ME FOR?!
THOK
JUST FELT LIKE IT.
ANYWAY, ABOUT TSUKUNE... HOW IS HE?
STAB
!
OW...
KURUMU ...?
FUMP
...
HUH?! ARE YA STILL...?
WHAT'S THE MATTER WITH YA, FOR PETE'S SAKE...

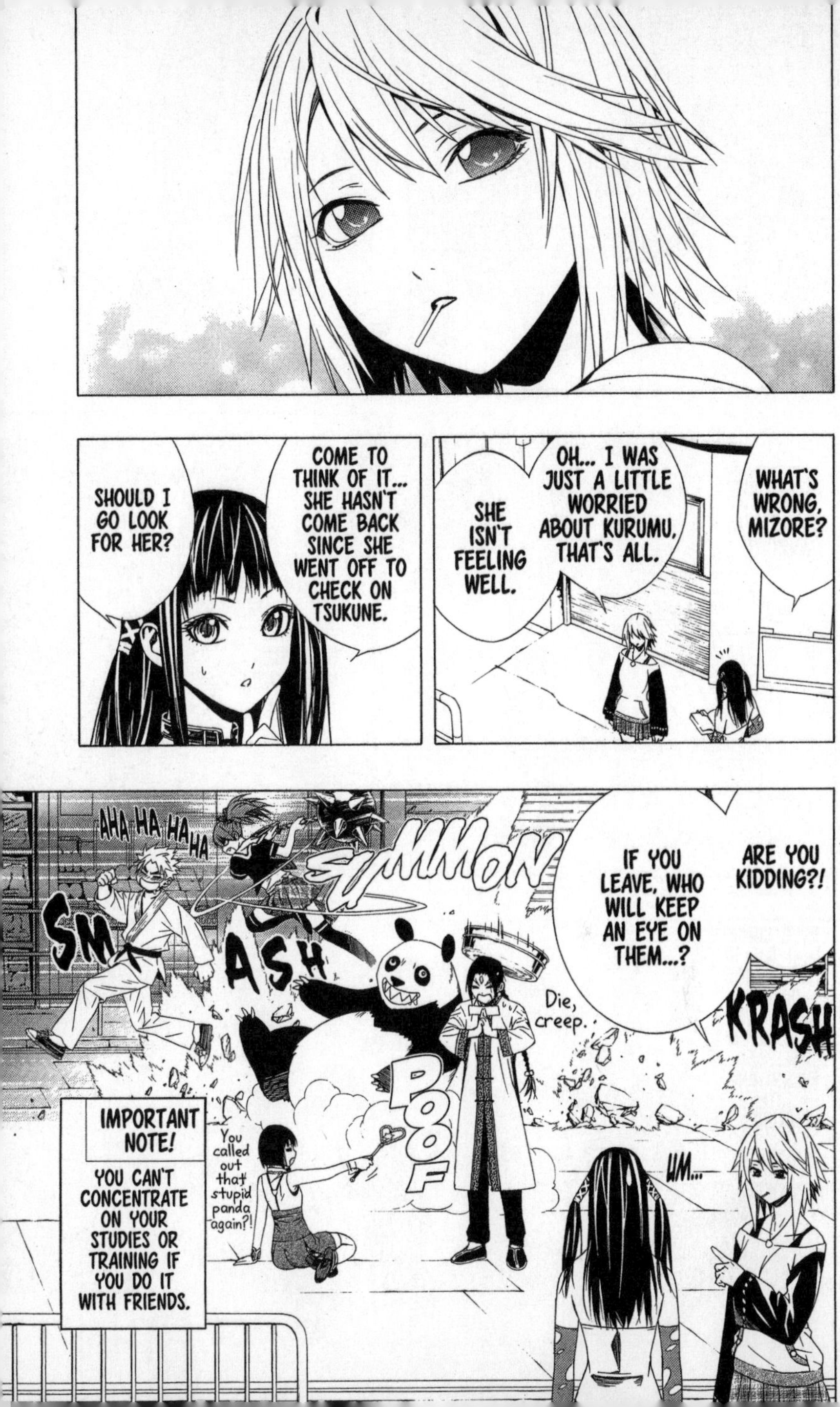
WHAT'S WRONG, MIZORE?
OH... I WAS JUST A LITTLE WORRIED ABOUT KURUMU, THAT'S ALL.
SHE ISN'T FEELING WELL.
COME TO THINK OF IT... SHE HASN'T COME BACK SINCE SHE WENT OFF TO CHECK ON TSUKUNE.
SHOULD I GO LOOK FOR HER?
ARE YOU KIDDING?!
IF YOU LEAVE, WHO WILL KEEP AN EYE ON THEM...?
KRASH
SUMMON
Die, creep.
AHA HA HA HA
SMASH
POOF
UM...
You called out that stupid panda again?!
IMPORTANT NOTE!
YOU CAN'T CONCENTRATE ON YOUR STUDIES OR TRAINING IF YOU DO IT WITH FRIENDS.

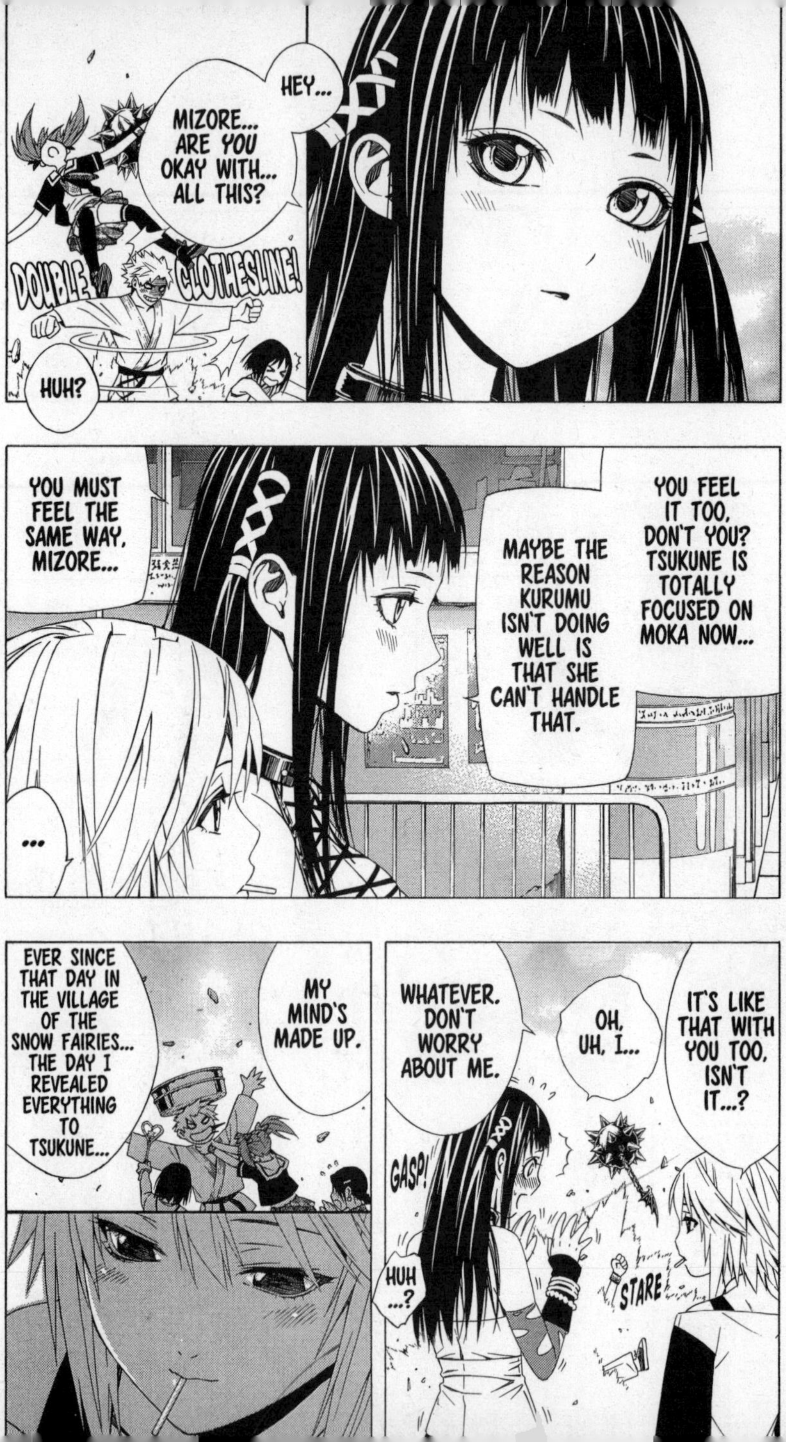
HEY... MIZORE... ARE YOU OKAY WITH... ALL THIS?
DOUBLE CLOTHESLINE!
HUH?
YOU FEEL IT TOO, DON'T YOU? TSUKUNE IS TOTALLY FOCUSED ON MOKA NOW...
MAYBE THE REASON KURUMU ISN'T DOING WELL IS THAT SHE CAN'T HANDLE THAT.
YOU MUST FEEL THE SAME WAY, MIZORE...
...
IT'S LIKE THAT WITH YOU TOO, ISN'T IT...?
OH, UH, I...
WHATEVER. DON'T WORRY ABOUT ME.
GASP!
STARE
HUH ...?
MY MIND'S MADE UP.
EVER SINCE THAT DAY IN THE VILLAGE OF THE SNOW FAIRIES... THE DAY I REVEALED EVERYTHING TO TSUKUNE...

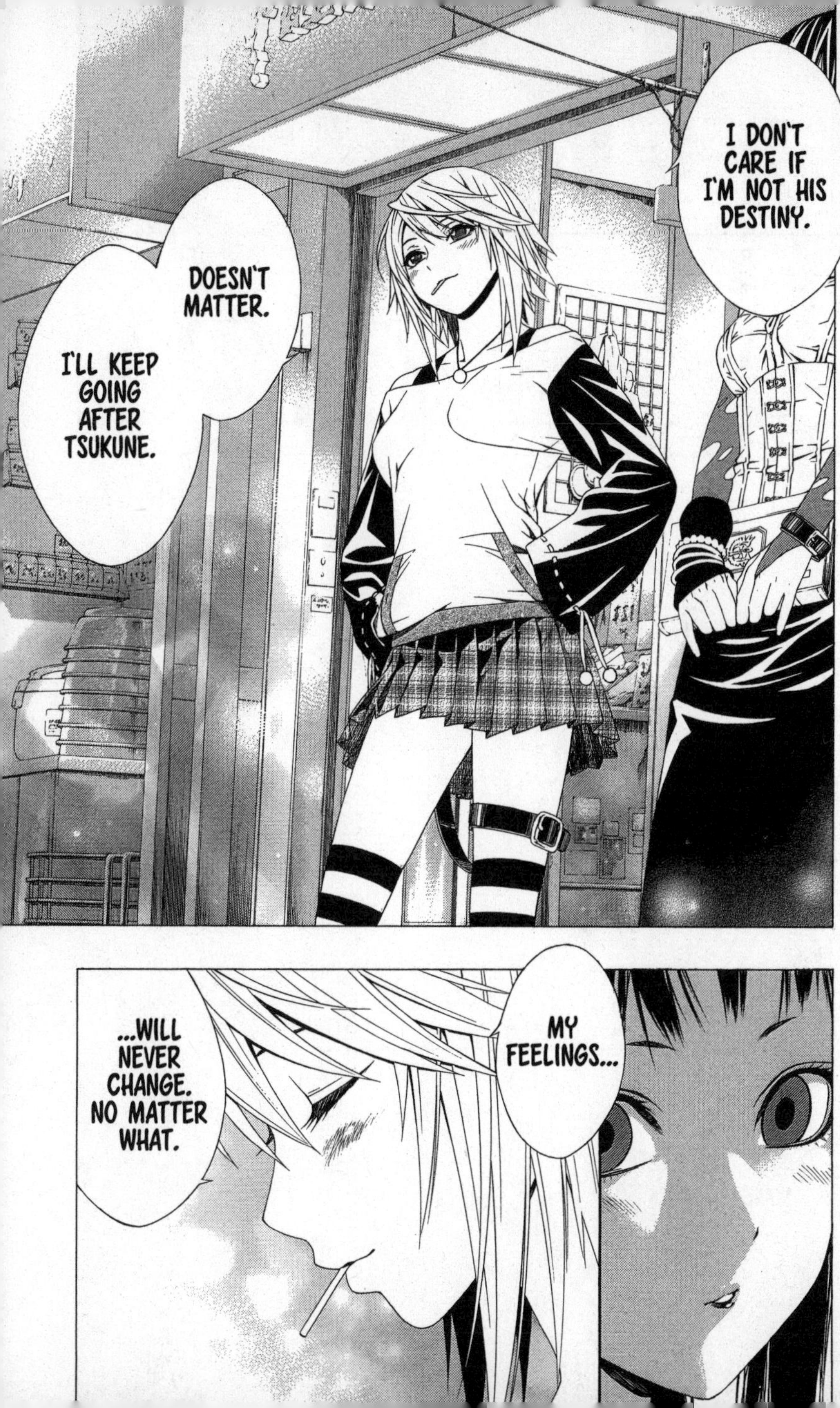
I DON'T CARE IF I'M NOT HIS DESTINY.
DOESN'T MATTER.
I'LL KEEP GOING AFTER TSUKUNE.
MY FEELINGS...
...WILL NEVER CHANGE. NO MATTER WHAT.

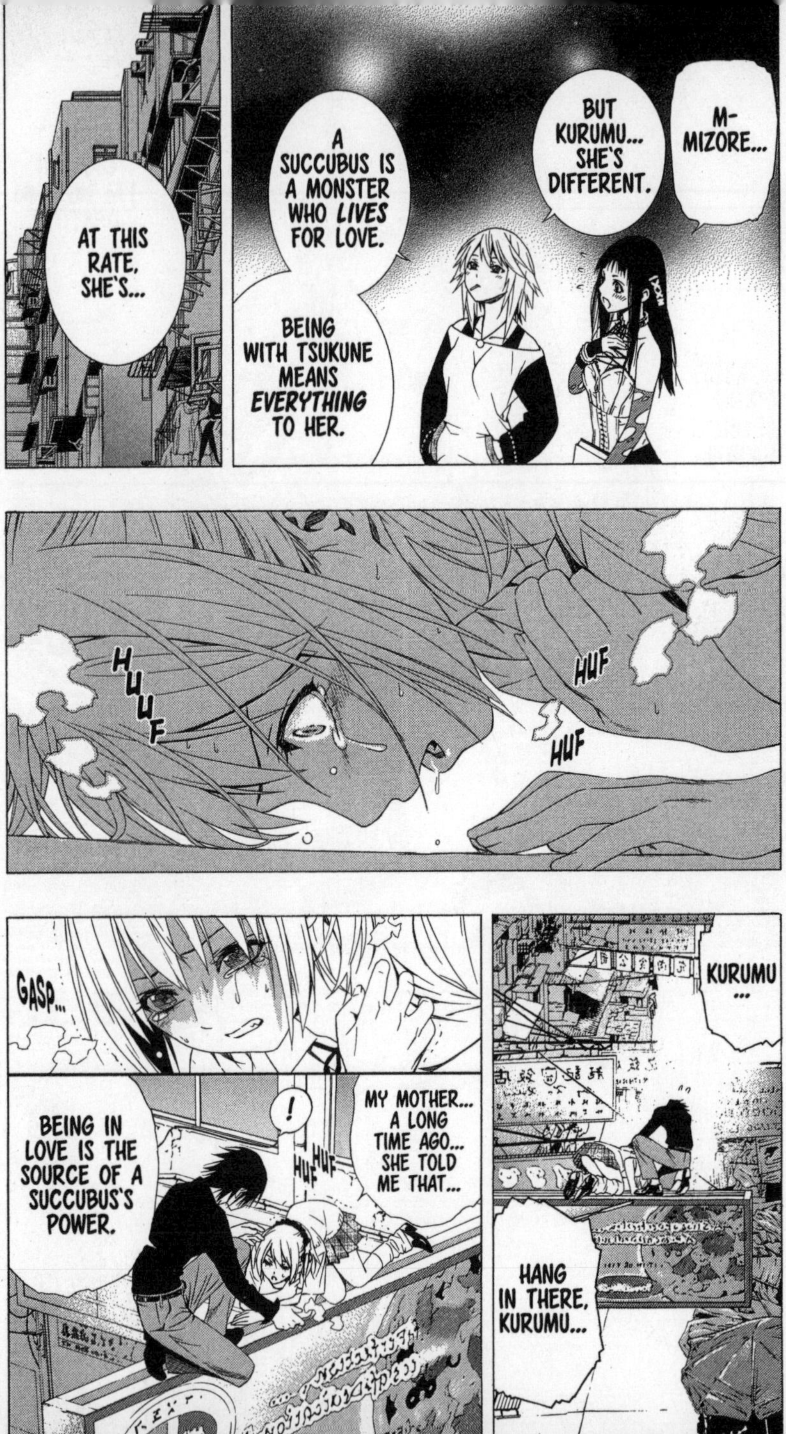
M-MIZORE...
BUT KURUMU... SHE'S DIFFERENT.
A SUCCUBUS IS A MONSTER WHO *LIVES* FOR LOVE.
BEING WITH TSUKUNE MEANS *EVERYTHING* TO HER.
AT THIS RATE, SHE'S...
HUF
HUF
HUUF
KURUMU ...
HANG IN THERE, KURUMU...
GASP...
MY MOTHER... A LONG TIME AGO... SHE TOLD ME THAT...
!
HUF HUF
BEING IN LOVE IS THE SOURCE OF A SUCCUBUS'S POWER.

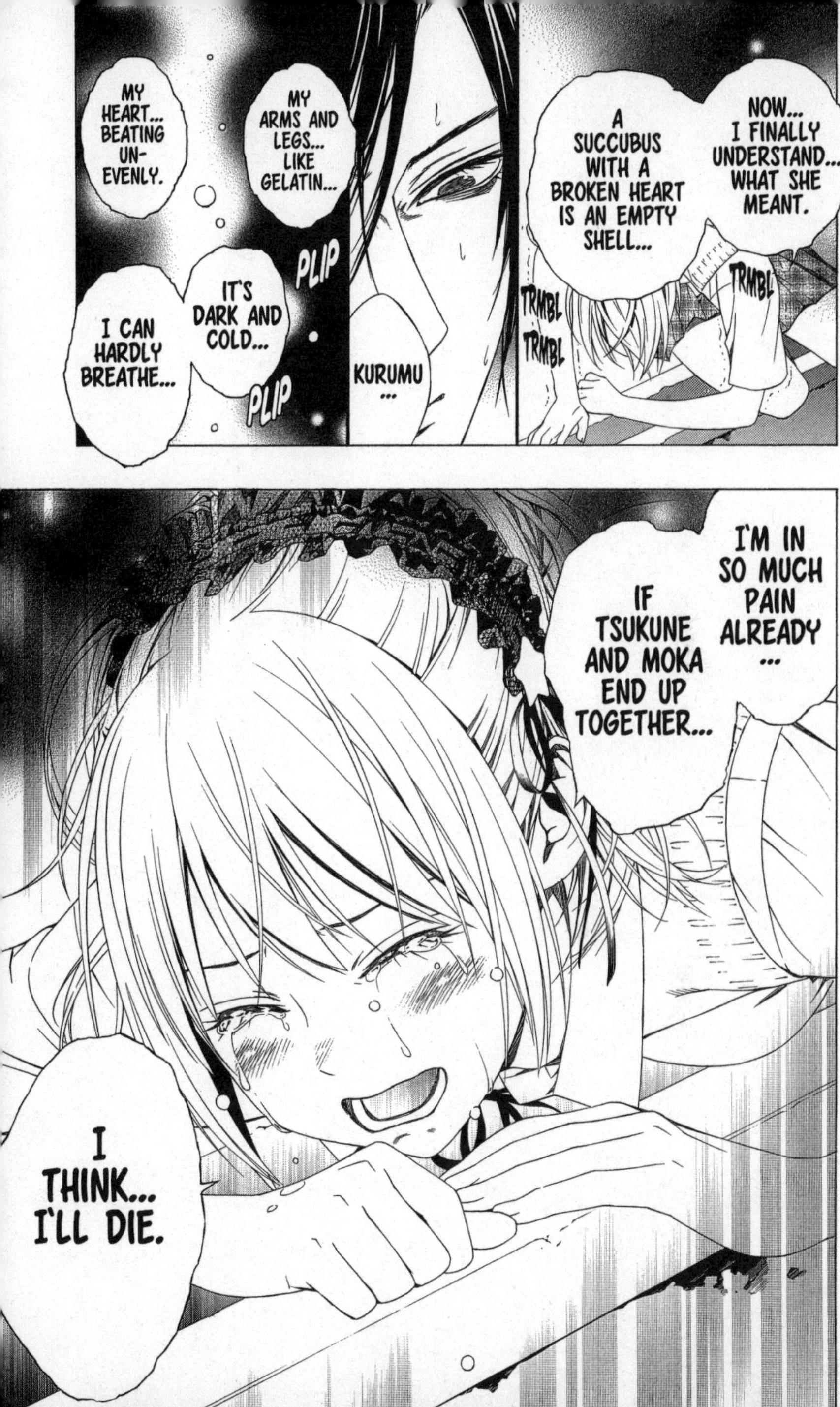
NOW... I FINALLY UNDERSTAND... WHAT SHE MEANT.
A SUCCUBUS WITH A BROKEN HEART IS AN EMPTY SHELL...
TRMBL
TRMBL
TRMBL
KURUMU...
MY ARMS AND LEGS... LIKE GELATIN...
MY HEART... BEATING UN-EVENLY.
PLIP
IT'S DARK AND COLD...
PLIP
I CAN HARDLY BREATHE...
I'M IN SO MUCH PAIN ALREADY...
IF TSUKUNE AND MOKA END UP TOGETHER...
I THINK... I'LL DIE.

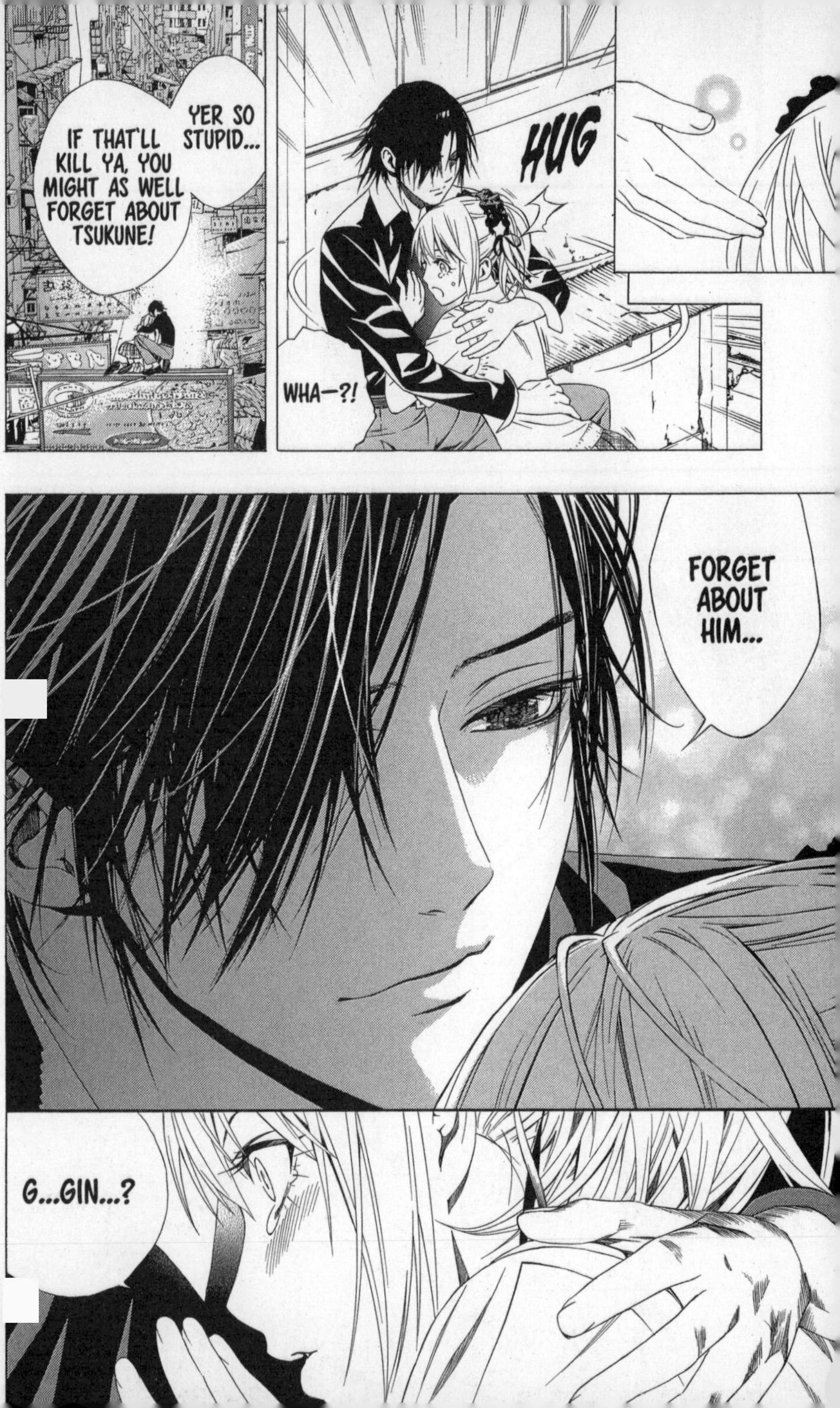
HUG
WHA—?!
YER SO STUPID...
IF THAT'LL KILL YA, YOU MIGHT AS WELL FORGET ABOUT TSUKUNE!
FORGET ABOUT HIM...
G...GIN...?

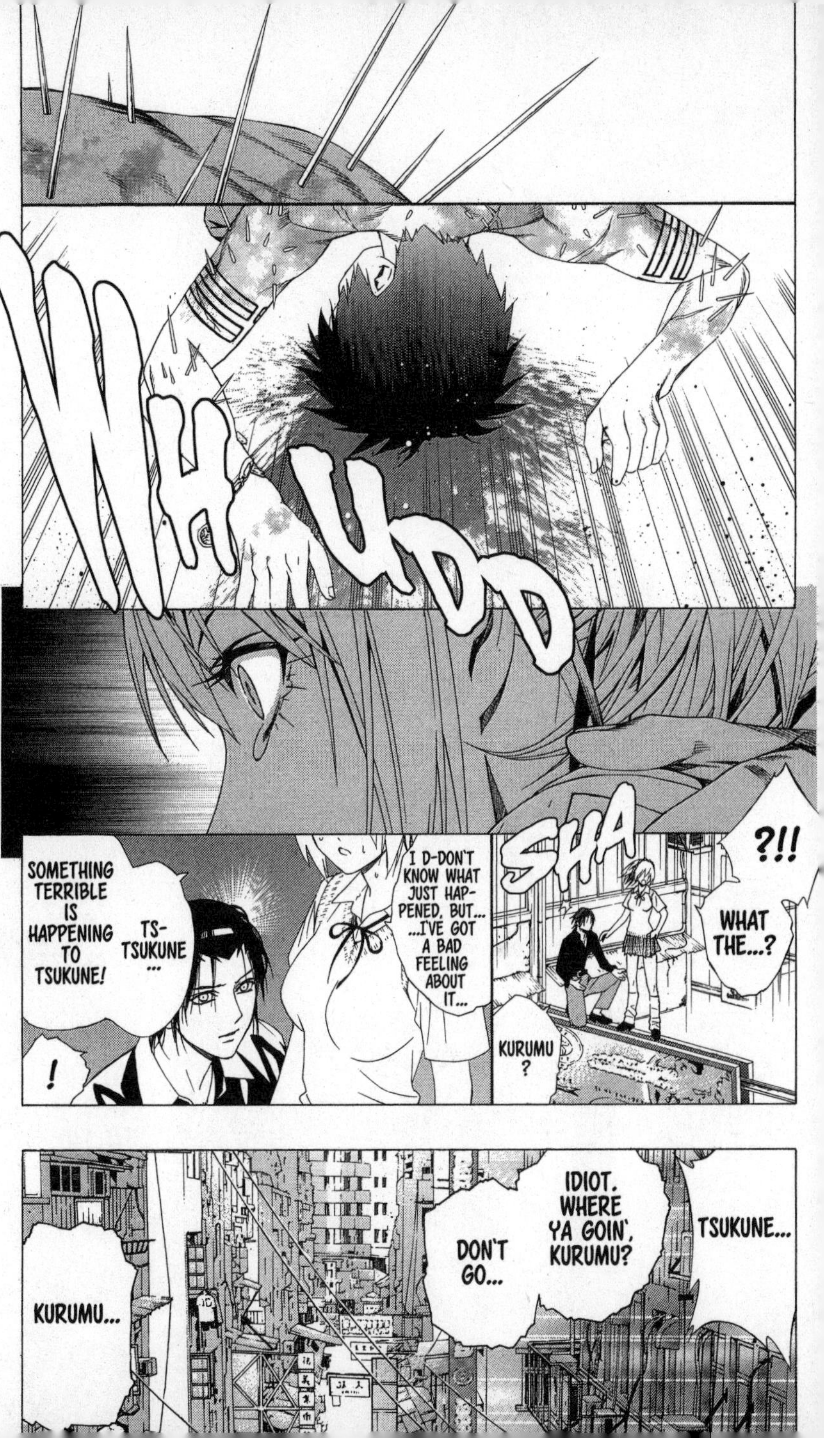
WHUDD
?!!
WHAT THE...?
SHA
KURUMU?
I D-DON'T KNOW WHAT JUST HAPPENED, BUT... ...I'VE GOT A BAD FEELING ABOUT IT...
TS-TSUKUNE...
SOMETHING TERRIBLE IS HAPPENING TO TSUKUNE!
!
TSUKUNE...
IDIOT. WHERE YA GOIN', KURUMU?
DON'T GO...
KURUMU...

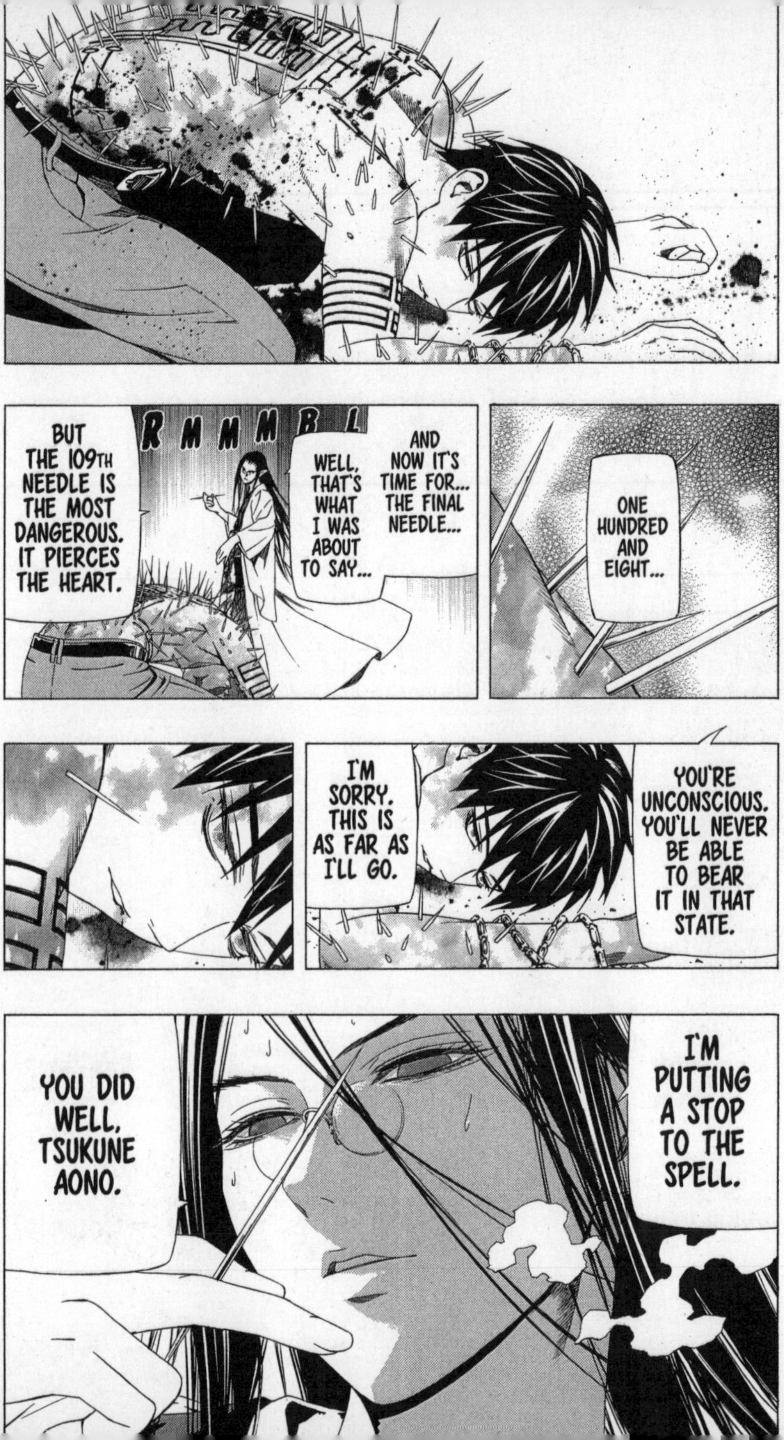
ONE HUNDRED AND EIGHT...
AND NOW IT'S TIME FOR... THE FINAL NEEDLE...
RMMMBL
WELL, THAT'S WHAT I WAS ABOUT TO SAY...
BUT THE 109TH NEEDLE IS THE MOST DANGEROUS. IT PIERCES THE HEART.
YOU'RE UNCONSCIOUS. YOU'LL NEVER BE ABLE TO BEAR IT IN THAT STATE.
I'M SORRY. THIS IS AS FAR AS I'LL GO.
I'M PUTTING A STOP TO THE SPELL.
YOU DID WELL, TSUKUNE AONO.

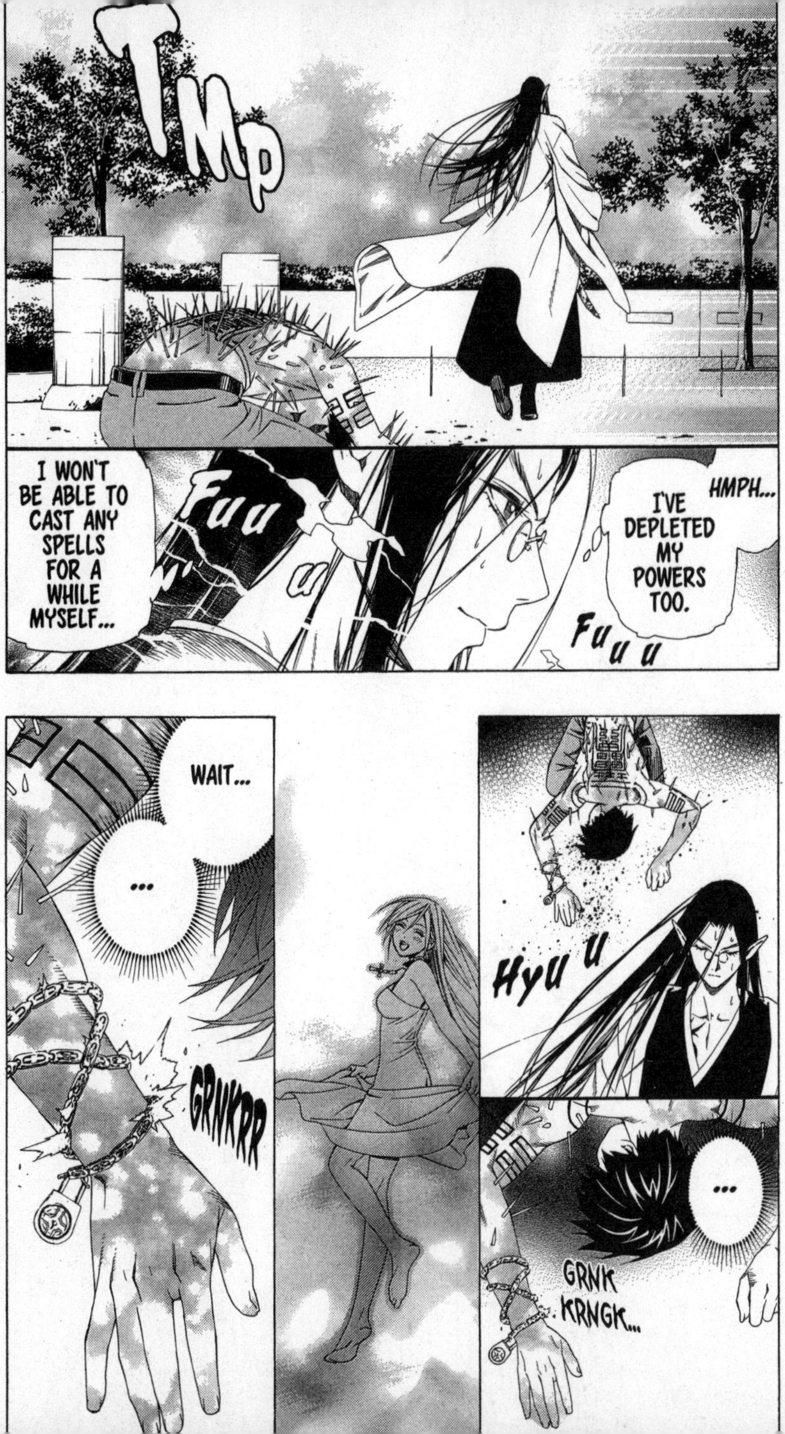
TMP
HMPH...
I'VE DEPLETED MY POWERS TOO.
FUUU
FUUU
I WON'T BE ABLE TO CAST ANY SPELLS FOR A WHILE MYSELF...
HYUU
...
GRNK KRNGK...
WAIT...
...
GRNKRR

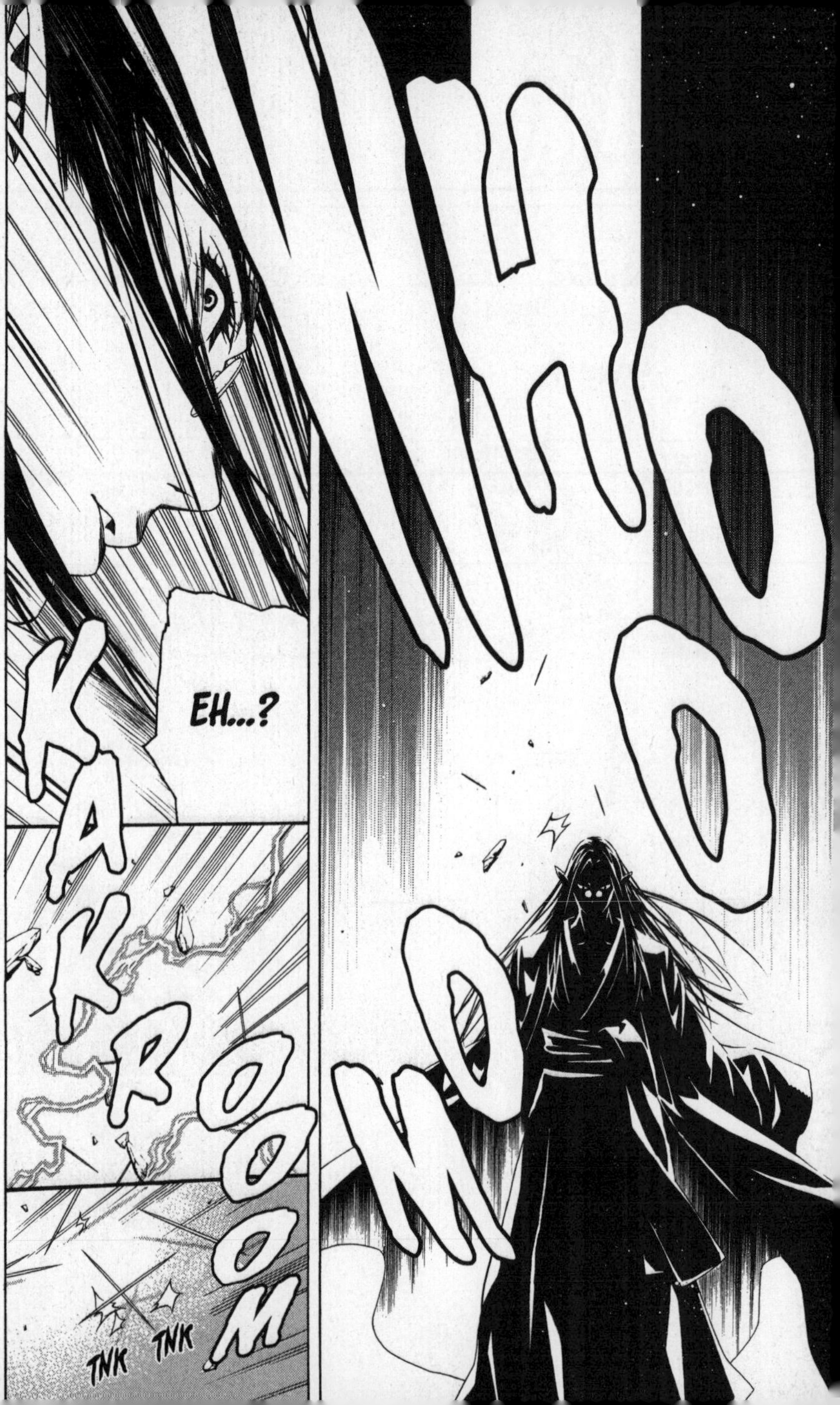
WHOOOM
EH...?
KAKROOOM
TNK
TNK

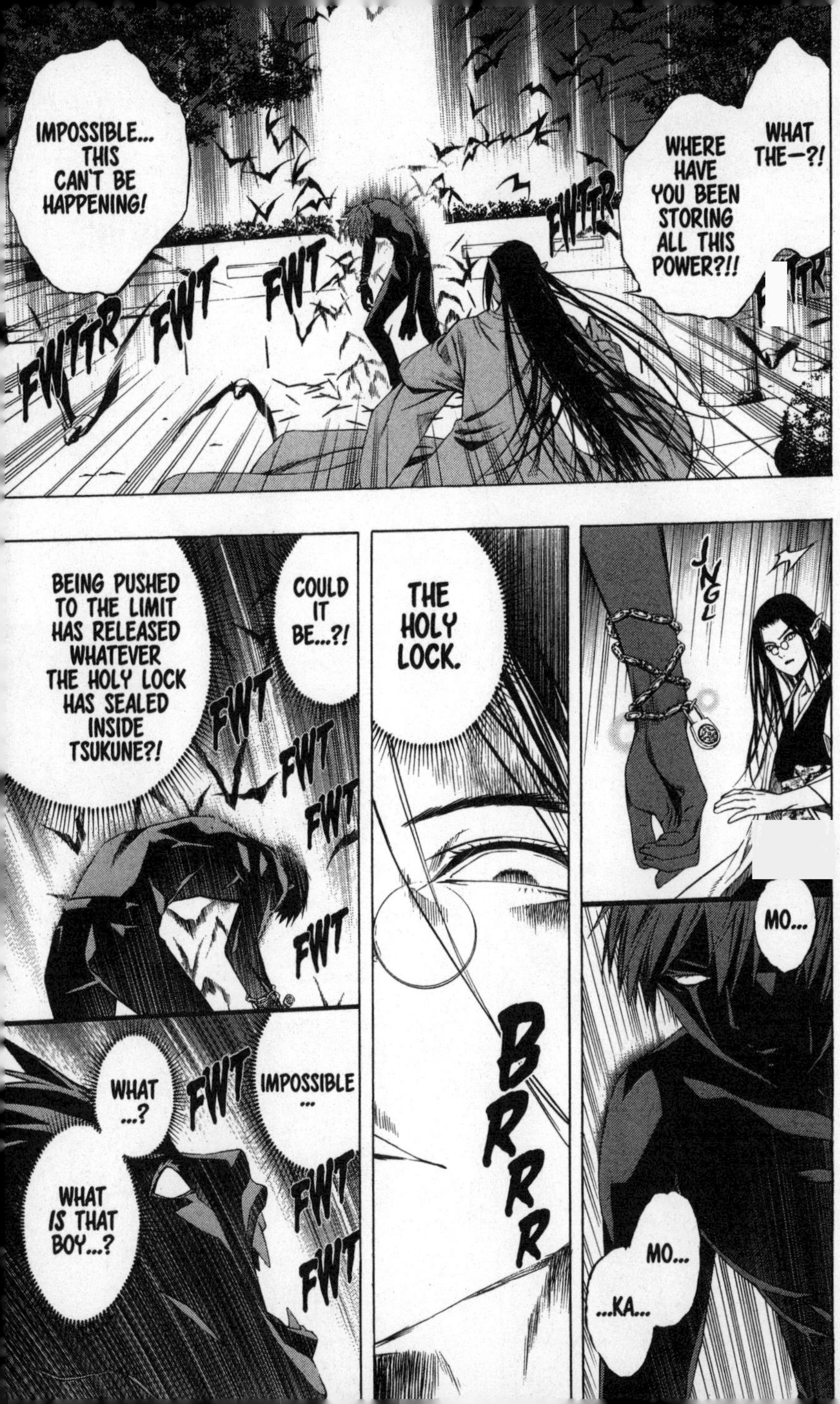
WHAT THE—?!
WHERE HAVE YOU BEEN STORING ALL THIS POWER?!!
FWTTR
FWT
FWT
FWTTR
IMPOSSIBLE... THIS CAN'T BE HAPPENING!
JNGL
THE HOLY LOCK.
COULD IT BE...?!
BEING PUSHED TO THE LIMIT HAS RELEASED WHATEVER THE HOLY LOCK HAS SEALED INSIDE TSUKUNE?!
FWT
FWT
FWT
FWT
MO...
MO...
...KA...
BRRR
IMPOSSIBLE...
FWT
WHAT...?
WHAT IS THAT BOY...?
FWT
FWT

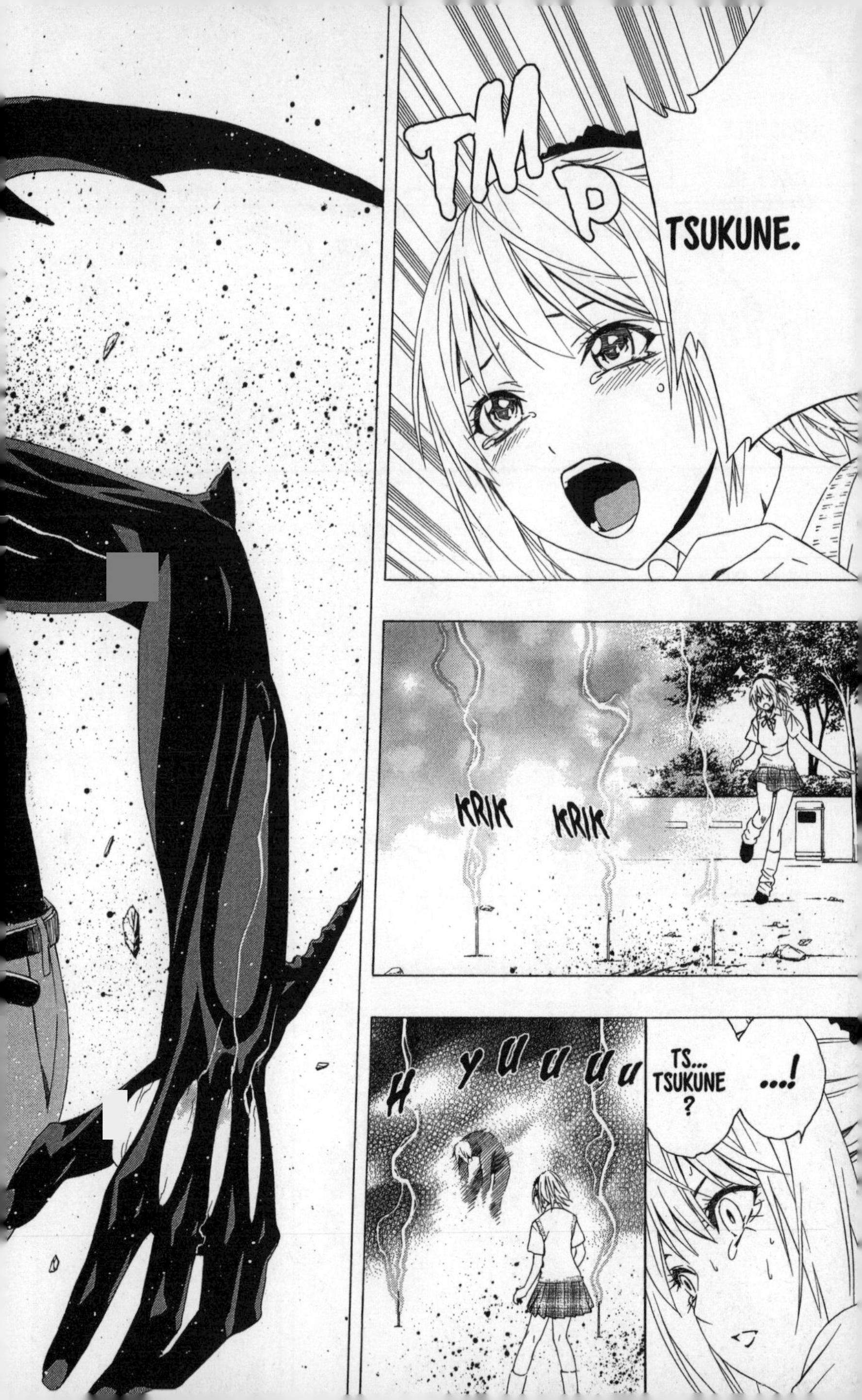
TMP
TSUKUNE.
KRIK KRIK
TS... TSUKUNE ?
...!
HYUUUUU

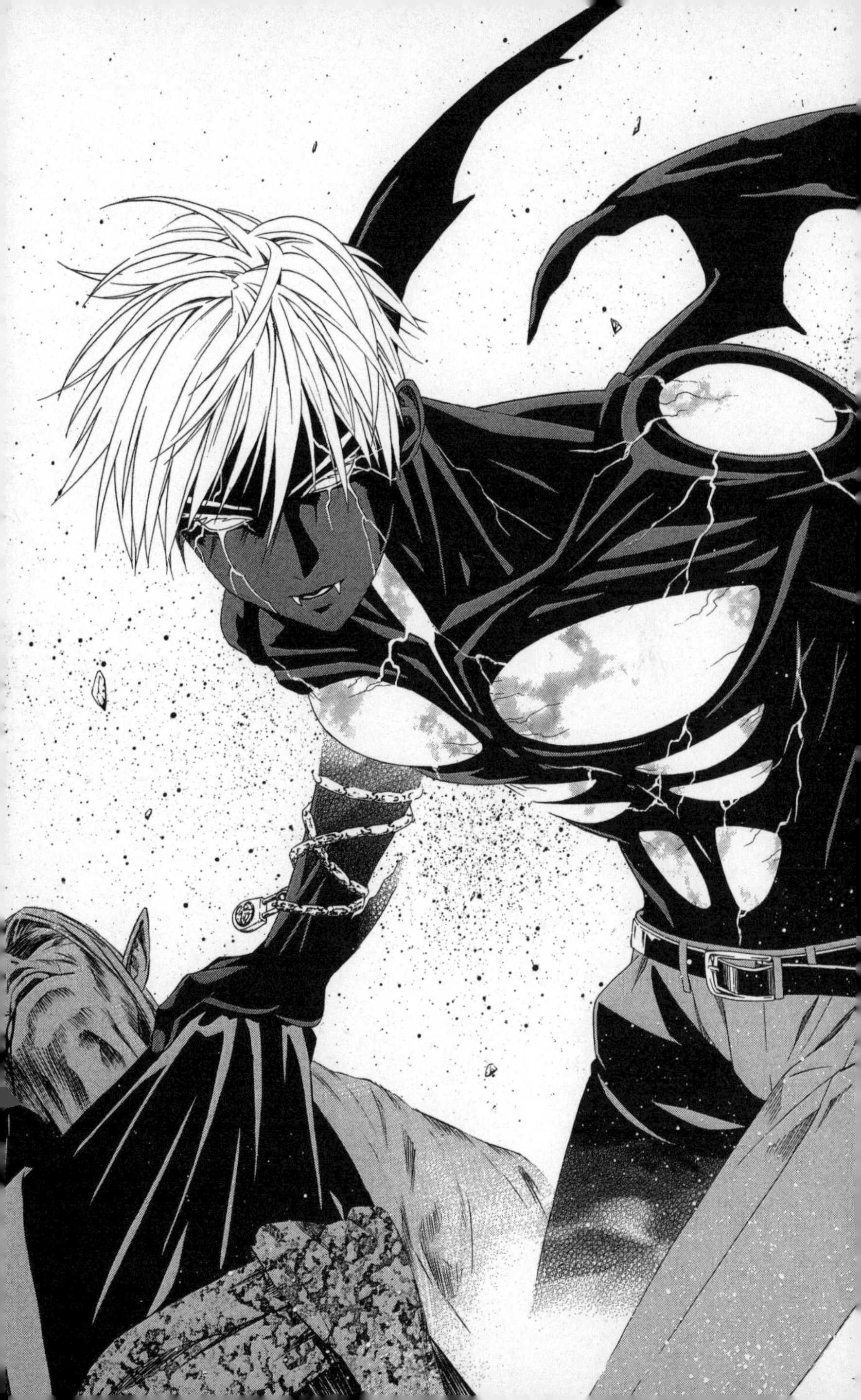

41: Bond

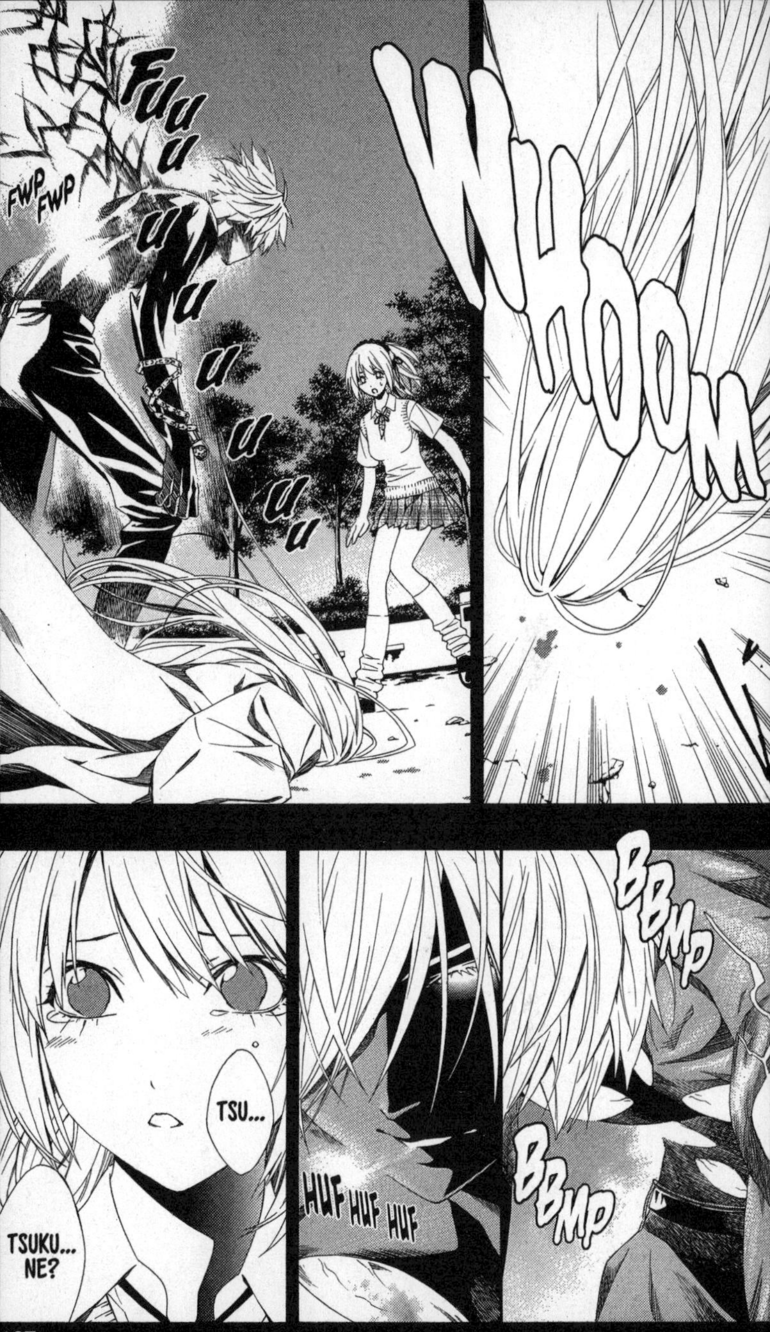
WHOOOM
FUUUUUUUUUUU
FWP FWP
BBMP
BBMP
HUF HUF HUF
TSU...
TSUKU... NE?

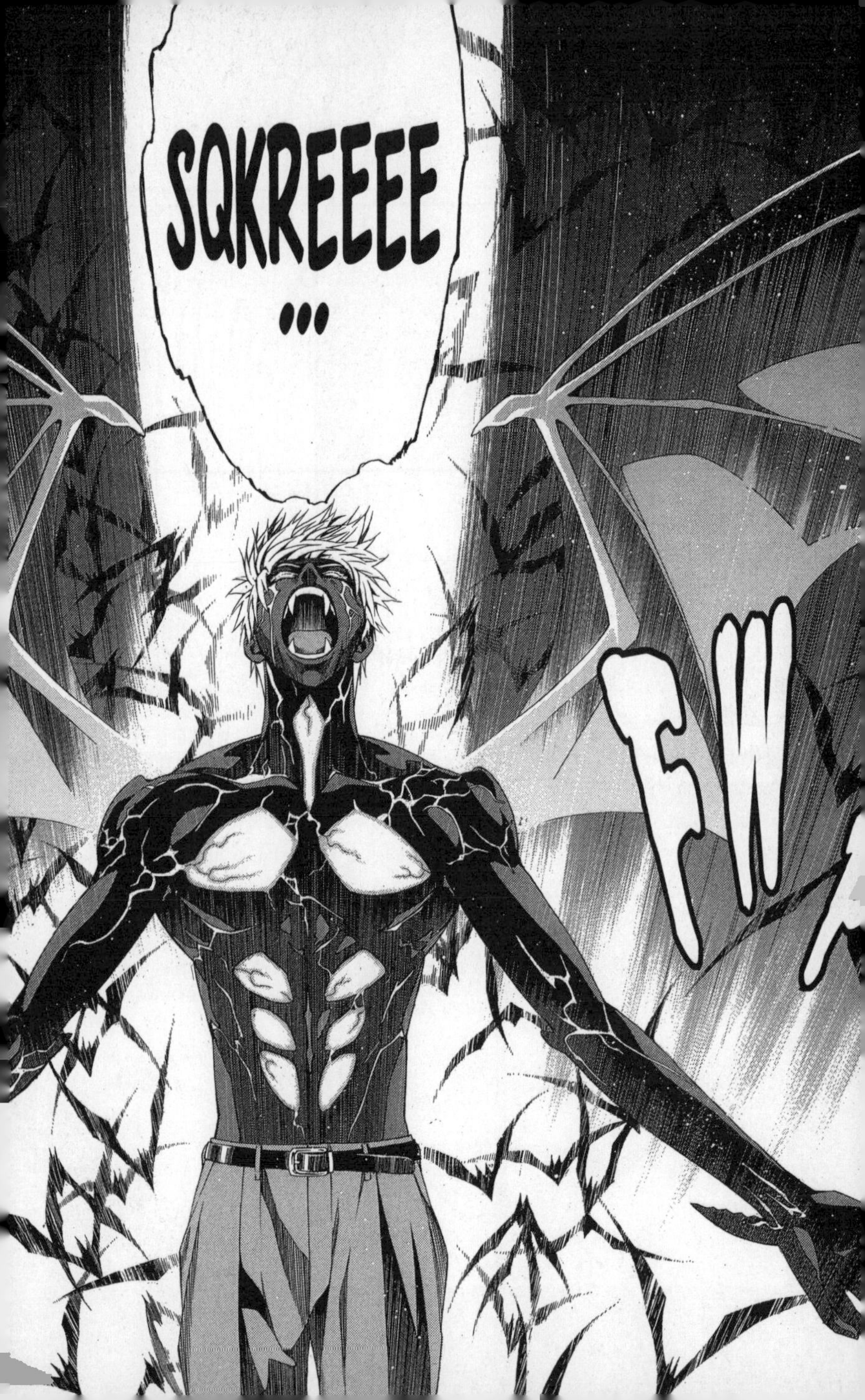
SQKREEEE
...
FW

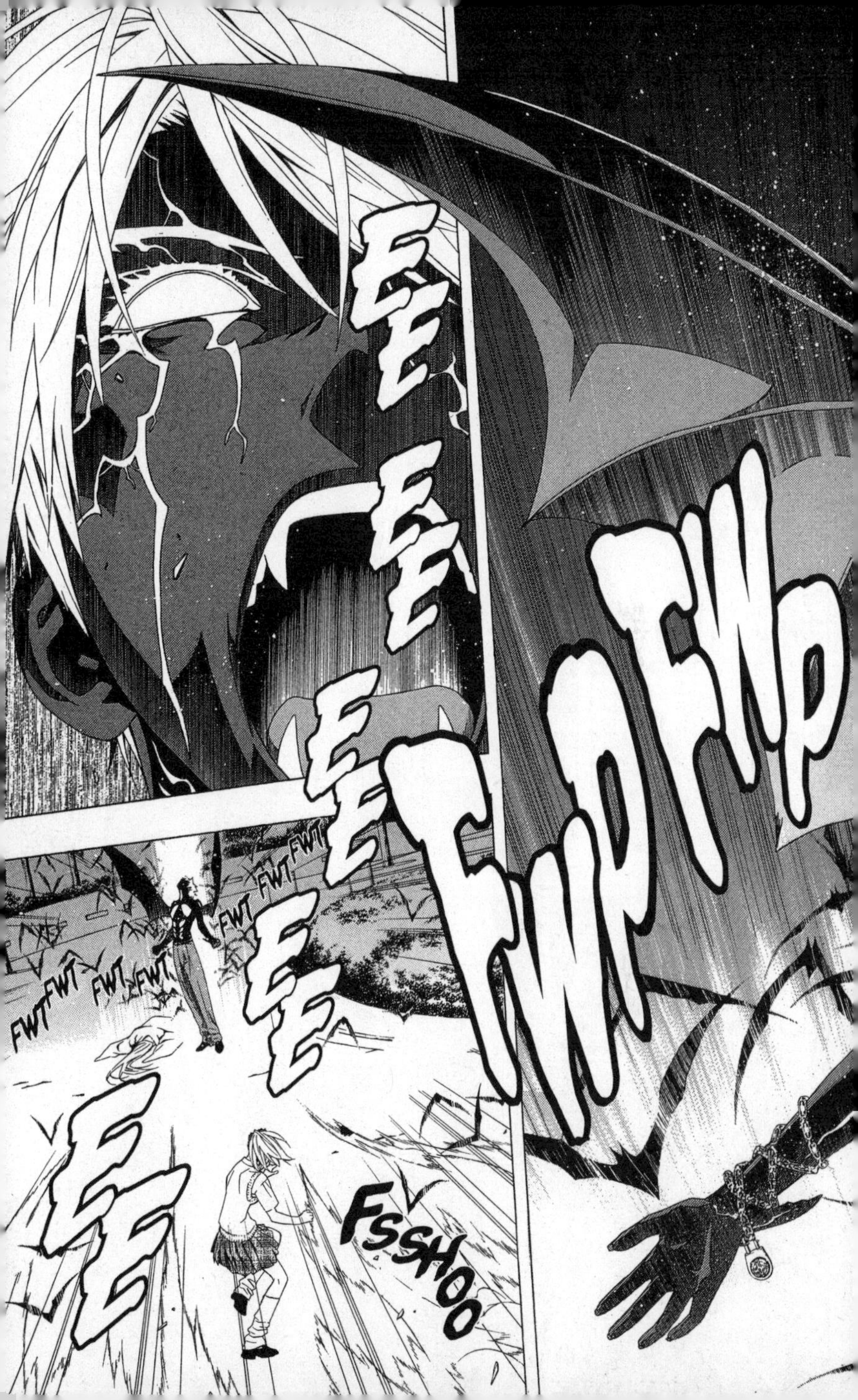

EEEEEEEEEEEE
FWP FWP
FWT FWT FWT FWT
FWT FWT FWT FWT
EEE
FSSHOO

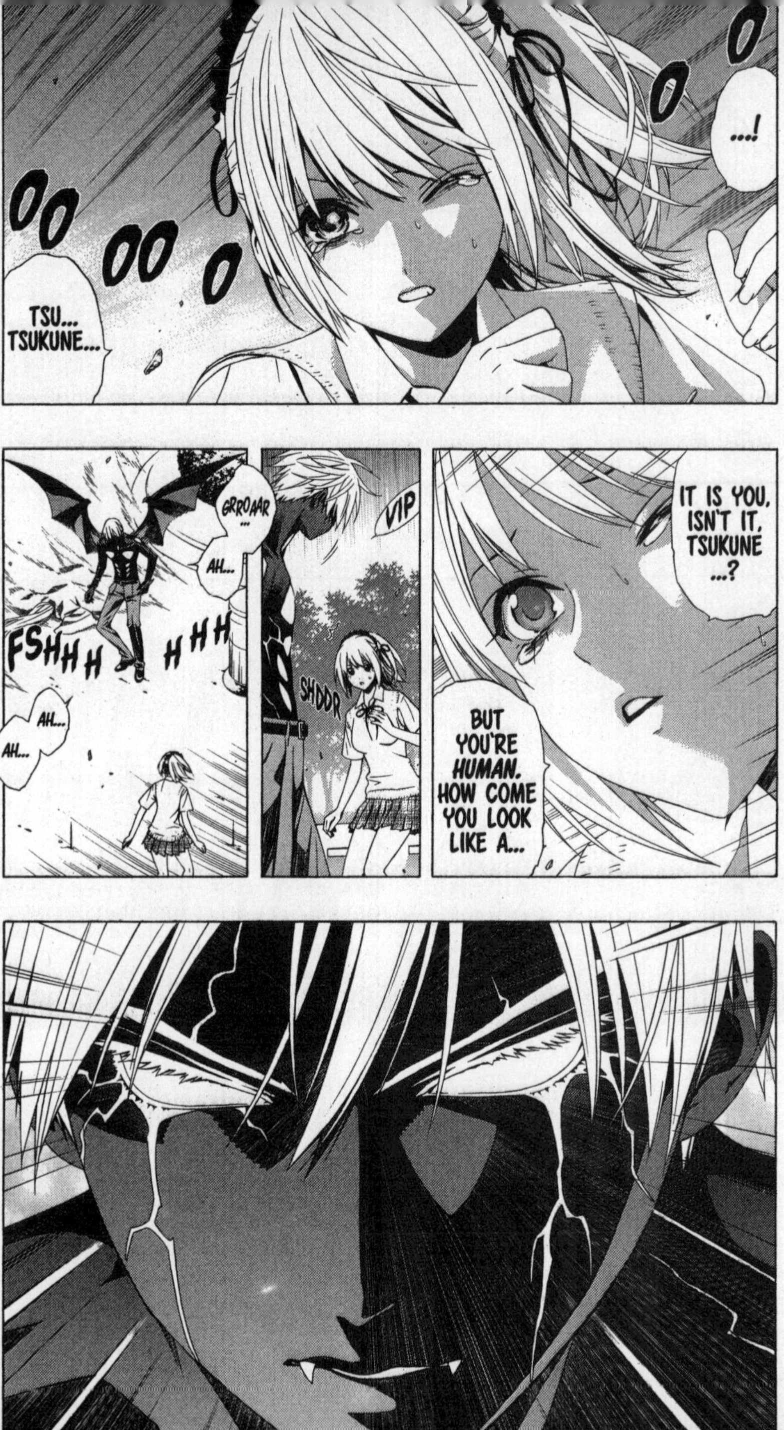
...!
OO OOO OO O
TSU... TSUKUNE...
IT IS YOU, ISN'T IT, TSUKUNE ...?
BUT YOU'RE HUMAN. HOW COME YOU LOOK LIKE A...
VIP
SHDDR
GRROAAR ...
AH...
FSHHHHHHH
AH... AH...

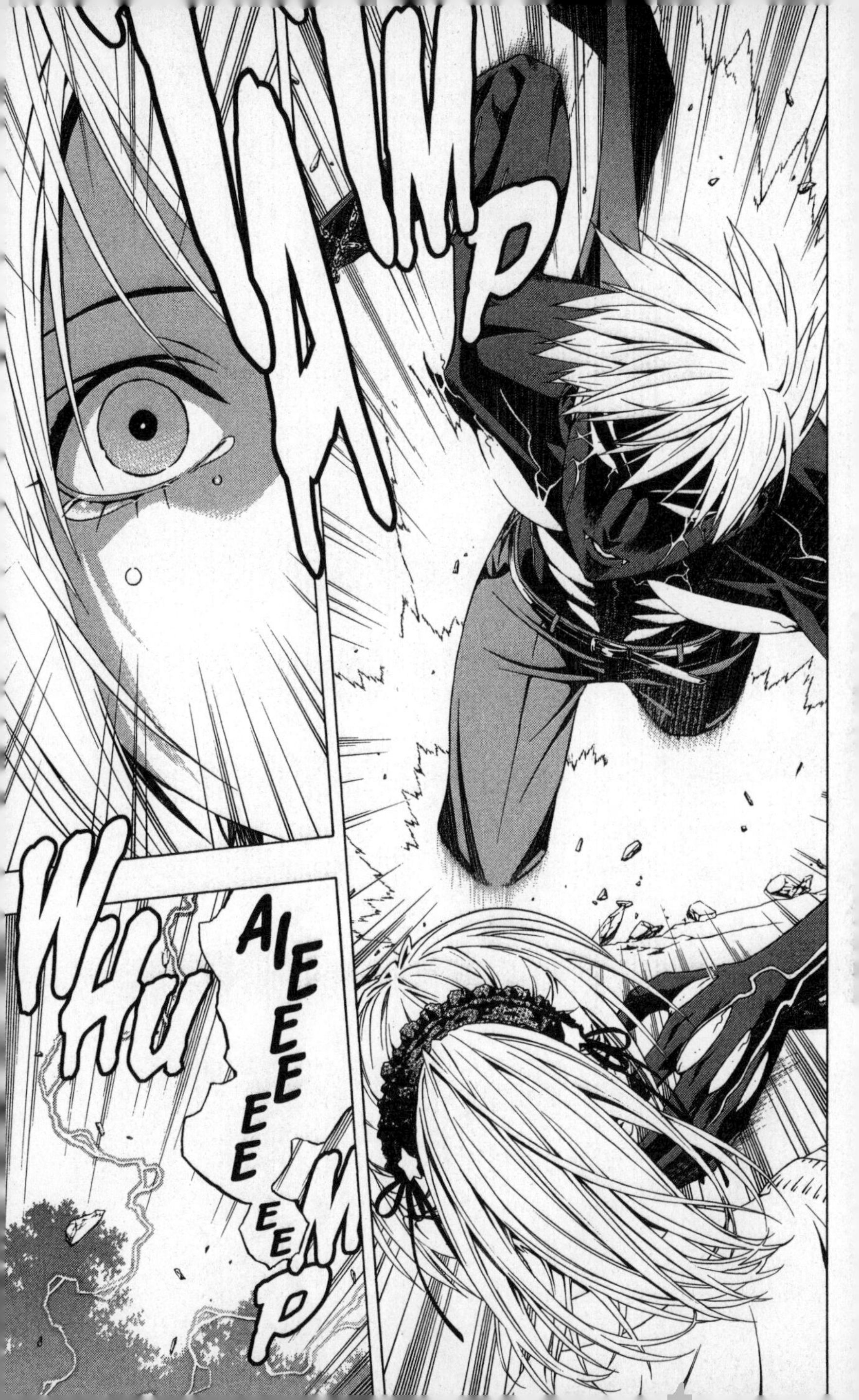
Wha
AIEEEEEEE

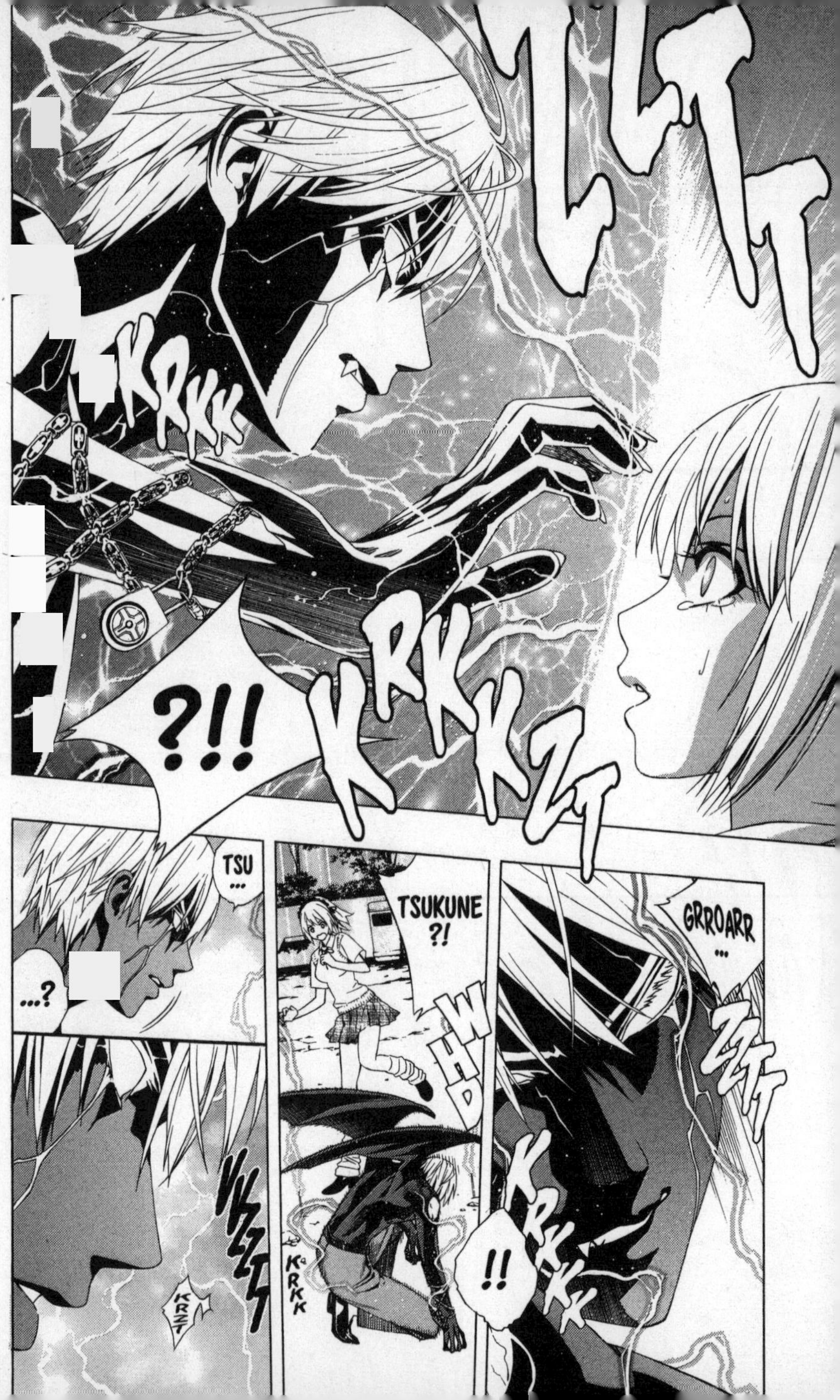
KRKK
?!!
KRKKZZT
GRROARR ...
KRKKK
!!
TSUKUNE ?!
KRKK
TSU ...
...?
KRZT

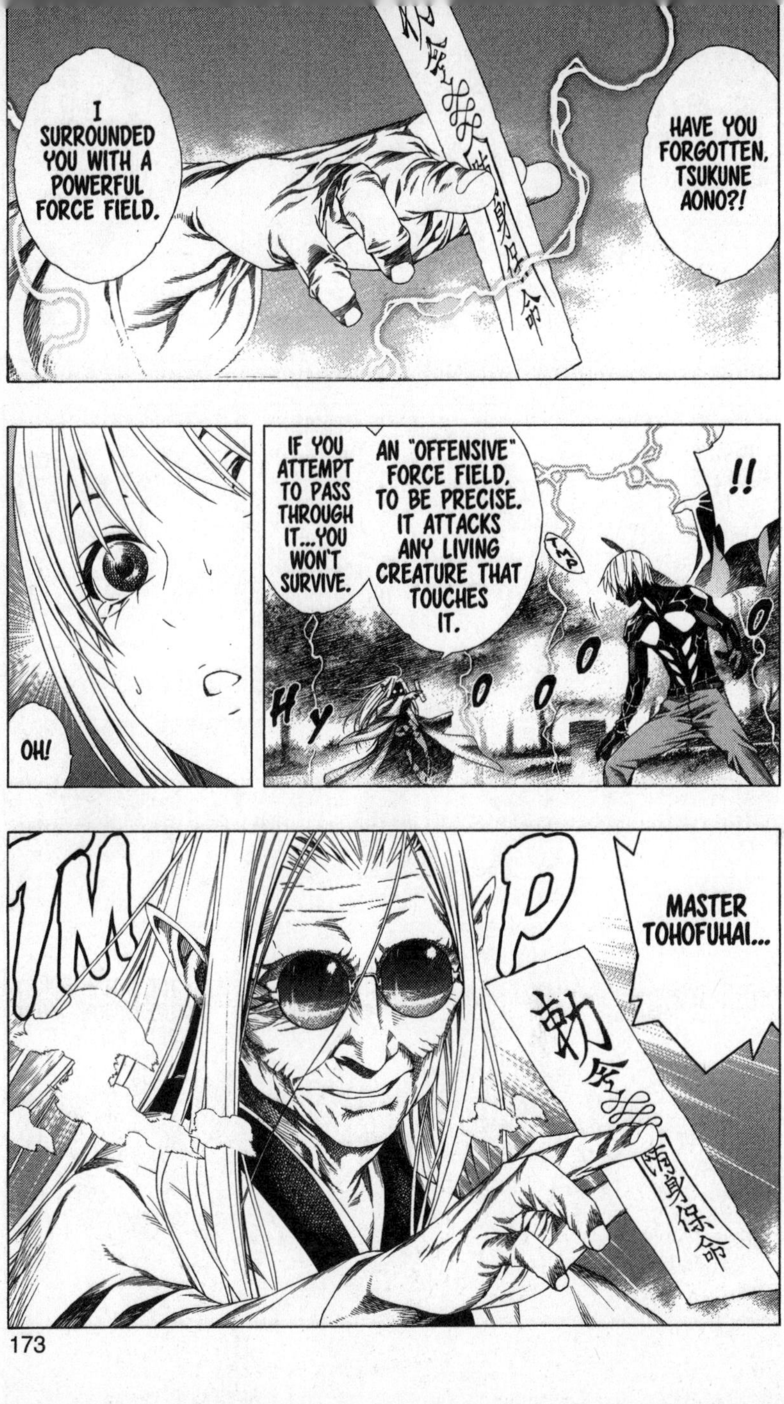
HAVE YOU FORGOTTEN, TSUKUNE AONO?!
I SURROUNDED YOU WITH A POWERFUL FORCE FIELD.
!!
AN "OFFENSIVE" FORCE FIELD, TO BE PRECISE. IT ATTACKS ANY LIVING CREATURE THAT TOUCHES IT.
IF YOU ATTEMPT TO PASS THROUGH IT...YOU WON'T SURVIVE.
TMP
HYOOOO
OH!
MASTER TOHOFUHAI...
TMP

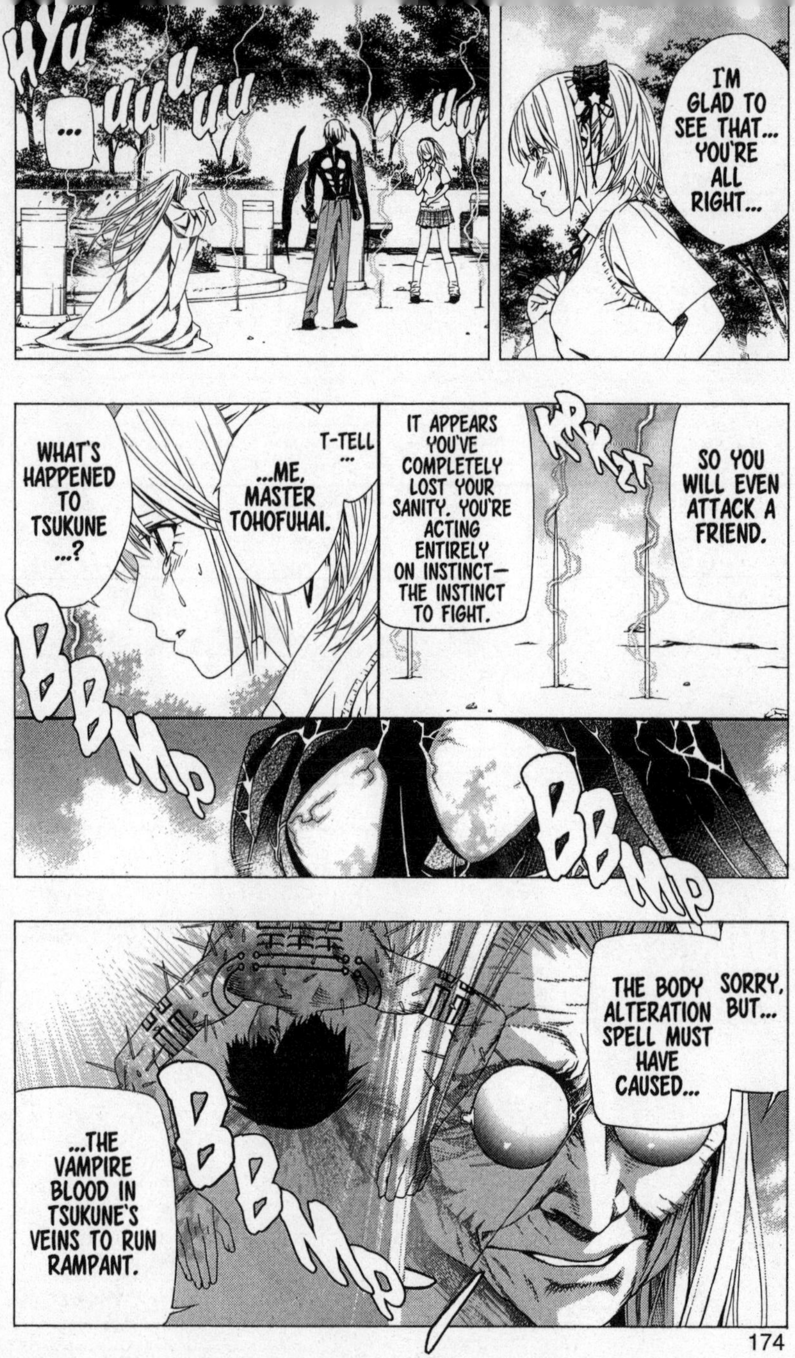
I'M GLAD TO SEE THAT... YOU'RE ALL RIGHT...
HYUUUUUUU
...
UU
SO YOU WILL EVEN ATTACK A FRIEND.
KRKZT
IT APPEARS YOU'VE COMPLETELY LOST YOUR SANITY. YOU'RE ACTING ENTIRELY ON INSTINCT— THE INSTINCT TO FIGHT.
T-TELL...
...ME, MASTER TOHOFUHAI.
WHAT'S HAPPENED TO TSUKUNE...?
BBMP
BBMP
SORRY, BUT...
THE BODY ALTERATION SPELL MUST HAVE CAUSED...
...THE VAMPIRE BLOOD IN TSUKUNE'S VEINS TO RUN RAMPANT.
BBMP

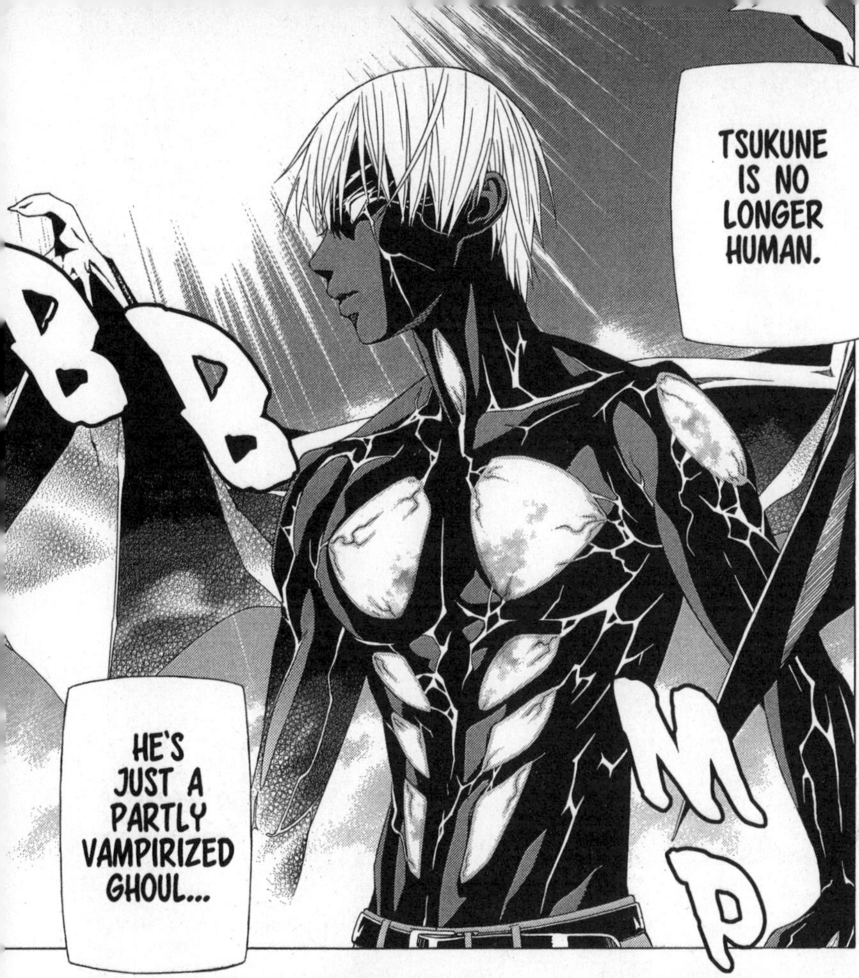
TSUKUNE IS NO LONGER HUMAN.
HE'S JUST A PARTLY VAMPIRIZED GHOUL...

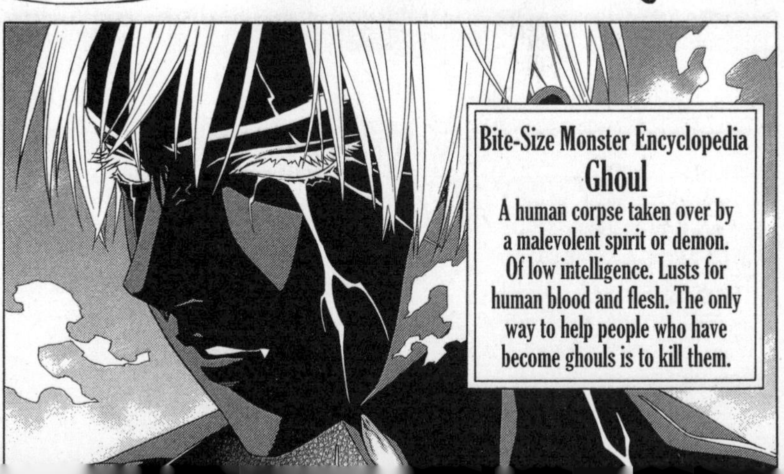
Bite-Size Monster Encyclopedia
Ghoul
A human corpse taken over by a malevolent spirit or demon. Of low intelligence. Lusts for human blood and flesh. The only way to help people who have become ghouls is to kill them.

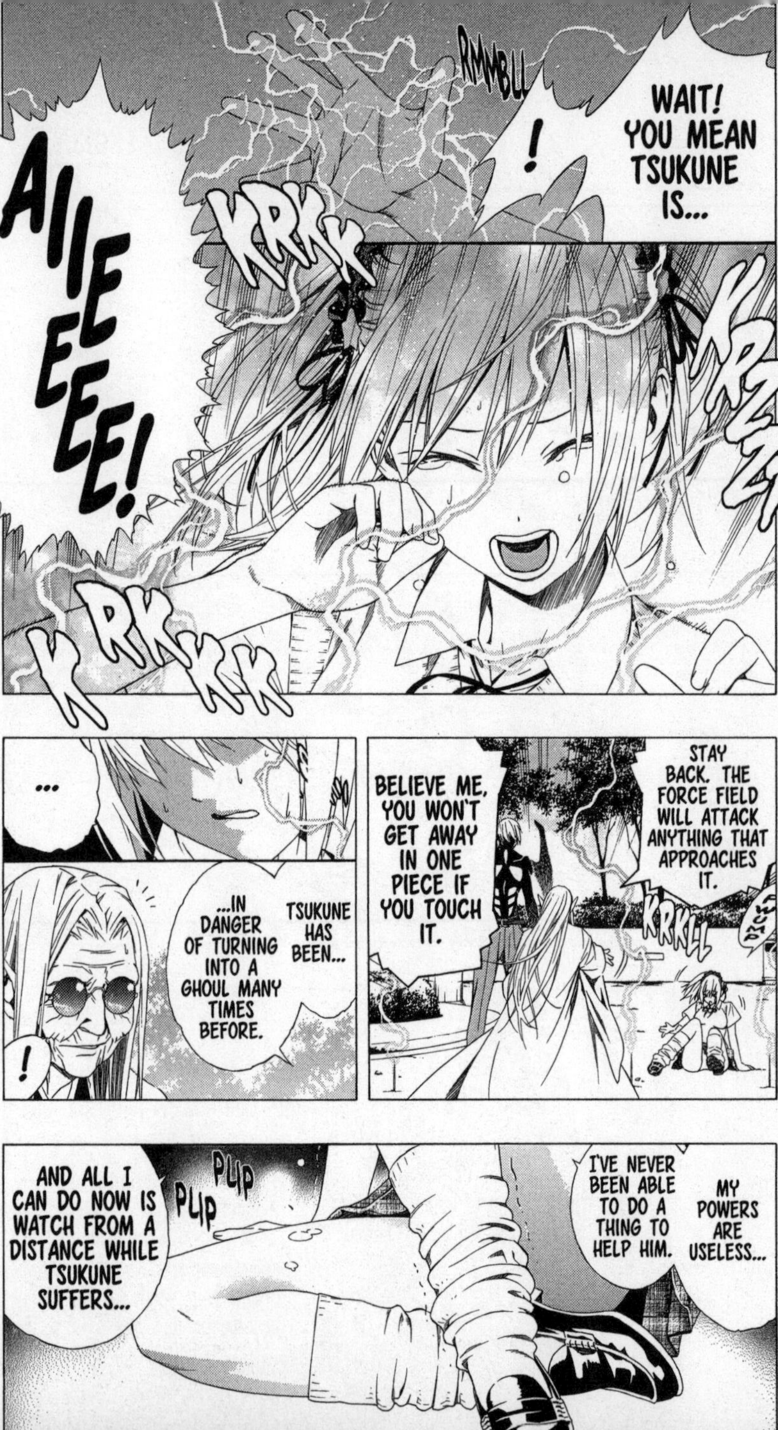
WAIT! YOU MEAN TSUKUNE IS...
!
RMMBLL
AIIEEEEE!
KRKK
KRZZT
KRKKKK
STAY BACK. THE FORCE FIELD WILL ATTACK ANYTHING THAT APPROACHES IT.
BELIEVE ME, YOU WON'T GET AWAY IN ONE PIECE IF YOU TOUCH IT.
KRKLL
...
TSUKUNE HAS BEEN...
...IN DANGER OF TURNING INTO A GHOUL MANY TIMES BEFORE.
!
MY POWERS ARE USELESS...
I'VE NEVER BEEN ABLE TO DO A THING TO HELP HIM.
PLIP
PLIP
AND ALL I CAN DO NOW IS WATCH FROM A DISTANCE WHILE TSUKUNE SUFFERS...

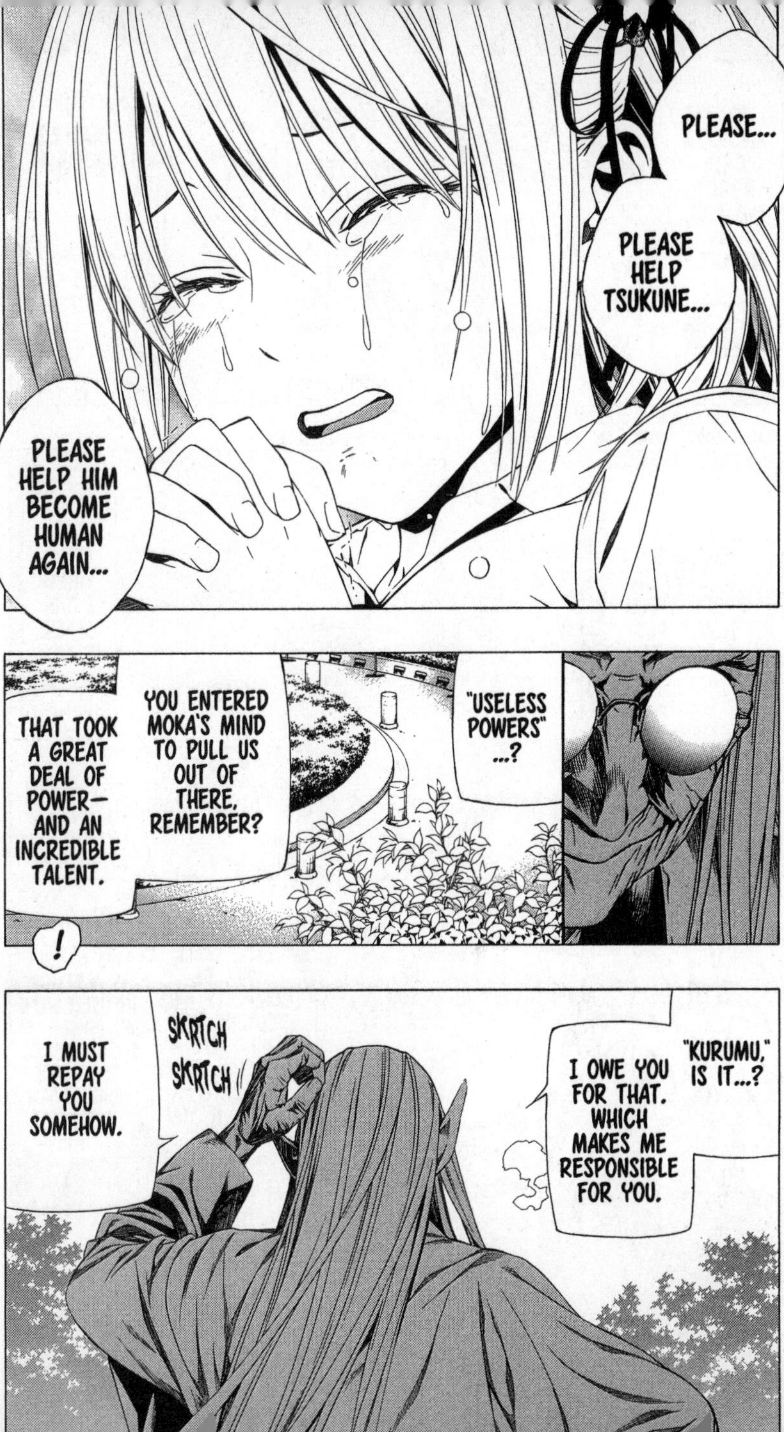
PLEASE...
PLEASE HELP TSUKUNE...
PLEASE HELP HIM BECOME HUMAN AGAIN...
"USELESS POWERS" ...?
YOU ENTERED MOKA'S MIND TO PULL US OUT OF THERE, REMEMBER?
THAT TOOK A GREAT DEAL OF POWER— AND AN INCREDIBLE TALENT.
!
"KURUMU," IS IT...?
I OWE YOU FOR THAT. WHICH MAKES ME RESPONSIBLE FOR YOU.
SKRTCH SKRTCH
I MUST REPAY YOU SOMEHOW.

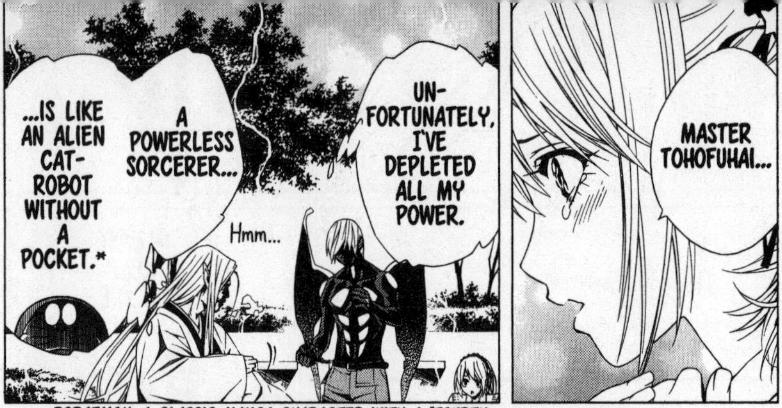
MASTER TOHOFUHAI...
UN-FORTUNATELY, I'VE DEPLETED ALL MY POWER.
Hmm...
A POWERLESS SORCERER...
...IS LIKE AN ALIEN CAT-ROBOT WITHOUT A POCKET.*

*DORAEMON, A CLASSIC MANGA CHARACTER WITH A "FOURTH-DIMENSIONAL POCKET" OUT OF WHICH HE PULLS ANYTHING IMAGINABLE.

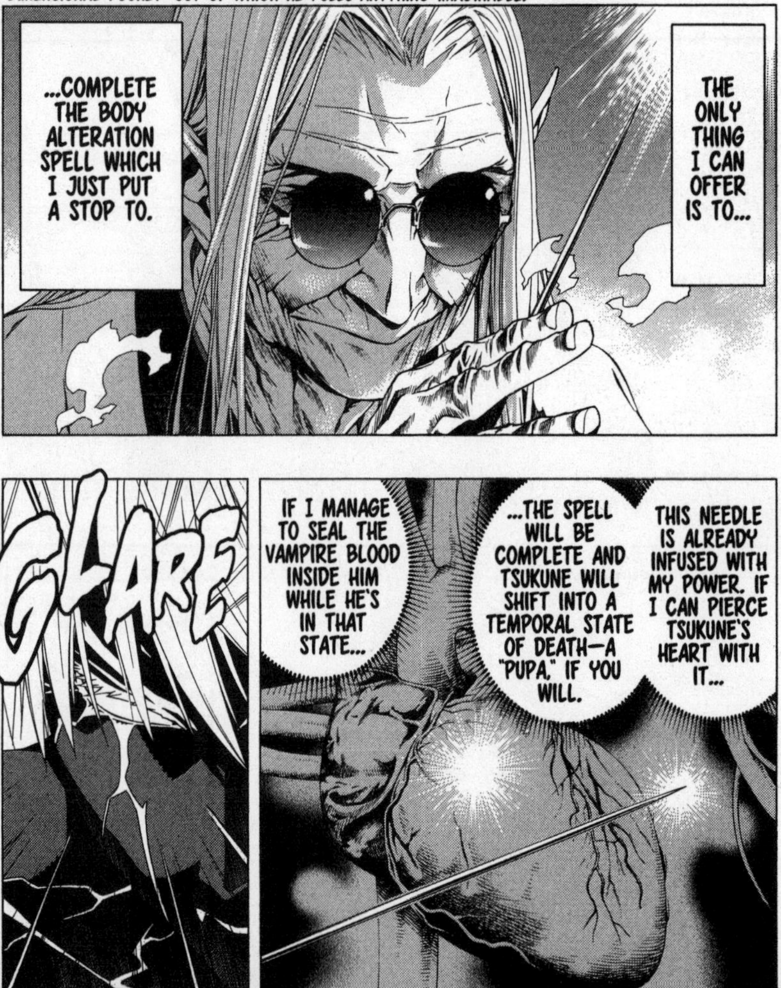
THE ONLY THING I CAN OFFER IS TO...
...COMPLETE THE BODY ALTERATION SPELL WHICH I JUST PUT A STOP TO.
THIS NEEDLE IS ALREADY INFUSED WITH MY POWER. IF I CAN PIERCE TSUKUNE'S HEART WITH IT...
...THE SPELL WILL BE COMPLETE AND TSUKUNE WILL SHIFT INTO A TEMPORAL STATE OF DEATH—A "PUPA," IF YOU WILL.
IF I MANAGE TO SEAL THE VAMPIRE BLOOD INSIDE HIM WHILE HE'S IN THAT STATE...
GLARE

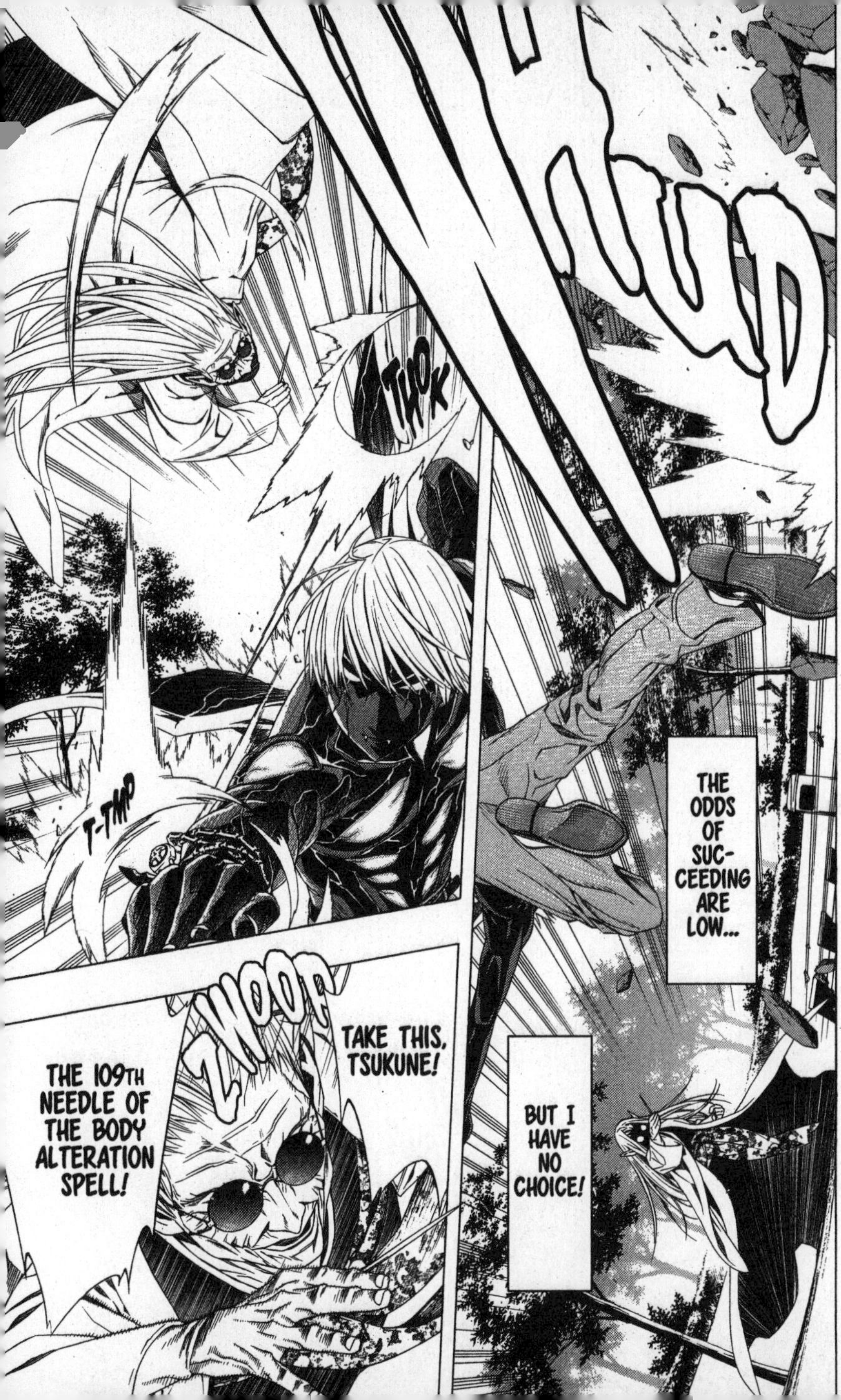
THOK
T-TMP
THE ODDS OF SUC-CEEDING ARE LOW...
BUT I HAVE NO CHOICE!
ZWOOF
TAKE THIS, TSUKUNE!
THE 109TH NEEDLE OF THE BODY ALTERATION SPELL!

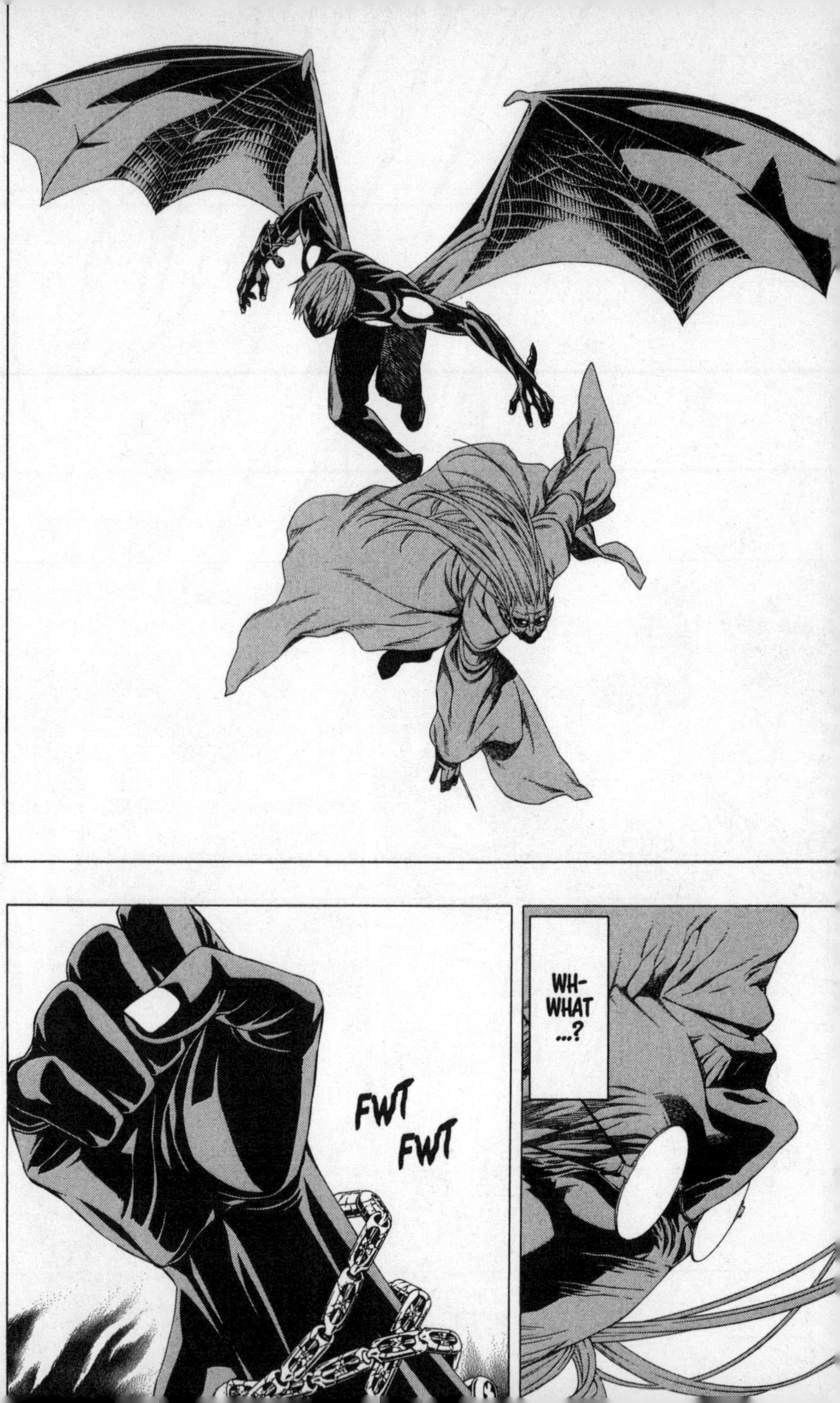
WH-WHAT ...?
FWT FWT

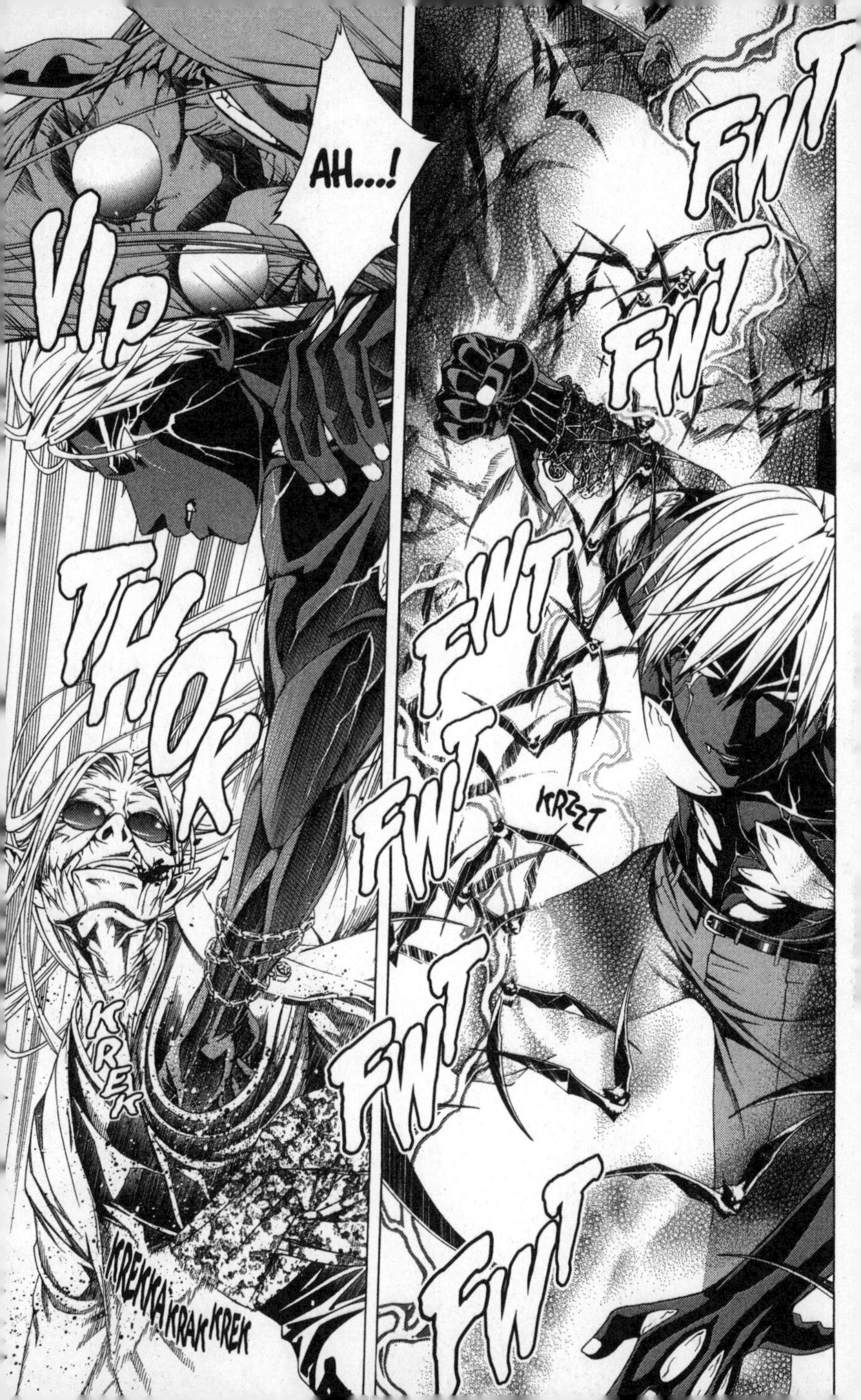
FWT
FWT
FWNT
FWT
KRZZT
FWT
FWT
AH...!
VIP
THOK
KREK
KREKKA KRAK KREK

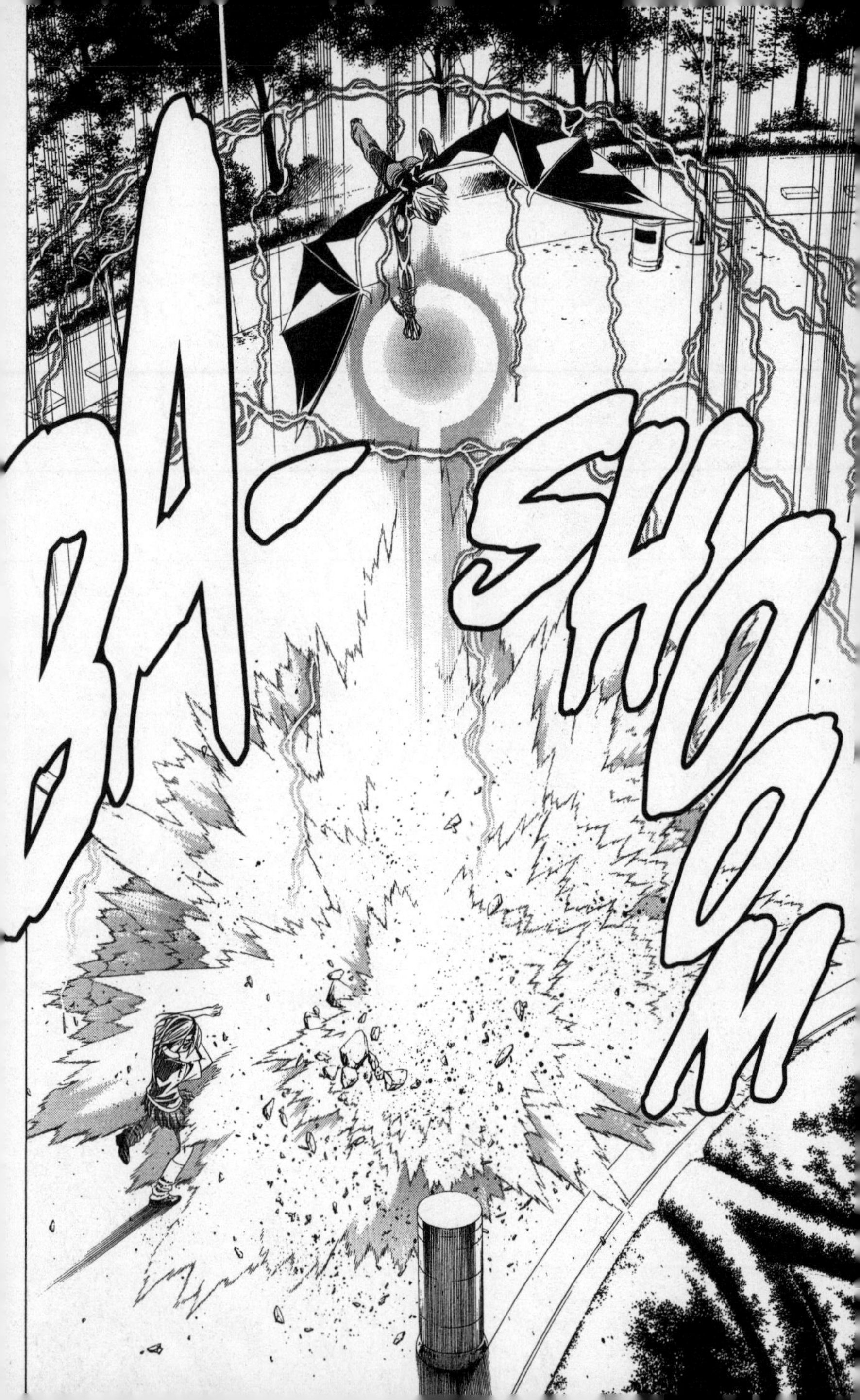
BA-SHOOOM

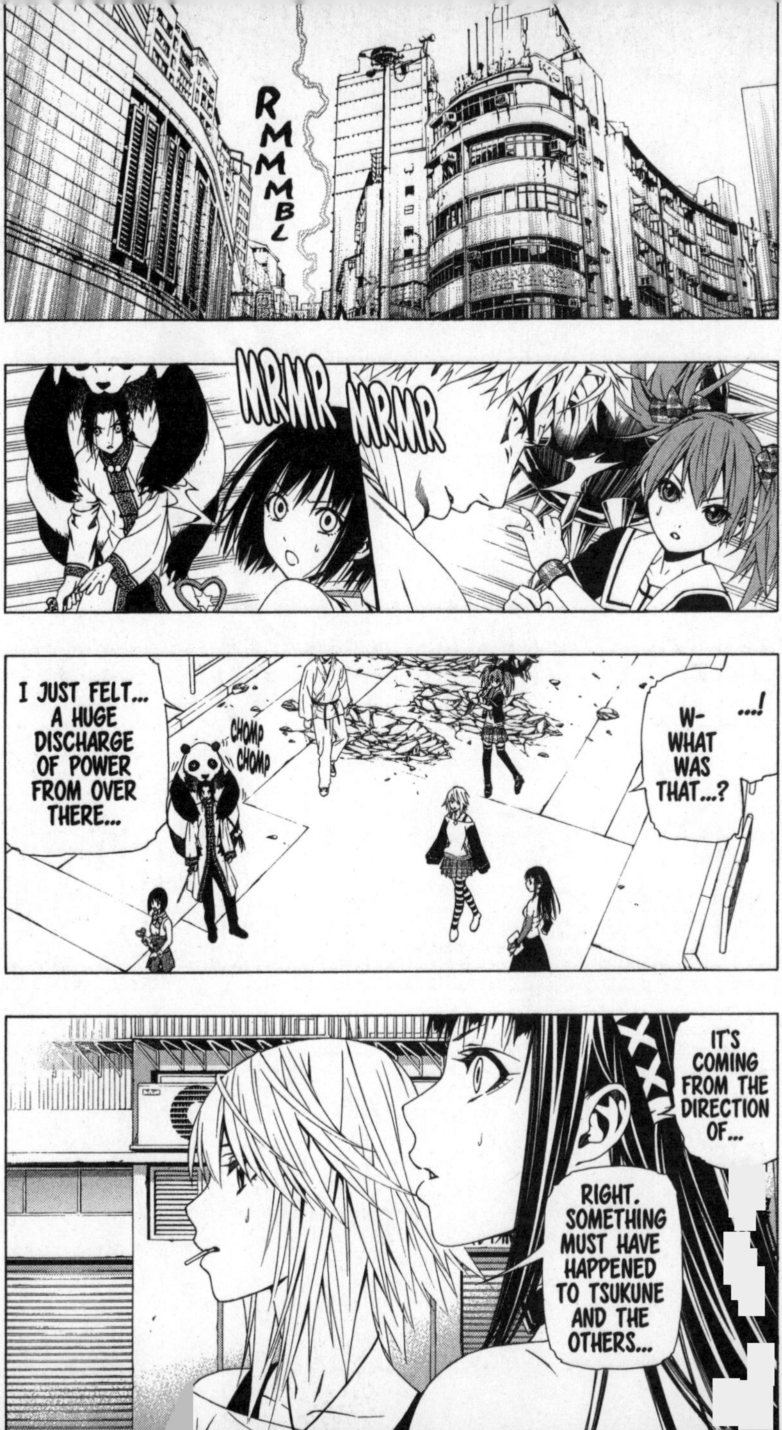
RMMMBL
MRMR MRMR
...!
W- WHAT WAS THAT...?
CHOMP CHOMP
I JUST FELT... A HUGE DISCHARGE OF POWER FROM OVER THERE...
IT'S COMING FROM THE DIRECTION OF...
RIGHT. SOMETHING MUST HAVE HAPPENED TO TSUKUNE AND THE OTHERS...

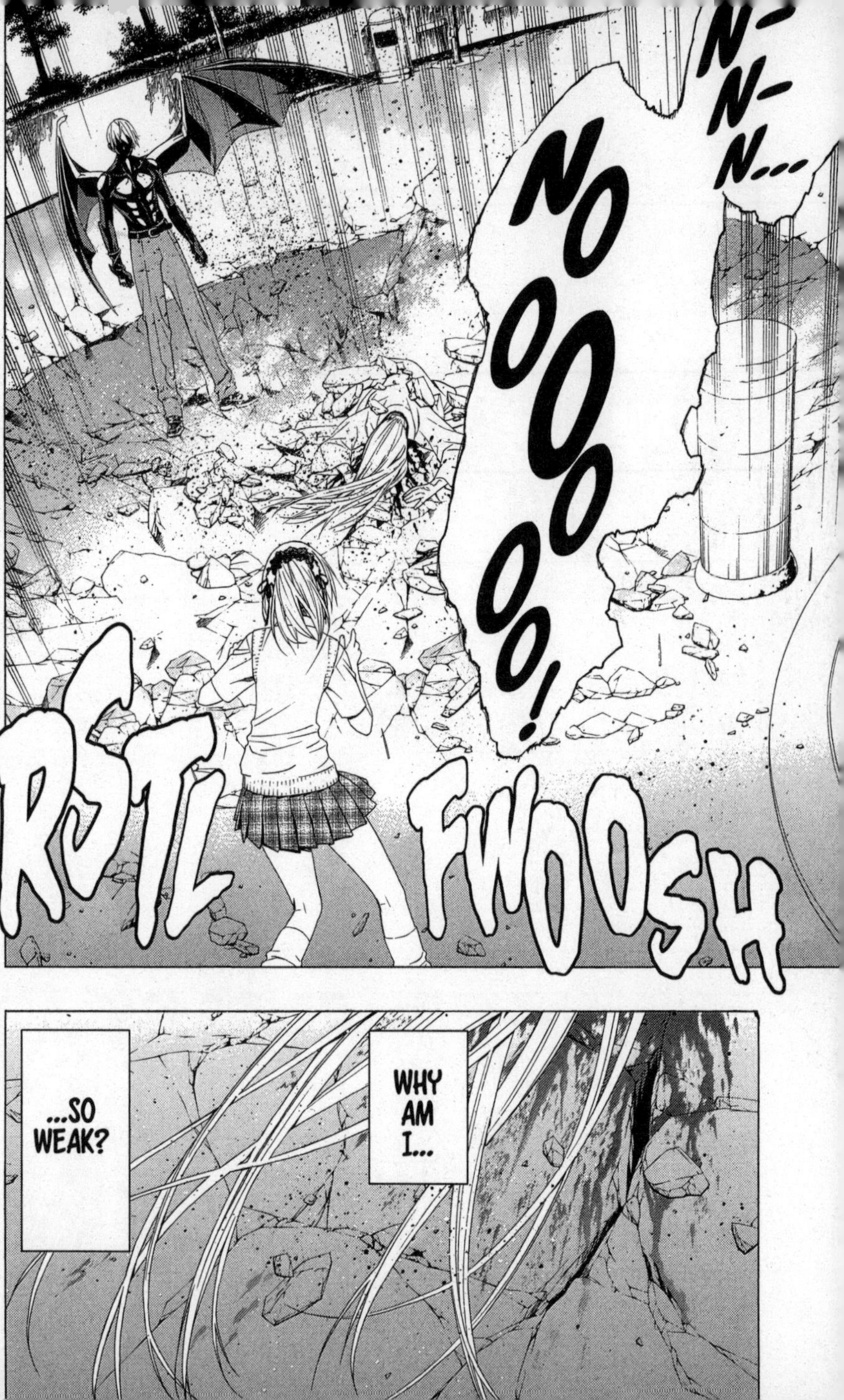
N-N-N...
NOOOOOOO!
FWOOSH
RSTL
WHY AM I...
...SO WEAK?

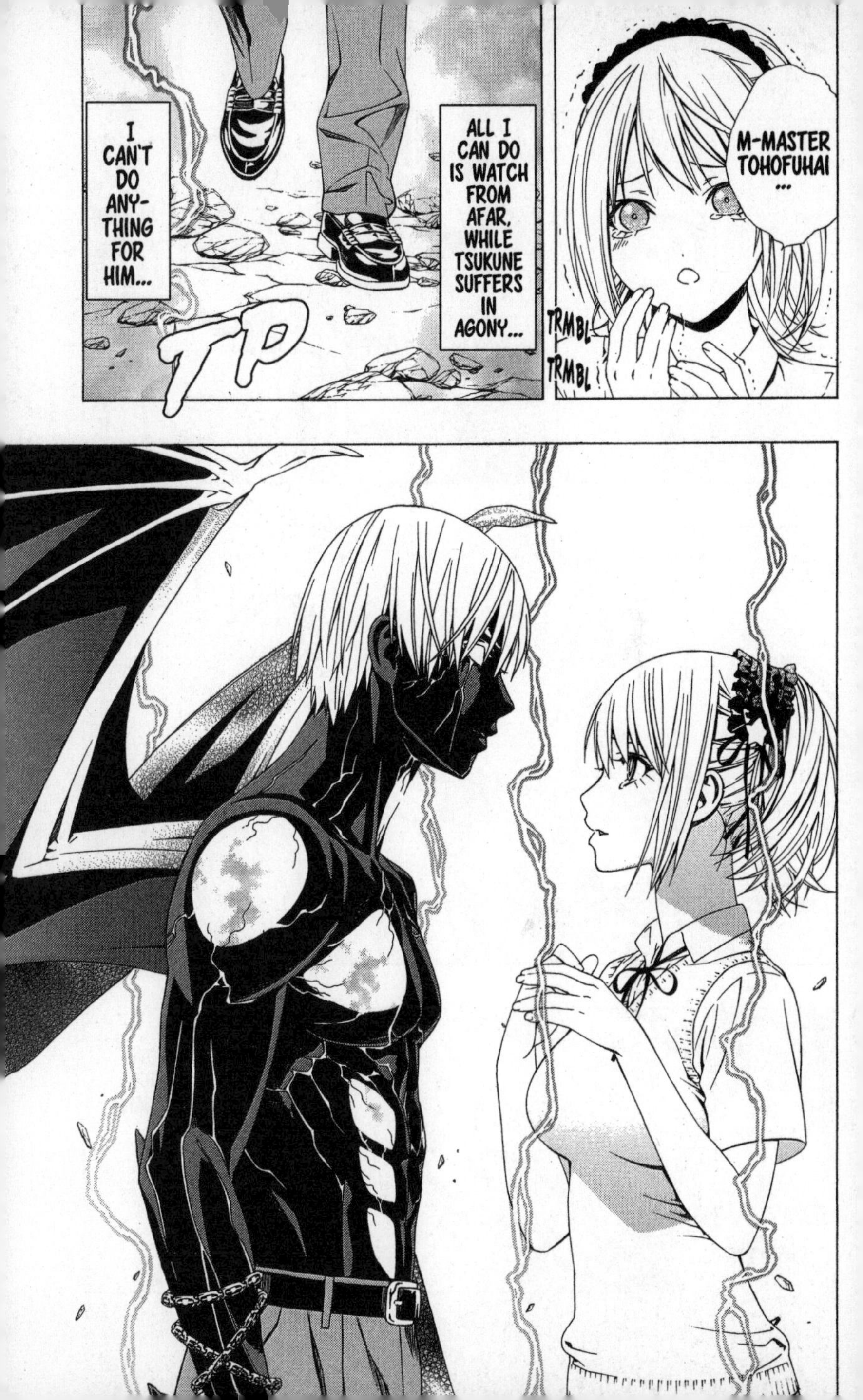
M-MASTER TOHOFUHAI ...
TRMBL
TRMBL
ALL I CAN DO IS WATCH FROM AFAR, WHILE TSUKUNE SUFFERS IN AGONY...
I CAN'T DO ANY-THING FOR HIM...
TP

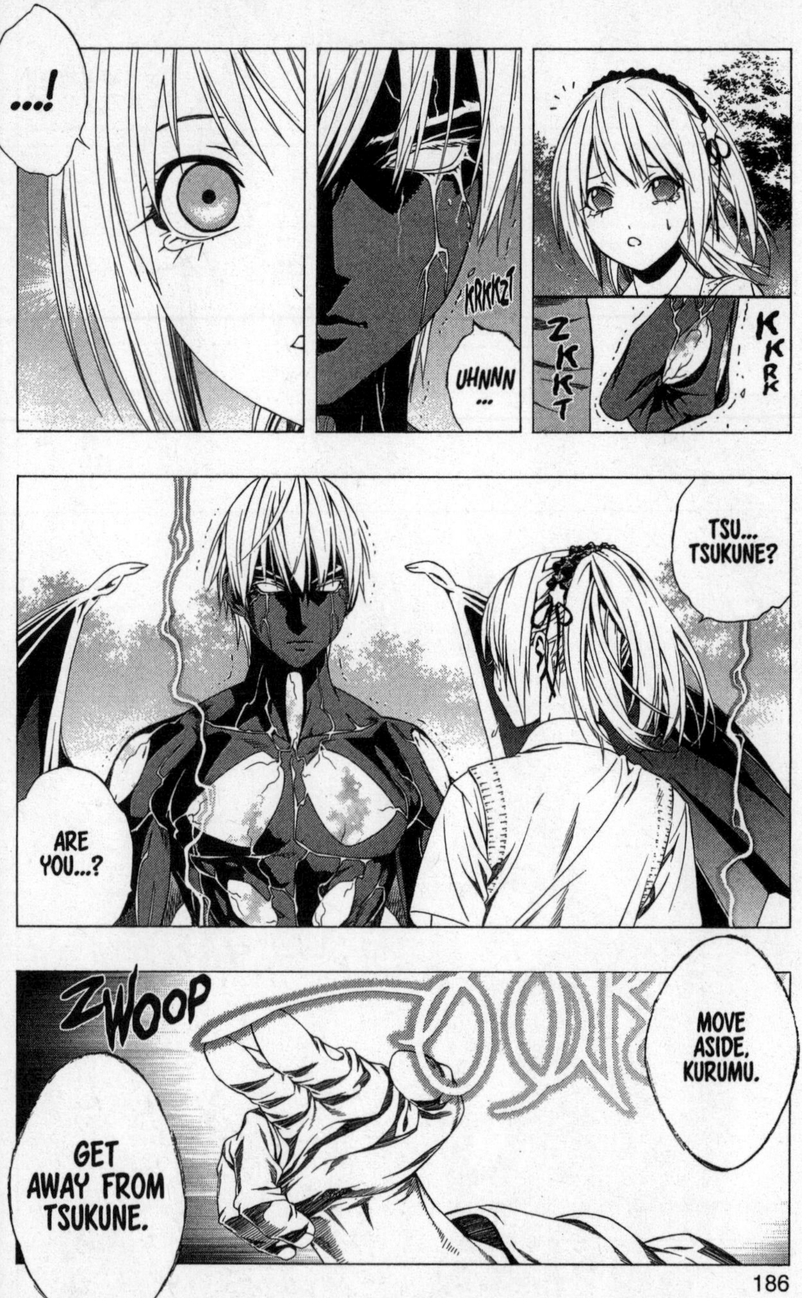
KKRK
ZKKT
KRKKZT
UHNNN...
...!
TSU... TSUKUNE?
ARE YOU...?
MOVE ASIDE, KURUMU.
ZWOOP
GET AWAY FROM TSUKUNE.

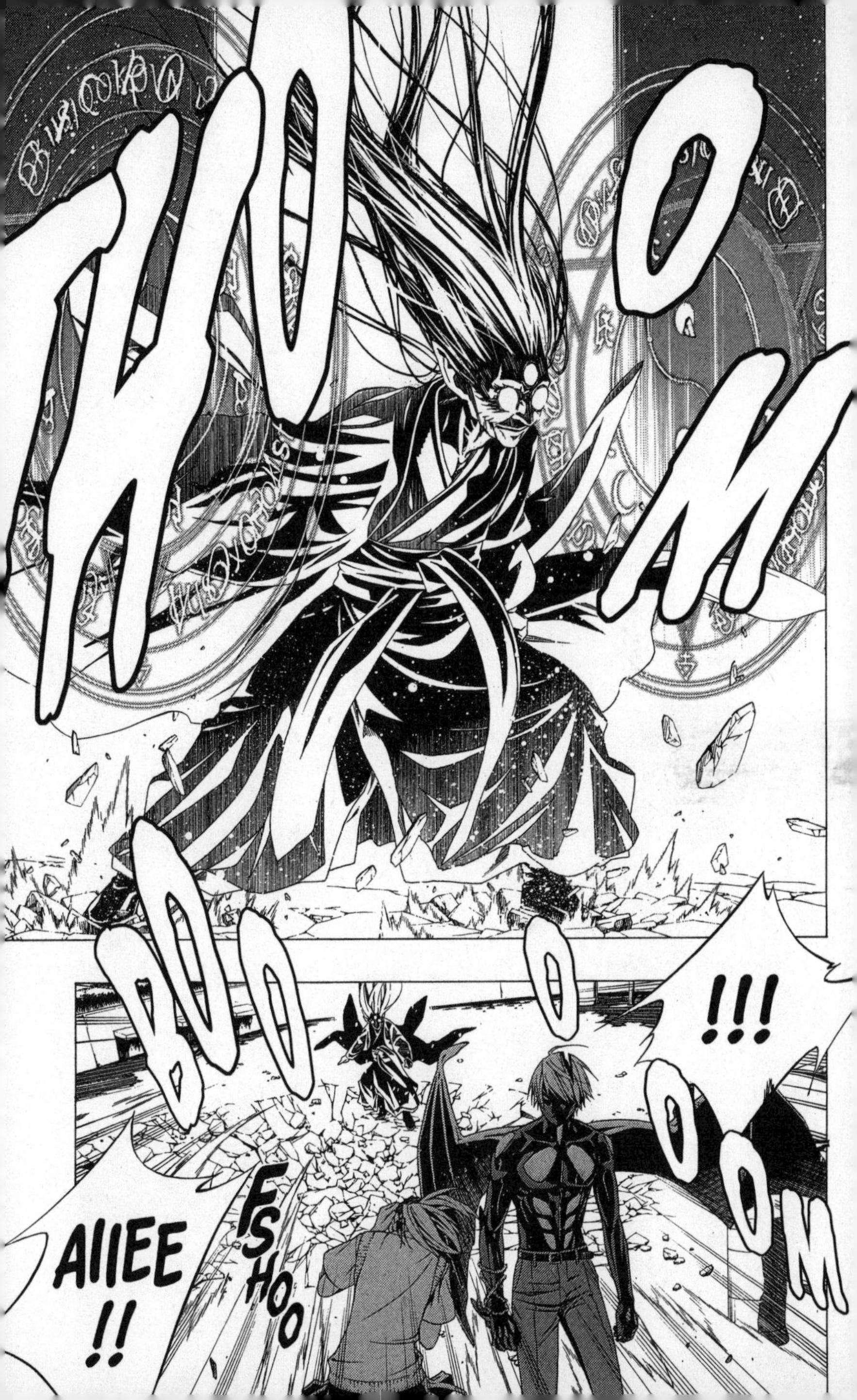
ZHOOM
BOOOOOOM
!!!
AIIEE !!
FSHOO

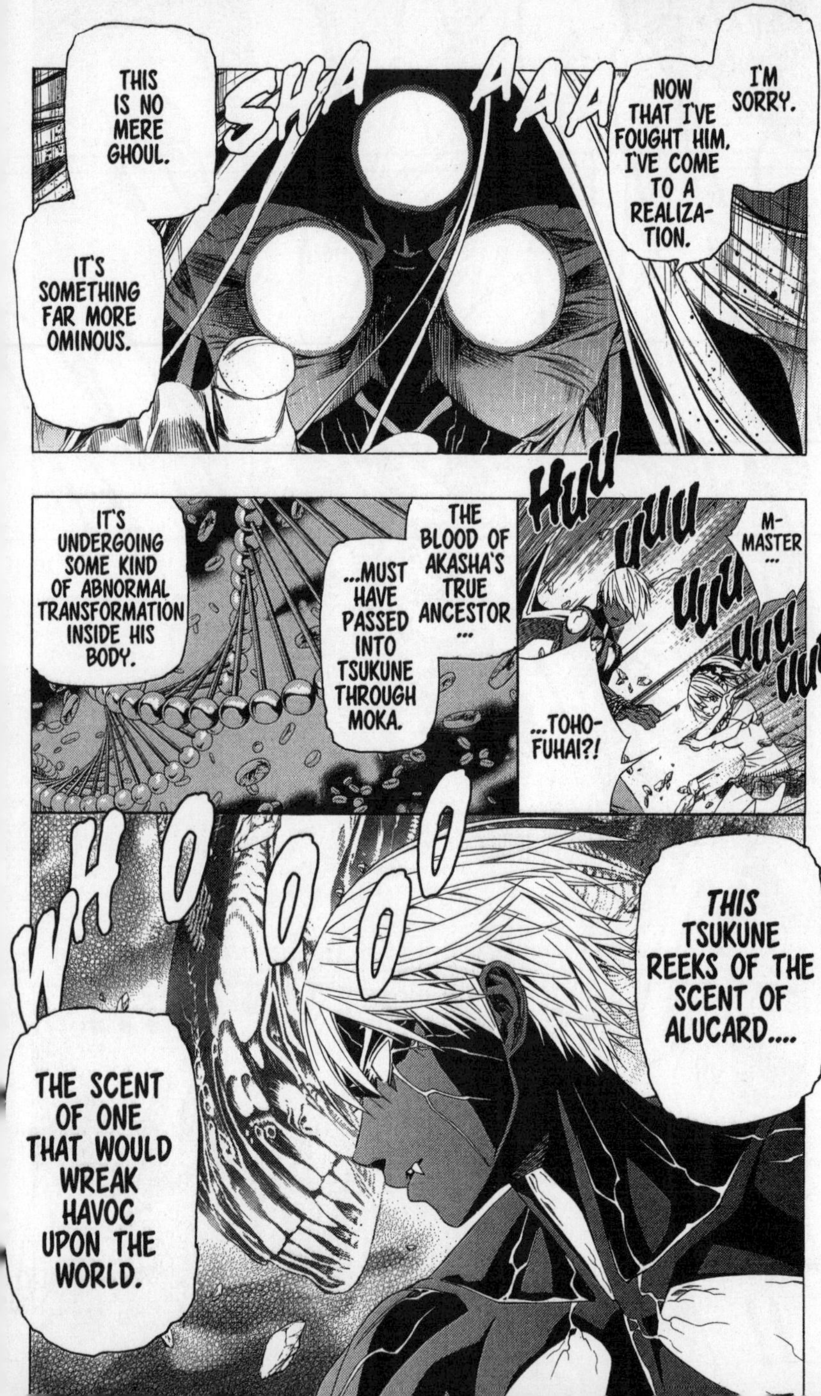
I'M SORRY.
NOW THAT I'VE FOUGHT HIM, I'VE COME TO A REALIZATION.
SHAAAA
THIS IS NO MERE GHOUL.
IT'S SOMETHING FAR MORE OMINOUS.
HUUUUUUUUUUUUUUU
M-MASTER...
...TOHO-FUHAI?!
THE BLOOD OF AKASHA'S TRUE ANCESTOR...
...MUST HAVE PASSED INTO TSUKUNE THROUGH MOKA.
IT'S UNDERGOING SOME KIND OF ABNORMAL TRANSFORMATION INSIDE HIS BODY.
THIS TSUKUNE REEKS OF THE SCENT OF ALUCARD....
WHOOOOOO
THE SCENT OF ONE THAT WOULD WREAK HAVOC UPON THE WORLD.

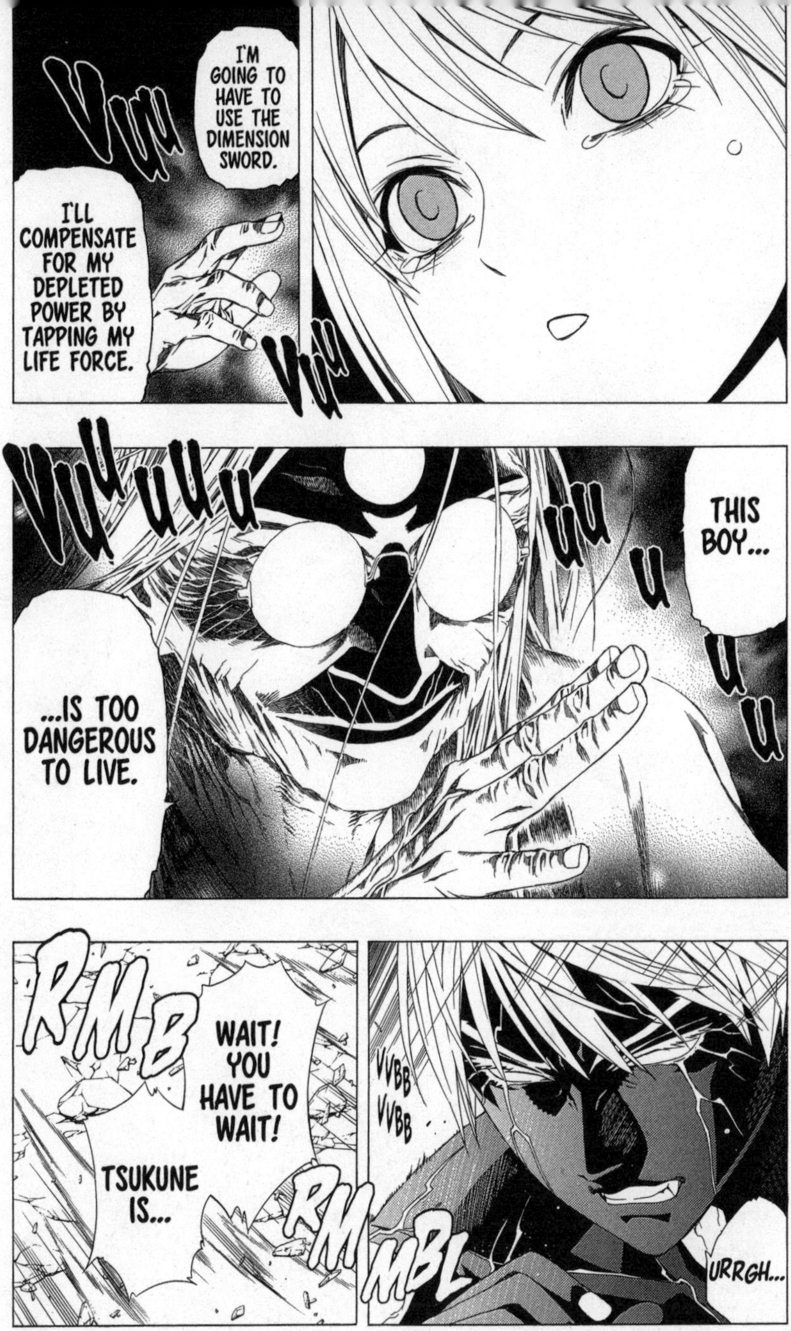
VVU
VVU
I'M GOING TO HAVE TO USE THE DIMENSION SWORD.
I'LL COMPENSATE FOR MY DEPLETED POWER BY TAPPING MY LIFE FORCE.
THIS BOY...
VVUUUUU
UUUUUU
...IS TOO DANGEROUS TO LIVE.
VVBB VVBB
URRGH...
RMMBL
RMB
WAIT! YOU HAVE TO WAIT!
TSUKUNE IS...

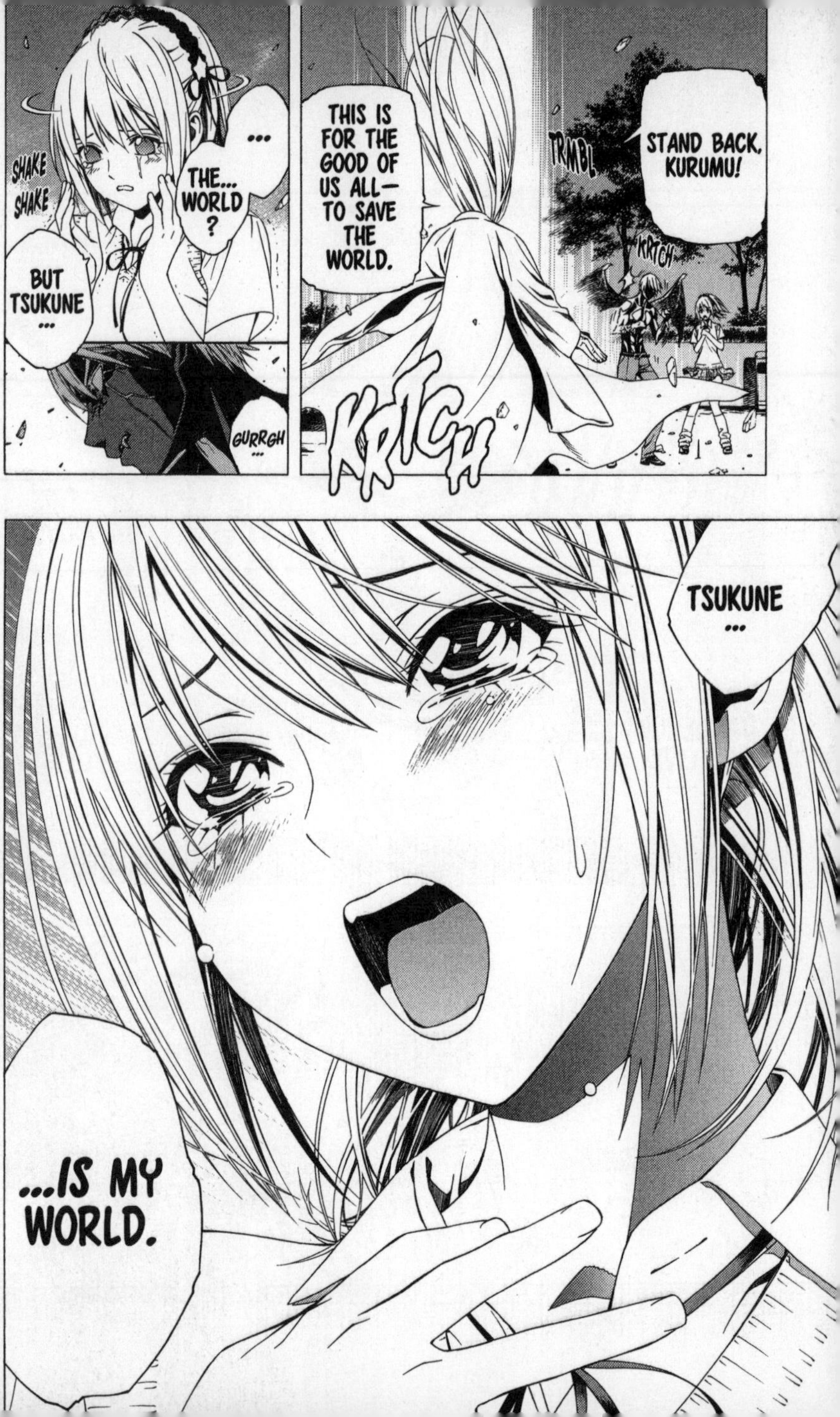
TRMBL
STAND BACK, KURUMU!
KRTCH
THIS IS FOR THE GOOD OF US ALL—TO SAVE THE WORLD.
KRTCH
...
THE... WORLD?
SHAKE SHAKE
BUT TSUKUNE...
GURRGH...
TSUKUNE...
...IS MY WORLD.

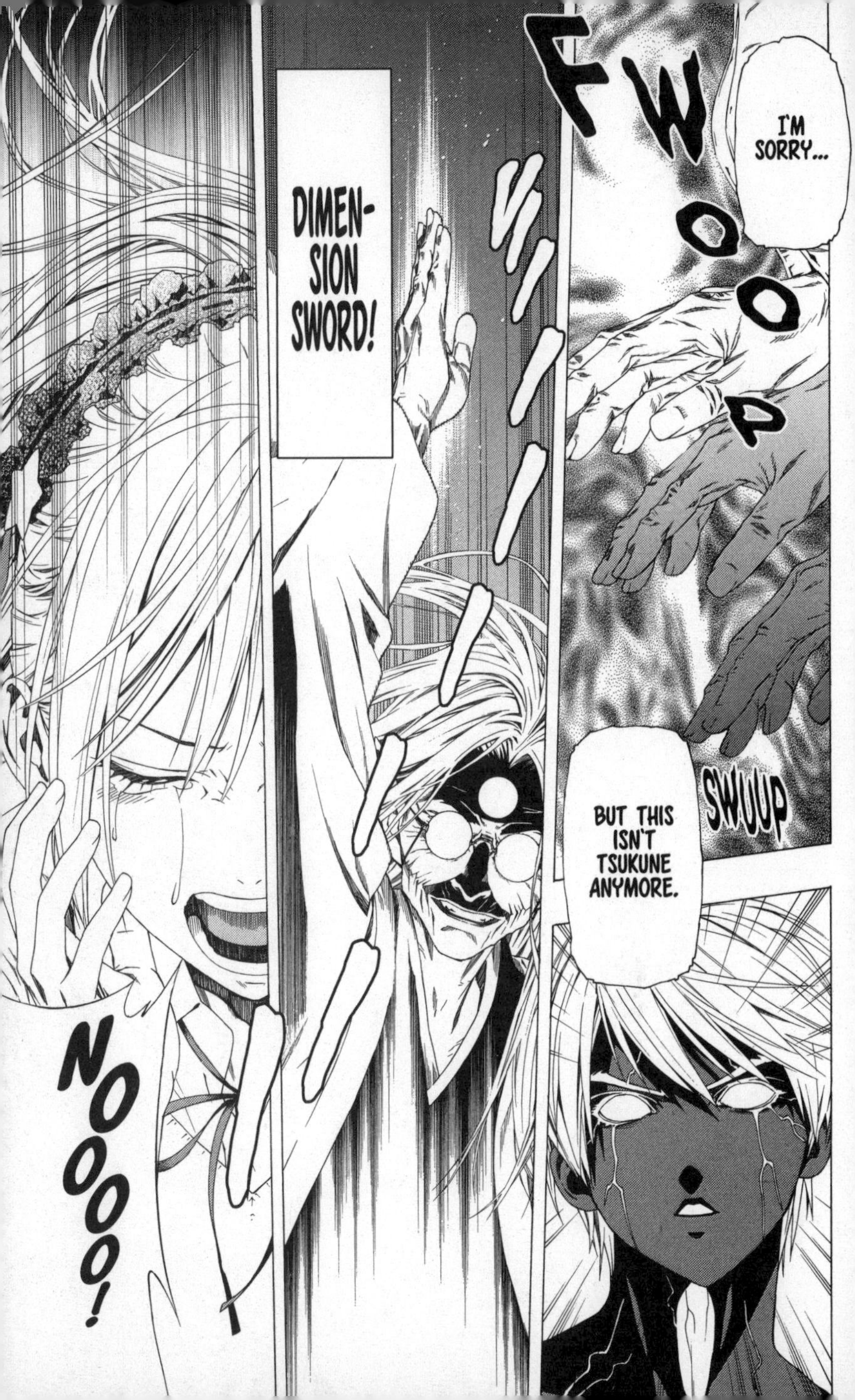
I'M SORRY...
FWOOR
SWUUP
BUT THIS ISN'T TSUKUNE ANYMORE.
DIMEN-SION SWORD!
NOOOO!

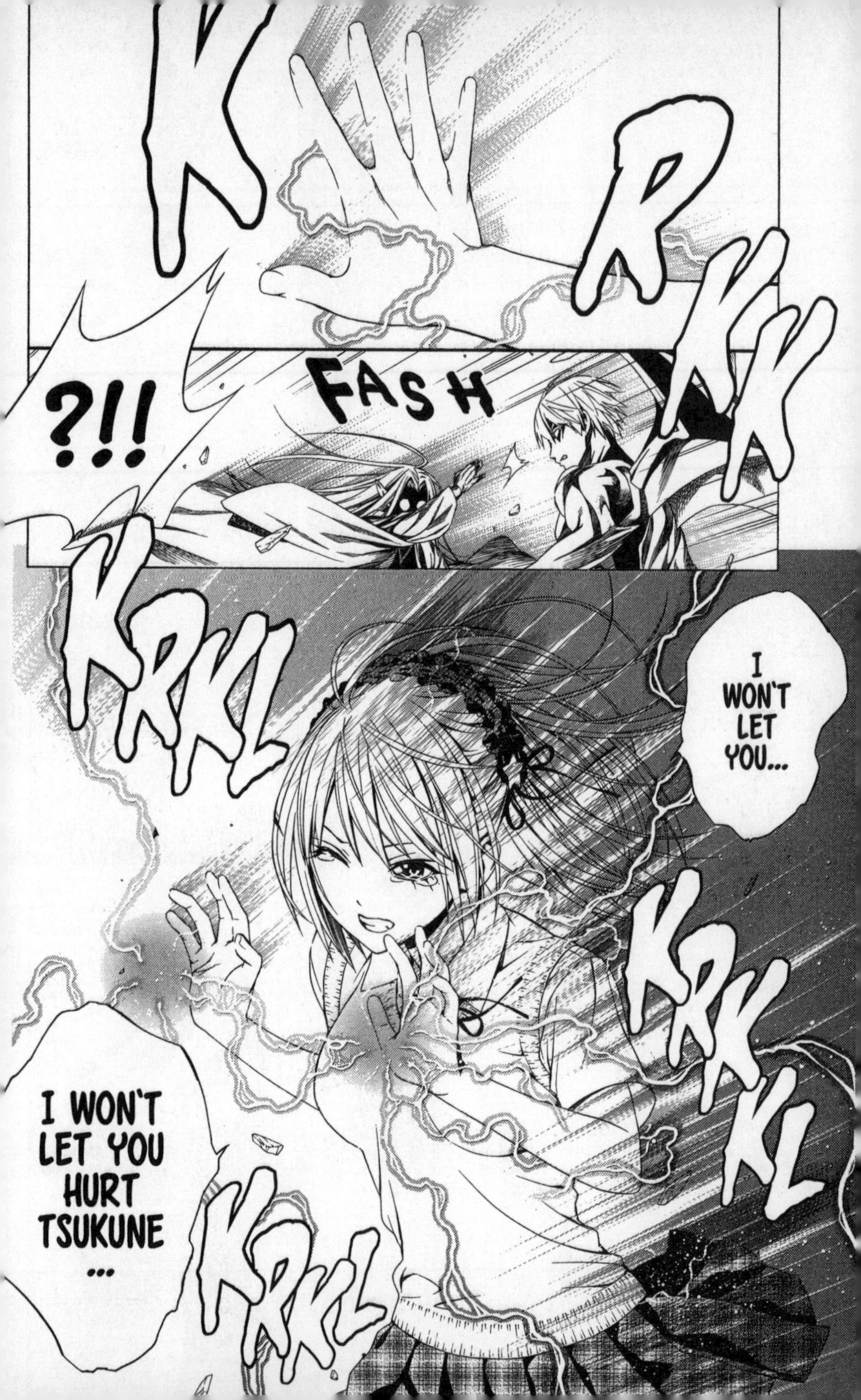

RKK
K
FASH
?!!
I WON'T LET YOU...
KRKL
KRKKL
I WON'T LET YOU HURT TSUKUNE ...
KRKL

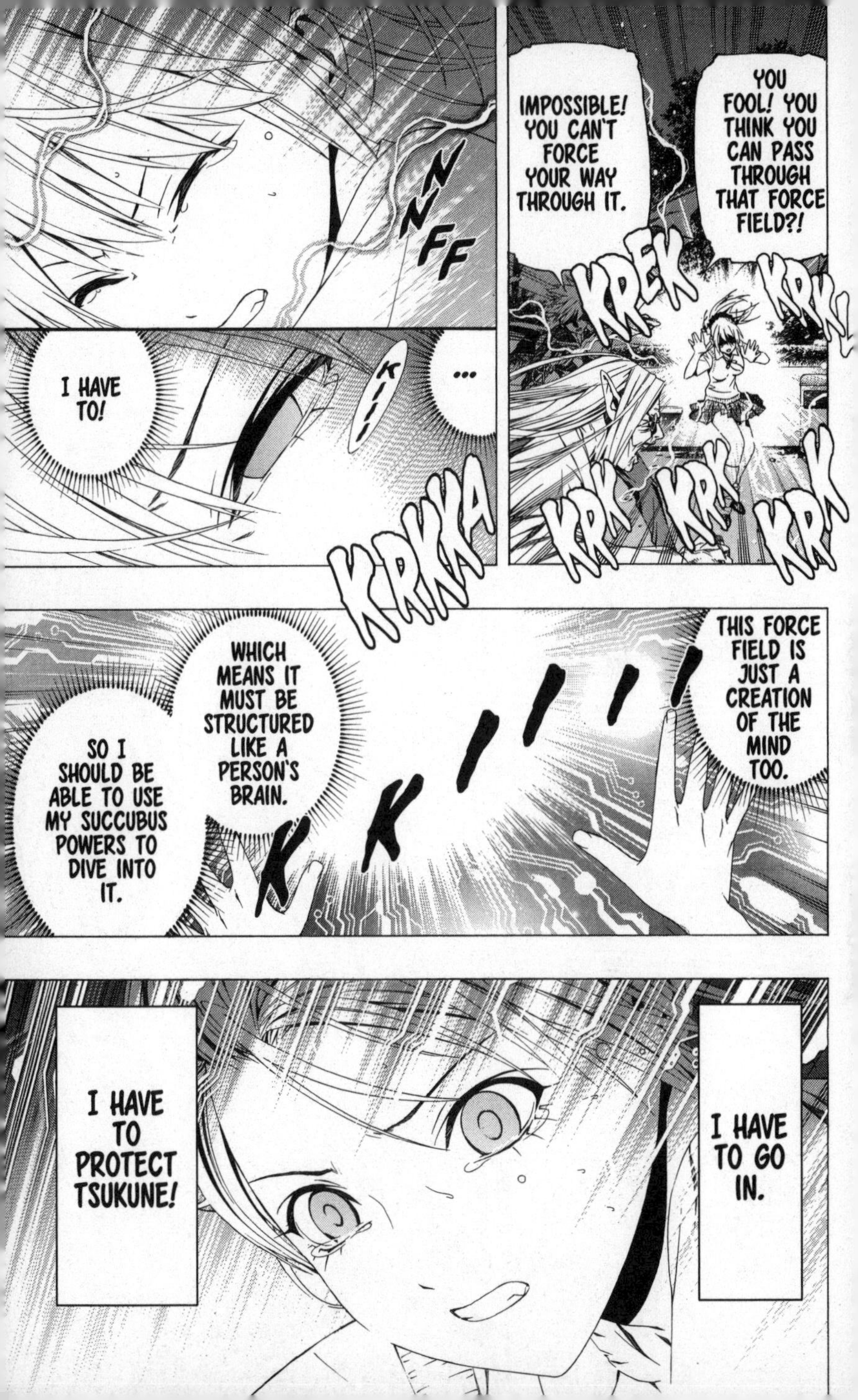
YOU FOOL! YOU THINK YOU CAN PASS THROUGH THAT FORCE FIELD?!
IMPOSSIBLE! YOU CAN'T FORCE YOUR WAY THROUGH IT.
KREK
KRK
KRK KRK KRK
NNFF
...
KIII
I HAVE TO!
KRKKA
THIS FORCE FIELD IS JUST A CREATION OF THE MIND TOO.
WHICH MEANS IT MUST BE STRUCTURED LIKE A PERSON'S BRAIN.
SO I SHOULD BE ABLE TO USE MY SUCCUBUS POWERS TO DIVE INTO IT.
KKIIII
I HAVE TO GO IN.
I HAVE TO PROTECT TSUKUNE!

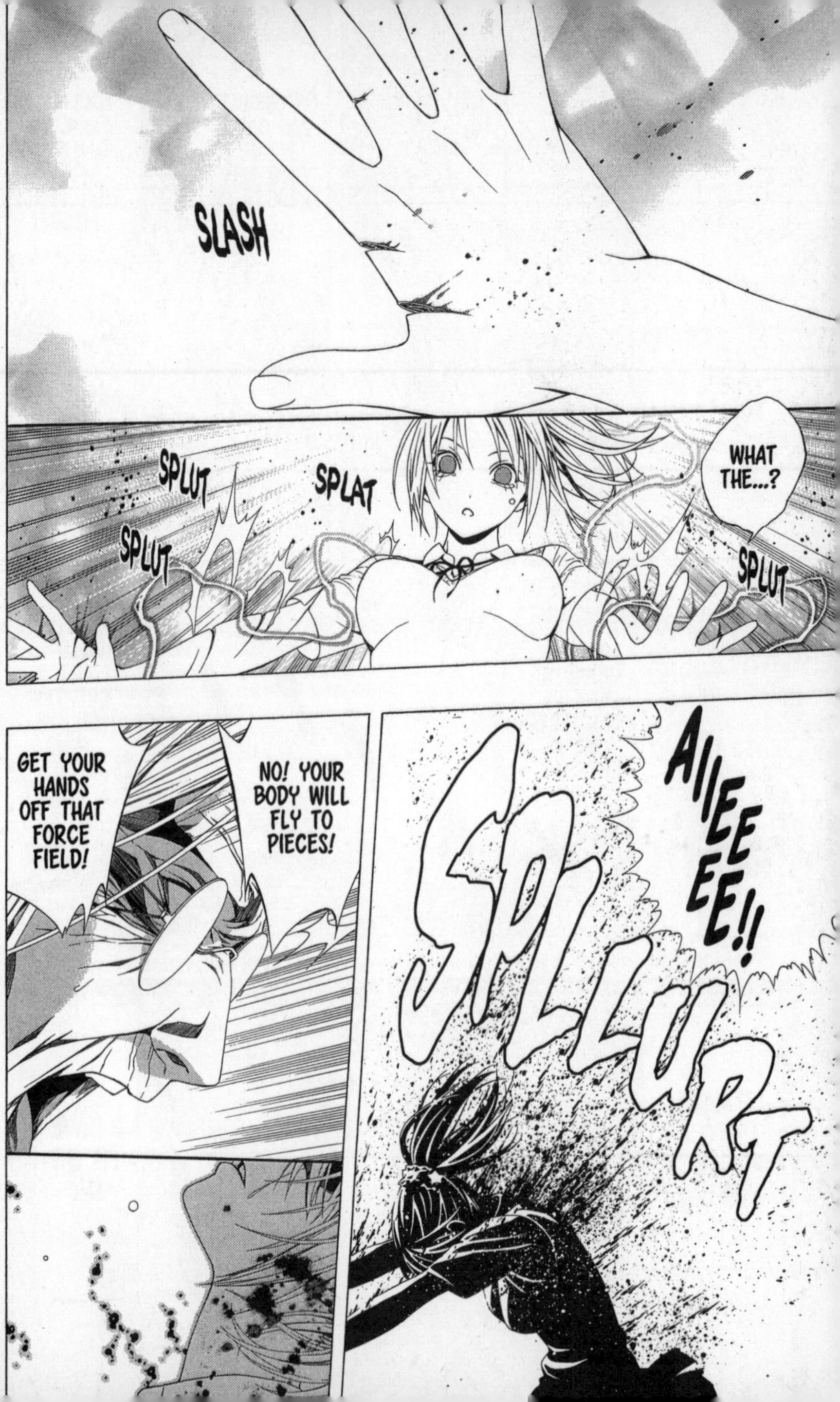
SLASH
WHAT THE...?
SPLUT
SPLAT
SPLUT
SPLUT
AIIEEEE!!
SPLLURT
NO! YOUR BODY WILL FLY TO PIECES!
GET YOUR HANDS OFF THAT FORCE FIELD!

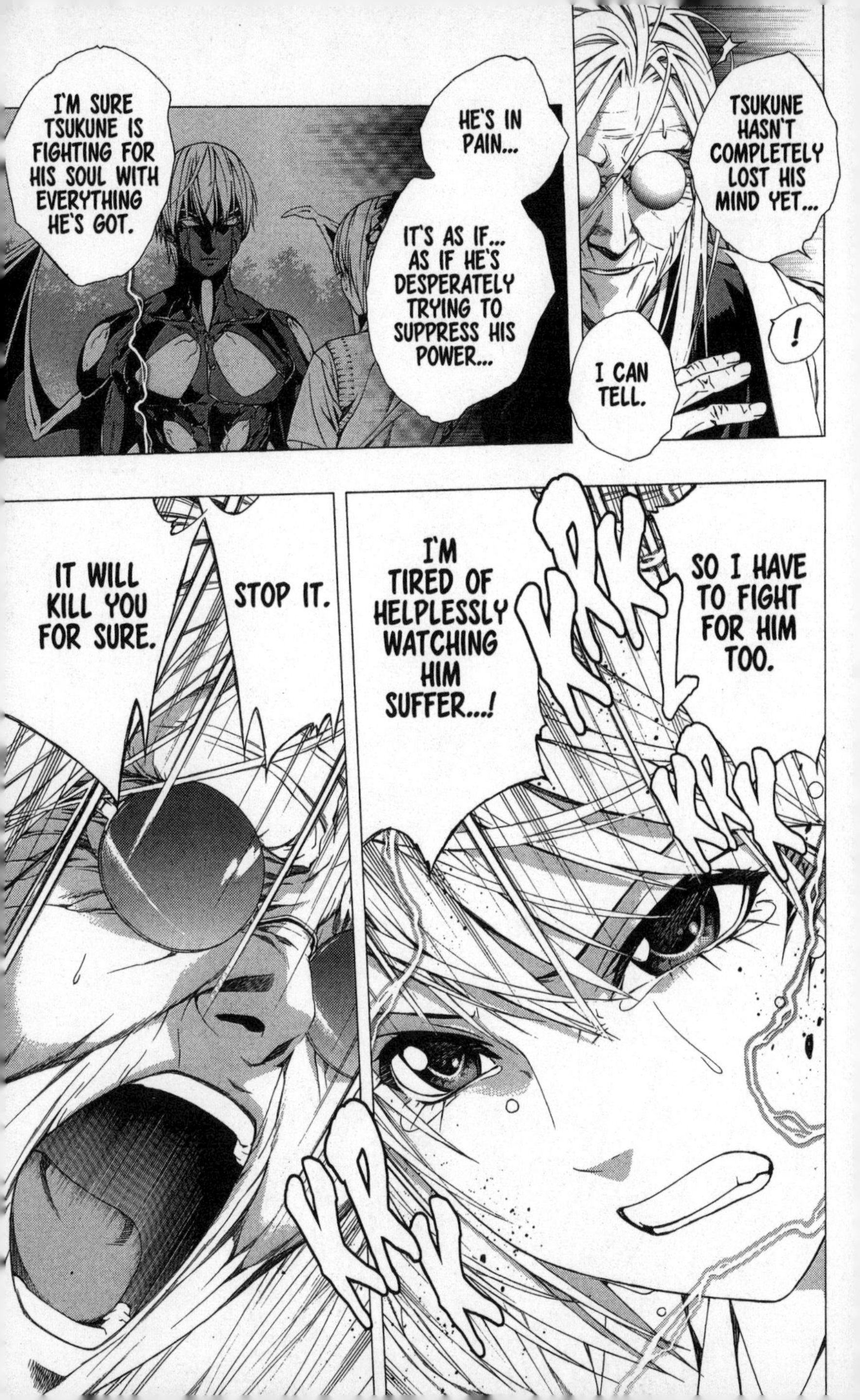
TSUKUNE HASN'T COMPLETELY LOST HIS MIND YET...
!
I CAN TELL.
HE'S IN PAIN...
IT'S AS IF... AS IF HE'S DESPERATELY TRYING TO SUPPRESS HIS POWER...
I'M SURE TSUKUNE IS FIGHTING FOR HIS SOUL WITH EVERYTHING HE'S GOT.
SO I HAVE TO FIGHT FOR HIM TOO.
I'M TIRED OF HELPLESSLY WATCHING HIM SUFFER...!
STOP IT.
IT WILL KILL YOU FOR SURE.

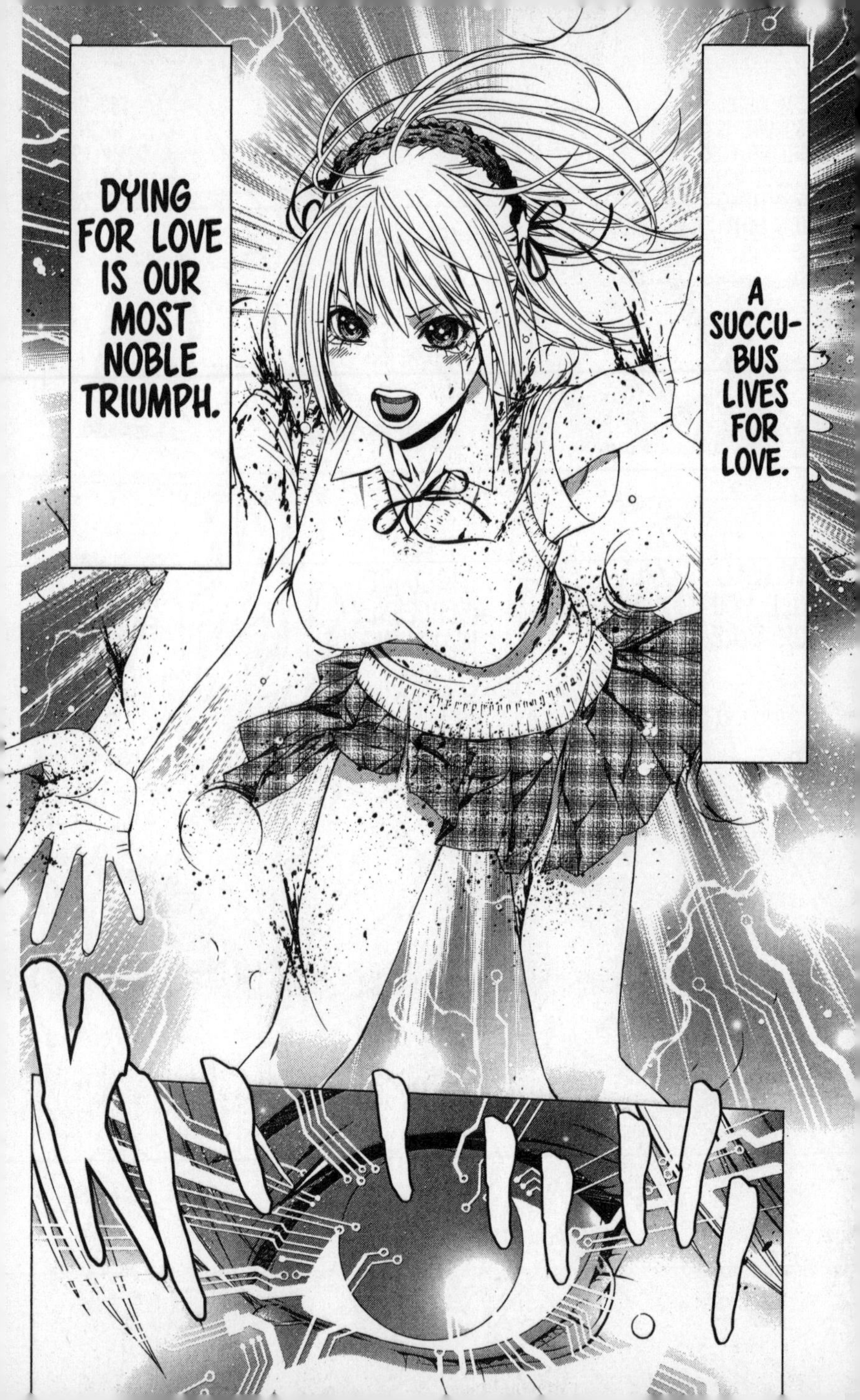
A SUCCU-BUS LIVES FOR LOVE.
DYING FOR LOVE IS OUR MOST NOBLE TRIUMPH.

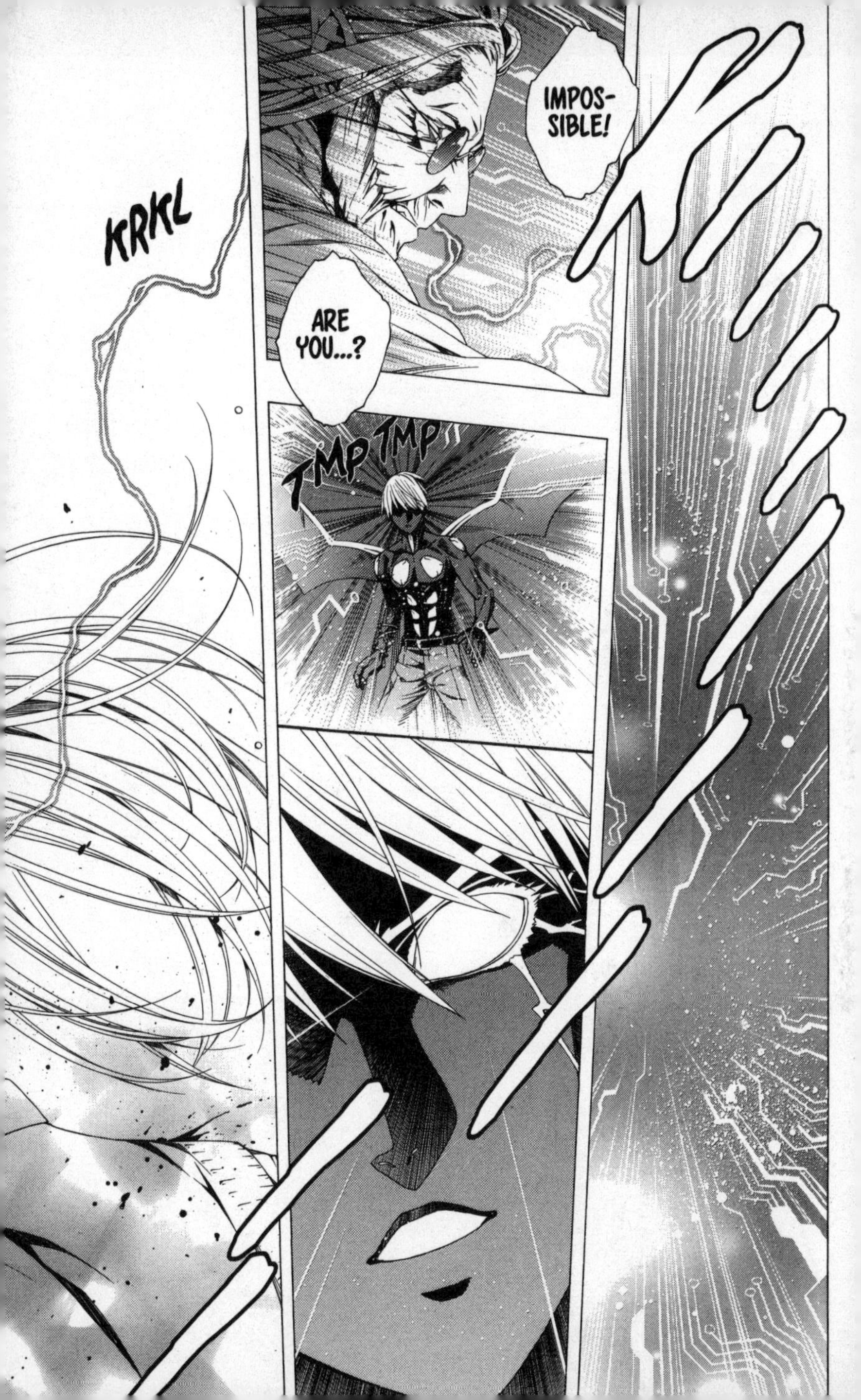
IMPOS-
SIBLE!
ARE
YOU...?
TMP TMP
KRKL

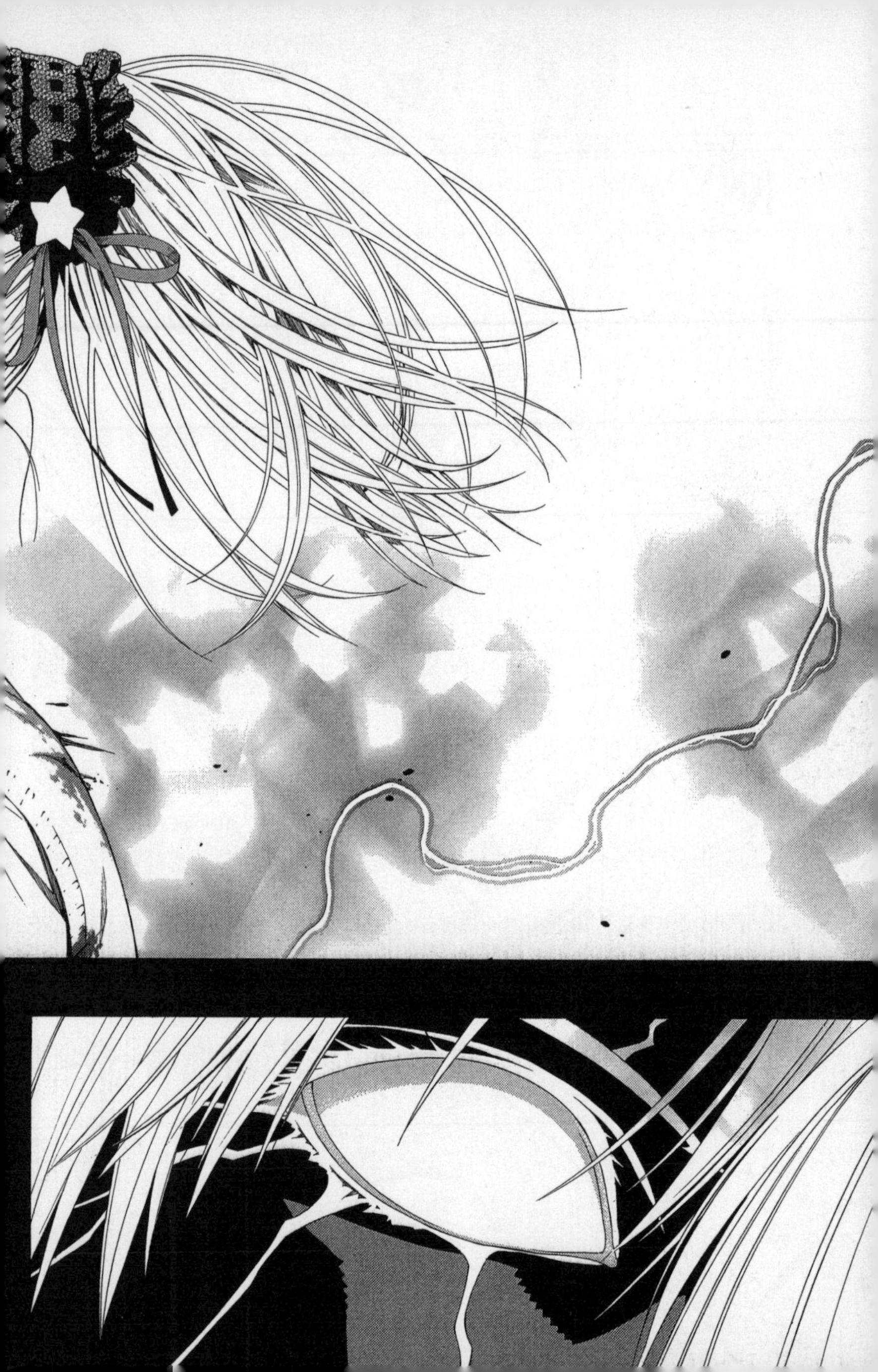

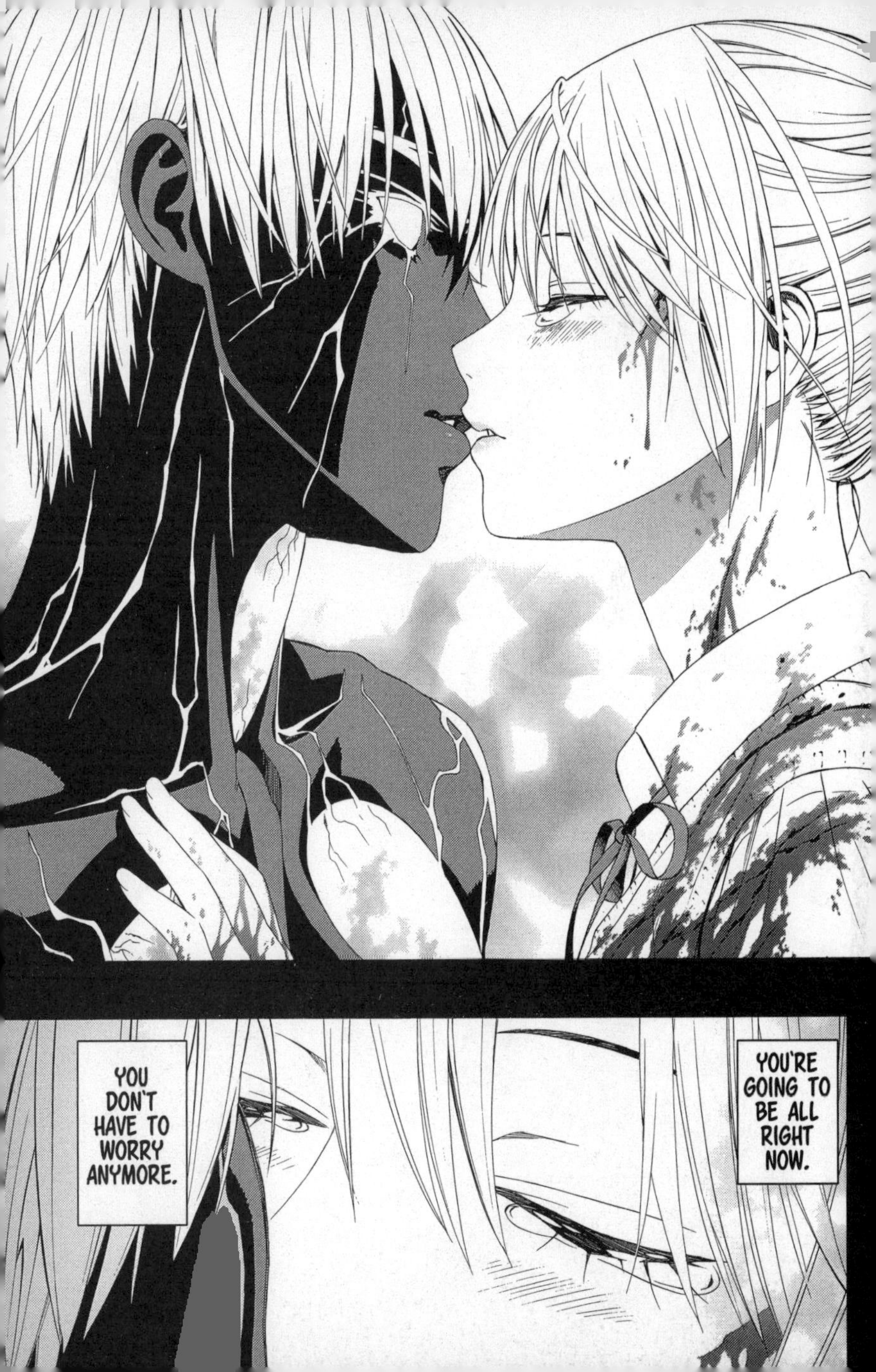
YOU'RE GOING TO BE ALL RIGHT NOW.
YOU DON'T HAVE TO WORRY ANYMORE.

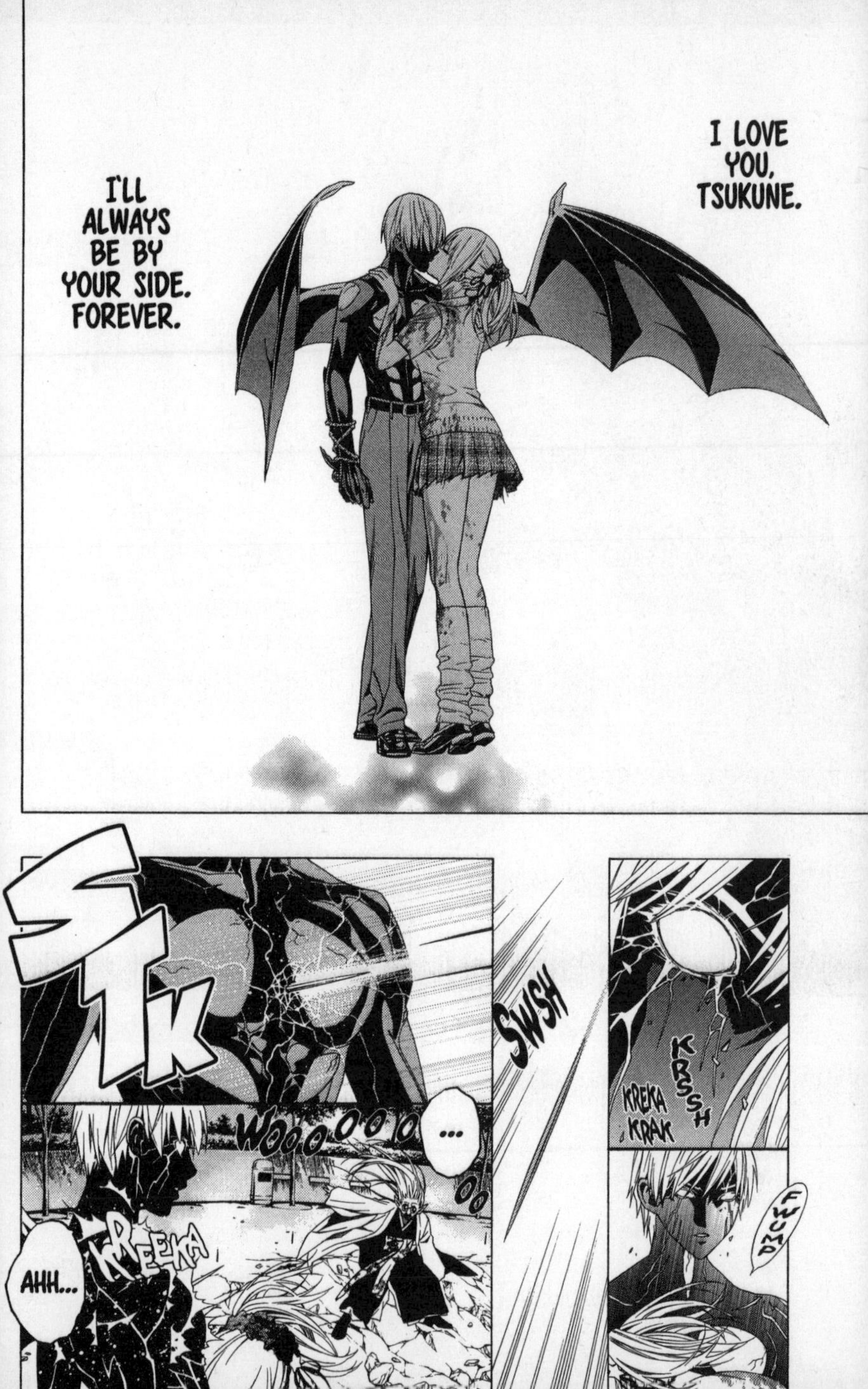

I LOVE YOU, TSUKUNE.
I'LL ALWAYS BE BY YOUR SIDE. FOREVER.
KRSSH
KREKA KRAK
FWUMP
SWSH
STK
...
WOOOOOOOO
KREEKA
AHH...

TNK
TNK
TNK

WHUD

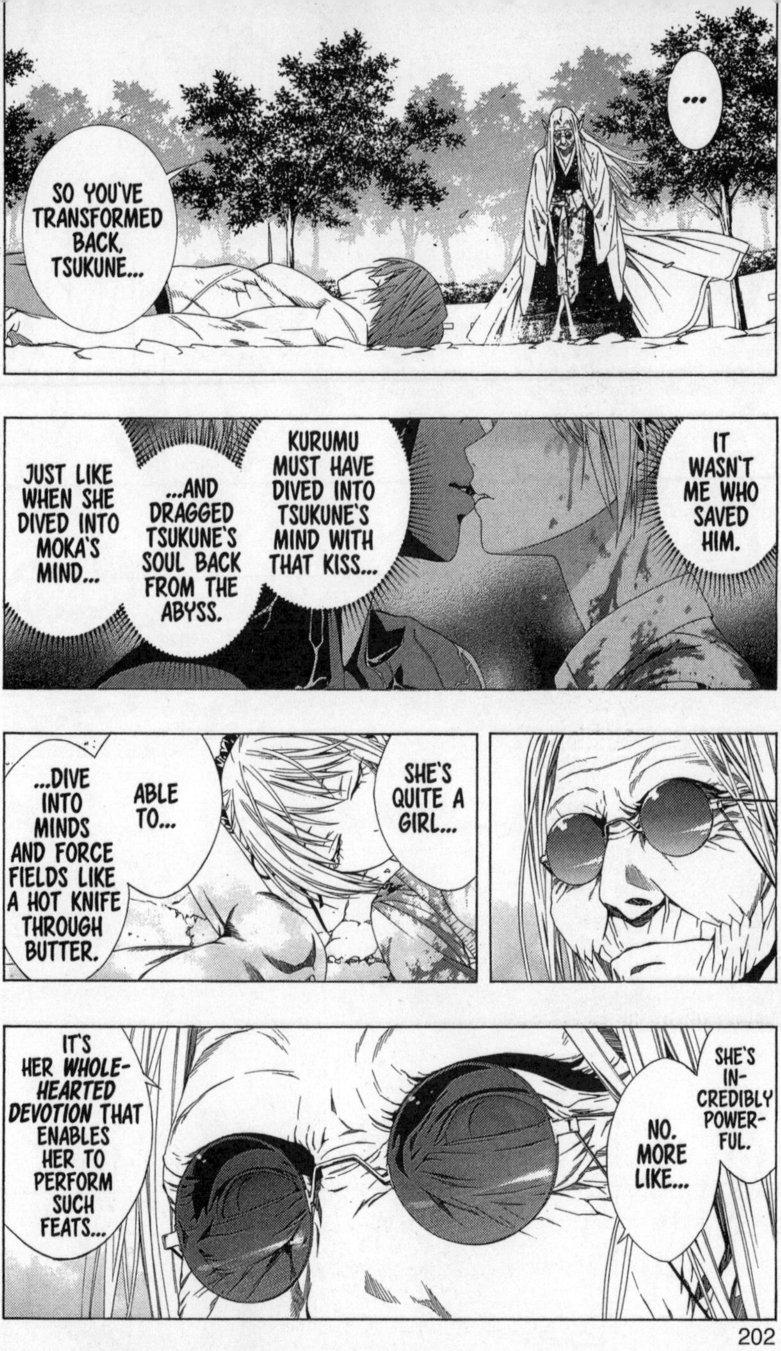
...
SO YOU'VE TRANSFORMED BACK, TSUKUNE...
IT WASN'T ME WHO SAVED HIM.
KURUMU MUST HAVE DIVED INTO TSUKUNE'S MIND WITH THAT KISS...
...AND DRAGGED TSUKUNE'S SOUL BACK FROM THE ABYSS.
JUST LIKE WHEN SHE DIVED INTO MOKA'S MIND...
SHE'S QUITE A GIRL...
ABLE TO...
...DIVE INTO MINDS AND FORCE FIELDS LIKE A HOT KNIFE THROUGH BUTTER.
SHE'S IN-CREDIBLY POWER-FUL.
NO. MORE LIKE...
IT'S HER *WHOLE-HEARTED DEVOTION* THAT ENABLES HER TO PERFORM SUCH FEATS...

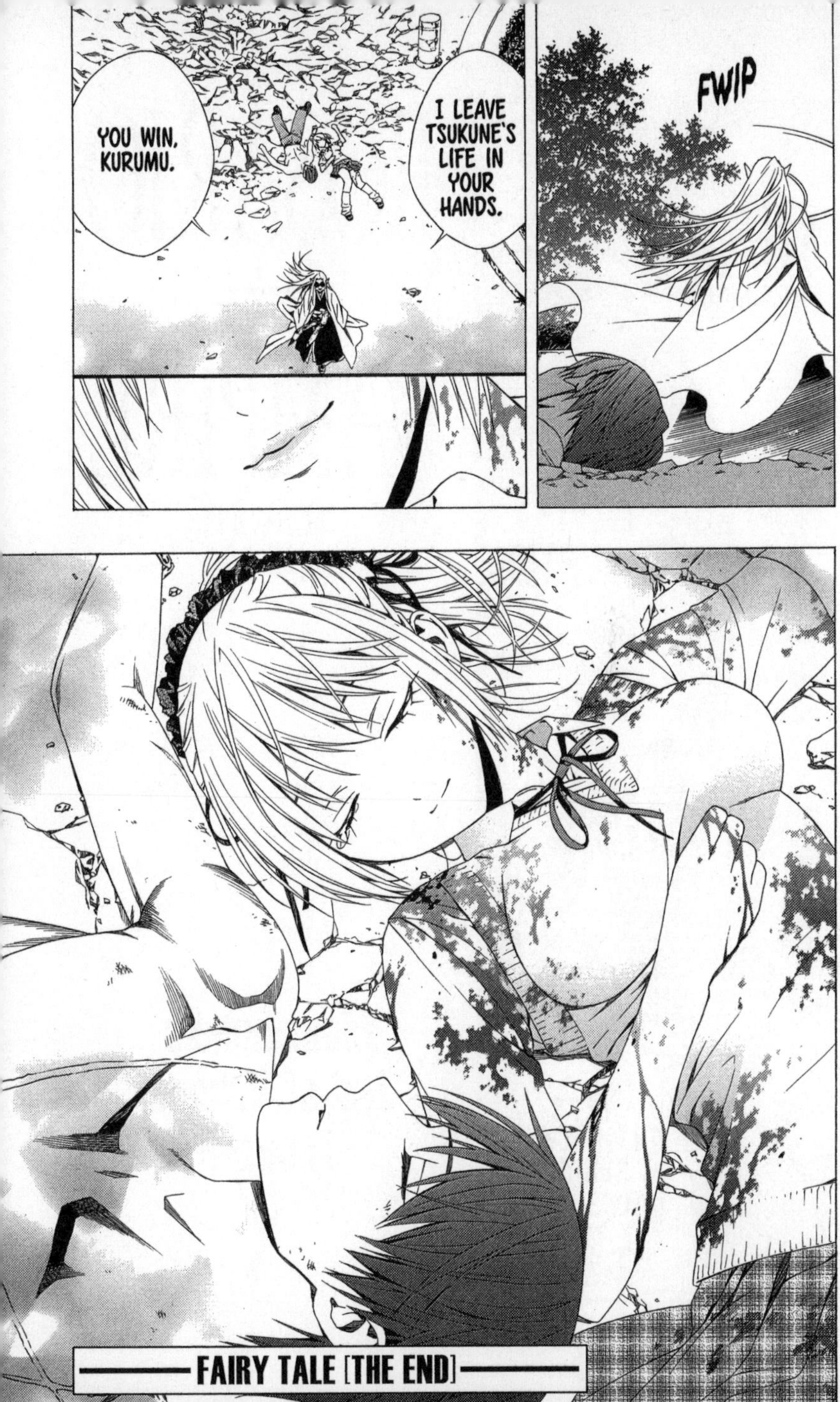
FWIP
I LEAVE TSUKUNE'S LIFE IN YOUR HANDS.
YOU WIN, KURUMU.
FAIRY TALE [THE END]

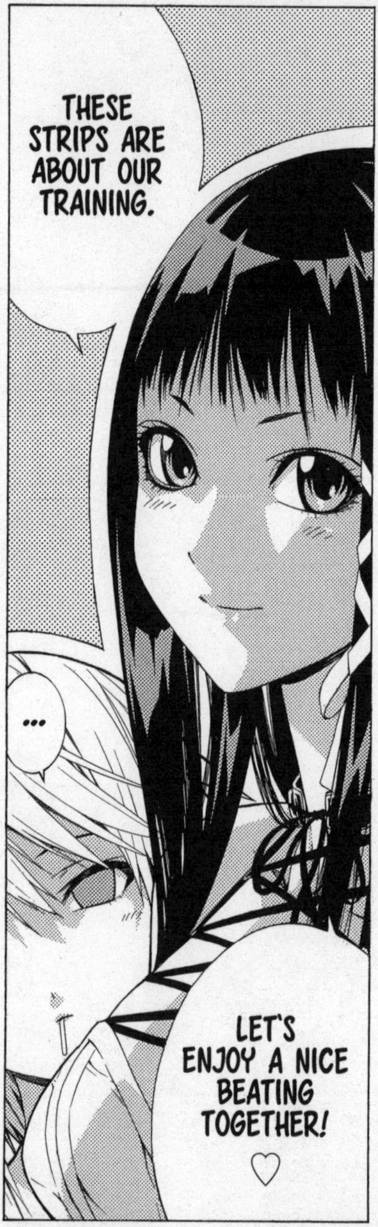
THESE STRIPS ARE ABOUT OUR TRAINING.
...
LET'S ENJOY A NICE BEATING TOGETHER! ♡

ROSARIO + VAMPIRE

Season II

Meaningless End-of-Volume Theater

IX

• Image Training •

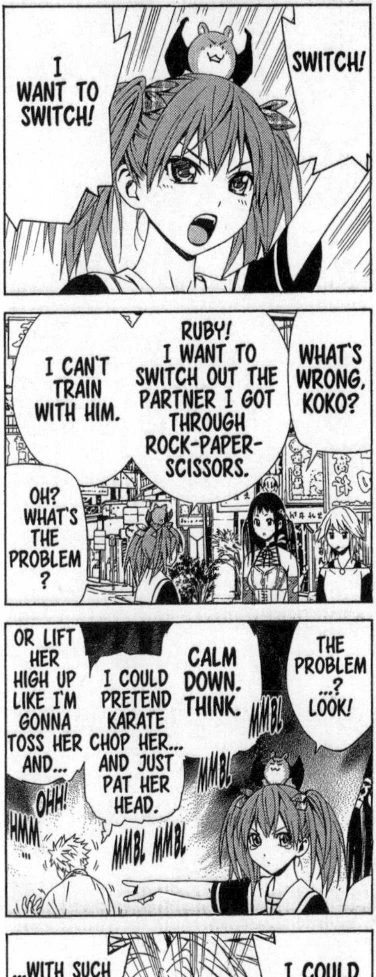
SWITCH!
I WANT TO SWITCH!
WHAT'S WRONG, KOKO?
RUBY! I WANT TO SWITCH OUT THE PARTNER I GOT THROUGH ROCK-PAPER-SCISSORS.
I CAN'T TRAIN WITH HIM.
OH? WHAT'S THE PROBLEM?
THE PROBLEM...? LOOK!
CALM DOWN. THINK.
I COULD PRETEND KARATE CHOP HER... AND JUST PAT HER HEAD.
OR LIFT HER HIGH UP LIKE I'M GONNA TOSS HER AND...
MMBL
MMBL
OHH!
MMBL MMBL
HMM...
I COULD DO ANYTHING...
...WITH SUCH A CUTE GIRL FOR A TRAINING PARTNER.

• Power-up Item •

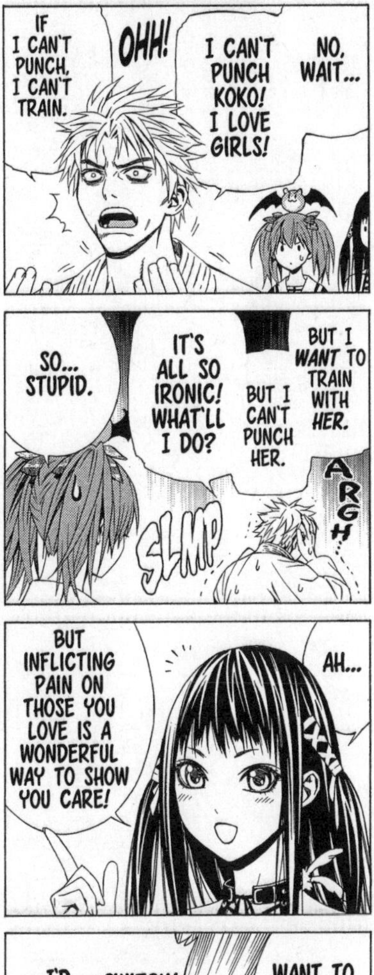
NO, WAIT...
I CAN'T PUNCH KOKO! I LOVE GIRLS!
OHH!
IF I CAN'T PUNCH, I CAN'T TRAIN.
BUT I WANT TO TRAIN WITH HER.
BUT I CAN'T PUNCH HER.
IT'S ALL SO IRONIC! WHAT'LL I DO?
SO... STUPID.
ARGH
SLMP
AH...
BUT INFLICTING PAIN ON THOSE YOU LOVE IS A WONDERFUL WAY TO SHOW YOU CARE!
WANT TO BORROW MY ACCESSORIES?
OH!
SWITCH!
I'D LIKE TO SWITCH PARTNERS, PLEASE!

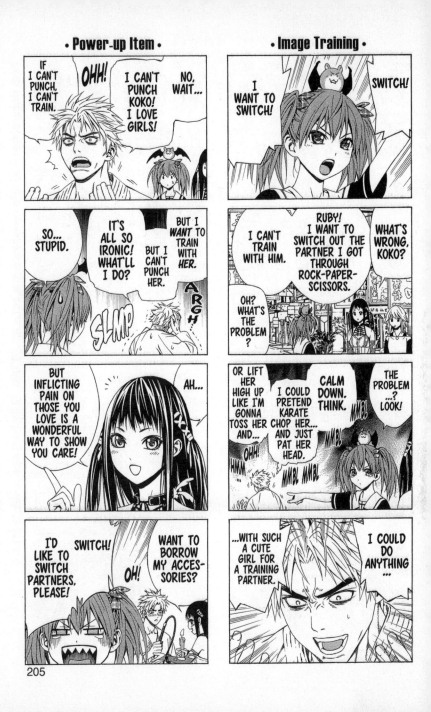

• Another Guy •

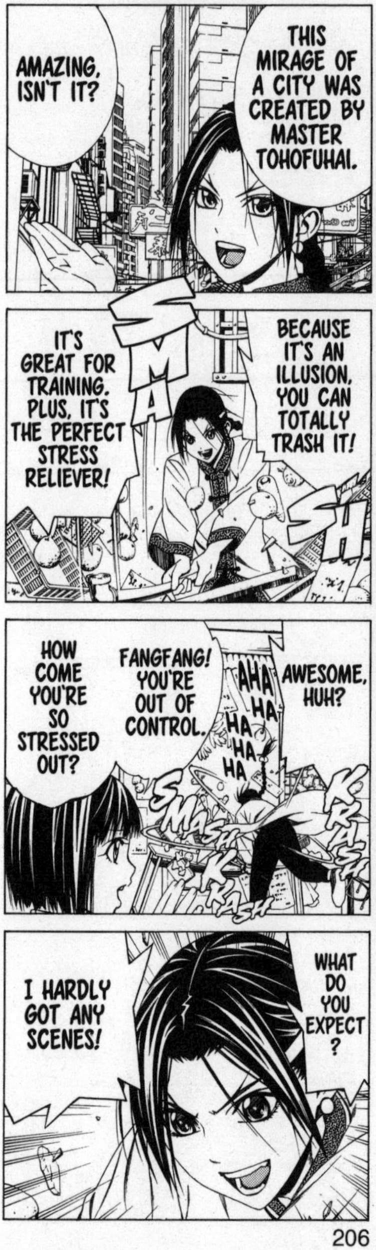
THIS MIRAGE OF A CITY WAS CREATED BY MASTER TOHOFUHAI.
AMAZING, ISN'T IT?
SMA
BECAUSE IT'S AN ILLUSION, YOU CAN TOTALLY TRASH IT!
SH
IT'S GREAT FOR TRAINING. PLUS, IT'S THE PERFECT STRESS RELIEVER!
AWESOME, HUH?
AHA HA HA HA HA HA
FANGFANG! YOU'RE OUT OF CONTROL.
HOW COME YOU'RE SO STRESSED OUT?
KRASH
SMASH
KRASH
WHAT DO YOU EXPECT?
I HARDLY GOT ANY SCENES!

• Mizore × Ruby •

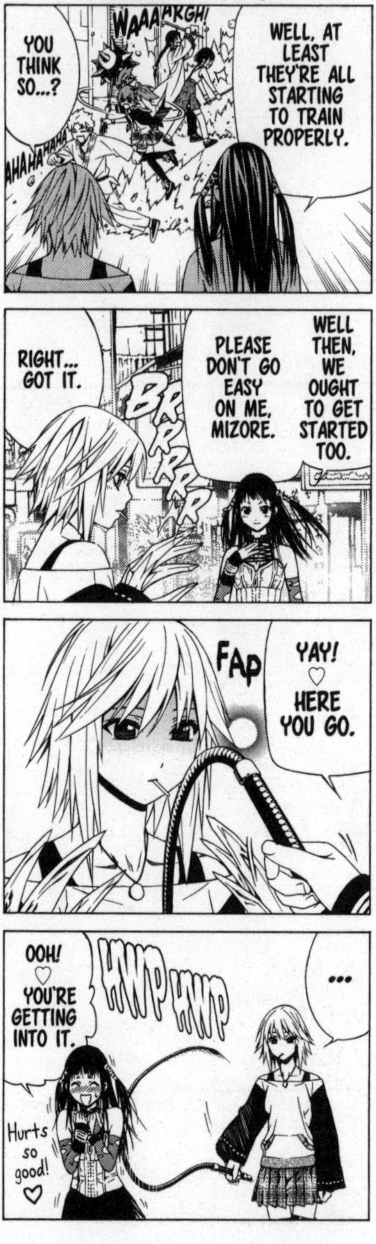
WELL, AT LEAST THEY'RE ALL STARTING TO TRAIN PROPERLY.
WAAAARGH!
YOU THINK SO...?
AHAHAHAHA
WELL THEN, WE OUGHT TO GET STARTED TOO.
PLEASE DON'T GO EASY ON ME, MIZORE.
BRRRRR
RIGHT... GOT IT.
YAY! ♡ HERE YOU GO.
FAP
...
HWP HWP
OOH! ♡ YOU'RE GETTING INTO IT.
Hurts so good! ♡

Please send questions and fan letters to ➡ Rosario+Vampire Fan Mail, VIZ Media, P.O. Box 77010, San Francisco, CA 94107

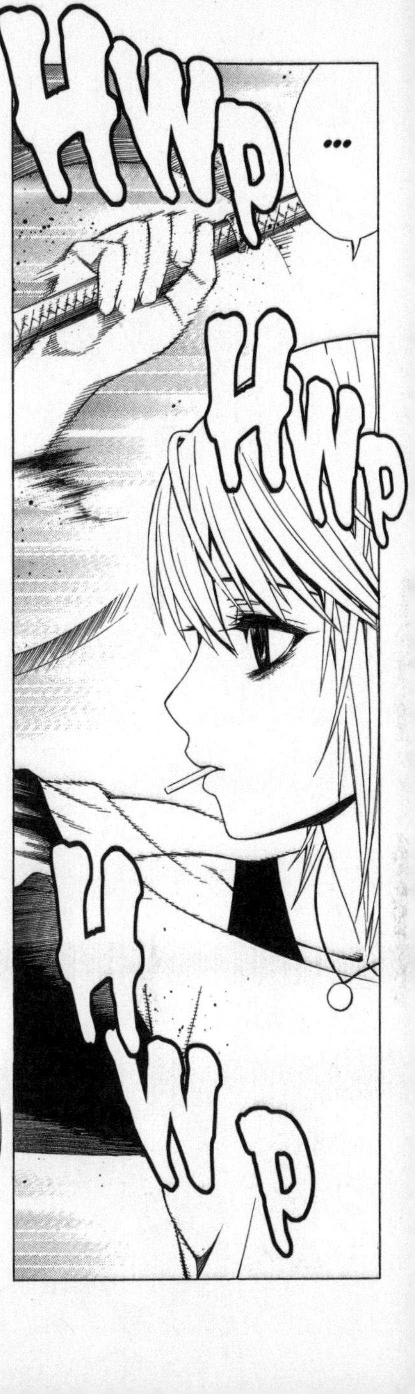
HWP
...
HWP
HWP

Rosario+Vampire

Akihisa Ikeda

• Staff •

Makoto Saito
Nobuyuki Hayashi
Rika Shirota

• Assistants •

Tomoharu Shimomura
Yuki Sato
Tatsuro Sakaguchi
Kotaro Suzuki

• Editor •

Junichi Tamada

• Comic •

Kenju Noro

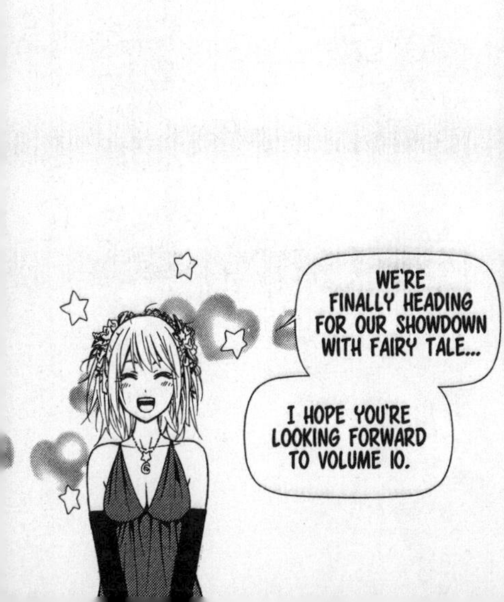
WE'RE FINALLY HEADING FOR OUR SHOWDOWN WITH FAIRY TALE...
I HOPE YOU'RE LOOKING FORWARD TO VOLUME 10.

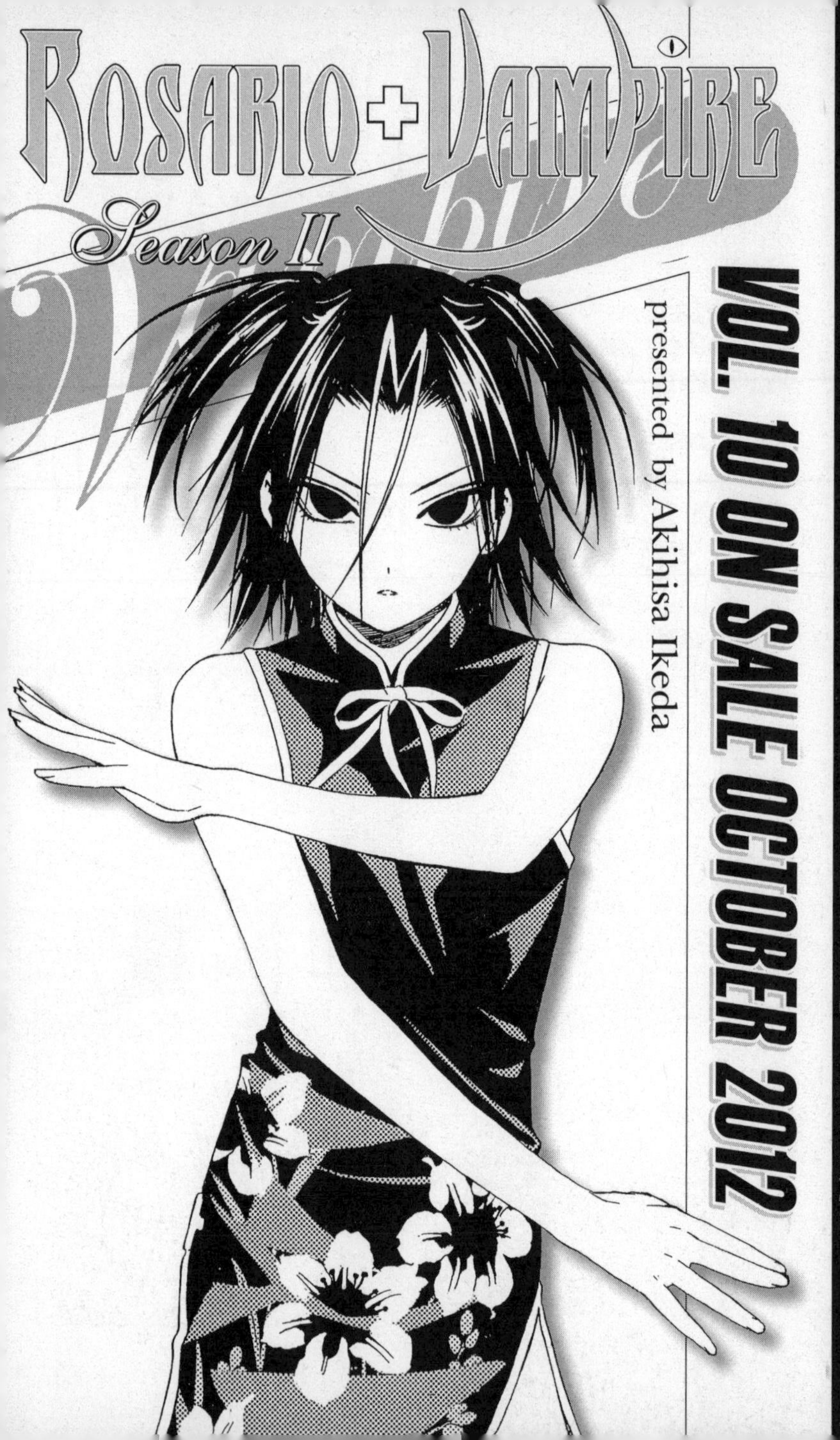
ROSARIO+VAMPIRE
Season II
VOL. 10 ON SALE OCTOBER 2012
presented by Akihisa Ikeda

NEXT VOLUME...
REUNIONS, MORE ORDEALS, PLUS...
A NEW POWER!

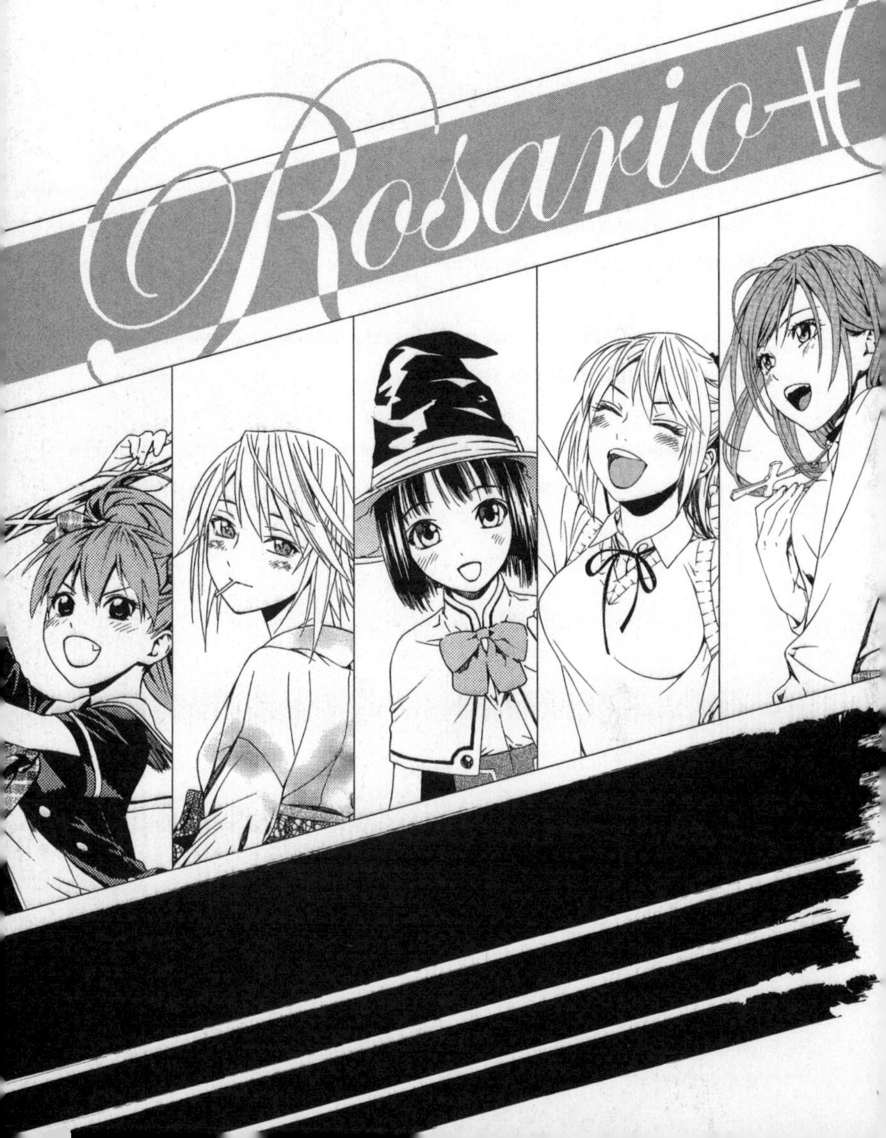
Rosario+

AKIHISA IKEDA

Ideally, I don't want money. And I don't want fame. I just want to create something good. My ambition basically boils down to that.

Um... So I guess I just need enough time to create something good, enough money to stay alive, and the smiles of my fans. Yeah, right...

We're already at volume 9 of Season II! I took pains drawing the characters so that their hopes and dreams are revealed on their faces as they prepare for their final battle.

I hope you all enjoy this volume!

Akihisa Ikeda was born in 1976 in Miyazaki. He debuted as a mangaka with the four-volume magical warrior fantasy series *Kiruto* in 2002, which was serialized in *Monthly Shonen Jump*. *Rosario+Vampire* debuted in *Monthly Shonen Jump* in March of 2004 and is continuing in the magazine *Jump Square (Jump SQ)* as *Rosario+Vampire: Season II*. In Japan, *Rosario+Vampire* is also available as a drama CD. In 2008, the story was released as an anime. Season II is also available as an anime now. And in Japan, there is a Nintendo DS game based on the series.

Ikeda has been a huge fan of vampires and monsters since he was a little kid. He says one of the perks of being a manga artist is being able to go for walks during the day when everybody else is stuck in the office.

ROSARIO+VAMPIRE: Season II
9

SHONEN JUMP ADVANCED Manga Edition

STORY & ART BY AKIHISA IKEDA

Translation/Tetsuichiro Miyaki
English Adaptation/Annette Roman
Touch-up Art & Lettering/Stephen Dutro
Cover & Interior Design/Ronnie Casson
Editor/Annette Roman

Printed in the U.S.A.

Published by VIZ Media, LLC
P.O. Box 77010
San Francisco, CA 94107

10 9 8 7 6 5 4 3 2
First printing, July 2012
Second printing, May 2015

www.viz.com

www.shonenjump.com

PARENTAL ADVISORY
ROSARIO+VAMPIRE is rated T+ for Older Teen and is recommended for ages 16 and up. It contains suggestive situations and violence.

ratings.viz.com

CRYPT SHEET FOR
ROSARIO+VAMPIRE: SEASON II, VOL. 10
KIDNAPPED

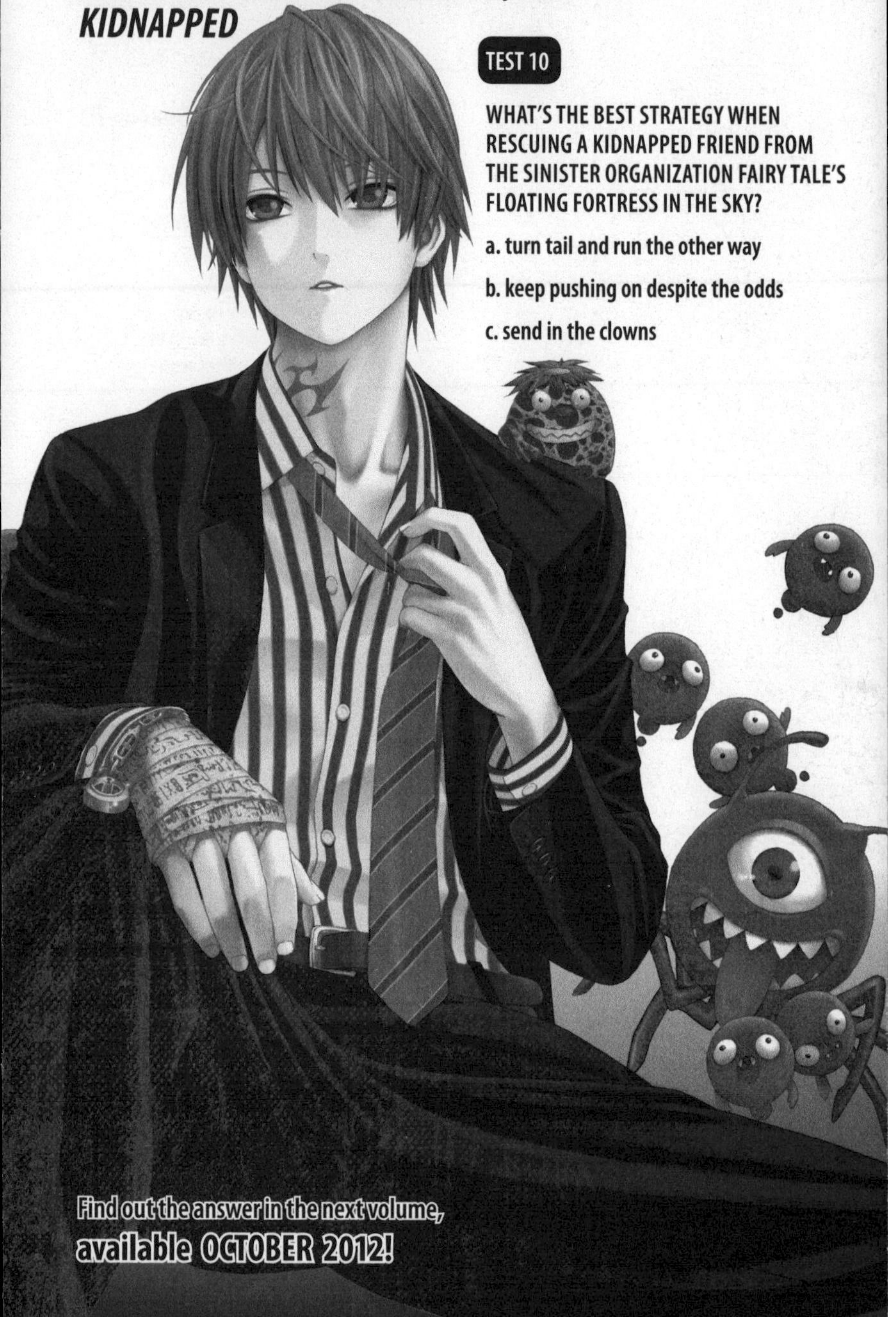

TEST 10

WHAT'S THE BEST STRATEGY WHEN RESCUING A KIDNAPPED FRIEND FROM THE SINISTER ORGANIZATION FAIRY TALE'S FLOATING FORTRESS IN THE SKY?

a. turn tail and run the other way

b. keep pushing on despite the odds

c. send in the clowns

Find out the answer in the next volume, available OCTOBER 2012!

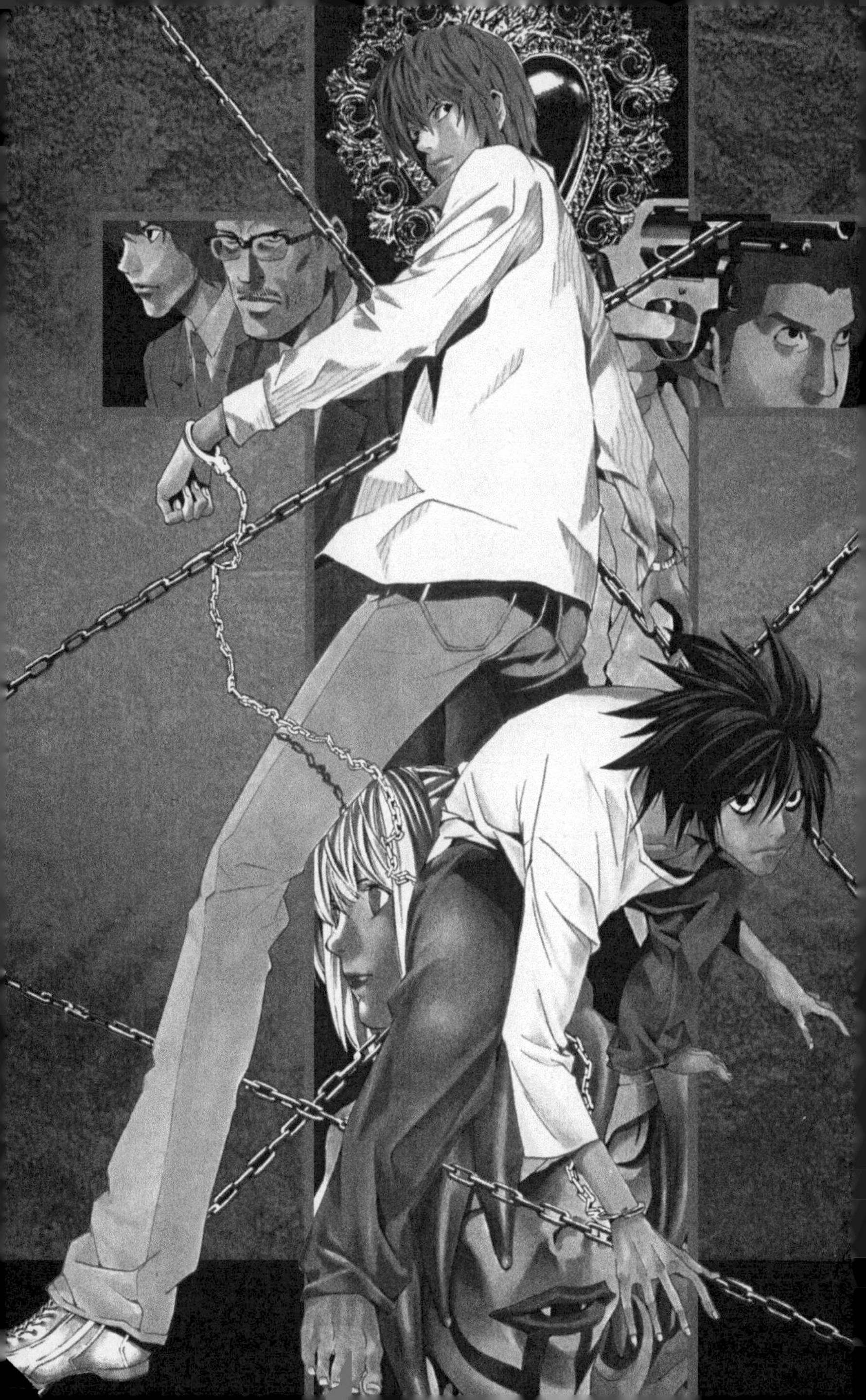

You're Reading in the Wrong Direction!!

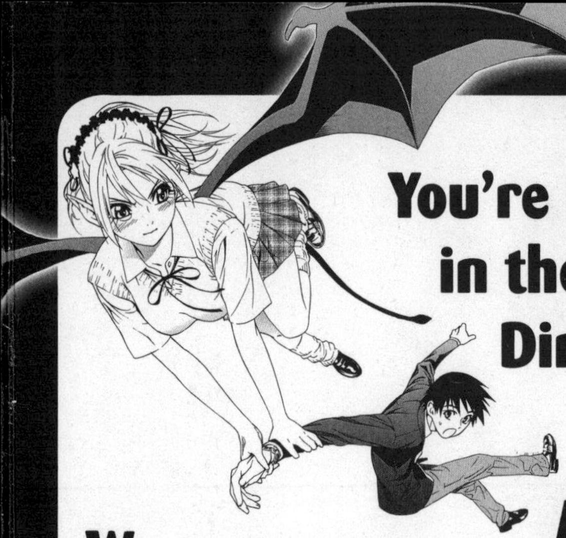

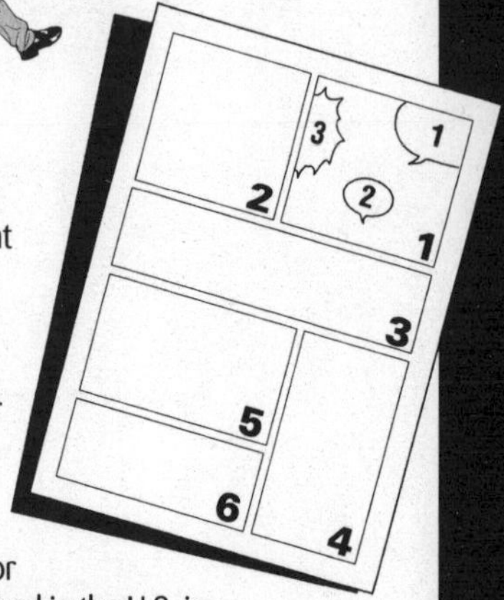
1
2
3
1
2
3
4
5
6

Whoops! Guess what? You're starting at the wrong end of the comic!

...It's true! In keeping with the original Japanese format, **Rosario+Vampire** is meant to be read from right to left, starting in the upper-right corner.

Unlike English, which is read from left to right, Japanese is read from right to left, meaning action, sound effects and word-balloon order are completely reversed... something which can make readers unfamiliar with Japanese feel pretty backwards themselves. For this reason, manga or Japanese comics published in the U.S. in English have sometimes been published "flopped"—that is, printed in exact reverse order, as though seen from the other side of a mirror.

By flopping pages, U.S. publishers can avoid confusing readers, but the compromise is not without its downside. For one thing, a character in a flopped manga series who once wore in the original Japanese version a T-shirt emblazoned with "M A Y" (as in "the merry month of") now wears one which reads "Y A M"! Additionally, many manga creators in Japan are themselves unhappy with the process, as some feel the mirror-imaging of their art skews their original intentions.

We are proud to bring you Akihisa Ikeda's **Rosario+Vampire** in the original unflopped format. For now, though, turn to the other side of the book and let the haunting begin...!

—Editor